KT-116-858

Brilliant Guides

What you need to know and how to do it

When you're working on your computer and come up against a problem that you're unsure how to solve, or want to accomplish something in an application that you aren't sure how to do, where do you look?? Manuals and traditional training guides are usually too big and unwieldy and are intended to be used as an end-to-end training resource, making it hard to get to the info you need right away without having to wade through pages of background information that you just don't need at that moment – and helplines are rarely that helpful!

Brilliant guides have been developed to allow you to find the info you need easily and without fuss and guide you through the task using a highly visual, step-by-step approach – providing exactly what you need to know when you need it!!

Brilliant guides provide the quick easy-to-access information that you need, using a detailed index and troubleshooting guide to help you find exactly what you need to know, and then presenting each task on one or two pages. Numbered steps then guide you through each task or problem, using numerous screenshots to illustrate each step. Added features include "See Also …" boxes that point you to related tasks and information in the book, whilst "Did you know?..." sections alert you to relevant expert tips, tricks and advice to further expand your skills and knowledge.

In addition to covering all major office applications, and related computing subjects, the *Brilliant* series also contains titles that will help you in every aspect of your working life, such as writing the perfect CV, answering the toughest interview questions and moving on in your career.

Brilliant guides are the light at the end of the tunnel when you are faced with any minor or major task!

a

Acknowledgements

Perspection, Inc.

Brilliant Adobe Dreamweaver CS3 has been created by the professional trainers and writers at Perspection, Inc.

Perspection, Inc. is a software training company committed to providing information and training to help people use software more effectively in order to communicate, make decisions, and solve problems. Perspection writes and produces software training books, and develops multimedia and Web-based training. Since 1991, we have written more than 80 computer books, with several bestsellers to our credit, and sold over 5 million books.

This book incorporates Perspection's training expertise to ensure that you'll receive the maximum return on your time. You'll focus on the tasks and skills that increase productivity while working at your own pace and convenience.

We invite you to visit the Perspection Web site at:

www.perspection.com

Acknowledgements

The task of creating any book requires the talents of many hard-working people pulling together to meet impossible deadlines and untold stresses. We'd like to thank the outstanding team responsible for making this book possible: the writers, Steve Johnson and Andy Anderson; the technical editor, Beth Teyler; the production editors, James Teyler and Beth Teyler; the proofreader, Holly Johnson; and the indexer, Katherine Stimson.

At Que publishing, we'd like to thank Greg Wiegand and Laura Norman for the opportunity to undertake this project, Michelle Newcomb for administrative support, and Sandra Schroeder for your production expertise and support.

Perspection

Brilliant Adobe® Dreamweaver CS3

Steve Johnson

with Andy Anderson

Perspection, Inc.

PEARSON
Prentice Hall

Harlow, England • London • New York • Boston • San Francisco • Toronto
Sydney • Tokyo • Singapore • Hong Kong • Seoul • Taipei • New Delhi
Cape Town • Madrid • Mexico City • Amsterdam • Munich • Paris • Milan

Pearson Education Limited
Edinburgh Gate
Harlow
Essex CM20 2JE
England

and Associated Companies throughout the world

Visit us on the World Wide Web at:
www.pearsoned.co.uk

Original edition, entitled Adobe® Dreamweaver CS3 ON DEMAND, 1st edition, 9780789736932 by ANDERSON, ANDY JOHNSON, STEVE; PERSPECTION, INC., published by Pearson Education, Inc, publishing as Que/Sams, Copyright © 2007 Perspection, Inc.

This UK edition published by PEARSON EDUCATION LTD, Copyright © 2007

This edition is manufactured in the USA and available for sale only in the United Kingdom, Europe, the Middle East and Africa

The right of Andy Anderson and Steve Johnson to be identified as author of this work has been asserted by him in accordance with the Copyright, Designs and Patents Act 1988.

ISBN: 978-0-273-71437-8

British Library Cataloguing-in-Publication Data
A catalogue record for this book is available from the British Library

10 9 8 7 6 5 4 3 2
11 10 09 08

Printed and bound in the United States of America

The publisher's policy is to use paper manufactured from sustainable forests.

About The Authors

Steve Johnson has written more than 45 books on a variety of computer software, including Microsoft Office 2003 and XP, Microsoft Windows Vista and XP, Apple Mac OS X Panther, Macromedia Flash MX 2004 and 8, Macromedia Director MX 2004, Macro media Fireworks, and Adobe Photoshop CS and CS2. In 1991, after working for Apple Computer and Microsoft, Steve founded Perspection, Inc., which writes and produces software training. When he is not staying up late writing, he enjoys
playing golf, gardening, and spending time with his wife, Holly, and three children, JP, Brett, and Hannah. When time permits, he likes to travel to such places as New Hampshire in October, and Hawaii. Steve and his family live in Pleasanton, California, but can also be found visiting family all over the western United States.

Andy Anderson is a Web and graphics designer and illustrator who has worked with Dreamweaver since it was released. A university professor, Andy is a sought-after lecturer in the U.S., Canada, and Europe. The remainder of his time is split between writing graphics and fiction books, and developing graphics, animations, and resource materials for various corporations and seminar companies. His clients include designers and trainers from the U.S. Government, Boeing, Disneyland, and other Fortune 500 companies.

Contents

Introduction

Welcome to *Adobe Dreamweaver CS3 On Demand*, a visual quick reference book that shows you how to work efficiently with Dreamweaver CS3. This book provides complete coverage of basic to advanced Dreamweaver skills.

How This Book Works

You don't have to read this book in any particular order. We've designed the book so that you can jump in, get the information you need, and jump out. However, the book does follow a logical progression from simple tasks to more complex ones. Each task is presented on no more than two facing pages, which lets you focus on a single task without having to turn the page. To find the information that you need, just look up the task in the table of contents or index, and turn to the page listed. Read the task introduction, follow the step-by-step instructions in the left column along with screen illustrations in the right column, and you're done.

What's New

If you're searching for what's new in Dreamweaver CS3, just look for the icon: New!. The new icon appears in the table of contents and through out this book so you can quickly and easily identify a new or improved feature in Dreamweaver CS3. A complete description of each new feature appears in the New Features guide in the back of this book.

Keyboard Shortcuts

Most menu commands have a keyboard equivalent, such as Ctrl+P (Win) or ⌘+P (Mac), as a quicker alternative to using the mouse. A complete list of keyboard shortcuts is available in the back of this book and on the Web at *www.perspection.com*.

Step-by-Step Instructions

This book provides concise step-by-step instructions that show you "how" to accomplish a task. Each set of instructions include illustrations that directly correspond to the easy-to-read steps. Also included in the text are time-savers, tables, and sidebars to help you work more efficiently or to teach you more in-depth information. A "Did You Know?" provides tips and techniques to help you work smarter, while a "See Also" leads you to other parts of the book containing related information about the task.

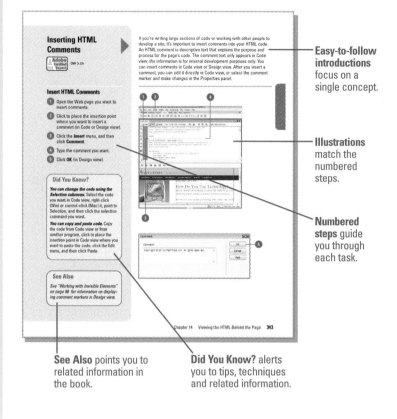

Easy-to-follow introductions focus on a single concept.

Illustrations match the numbered steps.

Numbered steps guide you through each task.

See Also points you to related information in the book.

Did You Know? alerts you to tips, techniques and related information.

Real World Examples

This book uses real world examples files to give you a context in which to use the task. By using the example files, you won't waste time looking for or creating sample files. You get a start file and a result file, so you can compare your work. Not every topic needs an example file, such as changing options, so we provide a complete list of the example files used through out the book. The example files that you need for project tasks along with a complete file list are available on the Web at *www.perspection.com*.

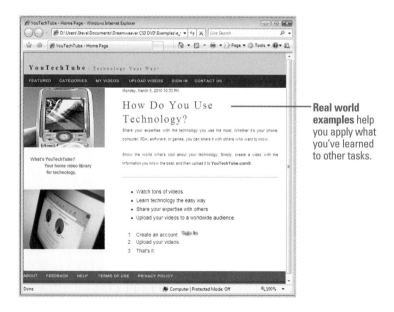

Real world examples help you apply what you've learned to other tasks.

Workshop

This book shows you how to put together the individual step-by-step tasks into indepth projects with the Workshop. You start each project with a sample file, work through the steps, and then compare your results with project results file at the end. The Workshop projects and associated files are available on the Web at *www.perspection.com.*

Workshop

Introduction

The Workshop is all about being creative and thinking outside of the box. These workshops will help your right-brain soar, while making your left-brain happy, by explaining why things work the way they do. Exploring Dreamweaver's possibilities is great fun; however, always stay grounded with knowledge of how things work. Knowledge is power.

Getting and Using the Project Files

Each project in the Workshop includes a start file to help you get started with the project, and a final file to provide you with the results so you can see how well you accomplished the task.

Before you can use the project files, you need to download them from the Web. You can access the files at *www.perspection.com.* After you download the files from the Web, uncompress the files into a folder on your hard drive to which you have easy access from Dreamweaver.

Project 1: Creating a Web Site from Scratch

Skills and Tools: Use Dreamweaver tools to create a Web site

Dreamweaver provides the tools you need to create a professional Web site that meets industry standards, which means Web browsers everywhere can display your site.

The Project

In this project, you'll learn how to create a Web site from scratch, which includes starting a new site, creating Web pages, creating page layouts with layers, adding and adjusting layers, inserting text and graphics, linking pages and other sites, adding interactivity and navigation, creating and attaching cascading style sheets, and publishing your Web site to a remote Web server for public viewing on the Web.

The Process

1 Start Adobe Dreamweaver CS3.

2 Click the **File** menu, and then click **New.**

1

The **Workshop** walks you through indepth projects to help you put Dreamweaver to work.

Adobe Certified Expert

This book prepares you fully for the Adobe Certified Expert (ACE) exam for Adobe Dreamweaver CS3. Each Adobe Certified Expert certification level has a set of objectives, which are organized into broader skill sets. To prepare for the certification exam, you should review and perform each task identified with a Adobe Certified Expert objective to confirm that you can meet the requirements for the exam. Throughout this book, content that pertains to an objective is identified with the Adobe Certified Expert logo and objective number next to it.

Adobe Certified Expert

About the Adobe Certified Expert (ACE) Program

The Adobe Certified Expert (ACE) program is for graphic designers, Web designers, systems integrators, value-added resellers, developers, and business professionals seeking official recognition of their expertise on Adobe products.

What Is an ACE?

An Adobe Certified Expert is an individual who has passed an Adobe Product Proficiency Exam for a specific Adobe software product. Adobe Certified Experts are eligible to promote themselves to clients or employers as highly skilled, expert-level users of Adobe software. ACE certification is a recognized worldwide standard for excellence in Adobe software knowledge. There are three levels of ACE certification: Single product certification, Specialist certification, and Master certification. To become an ACE, you must pass one or more product-specific proficiency exam and sign the ACE program agreement. When you become an ACE, you enjoy these special benefits:

*   Professional recognition
*   An ACE program certificate
*   Use of the Adobe Certified Expert program logo

What Does This Logo Mean?

It means this book will prepare you fully for the Adobe Certified Expert exam for Adobe Dreamweaver CS3. The certification exam has a set of objectives, which are organized into broader skill sets. Throughout this book, content that pertains to an ACE objective is identified with the following Adobe Certified Expert logo and objective number below the title of the topic:

DW 3-1

557

Logo indicates a task fulfills one or more Adobe Certified Expert objectives.

Get More on the Web

In addition to the information in this book, you can also get more information on the Web to help you get up to speed faster with Dreamweaver CS3. Some of the information includes:

Transition Helpers

◆ **Only New Features.** Download and print the new feature tasks as a quick and easy guide.

Productivity Tools

◆ **Keyboard Shortcuts.** Download a list of keyboard shortcuts to learn faster ways to get the job done.

More Content

◆ **Photographs.** Download photographs and other graphics to use in your Dreamweaver documents.

◆ **More Content.** Download new content developed after publication.

You can access these additional resources on the Web at *www.perspection.com.*

Keyboard Shortcuts

Adobe Dreamweaver CS3

If a command on a menu includes a keyboard reference, known as a keyboard shortcut, to the right of the command name, you can perform the action by pressing and holding the first key, and then pressing the second key to perform the command quickly. In some cases, a keyboard shortcut uses three keys. Simply press and hold the first two keys, and then press the third key. Keyboard shortcuts provide an alternative to using the mouse and make it easy to perform repetitive commands.

If you're searching for new keyboard shortcuts in Dreamweaver CS3, just look for the letter: N. The N appears in the Keyboard Shortcuts table so you can quickly and easily identify new or changed shortcuts.

Dreamweaver CS3 Keyboard Shortcuts		
Command	**Windows**	**Macintosh**
Menu Commands		
File		
New	Ctrl+N	⌘+N
Open	Ctrl+O	⌘+O
Browse in Bridge	Ctrl+Alt+O	⌘+Option+O
Open Recent		
Open in Frame	Ctrl+Shift+O	⌘+Shift+O
Close	Ctrl+W	⌘+W
Close All	Ctrl+Shift+W	⌘+Shift+W
Save	Ctrl+S	⌘+S
Save As	Ctrl+Shift+S	⌘+Shift+S
Print Code	Ctrl+P	⌘+P
Check Page		
Links	Shift+F8	Shift+F8

547

Additional content is available on the Web.

Preparing and Planning a Web Site

Introduction

You might have heard the expression: A journey of a thousand miles begins with the first step. While that makes perfect sense, there is one other thing that must be accomplished before taking that fateful step... proper planning.

Attempting to design a complex Web site without proper planning would be akin to taking a trip from New York to California without the benefit of any roadmaps. You might understand that you need to travel in a westerly direction; however, without proper planning, you would probably make a lot of wrong turns before arriving at your final destination. Planning therefore is a fundamental part of any journey, and it's a fundamental part of any Web design project.

Planning for a new Web site involves understanding in two key areas: knowledge of the applications you will be using (the logical side), and knowledge of what direction you want to take this new Web project (the creative side).

Dreamweaver will help any Web design project run more smoothly; whether you are building a Web site from scratch, collaborating with a Web-design team, or anywhere in between. So, before starting the planning process, you need knowledge of Dreamweaver and what's it's capable of doing.

Regardless of the scope of your project, take some time in advance to think through the architecture of your site (the layout structure of the pages as a whole, and the options for navigating the site), develop a look-and-feel (graphic design and interface), and gather the content (the information you want to include on the site pages). When this preliminary work is done, you can plunge into the development, staging, launching, and the very important maintenance of the site.

Creating a comprehensive plan of the project will simplify the process of creating a complex Web site, and like a road map, will help to keep you on track as you make that journey of a thousand miles.

Beginning with a Plan

Before you fire up the software and start cranking out Web pages, take a step back from the process, and ask yourself what you're aiming at by designing this Web site. You can get help in answering that question by asking yourself five more questions. Just turn to journalism 101, and ask yourself the 5 basic W questions: Who, What, When, Where, and the all-important, Why.

- **Who** is designing this site?
- **What** are the goals of the site?
- **When** will the site be completed?
- **Where** is my target audience?
- **Why** am I doing this?

Who is designing this site?

In this case the answer would be you. You're responsible for everything from the creation of the graphics, to the typing of the text: even to the compression of the video. Since you know Dreamweaver, the construction of the site... from the ground up, is all up to you. At least you think it is...

For example, you might know Dreamweaver from top to bottom, but do you also know some of the other applications you might need to use, such as: Photoshop, Illustrator, Flash, and Fireworks; just to name a few. If your knowledge of other essential applications is lacking, you might need to bring other experts into the mix. In addition, many Web designers can assemble Web pages with their eyes closed, but lack a fundamental understanding of how to load and manage the site out to the server. And what about marketing your site? Did you ever hear the expression, build it and they will come? Well, a lot of people built Web sites and nobody comes. Why? No one knew they

existed. The question: *Who is designing this site* helps you focus not only on the end game, but who is going to help you get there.

What are the goals of the site?

You would be surprised (or maybe you wouldn't) how many people want to build a Web site, but have no clear goals as to what they want the site to accomplish (just talk to some of my clients). A Web site is about communication, plain and simple. For example my goal for this book is to teach you how to use Dreamweaver in a logical and creative way, plain and simple. We could say that the goal of our fictional Web site is to obtain more business, that's what most business sites are designed to do. However, we also want an element of the site devoted to pure and free information; maybe an area devoted to tips and tricks on taking good photographs. A Web site can have more than one goal, but it's important to define them at the get go. If you don't have any clearly defined goals for your site, how are you going to be able to tell if you're successful? When my dad would take us on one of his famous across-the-country vacations, my sister and I would be in the back seat singing the mantra of all children everywhere: Are we there yet? Without a good, well-defined set of goals, how are you ever going to know if you've arrived? Later we'll talk about how you monitor those goals; for now just set them. If you don't know, or understand, the ultimate goals of your site, then stop right now, and don't move forward until you can define them.

When will the site be completed?

While this may seem trivial, I've known many a good Web designer who have gone out of business because they promised and never delivered. Since you'll be designing this site on your own, this question becomes even more important because it gives you a date to strive. Believe me it's very easy to let other considerations interfere with the completion of the site. And here's another good reason… in the business world a make or break for many is the holiday shopping season. From the end of November to the end of December many retailers make most of their money.

You believe that you can sell a lot of your photographs during this time of the year, so you plan for the site to be up and running for the holidays. But what does that really mean? In truth it means having the site up and running by August, at the latest. This gives the site time to be indexed by all the search engines, and it gives you time to iron out any possible kinks in the operation of the site. The worst thing you want to happen is to get the site up by mid November, and then discover that your shopping cart module is full of problems. Set a reasonable, reachable date, and then work toward that goal. Reasonable and reachable is obtained based on your knowledge of the site, its complexity, how long it will take you to do things, and how much time in the day you have to devote to the project.

Where is my target audience?

How are you going to know what to put into your site unless you understand where your audience is coming from? By coming from, I don't mean their geographical location (although that can be important). When I design a Web site for a client, I want to get to know the people that will be visiting the site. In reality, that's not very practical. After all, you're not going to knock on the front door of each and every possible visitor, sit down with a cup of tea, and discuss his or her likes and dislikes.

What I'm looking for in the discovery phase is a general idea of who my visitors might be: What kind of people would buy my photos and videos? Once I've got a handle on the demographics of my audience, I can design the site around those parameters. For example, I would design a Web site for six-year olds much differently than a site for a major corporation such as: General Electric, or Williams-Sonoma. We'll talk more about how you'll accomplish this later in this chapter; however, it's important to understand your target audience.

Why am I doing this?

While this may seem close to the goals for the site, it's simply a motivating tool. For example, the goal of the site is to increase my business, but in the end my goal is to share my photographic work with the world. It might also be security. For example, you work for someone else as a photographer in his or her studio, and because business is not that great, you feel that you could be in the unemployment queue before long. Your objective for designing this Web site is a personal goal you've had for years: To start you own business and become a photographer in your own rights.

Designing a Web site is not just about making money. You would be surprised how simply asking yourself the question: *Why am I doing this*, will motivate you to not only to get the job completed on time, but to do the absolute best job possible. Hey, this could just be your dream come true.

Creating a Visual Mind Map

There are many ways to expand a simple idea into a complex design. My personal favorite way is through the creation of a mind map.

Mind maps have many applications in personal, family, education, and business. Ideas are inserted into the map around a center thought (the seed), without the organization that comes from hierarchy or sequential arrangements (grouping and organizing is reserved for later stages).

A Mind Map consists of four essential elements:

◆ The **idea** (seed) is placed in the center of a blank page.

◆ The main **themes** of the central idea radiate from the central image on connecting lines or branches.

◆ Each branch holds a **key word**, and secondary ideas radiate out from each branch.

◆ The branches form a **connected structure** back to the central idea.

I find the best time to create a mind map of a project is when I'm fully rested and calm with the world. Remember, a mind map is all about free association.

Getting back to the mind map of our fictional Web site... The name of your business is YouTechTube, a place to store and display home videos on technology. Start the process by getting away from any possible distractions; turn off the television, get away from cell phones. Music is totally optional, and might help to focus your mind by eliminating any distracting background noise. The supplies you need are some plain white paper, and few colored pencils, the answers to the 5 W questions, and an uncluttered mind.

Start by drawing a circle in the middle of the page, and write the title of your site in the circle. You draw a line out from the center circle, like the branch of a tree, and on the branch you write the word, Applications. Then, using smaller branches, you begin listing the applications you believe will be needed to accomplish your goal: Dreamweaver, Flash, Photoshop, Final Cut Pro, etc. As you write down Final Cut Pro, you realize that you don't have much experience with that application; however, it will be very important in the design and compression of your video files. A good friend of yours, Harold Driver, is an expert and so you make a smaller branch next to Final Cut Pro and write, Contact Harold.

The process of free association is that one thought will inevitably lead to another related thought. If at any time you seem at a standstill, simply reread the answers you gave to the 5 basic W questions, and it should give you the mental inspiration to continue.

Once the mind map is complete, you might want to clean it up by entering the information from the hand-drawn sketch into a word processor. Sometimes by retyping the details of the mind map, it helps to spot things you might have forgotten. If you prefer doing your mind maps on a computer, check out the following Web sites:

◆ **Mindmap.** http://www.mindmap.com/EN/mindmaps/definition.html

◆ **Inspiration.** http://www.inspiration.com/

◆ **MindGenius.** http://www.mindgenius.com/

◆ **Mind manager.** http://www.mindjet.com/uk/

◆ **Mind tools.** http://www.mindtools.com/

◆ **Open source Freemind.**
http://freemind.sourceforge.net/wiki/
index.php/Main_Page

Remember that a mind map does not lock you in stone; it's simply ideas on how you are going to proceed with construction of your Web site.

The process of mind mapping a simple project can go very quickly. The more complex the project, the more involved the mind map. However it is time well spent. Most studies show that planning complex project will wind up saving you time... up to twenty percent.

Mind map

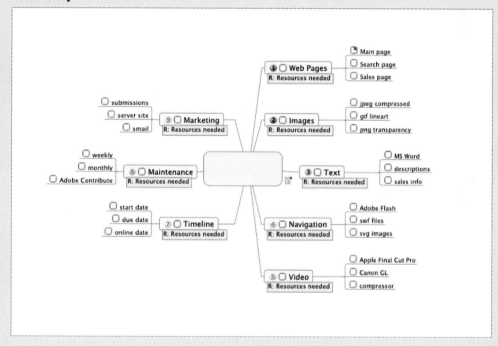

Creating Sample Page Sketches

Once the mind map is complete, take some time to hand draw some sketches of what the pages of your Web site will look like. You can start out (like I do) by drawing rectangles on a piece of paper, and crudely outlining where you want to place elements on the page; like arranging the furniture in a room, place page elements where they will be most comfortable and accessible to your visitors.

You don't have to be pretty; just get a general idea of how the site will be visually laid out. You might even add notations as to colors and text. Eventually you'll clean up these crude sketches by creating them on graph paper that matches the width to height ratio for each page, but more on that later.

The final step after the creation of the sketches is to give them the names you will use when you create them in Dreamweaver. Since these are file names, they should conform to standard file-naming conventions.

Sample Sketch

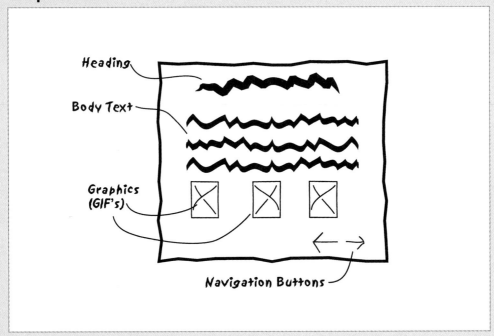

Generating a Timeline

You've generated a comprehensive mind map, and you've got some page sketches... you're doing great. You now have the information you need to proceed to the next step, and that's the creation of a flow chart. While the mind map gives you all the details of how your Web site is to be constructed, it does not give you that information in chronological order.

The flow chart takes the information obtained from the mind map and places it into an ordered timeline. For example, what do you work on first, second, third? Do you call Harold and ask for his help today on Final Cut Pro, or can it wait a bit. The flow chart is like the construction of a house; you start with the foundation, and move on. What do you think would happen if the drywall workers sealed up the walls to a new home before the electrician's had a chance to install the internal wiring?

In our case, you might design a really cool navigation system in Flash (took days of time); however, as you build the site, you realize that you left several pages out. Now, you've got to consume more time by going back and changing the Flash Navigation. The flow chart will help to reduce or eliminate such problems. It will also let you know where you stand in the construction of the site, and will help you complete your site successfully and on time.

Sample Timeline

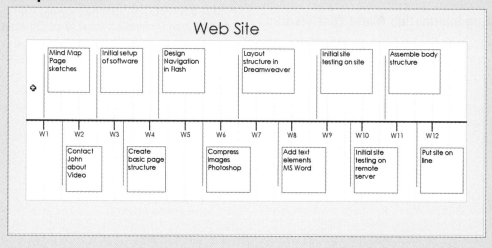

Assembling the Site

The majority of what you've accomplished so far is without the use of your computer (Unless you're using your computer to generate the mind maps or flow charts). While the process may seem tedious, in reality it's quite straightforward. As a matter of fact, once you have experienced the benefits of proper site planning, you'll never design another project without having a plan.

The next part of this process involves the gathering together of the "stuff" you will need to complete the project. That will include applications, images, animations, text; all the things that make up a proper site. Believe it or not, in a typical Web project, Dreamweaver might be one of the last places you go; not the first. Think of it this way, Dreamweaver is a Web design layout application. In order to use it, you need things to "lay out."

Gathering Information About Your Visitors

I mentioned earlier that the statement: Build it and they will come, is not necessarily true, especially when it comes to Web design. You need information. If you haven't already done a demographic study (also called the discovery phase) based on your target audience, do

so now. If this seems a bit overwhelming, there are a lot of sites that specialize in giving you exactly this sort of information.

The following list is just a few of the existing discovery sites:

- http://www.omniture.com/
- http://www.pewinternet.org/
- http://internet-statistics-guide.netfirms.com/
- http://www.w3.org/

A demographic study will give you an idea of what kind of people will visit your site, who they are, and what kind of Web knowledge they have. This information is invaluable in creating the design of your site. For example, the portion of your site that deals with video, could be made much more efficient if you used the latest compression codec from Adobe Flash; however, your study shows that most of your potential visitors do not have the current version of the Flash player, so you decide to downsize the videos to match what your visitors have. A demographic study is all about giving your visitors an enjoyable experience. If they like it they'll be back.

Creating a Marketing Plan

While you haven't started the actually creation of the site, it's not too early to start your marketing plans. There are thousands of new Web sites going up on the Internet every week. How do you get known? Well, first off Web search engines will find you; they employ programs called Web robots that go to all the Web servers on the planet, and patiently index each site. That way they can offer their visitors the ability to access information from any site, anywhere on or off the planet. The more sites like yours they index, the more money they can charge their advertisers. That means they are aggressive and they will find you. That doesn't mean that you sit by and wait, submission of your site to search engines is one of the first steps in getting your name out there to the world.

If you have the bucks, there are companies out there that will help you with the submission process. For example, the following sites will get you going, but for a price:

◆ http://www.wpromote.com/

◆ http://www.addpro.com/

◆ http://www.prioritysubmit.com/

If you would rather take a crack at the process yourself, there are a lot of ways to shout "Here I Am" without spending any of your hard-earned cash.

Search engine submission, or registration refers to the act of getting your Web site listed with search engines. Unfortunately, getting listed does not mean that you will necessarily rank well for particular terms. It simply means that the search engine knows your pages

exist, and if your visitors type in the right search words, they will find you.

For example, Yahoo has two submission options: "Standard," which is free, and "Yahoo Express," which involves a submission fee. Anyone can use Standard submission to submit for free to a non-commercial category.

How do you submit? Type the following URL into your browser:

http://search.yahoo.com/info/submit.html

That will bring up a list of submission options. Select you option, fill out the form, and you're finished.

Most search engines give you the ability to submit your site for free, or for a price. In many cases the only difference is how long it takes for your site to appear.

You should always prepare before submitting. This preparation means that you have written a 25 word or less description of your entire Web site. That description should make use of the two or three key terms that you hope to be found for. In our fictitious site you would use words like Photography and Video.

You should consider researching what are the best terms for your site, rather than guessing at these. The site:

http://searchenginewatch.com/

has a list of resources that will allow you to do such research. Avoid the use of marketing language in your description. You should use distinct keyworks instead. So, your description might go something like: *video, technology, training, and social network, etc.*

Creating a Storyboard

Many Web professionals use a technique called **storyboarding**. Storyboarding gives you a visual look at the layout of the site, and what type of organization you need to use. This will also give you a first look at how you want to build your navigational system.

A Linear Storyboard

The linear method connects pages one to another in an almost book-like fashion. The visitor has two choices: to move forward, or to move back... one page at a time.

A Hierarchical Storyboard

Hierarchical navigation models have a distinct top-down design. The idea is that there is an index or home page, and that pages branches to other main pages, on and on. It's resembles a business organizational chart, with the most important person at the top. This gives the visitor to your site a sense of direction, and is a popular Web organizational model.

A Wheel Storyboard

The wheel method is like spokes connected to a main hub. The main hub would have links to all the other pages within the site; however, it does require the visitor to return to the hub before moving to another page.

The Complete Storyboard

The Complete method takes into account the dynamic nature of the Web and its ability to navigate anywhere at any time. Typically it involves a main or index page, connected with a sophisticated menu system that allows the visitor to access any portion of the Web with 2 to 3 clicks, and a single click will always take them back to the main page. This is the most widely used navigational method.

Once you've chosen and created a storyboard, you should have a thumbnail of each of the proposed pages within your Web site, and the file name for each page.

Creating a Site Local Root Folder

Adobe Certified Expert   DW 2.4

The final act to perform is the creation of work folders. The work folders should contain all the elements of the Web site. You first start with a local root folder for the site. The **local root folder** contains all the elements of the Web site; every single piece of the site is included within this folder.

For example, your site local root folder is named, *youtechtube*, and there would be subfolders for the elements of the Web site, like: *Web Pages* and all the Web pages you designed in Dreamweaver would be placed within this subfolder. You use Photoshop and Fireworks to manage all of the site's images, and they are placed in the folder name, *Images*. Flash Objects, CSS, PDF documents; each kind of document is placed within its own personal folder. Later in this book you'll learn how to link this *site root folder* to Dreamweaver and create a working site.

Image the control you'll exert over the construction of a site when you create this type of organization. Even a modest Web site can have hundreds of parts. Let's say that you need to modify one of your PDF documents; however, you didn't create separate files, you put everything into one folder. Now, you have to scroll through over one hundred file names, looking for that one PDF file. Fortunately, you work smart, you simply open the PDF folder and, BANG, there it is, ready to be double-clicked. Work smart...

Creating a site root folder is not just a requirement of using Dreamweaver; in addition, it will help you in the creation, and of the moving of the site. If everything involving the construction of your Web site is contained within a single folder, it helps to keep you organized and in control... and being in control is an important part of being creative.

Although planning may seem like a lot of work, it really isn't. Especially when you add in the amount of time and frustration you'll save when the site is complete.

Have fun, and don't forget to enjoy the journey.

Create a Local Root Folder

1. Right click your mouse on the desktop, and then select **New Folder** from the popup menu (Macintosh) or right-click the desktop, point to **New**, and then click the **Folder** button from the popup menu.

2. Name the folder according to the site you're working (in this example, *youtechtube*).

3. Double click to open the folder, and then add additional subfolders to the local root folder.

All elements dealing with the construction of this Web site should be contained within this local root folder, and its corresponding subfolders.

Getting Started with Dreamweaver CS3

2

Introduction

Adobe Dreamweaver CS3 is the industry leading Web development tool for building Web sites and applications. It provides a combination of visual layout tools, application development features, and code editing support, enabling developers and designers at every skill level to create visually appealing, standards-based sites and applications quickly and easily. From leading support for Cascading Style Sheet (CSS) design to hand-coding features, Dreamweaver provides the tools professionals need to get the job done. In addition, developers can use Dreamweaver with the server technology of their choice to build powerful Internet applications that connect users to databases, live data feeds, and legacy systems.

Dreamweaver is an application that's rooted in the real world. In the real world, new or updated browsers come into the marketplace every year, and this creates problems in compatibility. Dreamweaver solves this problem by giving you powerful error-checking tools, and even gives you the ability to use Live Data View, and see exactly how your pages will perform on virtually any browser.

In the real world, server technologies change quickly. Dreamweaver's extensible architecture makes server compatibility a snap by giving you the tools to customize for third-party server models. In the real world computer operating systems change. Dreamweaver's CS3 not only supports use on Windows and Macintosh systems; in addition, there is now support for the new Intel-based Macintosh computers.

Web designers come at all levels of experience. Dreamweaver's user-friendly interface helps you out. If you're relatively new to the application, you can jump right in and begin designing simple Web pages. If you are an experienced designer, you will be able to access the power and control that this application offers, and take your Web designs where no one has gone before.

What You'll Do

Understand System Requirements

Install Dreamweaver CS3

Launch Dreamweaver

View the Dreamweaver Window

Create a Web Site

Open a Web Site

Create a Blank Web Page

Create Web Pages from Templates

Create a Web Page from a Sample

Save a Web Page

Open an Existing Web Page or File

Work with Views

Switch Between Pages and Views

Preview a Web Page

Get Help While you Work

Get Dreamweaver Updates on the Web

Close a Web Site or File

Exit or Quit Dreamweaver

Understanding System Requirements

System Requirements

Before you can install Dreamweaver, you will need to make sure that your computer meets the minimum system requirements. Dreamweaver CS3 is supported on both Windows and Macintosh computers, including the new Intel-based Macintosh systems.

While many designers bemoan the fact that their older computer systems will not support the newer applications, in the long run it's all for the best. The original versions of Dreamweaver (many years ago) were simply non-visual HTML editing applications. Dreamweaver CS3 is not only doing things that were not even dreamed of in years past; it's also faster. As a Web designer, time is an important part of getting the job done, and getting it done quickly.

If I can accomplish more work in less time, it gives me more time to be creative, and able to meet my deadlines. And that's a good thing. So think of system requirements as the power behind the applications, that's going to help you do more, better work, and all in less time.

For Windows Computers

You need to have a computer with the following minimum configuration:

- Intel Pentium 4, Intel Centrino, Intel Xeon, or Intel Core Duo (or compatible) processor
- Microsoft Windows XP with Service Pack 2 or Windows Vista Home Premium, Business, Ultimate, or Enterprise (certified for 32-bit editions)
- 512 MB of RAM, 1 GB or above recommended
- 1GB of available hard-disk space (additional free space required during installation)
- 1,024 x 768 monitor resolution with 16-bit video card
- DVD-ROM drive
- Internet or phone connection required for activation.
- Broadband Internet connection required for Adobe Stock Photos and other services

For Macintosh Computers

You need to have a computer with the following minimum configuration:

- 1 GHz PowerPC G4 or G5 or multicore Intel processor; Intel-based Macintosh
- Mac OS X 10.4.8, or later
- 512 megabytes (MB) of RAM, 1 GB or above recommended
- 1GB of available hard-disk space (additional free space required during installation)
- 1,024 x 768 monitor resolution with 16-bit video card
- DVD-ROM drive
- Internet or phone connection required for activation
- Broadband Internet connection required for Adobe Stock Photos and other services

Installing Dreamweaver CS3

The process of installing the Dreamweaver application is fairly straight-forward; you insert the Dreamweaver disc into your disc drive, double-click the installer application and simply follow the on-screen instructions. The first thing that will happen is that the installer will check to see if you have the minimum system requirements. If you meet the minimums, the installer will guide you through the steps to complete the installation. The whole process takes about ten minutes, and at the end of the process you can launch Dreamweaver for the first time. Remember to have your serial number handy, because you will have to type it in before you can open the application. It's a good idea to have that serial number in a safe place, just in case you would need to reinstall Dreamweaver.

Install Dreamweaver CS3

1️⃣ Insert the Dreamweaver CS3 disc into your disc drive.

2️⃣ Double-click the **Dreamweaver** icon, and then double-click the installer application (in Windows the installer application launches automatically).

   The installer screen will open, displaying the Dreamweaver CS3 installer window.

3️⃣ Follow the on-screen instructions and enter the information required for installation.

4️⃣ When the process is finished, close the installer.

   Congratulations, you've just installed Adobe Dreamweaver CS3 on your computer.

Did You Know?

Most Adobe applications can be downloaded. It's all very simple, you go to the http://www.adobe.com, click the Products menu item, and then select the application you want to purchase. You will need a credit card (of course), and a lot of bandwidth.

Launching Dreamweaver

The launching of Dreamweaver can be accomplished in one of several ways. You could access the application by opening the Dreamweaver folder and double-clicking on the application icon (Macintosh or Windows). You could create an alias of the application, by right clicking on the Dreamweaver program icon and selecting Make Alias (Macintosh) or Create Shortcut (Windows).

Launch Dreamweaver in Windows

① Click the **Start** button on the taskbar.

② Point to **All Programs**, and then click **Adobe**.

③ Click **Adobe Dreamweaver CS3**.

④ If this is the first time opening Dreamweaver CS3 you will be prompted to specify the following initial settings:

◆ Enter your serial number, and activate the application.

◆ Select the check boxes with page types you want to set Dreamweaver at the default editor, and then click **OK**.

Dreamweaver opens displaying the program window and the Startup Page.

③ ② All Programs changes to Back when you point to it.

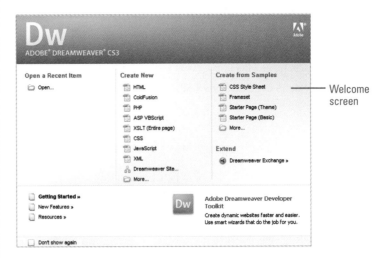

Welcome screen

Launch Dreamweaver in Macintosh

① Open the Applications folder (located on the main hard drive).

② Open the Adobe Dreamweaver CS3 folder.

③ Double-click the **Dreamweaver** icon.

④ If this is the first time opening Dreamweaver CS3 you will be prompted to specify the following initial settings:

◆ Enter your serial number, and activate the application.

◆ Select the check boxes with page types you want to set Dreamweaver at the default editor, and then click **OK**.

Dreamweaver opens displaying the program window and the Startup Page.

Shortcut for Adobe Dreamweaver CS3

Did You Know?

You can create a shortcut on the Macintosh. Drag and drop the Dreamweaver application icon to the bottom of the screen, and then add it to the shortcuts panel.

For Your Information

Activating Dreamweaver

In order to curb theft of their products, Adobe requires you to activate the Dreamweaver application. The first time you open it, you will be prompted to enter your serial number, and then activate Dreamweaver. You will be able to delay the activation process for up to 30 days; however, on day 31 the application will cease to run until activated. Activation can be accomplished by the Internet, or by phone.

You can launch Dreamweaver and open a document at the same time. Simply double-click on the document icon (i.e. index.html). If the document was originally created within Dreamweaver, the file automatically opens in the Dreamweaver application.

Viewing the Dreamweaver Window

The Dreamweaver Graphical User Interface or GUI (pronounced "GOOEY") is the Web designer's workplace. Inside its document window and 19 main work panels you will find all the tools you need to design everything from a simple Web page, to a complex site.

Welcome screen
Provides easy access links to create and open Dreamweaver documents.

Panel Windows
Gives you access to authoring tools and attribute settings for elements.

Document Window
Displays open Dreamweaver
documents, which includes
an Insert bar.

Insert Bar
Displays buttons for creating
and inserting objects in a
Dreamweaver document.

Property Inspector
Displays information about the properties and
attributes of tools and graphic elements.

Docking Channel
A place to attach and detach
panels. You can use the double-
arrow button at the top to
minimize and maximize the
docking channel.

Creating a Web Site

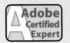

DW 2.4

Before you create a Web site, you need to create a local root folder where you'll store all the elements that make up the site. Web sites are more than just a bunch of Web pages. All the images, navigational buttons, document, etc., are separate files that must be uploaded into those pages. That's including any video, audio Java applets and scripts. Defining a Web site instructs Dreamweaver that the local root folder is the folder location that contains all the elements of your site. In turn, Dreamweaver will keep track of the files within the folder, automatically update them when necessary, and give you easy access to them, while you're working.

Create a New Web Site

1. Define a local root folder where you'll store all the elements that you will use to build your Web site.

2. Launch Dreamweaver.

3. Click the **Site** menu, and then click **New Site**.

   Dreamweaver gives you two choices on the creation of a Web site: Basic or Advanced.

4. Click the **Basic** tab (we'll deal with Advanced setting in Chapter 20).

5. Name your site (Site names are not file names, so feel free to use any naming convention you wish).

6. Enter in the URL (Uniform Resource Locator) for your site (the hosting server).

7. Click **Next** to continue.

8. Click the **No** option in response to the next screen's question: Do you want to work with a server technology such as ColdFusion, ASP, NET, ASP, JSP, or PHP.

9. Click **Next** to continue.

10. Click the **Edit Local Copies On My Machine, Then Upload To Server When Ready** option.

11 Enter the location of your local root folder, or click the **folder** icon, located to the right of the input box, and then select the folder from the Find window.

12 Click **Next** to continue.

13 Click the popup menu, and choose **None** from the available options.

14 Click **Next** to continue.

You'll see a listing of all the options you've chosen for this site.

15 Click **Back** to make changes, or click **Done** to complete the process.

Dreamweaver creates a site definition based on your options and your choice of the local root folder (In our example, youtechtube).

When you define a site in Dreamweaver, the Assets and Files panels will now display a list of all your folders and files.

Summary of selected settings

See Also

See "Setting Advanced Site Definitions" on page 478 for information on using the Advanced tab in the Site Definition dialog box.

For Your Information

Creating a Local Root Folder

The first step to a successful Web site is careful planning, and the creation of a local root folder. Since this is covered in Chapter 1, we'll assume that you've already taken care of this very important part of the design process. Remember, the local root folder contains all the elements that you use to build your Web site and all the individual pages and parts that it contains. It's very possible that you've already put in a lot of computer time before coming to this very important first step in Dreamweaver. For example, you may have created many of the images and graphics that you're going to use by working in Adobe Photoshop and Illustrator. You may have designed some Adobe Flash animations, and you might have even used Microsoft Word and Excel to generate some text documents and spreadsheets. All of these elements would be in the local root folder. In keeping with Chapter 1, we call this local root folder, *youtechtube*. Now that you have your local root folder, the next step is to inform Dreamweaver that this is the folder you'll be using for the creation of this particular Web site.

Opening a Web Site

Adobe Dreamweaver allows you to manage multiple sites. When you open Dreamweaver it will load the Web site last used. If, however, you need to work on another Web site it's a simple matter to redirect Dreamweaver to the needed site using the Manage Sites dialog box, which you can also use to create, edit, duplicate, remove, export, and import sites.

Open Predefined Sites

1 Click the **Site** menu, and then click **Manage Sites**.

2 Select the site from the listed options.

3 Click **Done**.

Dreamweaver closes the first site and loads all the assets for the selected site.

Creating a Blank Web Page

 DW 3.9

The whole point of using Dreamweaver is the creation of Web pages. In turn, these pages will load static and dynamic content, and be bundled together with a good navigational system; finally winding up as a complete Web site. The process of creating a site can become quite involved; however, it all begins with the creation of the first page. A new page is a blank slate for you to draw. A new Web page can be literally anything from a text page to a high-end page dealing with animation, video, audio, CSS, or any combination of the above. Please don't take this step too lightly. In other words don't start with a plan, just put the first page together and see where it goes from there. It's the plan that will make it all come together.

Create a Blank Web Page

1. Click the **File** menu, and then click **New**.

   TIMESAVER *Press Ctrl+N (Win) or* ⌘*+N (Mac).*

   The New Document dialog box opens.

   TIMESAVER *To create a Web page without the dialog box, click the file type you want at the Welcome Screen.*

2. Click the **Blank Page** category.

3. Select the Page Type you want (in this example, HTML).

4. Select the Layout you want (in this example, 1 column, elastic, centered).

5. Click the **DocType** popup and select the option you want.

   In this example, leave steps 5 thru 7 at their default values.

6. Click the **Layout CSS** popup, if available, and select the option you want.

7. Click the **Link** button to attach a CSS file to the current document.

8. Click **Create**.

   Dreamweaver creates the new page and opens it.

Creating a Web Page from a Blank Template

 DW 3.9

A Dreamweaver template is a common structure created and used for all or some pages of a Web site. Each section of a Web site can have its own template with variations in structure or color from the others. Templates are fantastic timesaving tools because they allow you to create pages that share the same design but different content, and if you modify a template document, you immediately update the design of all pages that were created from that template. Dreamweaver templates are special master files that contain editable and locked regions. Pages based on a template enable Dreamweaver users to edit parts of a Web page within the editable regions without the risk of accidentally changing the locked regions. This is a major advantage, because if you are creating a site that will be maintained by other users you can specify which parts of pages editors can and cannot change.

Create a Blank Template

1. Click the **File** menu, and then click **New**.

2. Click the **Blank Template** category.

3. Select the Template Type you want (in this example, HTML Template).

4. Select the Layout you want (in this example, 2 column, elastic, left sidebar).

   In this example leave the Doc Type and Layout CSS at their default values of XHTML 1.0 Transitional, and Add to Head, respectively.

5. Click **Create**.

   Dreamweaver opens the template.

6. Click the **File** menu, click **Save**, click **OK** if necessary to dismiss the no editable region alert, specify a name, and then click **Save**.

For Your Information

Storing Templates

When you work with templates, Dreamweaver automatically creates a folder called Templates, and all template files are stored in this folder. If you move a template file outside that folder, Dreamweaver will not be able to create new files based on that template. In addition, it creates problems when you insert paths for hyperlinks. Keep your templates within the Templates folder.

Create Editable Regions

1. Use your cursor to select an area of the image that you want to have the ability to edit. An editable area can be defined as an AP element, or table, or table cell, etc.

2. Click the **Insert** menu, point to **Template Objects**, and then select from the following Region options:

   ◆ **Editable Region.** Use this option to allow contributors to the Web page the ability to change or modify that selected area.

   ◆ **Optional Region.** Use this option to define a section of the page that will or will not be shown, depending on what the content contributor decides.

   ◆ **Repeating Region.** Use this option to allow contributors to the Web page the ability to duplicate the region. For example, creating a table that holds customer comments, and the contributor needs the ability to generate new pages, and add more rows to the table, as needed.

3. Enter an appropriate name for the Region.

4. Click **OK**.

   The selected area now takes on the appropriate characteristics.

Editable region

Creating a Web Page from a Template

Instead of creating a Web page from scratch, you can create a new Web page based on the existing template, which can save you a lot of time and effort. In the New Document dialog box, you can select your own custom template designs available in the Page From Template category or click Get More Content to open the Dreamweaver Exchange on the Web to download more template page designs.

Create a Web Page from an Existing Template

1 Click the **File** menu, and then click **New**.

TIMESAVER *Press Ctrl+N (Win) or* ⌘*+N (Mac).*

The New Document dialog box opens.

2 Click the **Page From Template** category.

3 Select the site that contains the template you want: Flash Site and Project Site appear by default.

4 Select the template you want to use.

5 Select or clear the **Update Page When Template Changes** check box.

6 Click **Create**.

7 Click the **File** menu, click **Save**, specify a name, and then click **Save**.

Did You Know?

You can create a document from a template in the Assets panel. Open the Assets panel using the Windows menu, click the Templates icon to view the list of templates, right-click (Win) or Control-click (Mac) the template you want, click New From Template, and then save the document.

Creating a Web Page from a Sample

DW 3.9

If you're not sure where you start, you can use one of Dreamweaver's sample designs as a starting point for a new page and then make any changes you want to customize it to suite your specific needs. In the New Document dialog box, you can preview sample file designs and then create a new document based on the one you want to use. You can select from sample pages with CSS (Cascading Style Sheets), frames, themes (starter pages for Entertainment, Lodging, etc.), and basic types (starter pages for Commerce, Data, Images, etc.). When you create a new document, Dreamweaver makes a untitled copy of the sample file, which you can save with a new name.

Create a Web Page from a Sample

1. Click the **File** menu, and then click **New**.

   TIMESAVER *Press Ctrl+N (Win) or ⌘+N (Mac).*

   The New Document dialog box opens.

2. Click the **Page From Sample** category.

3. Select the type of sample file you want to use: CSS Style Sheet, Frameset, Starter Page (Theme), or Starter Page (Basic).

   TIMESAVER *At the Welcome Screen, click the type of sample file you want.*

4. Select the sample file you want.

5. If available, click the **DocType** popup, and then select from the available options.

6. Click **Create**.

   Dreamweaver creates the new page and opens it.

7. Click the **File** menu, click **Save**, specify a name, and then click **Save**.

8. If the Copy Dependent Files dialog box appears, set the options you want, and then click **Copy**.

Saving a Web Page

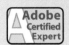

DW 3.9, 3.18

Web pages should be saved as soon as they're opened. Naming conventions should be according to a predefined list of names that you created during the planning stage of the project. It's important to save pages early, that way if there's any problem such as: the application locking up, you will be able to start again from the last-saved version. Another important reason is error checking and validating. Web pages must be in a saved state before performing any validation.

Save a Web Page

① Click the **File** menu, and then select from the following options:

◆ **Save.** If the file is new, you will be prompted to enter a proper file name and location for the new page. If the file has been previously saved, Dreamweaver saves the file, using the original file name and location (without prompting).

TIMESAVER *Press Ctrl+S (Win) or ⌘+S (Mac).*

◆ **Save As.** Use this option to make a copy of a file; you will be prompted to give the file a new name and location.

TIMESAVER *Press Ctrl+Shift+S (Win) or ⌘+Shift+S (Mac).*

◆ **Save All.** Use this option if you have more than one file open, and you want to save all of them at the same time. If any of the files are new, you will be prompted to enter a file name and location.

◆ **Save To Remote Server.** Use this option if you've set up your remote server, and you want to save the file directly to the server.

Local root site

Site folders

◆ **Save As Template.** Use this
option to save the open
document as a template. A
template is a reusable
document that contains
editable regions.

2 Navigate to the drive and folder
location where you want to save
the file.

3 Type a name for the file, or use the
suggested name.

When naming files, avoid using
spaces and special characters, or
punctuation.

For this example, leave the other
options at their default levels.

4 Click **Save** to finalize the process.

5 Click **Copy**.

Did You Know?

*You can revert to the last saved ver-
sion of a document.* Click the File
menu, click Revert, and then click Yes
to revert to the previous version, or
click No to keep your changes. If you
save a document and then exit
Dreamweaver, you cannot revert to the
previous version when you restart
Dreamweaver.

*Macintosh and Windows computers
systems are not case sensitive.*
Therefore when you create a file name
for a Web page (or the files loaded on
the page), you won't have a problem
validating that page on your computer;
however, when you move the site to
the server, many servers are case-sensitive, and the same pages may not
load correctly. For example, if a Web
page is named Index.html and you call
it using index.html. It validates on your
computer, but it might not work on the
server… pay attention to case.

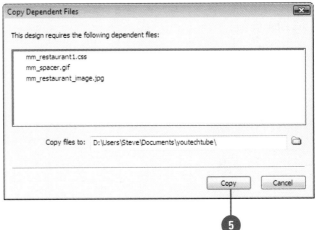

Opening an Existing Web Page or File

Opening a Web page is a simple procedure and can be accomplished using the Open command on the File menu. You can open a Web page from your local hard drive, a network drive, or a Web server using an Uniform Resource Locator (URL). By default, Dreamweaver opens the last Web site you worked on every time you open the program. If you open a new page while another site is still open, the new page opens in a new Dreamweaver window. Web pages using the HTML—Hypertext Markup Language—are the primary file types you open in Dreamweaver, however, you can open other types too. As a editor, you can use Dreamweaver to open many types of Web related files, including style sheets, scripts, text, xml, and libraries. For Web pages you recently opened, you can quickly reopen them again by pointing to Open Recent on the File menu, and then selecting the Web page you want to open.

Open an Existing Web Page or File

1. Click the **File** menu, and then click **Open**.

   TIMESAVER *Press Ctrl+O (Win) or ⌘+O (Mac).*

2. Navigate to the drive and folder location where you want to open the Web page.

3. Click the **Files Of Type** list arrow (Win) or **popup** (Mac), and then select the type of file you want to open.

4. Select the page you want to open in the working folder, or type the URL of the page you want.

5. Click **Open**.

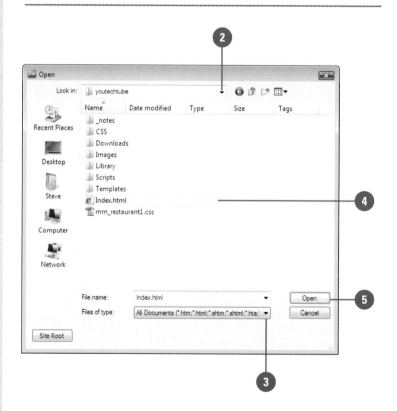

Open a Recently Opened Document

◆ **File Menu**. Click the **File** menu, point to **Open Recent**, and then click the file you want to open.

◆ **Welcome Screen**. At the Welcome Screen, click the file you want to open under Open a Recent Item.

Click to open recently opened files

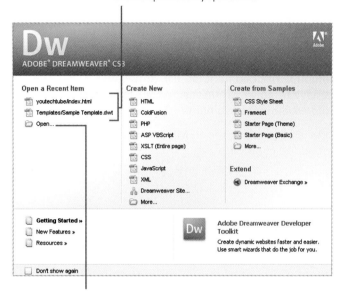

Click to access the Open dialog box

Dreamweaver File Types

File Type	Description
HTML	Hypertext Markup Language (.html or .htm) files display Web pages in a browser.
CSS	Cascading Style Sheet (.css) files are used to format and position HTML content in a consistent manner.
GIF	Graphics Interchange Format (.gif) files are used for graphic, such as logos, containing a max of 256 colors.
JPEG	Joint Photographic Expert Group (.jpeg) files are used for graphics, such as photographs, requiring more than 256 color.
XML	Extensible Markup Language (.xml) files contain data in raw form that can be formatted using XSL.
XSL	Extensible Stylesheet Language (.xsl or .xslt) files are used to style XML data.
CFML	ColdFusion Markup Language (.cfm) files are used to process dynamic Web pages.
ASPX	ASP.NET files (.aspx) files are used to process dynamic Web pages.
PHP	Hypertext Preprocessor (.php) files are used to process dynamic Web pages.

Working with Views

Dreamweaver displays the contents of a Web page in different ways to help you work efficiently with your content. When you click a Web page or document tab, Dreamweaver displays three view buttons on the Document toolbar below the tab name.

Code view displays the HTML and any embedded code for a page.

Split view displays the screen in half horizontally. The top half displays the current page in Code view and the bottom half displays the current page in Design view.

Design view displays Web pages in WYSIWYG (What You See Is What You Get) view for editing.

Code view

Split view

Design view

Switching Between Pages and Views

The tabs across the top of the Document window indicate the currently open Web pages. You can click the tab to display the page or site you want. Below the tab in the Document window, the view buttons—Code, Split, and Design—appear for the currently page tab. Design view displays the page or site as it appears on screen, while Code view displays the HTML code that makes up the page or site. Split view shows you Code view at the top and Design view at the bottom. This view is helpful for learning how the code and design elements work.

Switch Between Web Pages

◆ **Web Pages**. Click the tab with the name you want to display.

TIMESAVER *Press Ctrl+Tab or Ctrl+Shift+Tab to cycle thru tabs.*

Did You Know?

You can view multiple documents in a single Document window (Mac). Control-click the tab, and then click Move To New Window. To combine separate documents into tabbed windows, click the Window menu, and then click Combine As Tabs.

Click tabs to switch between open files

Switch Between Page Views

◆ **Switch Views**. Click the **Code**, **Split**, or **Design** button below the tab on the Document toolbar in the Document window, or click the **View** menu, and then click the view you want.

TIMESAVER *Press Ctrl+` (accent above Tab button) to cycle to the view you want.*

Click to switch views

Previewing a Web Page

As you work on the development of your site, you will probably want to occasionally stop and see what the individual pages look like when previewed within a specific browser. One of the most used features for testing your site is the Preview In Browser feature. This is one of the most used when working in Dreamweaver. It lets you see what your site will look like in a particular Internet browser. When testing a particular Web page, it's a good idea to check it out in more than one browser, and in more than one version of the browser. For example, on the Macintosh the native browser is called Safari, and on Windows, it's Explorer. The Safari browser will not work on a Windows machine, and Microsoft recently stopped supporting the Macintosh platform. Since your Web page will be loaded, interpreted, and run by the visitor's browser, it may look great in Safari, and not even work in Explorer. Therefore, make sure that you check your pages out in all the major versions of the browsers that you believe your visitors will use.

Preview a Web Page

1. Open the Web page you want to view.

2. Click the **File** menu, point to **Preview In Browser**, and then select a browser from the available options.

3. If the Web page needs to be saved, you will be prompted to save the page before continuing.

   The Web page opens and displays in the selected browser. Check the page out by clicking all the links, and making sure everything displays as planned.

4. When you're done, close the browser to return to Dreamweaver.

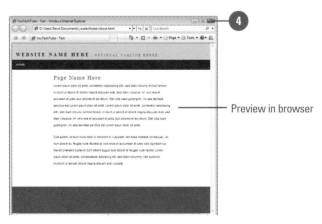

Preview in browser

> ### Did You Know?
>
> *What it means when you get an error previewing a Web page.* The preview in browser function may return a "page cannot be found" error if any of the characters in the path of the local folder have a different letter case than the path of the testing server folder.

Edit the Browser List in Preferences

1. Click the **File** menu, point to **Preview In Browser**, and then click **Edit Browser List**.

2. Click the **Plus** (+) button to add another browser to the list.

3. Give the new browser a name.

4. Click **Browse**, and then locate the browser you want to add to your list.

5. Select the browser, and then click **Open**.

6. Select the **Primary Browser** or **Secondary Browser** check box to decide whether this new browser is the primary or secondary browser.

7. Click **OK** to return to the Preferences dialog box.

8. Click **OK** to close the dialog box and save your changes.

9. Click the **File** menu, and move down to **Preview In Browser**.

   Your new browser option is added to the list.

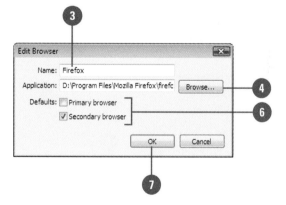

Did You Know?

You can use keyboard shortcuts to preview pages. The Primary Browser launches when you press the F12 key. The Secondary Browser launches when you press Ctrl+F12 (Win) or ⌘+F12 (Mac).

Getting Help While you Work

Everybody needs a bit of help now and then, and working in Dreamweaver is no exception to that rule. For example, you're working hard and fast on a Web page and it's time to insert a table; however, you're a bit fuzzy on that particular subject. Not to worry, all you have to do is ask Dreamweaver about adding tables, and you'll have the answer. It's that simple. Years ago, Help systems for applications were laborious, took forever to access, and half the time didn't give you the answer you were looking for. Thank goodness that the times have changed, and all you have to do is click the Help menu.

Get Dreamweaver Help

1. Click the **Help** menu, and then click **Dreamweaver Help**.

   TIMESAVER *Press F1.*

2. Click the **Browser** list arrow, and then select from the following options:

   - **Dreamweaver CS3.**

   - **Dreamweaver CS3 - API Reference.**

   - **Dreamweaver CS3 - Extending.**

3. Click to view help by Contents or Index.

4. Select the appropriate topic on the left, and view the corresponding help information on the right.

5. If you can't find help in the Contents or Index area, click in the **Search** field and type in a specific piece of information to search.

6. Click the **Print** button to print the current help information.

7. When you're done, click the **Close** button.

Help topic

Get Additional Help

1. Click the **Help** menu, and choose from the following options:

   ◆ **Dreamweaver Help.** Standard help systems for all areas of Dreamweaver.

   ◆ **Help Resources Online.** Gives you access to the Adobe online support center, and allows you to search through an extensive LiveDocs data base.

   ◆ **Extending Dreamweaver.** Gives you access to information about extending Dreamweaver capabilities using 3rd party extensions, and open-architecture programming.

   ◆ **Dreamweaver API (Application Program Interface) Reference.** A set of routines provided in libraries that extends a language's functionality.

   ◆ **What's New In Dreamweaver.** All about what's new in Dreamweaver CS3.

   ◆ **Spry Framework Help.** Online help for Spry, an open source Ajax framework developed by Adobe which is used in the construction of Rich Internet Applications.

   ◆ **ColdFusion Help.** Online help for CFML (ColdFusion Markup Language). CFML is a tag-based Web scripting language supporting dynamic Web page creation and Database access in a Web server environment.

   ◆ **Reference.** Gives you access to fourteen books and manuals with information of how to use Dreamweaver in a creative and logical way; this one is my favorite.

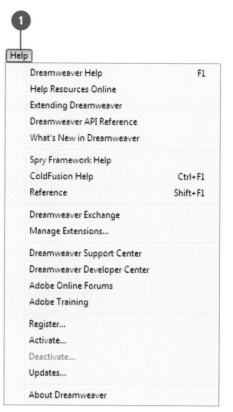

Getting Dreamweaver Updates on the Web

Applications are released to the public on a specific date, and as sure as the sun rises in the east; they will eventually come up with a new version. As a matter of fact, this is the ninth version of Dreamweaver. The problem is that we can't always wait for an update to fix a specific problem. For example, you just picked up Dreamweaver CS3 and loaded it onto your computer... three months later you get an update to your operating system, and load it. Ops... Dreamweaver is having problems, now that the new operating system is loaded. Do you wait another year for the next version update? The good news is that Adobe already knows about the potential problem, and in their immense wisdom created an update to fix the problem. It's not a bad idea to make a notation on your calendar and visit the update area on a monthly basis. You might be surprised what you find... and all updates are free. But how do you get that update? You're only a couple of clicks away.

Get Dreamweaver Updates on the Web

1 Click the **Help** menu, and then click **Updates**.

2 If the Adobe Updater dialog box appears, indicating updates are available, click the **Show Details** link to select the updates you want.

Adobe displays a listing of all available updates for every one of their applications.

3 Select the updates you want.

4 Select the appropriate update, click the **Download and Install Updates** button, and follow the onscreen instructions.

Closing a Web Page or File

After you finish working on a Web page, you can close it and open another one, or close it and exit Dreamweaver. Closing a Web page makes more computer memory available for other processes. Closing a Web page is different from exiting Dreamweaver: after you close a Web page, Dreamweaver is still running until you exit it.

Close a Web Page or File

1. Click the **File** menu, and then click **Close**.

    TIMESAVER *Click the Close button in the Document window or press Ctrl+W (Win) or ⌘+W (Mac).*

2. Click **Yes** to save any Web changes; click **No** to close the Web without saving any changes; or click **Cancel** to return to the Web without closing it.

Click to close file

Did You Know?

You can close all Web pages at one time. Click the File menu, and then click Close All Pages or press Ctrl+Shift+W (Win) or ⌘+Shift+W (Mac).

You can cascade or tile Document window. To cascade document windows, click the Windows menu, and then click Cascade. To tile documents, click the Windows menu, and then click Tile Horizontally or Tile Vertically (Windows), or Tile (Mac).

Exiting or Quitting Dreamweaver

As much as we enjoy working in Dreamweaver, the time will finally come when you want to shut down for the day. The process of closing out a Dreamweaver Web site, is not difficult; as a matter of fact, it's no more complicated than closing down any application. Dreamweaver is smart, if you attempt to exit or quit before saving that last file you were working on, Dreamweaver prompts you to save or ignore any changes.

Exit or Quit Dreamweaver

1 Use any of the following methods:

TIMESAVER *Press Ctrl+Q (Win) or* ⌘*+Q (Mac).*

◆ Click the **Close** button on the Dreamweaver program window title bar.

◆ In Macintosh, click the **Dreamweaver** menu, and then click **Quit Dreamweaver**.

◆ In Windows, click the **File** menu, and then click **Exit**.

2 Click **Yes** to save any Web changes, or click **No** to ignore any changes.

Dreamweaver performs an orderly shutdown of the program.

Click to exit Dreamweaver

Working Within the Dreamweaver Environment

Introduction

Getting to know the Dreamweaver authoring environment makes you more effective and efficient as you create Web pages and manage Web sites. You'll get to know the parts of the Dreamweaver window, which include toolbars and panels.

The Toolbars contain buttons that you can use to perform common tasks. Dreamweaver comes with five toolbars. The main two are the Insert and Document toolbars, which appear by default. The Insert toolbar, also known as the Insert bar, appears under the menu bar and provides the commands for inserting various types of objects, while the Document toolbar appears under an open document tab and allows you to change views, specify a title, manage files, preview pages, enable or disable page view options, and perform document validation. The Dreamweaver window also included panels. Panels are windows that allow you to view, organize, and change elements and related options in a document. The Properties panel is a specialize panel that allows you to change object specific attributes and options. To work efficiently in Dreamweaver you need information about the active document. Dreamweaver displays current information about the active document and common display tools on the Status bar, located at the bottom of the document window. For example, working with the Zoom tool on the Status bar gives you one more way to control the view size to exactly what you see in Dreamweaver. In addition, you can use rulers, guides, and the grid to help you lay out artwork and objects with precision.

Dreamweaver uses built-in keyboard shortcuts designed specifically for Dreamweaver. The built-in keyboard shortcuts are organized into sets, which you can duplicate and customize to create your own personalized set. Dreamweaver allows you to set preferences to customize the way you work in the program.

Examining the Dreamweaver Window

When you start Dreamweaver, the program window displays several windows of varying sizes you can use to create Web pages. These windows include the Program window, Document window, various panels, and the Properties panel. Depending on your installation and previous program usage, not all of

these windows may appear, or additional ones may be visible. You'll do the bulk of your work in Dreamweaver with these windows.

In Dreamweaver, windows appear in the workspace with a title bar, such as the program window, a document window tab, or in a panel.

Document Window
Displays open Dreamweaver documents, panels, and the Properties panel.

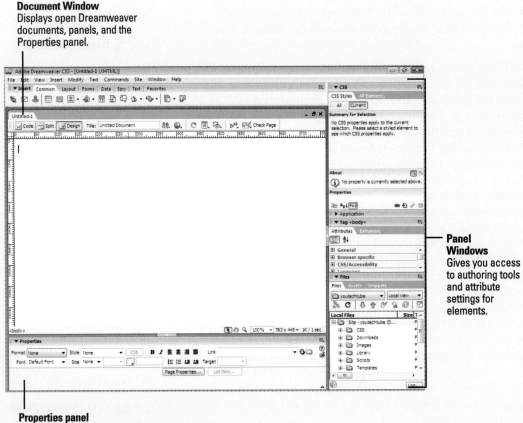

Panel Windows
Gives you access to authoring tools and attribute settings for elements.

Properties panel
Displays information about the properties and attributes of tools and graphic elements.

DW 3.1

The **Program window** displays a Title bar with the program name Adobe Dreamweaver CS3 and the filename of the active open file in brackets. The Title bar also contains a Close button and resizing buttons to the far right.

A menu bar appears below the title bar with menu names. A **menu** is a list of commands that you use to accomplish specific tasks. A **command** is a directive that accesses a feature of a program. Dreamweaver has its own set of menus, which are located on the menu bar along the top of the Dreamweaver window. On a menu, a check mark identifies a feature that is currently selected (that is, the feature is enabled or on). To disable (turn off) the feature, you click the command again to remove the check mark. A menu can contain several check marked features. A bullet (Win) or diamond (Mac) also indicates that an option is enabled, but a menu can contain only one bullet-or diamond-marked feature per menu section. To disable a command with a bullet or diamond next to it, you must select a different option in the section on the menu.

When you perform a command frequently, it's faster, and sometimes more convenient, to use a shortcut key, which is a keyboard alternative to using the mouse. When a shortcut key is available, it is listed beside the command on the menu, such as ⌘+F3 (Mac) or Ctrl+F3 (Win) for the Properties command on the Window menu.

Below the menu bar is the Insert toolbar, which appears by default and provides tabs with a variety of different buttons. A **Toolbar** contains a set of commonly used buttons you can quickly access to help you to create Web pages. Dreamweaver comes with five different toolbars, which you can show or hide to customize the Program window

The **Document window** displays open Dreamweaver documents. Dreamweaver uses tabs to make it easier to switch back and forth between documents. Below a Document tab is the Document toolbar. Each document window includes a Minimize, Maximize, and Close button at the top, and a **Status bar** at the bottom, which displays current information about the active document and common display tools.

A **panel** is a window you can collapse, expand, and group with other panels, known as a panel group, to improve accessibility and workflow. A panel appears with a shaded header bar, which includes the window title and additional options. A panel group consists of either individual panels stacked one on top of the other or related panels organized together with tabs, such as the Files panel, to navigate from one panel to another. Dreamweaver provides a wide variety of panels you can use to work with different aspects of a Web page, including CSS Styles, Databases, Tags, and Frames, which you can open and close from the Window menu. As you open, close, and move around windows and panels to meet your individual needs, you can save the location of windows and panels as a custom panel layout set, which you can display again later.

The **Properties panel**, known more commonly as the **Property Inspector**, at the bottom of the Program window provides a convenient way to view and change attributes of any selected object or multiple objects, such as graphics and shapes, on a Web page. After you select an object, relevant commands and associated fields for it appear in the Property Inspector.

Working with Toolbars

Toolbars contain buttons you can click to carry out commands you use frequently. Dreamweaver provides 5 different toolbars—Insert, Style Rendering, Document, Standard, and Coding—for you to use to execute commands. The Insert toolbar appears by default under the menu bar and provides the commonly used commands for inserting various types of objects. The Insert toolbar, which is a panel, displays tabs, such as Common, Layout, Forms, Data, Spry, Text, and Favorites, you can use to access toolbar buttons. The Style Rendering toolbar allows you to work with different media types. The Document toolbar appears by default under an open document tab and allows you to change views, specify a title, manage files, preview pages, enable or disable page view options, and perform document validation. The Standard toolbar provides common file and editing commands, such as Open, Save, Print, Cut, Copy, Paste, Undo, and Redo. The Coding toolbar is available in Code and Split views and makes it easier to work with code. You can quickly show or hide the toolbars you need or no longer using to customize the way you use Dreamweaver.

Show and Hide Toolbars

◆ To display a toolbar, click the **View** menu, point to **Toolbars**, and then click a toolbar to select the check mark.

   TIMESAVER *You can also right-click (Win) or Control+click (Mac) any of the toolbars and then click a toolbar.*

◆ To hide a toolbar, click the **View** menu, point to **Toolbars**, and then click a toolbar to deselect the check mark.

   TIMESAVER *To display or hide the Insert toolbar, press Ctrl+F2, or click the Window menu, and then click Insert.*

Click to select (show) or deselect (hide) the check mark.

Using the Docking Channel

If you use Windows and need more workspace, you can use the Drawer button on the channel separator bar (a thin line along the edge of a docking channel) to quickly minimize a docking channel. When you click the Drawer button, the docking channel collapses to increase the size of the workspace. When you click the Drawer button again, the docking channel reopens. If you need to increase or decrease the size of a docking channel, you can drag the channel separator bar to resize the docking channel as you would any window.

Minimize and Maximize a Docking Channel in Windows

1. To minimize or maximize a docking channel, click the **Drawer** button on the channel separator bar.

Drawer button; minimized docking channel

Drawer button; maximized docking channel

Working with Panels

Panels are windows that allow you to view, organize, and change elements and related options in a document. In Dreamweaver you work with several panel windows at one time. Instead of continually moving, resizing, or opening and closing windows, you can collapse or expand individual panels within a window with a single click to save space. A panel appears with a header bar, which includes the window title and three accessibility options: the panel gripper, the expander arrow, and an Options menu. You use the panel gripper to group or ungroup and dock or undock panel windows. You use the expander arrow to collapse or expand panels. The Options menu provides you with commands to group, rename, maximize, and close a panel, and use the Help system. The commands available on the Options menu vary depending on the panel.

Open and Close a Panel

1. Click the **Window** menu.

2. Click a panel name, such as Properties, Files, History, or CSS Styles.

Panels on Window menu

Collapse and Expand a Panel

1. To collapse or expand an open panel, click the triangle or window title on the header bar of the panel.

   TIMESAVER *To hide and show all panels, click the Window menu, and then click Hide Panels.*

Collapsed panels

Expanded panel

Collapse and Expand the Information Area in a Panel

1 Open or expand a panel.

IMPORTANT *Not all panels contain an information area.*

2 Click the triangle in the bottom right-corner of the panel.

Expanded

Use the Panel Options Menu

1 Open or expand a panel.

2 Click the **Options** button on the right side of the panel header bar.

3 Click a command from the list (commands vary). Common commands include:

◆ Help

◆ Group *panel name* With

◆ Close *panel name*

◆ Rename Panel Group

◆ Maximize Panel Group

◆ Close Panel Group

Docking and Undocking Panels

You can dock and undock, or temporarily attach and detach, panels or panel groups in docking channels. A docking channel is a region located on the left and right side of the Dreamweaver window to which you can temporarily attach and detach panels. You can only dock tool panels in a docking channel. Document panels and the Stage cannot be docked to a docking channel. When you drag a panel over a dockable area, an outline around the target dock appears. When you release the mouse button, the panel snaps to the dockable area and stays there until you move it. If you attempt to dock a panel over an undockable area, no outline appears. When a docking channel doesn't have any panels, the channel disappears until it is needed again.

Dock a Panel

1 Position the pointer on the panel gripper (the textured area left of the tile in the header bar).

2 Drag the window away from the panel to a docking channel.

Undock a Panel

1 Position the pointer on the panel gripper (the textured area left of the tile in the header bar).

2 Drag the window away from the panel to an empty area of the Dreamweaver window.

Grouping and Ungrouping Panels

You can group panels together to improve organization and workflow. When you group panels together, you can stack one on top of the other, or group related panels together as a tabbed panel group, such as the Component Inspector panel. You can add a panel to an existing panel group or you can create a new panel group. If you no longer need panels grouped together, you can ungroup them. You can use the panel gripper to group or ungroup as well as dock or undock panel windows.

Group Panels Together

1. Position the pointer on the panel gripper (the textured area to the left of the tile in the header bar).

2. Drag the window away from the panel to another panel window.

Did You Know?

You can group panels together using a menu. Click the Options button on the panel that you want to group, point to Group *Panel Name* With, and then select a panel.

Ungroup Panels

1. Position the pointer on the panel gripper (the textured area the left of the tile in the header bar).

2. Drag the window away from the panel to an empty area of the Dreamweaver window or a docking channel.

See Also

See "Working with Panels" on page 46 for information on using panels, or "Docking and Undocking Panels" on page 48 for information on moving panels around the screen.

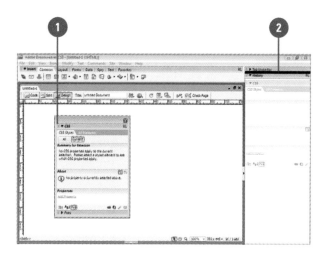

Creating a Panel Set

As you work with Dreamweaver, you'll open, close, and move around windows and panels to meet your individual needs. After you customize the Dreamweaver workspace, you can save the location of windows and panels as a custom panel layout set, which you can display using the Panel Sets command on the Window menu. You can create custom panel sets, or use the default panel set provided by Dreamweaver. If you no longer use a custom panel set, you can remove it at any time. You can also rename a custom panel set to better recognition and use.

Create a Panel Set

1. Open and position the panels you want to include in a panel set.

2. Click the **Window** menu, point to **Workspace Layout**, and then click **Save Current**.

   The Save Workspace Layout dialog box opens.

3. Type a name in the Name box.

4. Click **OK**.

   The panel set is now saved.

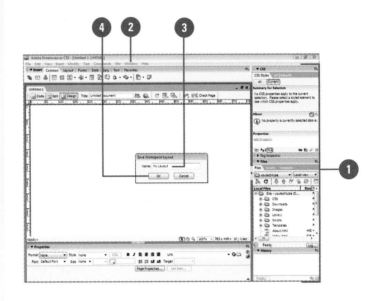

Display a Panel Set

1. Click the **Window** menu, point to **Workspace Layout**, and then select a panel option:

   ◆ **Custom Panel Name.** Displays a custom panel layout in which you created.

   ◆ **Predefined Layouts.** Displays the default panel layout: Coder (Win), Designer (Win), Default (Mac), or Dual Screen.

Custom panel

Delete a Panel Set

① Click the **Window** menu, point to **Workspace Layout**, and then click **Manage**.

The Manage Workspace Layouts dialog box opens.

② Select the panel set you want to delete.

③ Click **Delete**.

④ Click **Yes** to confirm the deletion.

⑤ Click **OK**.

The panel set is now deleted.

Did You Know?

You can hide all panels. Click the Window menu, and then click Hide Panels to select the check mark.

Rename a Panel Set

① Click the **Window** menu, point to **Workspace Layout**, and then click **Manage**.

The Manage Workspace Layouts dialog box opens.

② Select the panel set you want to rename.

③ Click **Rename**.

④ Type a new name, and then click **OK**.

The panel set is now renamed.

⑤ Click **OK**.

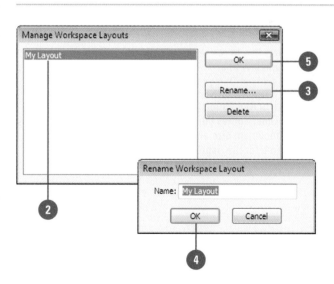

Using the Status Bar

DW 2.5

To work efficiently in Dreamweaver you need information about the active document. Details about the document's size and estimated download time all help in the design and preparation of the page. Dreamweaver displays current information about the active document and common display tools on the Status bar, located at the bottom of the document window. The Status bar displays the Tag selector for the current selection and the estimated document size and download time, and allows you to use the Select, Hand, or Zoom tools, set document magnification, or resize the Document window.

Use the Status Bar

1. View the display information or click a tool on the Status bar:

   ◆ **Tag Selector.** Shows the hierarchy of tags surrounding the current selection.

   ◆ **Select Tool.** Use to enable or disable the Hand tool.

   ◆ **Hand Tool.** Use to drag a document into the Document window.

   ◆ **Zoom Tool.** Use to increase or decrease the magnification level for a document.

   ◆ **Set Magnification.** Use to select a predefined magnification level.

   ◆ **Window Size.** Use to resize the Document window to a predefined value in Design view.

   ◆ **Document Size And Estimated Download Time.** Shows the estimated document size and download time for the page.

Tag selector   Status bar

Hand   Set Magnification   Document Size/Download Time

Select   Zoom   Window Size

Set Windows Size and Connection Speed from the Status Bar

① Click the **Dreamweaver** (Mac) or **Edit** (Win) menu, and then click **Preferences**.

② Click the **Status Bar** category.

③ Set the options you want:

◆ **Window Sizes.** Specify the window sizes you want to appears in the Status bar.

◆ **Connection Speed.** Select the connection speed (in kilobits per second) you want to use to calculate the download size that appears in the Status bar.

④ Click **OK**.

Did You Know?

You can display the download size for an image. When you select an image, the image's download size appears in the Properties panel.

Changing the View with the Zoom Tool

Working with the Zoom tool gives you one more way to control exactly what you see in Dreamweaver. The Zoom tool does not change the active image, it only lets you view the image at different magnifications. The Zoom tool is located on the Status bar, and resembles a magnifying glass. Increasing the magnification of an image gives you control over what you see and gives you control over how you work. Large documents are difficult to work with and difficult to view. Many documents, when viewed at 100 percent, are larger than the maximized size of the document window. When this happens, viewing the entire image requires reducing the zoom.

Zoom In or Out the View

① Select the **Zoom** tool on the Status bar.

② Use one of the following methods to zoom in:

◆ **Click On The Document.** The image increases in magnification centered on where you clicked.

◆ **Drag To Define An Area With The Zoom Tool.** The image increases in magnification based on the boundaries of the area you dragged.

TIMESAVER *Press Ctrl+= (Win) or ⌘+= (Mac) to zoom in.*

③ To zoom out, hold down the Alt (Win) or Option (Mac) key, and then click on the screen to reduce the zoom of the active document.

The zoom reduction centers on where you click on the active document.

TIMESAVER *Press Ctrl+- (Win) or ⌘+- (Mac) to zoom out.*

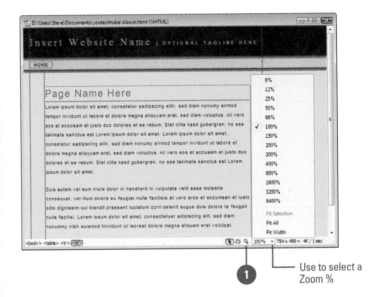

Use to select a Zoom %

Working with Rulers

Carpenters know that precise measurements are essential to making things fit, so they have a rule: Measure Twice, Cut Once. In keeping with the idea that precise measurements are essential, Dreamweaver gives you ruler bars. Ruler bars are located on the top and left sides of the active document window. Rulers serve a very important role. Ruler guides help you correctly align design elements. As a matter of fact, if you're not working on a flat glass or LCD monitor, the curvature of the monitor can give you a false impression of the vertical and horizontal. By using guides you have access to precise alignment systems.

Work with Rulers

1. Click the **View** menu, and then point to **Rulers**.

2. Select the options you want:

   ◆ **Show.** Click to show or hide the ruler.

   TIMESAVER *Press Ctrl+Alt+R (Win) or ⌘+Option+R (Mac) to show or hide the ruler.*

   ◆ **Reset Origin.** Click to set the ruler back to the default.

   ◆ **Change the Origin.** Drag the ruler-origin icon (at the upper-left corner) anywhere on the page.

   ◆ **Pixels**, **Inches**, or **Centimeters.** Click to select the type of measurement you want to appear on the ruler.

   TIMESAVER *Right-click in the ruler bar to open a menu you can use to change the measurement system.*

Did You Know?

You can choose what type of Point/Pica size to use. Click Postscript (72 points/inch) or click Traditional (72.27 points/inch). Postscript is more widely used, and Dreamweaver defaults to this option.

Working with the Grid and Guides

 DW 3.11

Dreamweaver comes with guides, grids, and rulers to help you lay out artwork and objects with precision. A grid is a series of crisscrossed lines that aid in aligning objects to each other on the Stage. A guide is a horizontal or vertical line you can position to align objects. Grids and guides are modifiable. You can change their visibility, position, color, and frequency. To align several elements to a grid or guide line, you first turn Snap to Grid or Snap to Guides on. Then you can drag the elements to align them to the grid or a guide. These items are invisible by default, but they can be easily turned on and adjusted. Though you see them in the Dreamweaver development environment, they are invisible on the viewable page. Use guides to align art and objects to each other on vertical or horizontal paths, or turn on the grid for use in designing a layout that is proportional and balanced.

Use the Grid

1. Click the **View** menu, and then point to **Grid**.

2. Select the option you want:

   ◆ **Show.** Click to show or hide the grid.

   TIMESAVER *Press Ctrl+Alt+G (Win) or ⌘+Option+G (Mac) to show or hide the grid.*

   ◆ **Snap To Grid.** Click to enable or disable objects aligning to a grid line.

   TIMESAVER *Press Ctrl+Alt+Shift+G (Win) or ⌘+Option+Shift+G (Mac) to enable or disable Snap To Grid.*

   ◆ **Grid Settings.** Click to open the Grid Settings dialog box, where you can set the grid color, settings, spacing, and display, either lines or dots.

Grid Settings

Use Guides

(1) Click the **View** menu, point to **Guides**, and then select the options you want:

◆ **Show Guides.** Click to show or hide the grid.

◆ **Snap To Guides** or **Guides Snap To Elements.** Click to enable or disable objects aligning to guides or guides to objects.

◆ **Edit Guides.** Click to set the guide color, distance color, and other settings.

◆ **Lock Guides.** Click to lock the existing guides in place.

◆ **Clear Guides.** Click to remove all guides.

(2) Move to the vertical or horizontal Ruler bar, and then click and drag into the document.

(3) Click the **Select** tool on the Status bar to drag existing guides to a new position (make sure Lock Guides is not selected).

Edit Guides

Did You Know?

You can remove one guide at a time. Make sure Lock Guides is clear, and then click the Move tool. Drag the existing guide you want removed back to the corresponding Ruler bar.

You can use keyboard shortcuts to work with guides. ⌘+; (Mac) or Ctrl+; (Win) shows and hides guides, Option+⌘+; (Mac) or Ctrl+Alt+; (Win) locks and unlocks guides, Shift+⌘+; (Mac) or Ctrl+ Shift+; (Win) to turn Snapping to guides on and off, and Shift+⌘+/ (Mac) or Ctrl+Shift+/ (Win) to turn Snapping guides to elements on and off.

Setting Precise Measurements Using Guides

If you want to use exact measurements while you work with guides to create a Web page design, you can set guides to a precise location or view the exact distance between guides. To view and move a guide to a specific location, double-click the guide, enter the exact location you want, and then click OK. To view the distance between guides, press Ctrl (Win) or (Mac), and hold down the mouse pointer anywhere between the two guides. The unit of measure that appears is the same as the unit of measure for the rulers.

Creating Keyboard Shortcuts

Dreamweaver uses built-in keyboard shortcuts designed specifically for Dreamweaver. A complete list of the keyboard shortcuts is available in the back of this book. The built-in keyboard shortcuts are organized into sets, which you can duplicate and customize to create your own personalized set. If you use other programs, such as Adobe Illustrator or Adobe Photoshop, and you are more comfortable using their keyboard shortcuts for common commands, you can select a built-in keyboard shortcut set from any of the graphics programs to use in Dreamweaver.

Create a Keyboard Shortcut Set

1. Click the **Dreamweaver** (Mac) or **Edit** (Win) menu, and then click **Keyboard Shortcuts**.

2. Click the **Current Set** popup, and then select a set.

3. Click the **Duplicate Set** button.

4. Type a name for the new shortcut set.

5. Click **OK**.

Did You Know?

You can delete a custom keyboard shortcut set. Click the Dreamweaver (Mac) or Edit (Win) menu, click Keyboard Shortcuts, select a shortcut set from the Current Set popup, and then click the Delete button. You cannot delete a built-in keyboard shortcut set that comes with Dreamweaver.

You can rename a custom keyboard shortcut set. Click the Dreamweaver (Mac) or Edit (Win) menu, click Keyboard Shortcuts, select a shortcut set from the Current Set popup, click the Rename Set button, enter a new name, and then click OK. You cannot rename a built-in keyboard shortcut set that comes with Dreamweaver.

Delete button

Add or Remove a Keyboard Shortcut

1. Click the **Dreamweaver** (Mac) or **Edit** (Win) menu, and then click **Keyboard Shortcuts**.

2. Click the **Current Set** popup, and then select the set in which you want to change.

3. Click the **Commands** popup, and then select a shortcut category, such as Drawing Menu Commands, Drawing Tools, Test Movie Menu Commands, and Workplace Accessibility Commands.

4. Select the command for which you want to add or remove a shortcut in the Commands list.

5. Do the following:
   - To add a shortcut, click the **Add Shortcut** (+) button, and then press the key combination to enter the new shortcut key in the Press Key box.
   - To remove a shortcut, click the **Remove Shortcut** (-) button.

6. Click **Change**.

7. To add or remove additional shortcuts, repeat Steps 2-6.

8. Click **OK**.

Keyboard shortcut

For Your Information

Export keyboard shortcuts as HTML

You can now export Dreamweaver keyboard shortcuts as an HTML file that you can view and print using a standard Web browser. To export the keyboard shortcuts, click the Dreamweaver (Mac) or Edit (Win) menu, click Keyboard Shortcuts, click the Current Set popup, select the set you want, click the Export Set As HTML button, enter a file name, specify a location, and then click Save.

Setting General Preferences

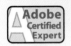

DW 2.11

Dreamweaver allows you to set general preferences to customize the way you work in the program. You can specify what you want to display or open when you launch Dreamweaver and how you want to edit content. Some of the preferences allow you to show or hide the Welcome Screen, allow multiple consecutive space when editing, use CSS or HTML tags when formatting, specify to the number of history steps (undo levels), and select a spelling dictionary.

Set General Preferences

1 Click the **Dreamweaver** (Mac) or **Edit** (Win) menu, and then click **Preferences**.

2 Click the **General** category.

3 Select from the following options:

- ◆ **Open Documents In Tabs (Mac)**. Select to open all documents in a single window with tabs.

- ◆ **Show Welcome Screen**. Select to show welcome screen (Default on).

- ◆ **Reopen Documents On Startup**. Select to open any documents that were opened the last time you closed Dreamweaver (Default off).

- ◆ **Warn When Open Read-Only Files**. Select to get an alert when you open a locked file (Default on).

- ◆ **Update Links When Moving Files**. Specify the action you want: Prompt (Default), Never, Always.

- ◆ **Show Dialog When Inserting Objects**. Select to prompt you when inserting objects using the Insert bar or Insert menu.

TIMESAVER *To temporarily override this setting, Ctrl-click (Win) or ⌘-click (Mac) when creating and inserting objects.*

- **Enable Double-Byte Inline Input.** Select to enter double-byte text, such as Japanese characters (Default on).

- **Switch To Plain Paragraph After Heading.** Select to press Enter (Win) or Return (Mac) after a heading paragraph to switch to a plain paragraph in Design view (Default on).

- **Allow Multiple Consecutive Spaces.** Select to allow typing two or more spaces in Design view to create nonbreaking spaces that appear as multiple spaces in a browser (Default off).

- **Use <strong> And <em> In Place Of <b> And <i>.** Select to apply <strong> instead of <b> and <em> instead of <i> (Default on).

- **Use CSS Instead Of HTML Tags.** Select to use CSS when you use the Properties panel's Style option, except for bold and italic (HTML) (Default on).

- **Warn When Placing Editable Regions Within <p> Or <h1><h6> Tags.** Select to display a warning when you save a template when true (Default on).

- **Centering.** Select the option you want when you click the Align Center button in the Properties panel (Default <div>).

- **Maximum Number Of History Steps.** Specify the number of steps the History panel keeps.

- **Spelling Dictionary.** Click to select a dictionary language. The dialect is in parenthesis.

④ Click **OK**.

Setting New Document Preferences

DW 2.11

Set New Document Preferences

1. Click the **Dreamweaver** (Mac) or **Edit** (Win) menu, and then click **Preferences**.

2. Click the **New Document** category.

3. Select from the following options:

   ◆ **Default Document.** Select the type of document you want to use as default (Default HTML).

   ◆ **Default Extension.** Enter the file extension you want to use for the HTML extension, either .html or .htm. (Default .html).

   ◆ **Default Document Type (DTD).** Select to the XHTML document type definition (DTD) you want.

   ◆ **Default Encoding.** Specify the encoding you want to use for new documents and opened documents without any specified encoding. This makes sure your Web browser and Dreamweaver use the right character set for the selected language. The default for HTML encoding is Unicode (UTF-8), which safely represents all characters.

When you create a new document, Dreamweaver allows you to set the default document type you want. The New Document preference options allow you to specify the default document, extension, document type definition (DTD), and file encoding. DTD allows you to select XHTML 1.0 Transitional or XHTML 1.0 Strict to make new Web pages XHTML-compliant. File encoding makes sure your Web browser and Dreamweaver use the right character set for the selected language.

- **Use When Opening Existing Files That Don't Specify An Encoding.** Select to apply encoding to when you open a file without encoding.

- **Unicode Normalization Form.** If you select Unicode (UTF-8) for encoding, select the form option you want: C, D, KC, or KD. Form C is the most common one used for the Web in the Character Model. The others are provided by Adobe.

- **Include Unicode Signature (BOM).** If you select Unicode (UTF-8) for encoding, you can select this option to include a Byte Order Mark (BOM), which is a 2-4 bytes at the beginning of a text file that identifies a file as Unicode, and order the bytes. This is optional.

- **Show New Document Dialog Box On Control+N.** Select to show the New Document dialog box or clear to automatically create a document with default settings when you use the shortcut key Ctrl+N (Win) or ⌘+N (Mac).

④ Click **OK**.

Setting Font Preferences

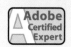

DW 2.11

You can use the Fonts section of the Preferences dialog box to view encoding for the selected font and size you want. File encoding makes sure your Web browser and Dreamweaver use the right character set for the selected language. The fonts you select in the Preferences dialog box don't affect the page display in a Web browser, however, it does affect the page display in Dreamweaver. You can specify the font and size you want to use in Code view, or as a proportional or fixed font.

Set Font Preferences

1. Click the **Dreamweaver** (Mac) or **Edit** (Win) menu, and then click **Preferences**.

2. Click the **Fonts** category.

3. Select the encoding type you want to view.

4. Select from the following check boxes:

   ◆ **Proportional Font.** Select the font and size you want to use to display normal text, such as paragraphs, headings, and tables.

   ◆ **Fixed Font.** Select the font and size you want to use to display text within pre, code, and tt tags.

   ◆ **Code View.** Select the font and size you want to use for all text in Code view.

5. Select the **Use Dynamic Font Mapping** check box.

6. Click **OK**.

Setting Highlighting Color Preferences

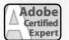 DW 2.11

You use the Highlighting section of the Preferences dialog box to specify the colors you want to use for the following items in Dreamweaver: Mouse-Over, Editable regions, Nested editable, Locked regions, Library items, Third-party tags, or untranslated or translated live data. You can select the color you want by using a color swatch or entering a color id number in Hexadecimal (Hex). In addition, you can also determine whether you can show or hide your color selection.

Set Highlighting Color Preferences

1. Click the **Dreamweaver** (Mac) or **Edit** (Win) menu, and then click **Preferences**.

2. Click the **Highlighting** category.

3. Click the color box and select a color or enter a color Hex number for the options you want.

4. Select or clear the **Show** check box next to an option to show or hide the color selection.

5. Click **OK**.

Working with Colors

Since Web pages appear in Web browsers, you want to use colors on your pages that are Web-safe, so they appear consistently on every browser. A **Web-safe** color appears the same in Microsoft Internet Explorer and Netscape Navigator on both Windows and Macintosh system when running in 256-color mode.

RGB (red, green, blue) is a set of color values that describe colors. RGB identifies a color by a set of hexadecimal numbers, an internal computer numbering scheme, that specify the amounts of red, green, and blue needed to create the color. RGB colors appear best over the Web (true color representation without dithers or substitutes) when you use only **browser safe colors**, which is a standard set of 216 color combinations. These RGB values are 0, 51, 102, 153, 204, or 255 in decimal or 00, 33, 66, 99, CC, or FF in hexadecimal. When you use the system color dialog boxes, you use decimal values. You use hexadecimal values in Code view, the Properties panel, and some dialog boxes, such as the Preferences dialog box.

Using the Color Picker

When you want to change a color, you can click any color box available in many dialog boxes, such as the Preferences dialog box, and the Property Inspector to open the color picker. The color picker allows you to select a color for different page elements.

When you click a color box, the color picker appears, displaying the eyedropper cursor and a palette with a bar at the top and a swatch of colors at the bottom. The bar displays the currently selected color and its hexadecimal number. To the right is the **Default Color button**, which clears the current

color without choosing a different color. Next to the Default Color button is the **Color Wheel button**, which opens the system color picker. The system color picker is the standard color selector provided by the operating system, either Windows or Macintosh. The popup menu in the upper-right corner of the color picker allows you to expand your color selection. You can select different color palettes, including Color Cubes, Continuous Tone, Windows OS, Mac OS, and Grayscale. The Color Cube (default color palette) and Continuous Tone palettes are Web-safe while the Windows OS, Mac OS, and Grayscale are not. If you are using a non Web-safe palette, you can use the Snap To Web Safe command to have Dreamweaver replace the selected color with the closest Web-safe color. You can use the eyedropper to select a color swatch from the palette or pick a color from anywhere on your screen inside or outside Dreamweaver.

Default color   Color wheel

Color Picker

Color palettes

Using the System Color Picker

When you click the Color Wheel button in the color picker, a system color picker dialog box opens. In Windows, you can use the Color dialog box, which displays basic and custom color squares and a color matrix with the full range of colors in the color spectrum, to help you select a color. You can enter RGB (Red, Green, Blue) values or hue, saturation, and luminosity (also known as brightness) values to specify a color. **Hue** is the color created by mixing primary colors (Red, Blue, and Yellow). **Saturation** is a measure of how much white is mixed in with the color. A fully saturated color is vivid; a less saturated color is washed-out pastel. **Luminosity** is a meas-ure of how much black is mixed with the color. A very bright color contains little or no black. You can also change the hue by moving the pointer in the color matrix box horizon-tally, the saturation by moving the pointer vertically, and the luminosity by adjusting the slider to the right of the color matrix box. On the Macintosh, you click one of the color modes and select a color, using its controls. You can select RGB values by selecting the color sliders at the top of the dialog box; or by entering values (color numbers) to select a color. You can select hue, saturation, and brightness (or luminosity) values by selecting the color sliders at the top of the dialog box or entering values (color numbers). The color you select appears in the ColorSolid box.

Drag to select color

Drag to select color range

RGB

HSL

Managing Web Site Files

4

Introduction

A Web site is made up of numerous files. As you continue to create more and more Web pages and other files for a Web site, keeping track of them becomes an important job. Managing Web site files is an important part of creating an organized site that one or more developers can work on.

In Dreamweaver, there are three main site folders: local root, remote, and testing server. The local root and testing server folders are the working development folders for your Web site, while the remote folder is the Web server folder that visitors access on the Web. Instead of using Windows Explorer (Win) or Finder (Mac) to manage and work with Web site files, you can use the Files panel. When you create or open a Web site, the Files tab in the Files panel displays all the site's files, which you can use to quickly and easily manage individual Web pages, files, and folders. If you can find a file on your site, you can also use the Files panel to help you locate it.

If you're creating a custom template or sharing files with someone who needs them for use in another program, you can use the Save As dialog box to change the file type for a Web page or other related file.

When you create a Web page, one of the first things to do is to apply some general settings to your page. The Page Properties dialog box lets you specify the default font family and font size, background color, margins, link styles, and many other aspects of page design. You can assign new page properties for each new page you create, and modify those for existing pages. Dreamweaver allows you to embed these changes to the page in using HTML or CSS (Cascading Style Sheets), depending on your preference.

Exploring Web Site Files and Folders

A Web site consists of linked documents and related files organized into folders. You can use Dreamweaver to organize and manage your site files and folders, and maintain your links. With Dreamweaver, you can create, develop, and work with site files and folders on your local hard disk and upload them to a Web server where visitors on the Web can access it.

Working with Site Folders

The development environment for a Dreamweaver site consists of three main folders: Local root, Remote, and Testing server. The **local root** folder, known as the "local site," stores your site files and folders you work on during development. You can store the local root folder on your local computer or a network server. The **remote** folder, known as the "remote site," stores your site files and folders for production on the Web. The remote folder is typically the Web server, known as a production server, where visitors access your site on the Web. If you plan to use dynamic pages—Web pages that changes based on circumstances—in your Web site, you need a **testing server** folder, which provides a place to generate and display dynamic content while you work. You can store the testing server folder on your local computer, development server, or production server. In order to set up a testing server folder, you need to define the local and remote folder first.

Web site development takes place in the local folder, while Web site final production takes place in the remote folder. After you finishing developing files and folder in your local folder, you can upload them to your remote folder. The folder structure in the local and remote folders should always be the same. If the folder structure is not the same, files upload to the wrong location and links to files don't work. So, making sure the folder structure of the local and remote are the same is very important.

You can name and specify the location of the local folder. However, the remote folder name and location is typically provided by your Web server administrator. After you find out the name and location of your remote folder, you can establish a connection to it from Dreamweaver. If the remote folder name and location is not available at the moment, you can still set up a local folder now and start creating Web site files, and then specify the remote and testing folders later.

Typically, you work on files in your local folder and then upload them to your remote folder. However, you can also work on files directly on your remote site in Dreamweaver. When you make a change to a remote site file make sure you also update the local site file too so they are both the same.

Setting Up Site Folders

In Dreamweaver, there are three main site folders: local root, remote, and testing server. The local root folder is the working development folder for your Web site. The remote folder is the Web server folder for your Web site. This is the location on the Web where visitors access your Web site. The testing server folder is a development folder for generating and displaying dynamic page content while you work. A **dynamic page** is a Web page that changes based on circumstances. The other type of Web page is a **static page**, which only changes when you edit it. You can set up site folders when you create a new site or edit an existing one. If you don't know the settings for the remote and testing server folders, you can set up a local folder now, start creating Web site files, and then specify the remote and testing folders later.

Set Up Site Folders

1. Use one of the following methods:

   ◆ **New Site.** Click the **Site** menu, and then click **New Site**.

   ◆ **Exist Site.** Click the **Site** menu, click **Manage Site**, select the site you want, and then click **Edit**.

2. Click the **Advanced** tab.

3. Click the **Local Info** category.

4. Click the **Local Root Folder** icon, locate the local folder you want to use, and then click **Select**.

5. Click the **Remote Info** category, and then select the access method you want to use to transfer files between local and remote folders.

6. Click the **Testing Server** category, and then select server model and access method you want to use to display dynamic page content.

7. Click **OK**.

Viewing the Files Panel

The Files panel is a useful place for managing files and folders. When you create or open a Web site, the Files tab in the Files panel displays all the site's files. If you want to change locations, you can use the Site popup in the Files panel to select a remote server, local drive, or desktop. The Files tab displays the file hierarchy of all the folders and files in your Web site in different views, either local, remote, testing, or map. Using the plus sign (+) and the minus sign (-) to the left of an icon in the Files tab allows you to display different levels of folders in your Web site without opening and displaying the contents of each folder. If you want to display two different views, you can expand the Files panel.

View Files in the Files Panel

1. Select the Web site in which you want to view.

2. Click the **Window** menu, and then click **Files** to display the Files panel.

3. Click the **Site** popup, and then select the location where you want to view files.

4. Click the **Site Files View** popup, and then select the view you want.

- **Local View.** Displays the folder structure of the site on your computer (Default view).

- **Remote View.** Displays the folder structure of the site on a Web server.

- **Testing View.** Displays the folder structure of the testing and local site.

- **Map View.** Displays a graphical map of the site.

5. Perform the commands you want to display folder structure and contents:

- To show the file and folder structure, click the **Plus** sign (+).

- To hide the file and folder structure, click the **Minus** sign (-).

- To display the contents of a folder, click the folder icon.

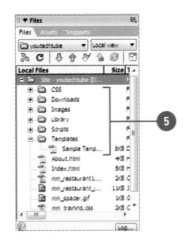

Work with the Files Panel in Expanded View

1 Select the Web site in which you want to view.

2 Click the **Window** menu, and then click **Files** to display the Files panel.

The Files panel appears, displaying the Files tab.

3 Click the **Expand** button to expand the Files panel.

The Files panel expands to display the remote site, testing site, or site map on the left and the local site on the right.

4 Click a button on the toolbar to display the view you want:

◆ **Site Files.** Displays the remote site.

◆ **Testing Server.** Displays the testing site.

◆ **Site Map.** Displays a graphical map of the site. When you click this button, click **Map Only** to view the site map only or **Map and Files** to view the site map with site files.

5 Click the **Collapse** button again to collapse the Files panel.

See Also

See "Managing Files and Folders in the Files Panel" on page 76 for information on working with site files in different views.

4   3 Click to expand and collapse

Opening and Creating Files in the Files Panel

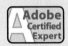

Instead of using Windows Explorer (Win) or Finder (Mac) to manage and work with Web site files, you can use the Files panel. After you open a Web site, you can quickly open files using the Files panel instead of using the Open command on the File menu. The Files panel displays all the files for the working site. If you want to open a file for another site, you need to use the Open command on the File menu, or switch the working site and use the Files panel. In addition, you can create a new file. When you do, Dreamweaver creates the new file in the same folder as the selected file.

Open a Files in Files Panel

1. Select the Web site in which you want to view.

2. Click the **Window** menu, and then click **Files** to display the Files panel.

3. Click the **Site** popup, and then select the location where you want to view files.

4. Click the **Site Files View** popup, and then select **Local View**.

5. Use any of the following methods:

   ◆ Double-click the file icon.

   ◆ Right-click (Win) or Control-click (Mac) the file icon, and then click **Open**.

Did You Know?

You can refresh the Files panel. If you don't see a file or folder you know is in the Files panel, click the Refresh button (Dreamweaver sites only) or right-click (Win) or Control-click (Mac), and then click Refresh.

Create a File in Files Panel

1 Select the Web site in which you want to view.

2 Click the **Window** menu, and then click **Files** to display the Files panel.

3 Click the **Site** popup, and then select the location where you want to view files.

4 Click the **Site Files View** popup, and then select **Local View**.

5 Select a file where you want to place the new one.

6 Right-click (Win) or Control-click (Mac), and then click **New File**.

7 Enter a name for the file or folder, and then press Enter (Win) or Return (Mac).

Did You Know?

You can control what applications open specific files. For example, you might want to open your .gif files using Fireworks, or you might want to use Photoshop. Click the Dreamweaver (Mac) or Edit (Win) menu, and then click Preferences. Click the File Types/Editors category, make your changes, and then click OK.

Managing Files and Folders in the Files Panel

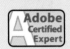 DW 4.5

After you create a Web site, you can use the Files panel to quickly and easily manage individual Web pages, files and folders. If a file or folder name is not exactly what you want, you can quickly rename it. You can create and name a new folder and move pages to a different location. If you no longer need or want a file or folder, you can remove it. In addition, you can move files and folders around in the same way you can in Windows Explorer (Win) or Finder (Mac). If you no longer need a file, you can quickly delete it.

Rename a Site File or Folder in Files Panel

① Select the Web site with the file or folder you want to rename.

② Click the **Window** menu, and then click **Files** to display the Files panel.

③ Right-click (Win) or Control-click the file or folder icon you want to rename, point to **Edit**, and then click **Rename**.

> **TIMESAVER** *Click the file name in the Files panel, and then click the file again to highlight it.*

④ Type a new name, and then press Enter (Win) or Return (Mac).

Did You Know?

You can delete a site file or folder. In the Files panel, right-click (Win) or Control-click (Mac) the file or folder you want to delete, click Delete, and then click Yes.

Create a New Site Folder in Files Panel

1. Select the Web site where you want to create a new folder.

2. Click the **Window** menu, and then click **Files** to display the Files panel.

3. Locate and select the file or folder where you want to place the new folder.

4. Right-click (Win) or Control-click (Mac), and then click **New Folder**.

5. Enter a name for the file or folder, and then press Enter (Win) or Return (Mac).

Move a Site File or Folder in Files Panel

1. Select the Web site with the file or folder you want to move.

2. Click the **Window** menu, and then click **Files** to display the Files panel.

3. In the Files panel, display the file or folder you want to use.

4. Drag the page icon to the position where you want it to occupy on your site.

Finding Files in the Files Panel

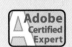 DW 4.5

If you can find a file on your site, you can use the Files panel to help you locate it. The Files panel allows you to quickly find files in your site. If you have a file open and your not sure which site it belongs to, you can find it using the Locate in Site command. If you want to find the newest files in your local or remote site, you can select them using commands on the Options menu in the Files panel. As you work on files, you can also use find commands to locate currently checked out or recently modified files.

Find Files in a Site

1 Select the Web site with the files you want to find.

2 Click the **Window** menu, and then click **Files** to display the Files panel.

3 Use any of the following methods to find a file:

◆ **Open File In Site.** Open the file in the Document window, click the **Site** menu, and then click **Locate In Site**, or click the **Options** menu, point to **Edit**, and then click **Locate In Site**.

The file appears selected in the Files panel.

◆ **Newer Local Files.** Click the **Options** menu, point to **Edit**, and then click **Select Newer Local**.

◆ **Newer Remote Files.** Click the **Options** menu, point to **Edit**, and then click **Select Newer Remote**.

◆ **Checked Out Files.** Click the **Options** menu, point to **Edit**, and then click **Select Checked Out Files**.

Options menu

See Also

See "Checking Site Files In and Out" on page 504 for information on checking out files.

Find Recently Modified Files in a Site

1. Select the Web site with the files you want to find.

2. Click the **Window** menu, and then click **Files** to display the Files panel.

3. Click the **Options** menu in the Files panel, point to **Edit**, and then click **Select Recently Modified**.

4. Do either of the following to indicate search dates you want:

   ◆ To report on all files modified in the last several dates, click the **Files Created Or Modified In The Last** option, and then enter the number of days you want.

   ◆ To report on all files modified within a specific time, click the **Files Created Or Modified Between** option, and then specify a data range.

5. If you are working on an Adobe Contribute site, enter a user name to limit your search to files modified by a specific user.

6. Click the option you want to specify where to view the files listed.

   ◆ **Local Machine.** Select if the site uses static pages.

   ◆ **Testing Server.** Select if the site uses dynamic pages.

   ◆ **Other Location.** Use to enter a specific location path.

7. Click **OK**.

   Dreamweaver saves your settings and highlights the files based on the search criteria.

Options menu

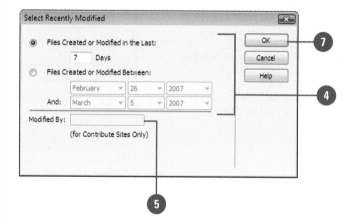

Saving a File with Different Formats

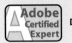
DW 3.9

A file type specifies the file format (for example, a Web page .htm or .html) as well as the program and version in which the file was created (for example, Dreamweaver). You might want to change the type if you're creating a custom template or sharing files with someone who needs them for use in another program. You can use the Save As dialog box to change the file type for a page. The Save As Type list arrow displays a list of the available formats for the program or current selection.

Save a File as a Different Type

1. Open and display the file you want to save in a different format.

2. Click the **File** menu, and then click **Save As**.

3. Locate the drive and folder location where you want to save the file.

4. Type a name for the file, or use the suggested name.

5. Click the **Save As Type** list arrow, and then click the file type you want.

6. Click **Save**.

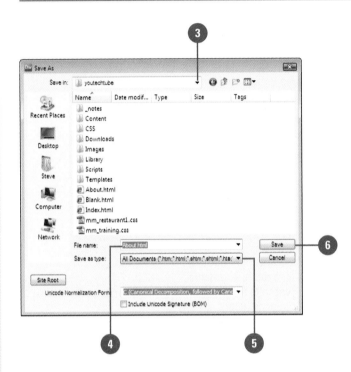

See Also

See "Identifying Dreamweaver File Formats" on page 81 for information on selecting the right file format.

Identifying Dreamweaver File Formats

 DW 3.9

Dreamweaver Open and Save File Formats

File type	Extension	Used to open or save
All Documents	*.*	Complete Web site
HTML Files	.htm, .html	Web pages as a HTML file
Server-Side Includes	.shtm, .shtml, .stm, .ssi, .inc	Web pages with incorporated files from a Web server
JavaScript Files	.js	Scripts in the JavaScript language
XML	.xml, .xsd,.xsl, .xslt, .dtd, .rss	Web pages as an XML file
Library Files	.lbi	Web page elements as a reusable file
Template Files	.dwt	Web pages as a changeable Dreamweaver template
Style Sheets	.css	Web pages as a cascading style sheet
Active Server Pages	.asp, .asa	Web pages as a Microsoft Active Server Page
Active Server Plus Pages	.aspx, .aspcx, .asmx, .cs, .vb, .config, .master	Web pages as a changeable Microsoft Active Server Page that utilizes ActiveX scripting usually VB Script or Jscript code
ColdFusion Templates	.ctm, .ctml, .cfc	Web pages as a changeable ColdFusion template that integrates databases and Web pages
ActionScript	.as, .asc, .asr	Scripts in the Flash scripting language, including Communication and Remote (Open only) files
Text	.txt	Web pages as a text file
PHP	.php	Web pages as a PHP script file
Lasso Files	.lasso	Scripts for internet applications development which use browsers to connect to HTTP and database servers
Java Server Pages	.jsp, .jst	Web pages as a JavaScript script file
Fireworks Script	.jsf	Scripts in the Fireworks scripting language (Open only)
Tag Library Descriptor Files	.tld	Tag library files (Open only)
Java Files	.java	Scripts in the Java language
WML	.wml	Web pages as an XML language used to specify content and user interface for WAP devices; WML (Wireless Markup Language)
EDML	.edml	Scripts for server behavior code
VB Script Files	.vbs	Scripts in the Visual Basic for Applications language
VTML	.vtm, .vtml	Tag library files that list every installed tag; VTML (Visual Tool Markup Language)

Setting the Home Page

A home page is the first page visitors see when they visit your site. The home page is typically named *index.htm*. If you already have a home page or want to create a different one, you can quickly set the one you want as the new home page using the Files panel.

Set a Web Page as the Home Page

① Select the Web site with the Web page you want to change.

② Click the **Window** menu, and then click **Files** to display the Files panel.

③ Right-click the page you want to set as the new home page, and then click **Set As Home Page**.

Did You Know?

You can also set the Home page using the Site Definition dialog box. Click the Site menu, click Manage Site, click the site you want to change, click Edit, click the Advanced tab, click the Site Map Layout category, click the Browse For File folder icon, select the home page file you want, click Open, click OK, and then click Done.

Preparing to Set Page Properties

 DW 3.10

When you create a Web page, one of the first things to do is to apply some general settings to your page. The Page Properties dialog box lets you specify the default font family and font size, background color, margins, link styles, and many other aspects of page design. You can assign new page properties for each new page you create, and modify those for existing pages. Dreamweaver provides the ability to embed these changes to the page in one of two ways: HTML or CSS.

Dreamweaver formats text using CSS (Cascading Style Sheets), by default, and it would prefer to set page preferences in this manner. If you use the default CSS setting, Dreamweaver uses CSS tags for all properties defined in the Appearance, Links, and Headings categories of the Page Properties dialog box. The CSS tags defining these attributes are embedded in the head section of the page. To view the tags, simply click the Code

button, located in the upper left corner of the document window, and Dreamweaver changes the view from Design to Code. Scroll up to the Head section of the document and view the property codes.

If, however, you want to use HTML tags, then you need to turn off the Use CSS instead of HTML tags option in the Preferences dialog box. To make the change, click click the Dreamweaver (Mac) or Edit (Win) menu, click Preferences, click the General category, clear the Use CSS instead of HTML tags check box. When you make changes in the Page Properties dialog box, Dreamweaver inserts the changes as standard HTML coding.

The page properties you choose apply only to the active document. If a page uses an external CSS style sheet, Dreamweaver doesn't overwrite the tags set in the style sheet, as this affects all other pages using that style sheet.

Setting Appearance Page Properties

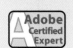

The Appearance category in the Page Properties dialog box allows you to set the default options you want for page font type and size, text and background color. You can also use a picture as the background for a page and specify how it appears. If you'd like to add some interest to your pages, you can add a background color. If the background image contains any transparent areas, the background color appears. When selecting background colors, some creative judgment is required. For example, if you choose a dark color for your background, make sure you use a light color for your text (the most commonly used is white) to generate the appropriate contrast required for easy reading.

Set Appearance Page Properties

1. Open the Web page you want to change.

2. Click the **Modify** menu, and then click **Page Properties**.

3. Click the **Appearance** category.

4. Select from the following options:

   ◆ **Page Font and Size.** Specify the font type and size you want.

   ◆ **Text and Background Color.** Specify the text and background color you want.

   ◆ **Background Image.** Specify the font type, size, and text color you want.

   ◆ **Repeat.** Specify how you want the background image to appear on the page. **No-repeat** appears once; **Repeat** appears tiled horizontally and vertically; **Repeat-x** appears horizontally; and **Repeat-y** appears vertically.

   ◆ **Margins.** Specify the page margins you want. Most designers place zeros in all four boxes (top, bottom, left, right), so when a visitor opens the page, all elements align to the upper left corner of the page.

5. Click **OK**.

Setting Link Page Properties

Set Link Page Properties

1. Open the Web page you want to change.

2. Click the **Modify** menu, and then click **Page Properties**.

3. Click the **Links** category.

4. Select any of the following font options:

   ◆ **Link Font.** Specifies the default font family to use for links. (Default uses entire page font set in the Appearance category)

   ◆ **Bold or Italic.** Specifies whether to use bold or italic for links.

   ◆ **Font Size.** Specifies the default size to use for links.

5. Select a color for the following options:

   ◆ **Link Color.** Displays color for linked text.

   ◆ **Visited Links.** Displays color for links you visit.

   ◆ **Rollover Links.** Displays color for links you point at.

   ◆ **Active Links.** Displays color for links you click.

6. Click the **Underline Style** popup, and then select the underline option you want.

7. Click **OK**.

The Links category in the Page Properties dialog box allows you to change the default nature of the links on a page. For example, a word defined as a link has a blue underline, by default. You could change the color to red. You can specify link colors for text, visited, rollover, and active links. In addition, you can even choose not to use an underline, or only have it appear when the visitor rolls over the text.

Setting Heading Page Properties

 DW 3.10

Set Heading Page Properties

1 Open the Web page you want to change.

2 Click the **Modify** menu, and then click **Page Properties**.

3 Click the **Headings** category.

4 Specify the Heading font you want.

5 Click the **Bold** and/or **Italic** buttons if you want.

6 Specify the specific font size and color of the H1 through H6 heading styles you want.

7 Click **OK**.

The Headings category in the Page Properties dialog box allows you to specify the default settings for up to six heading styles. You can specify the font type, size, color, and formatting. For example, you can specify that every H2 heading style that is applied to text is 14 points and red. In addition, you have the option of choosing whether the heading styles are Bold or Italic style.

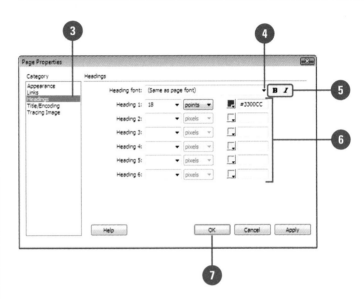

Changing Title and Encoding Page Properties

 DW 3.10

Change Title and Encoding Page Properties

1. Open the Web page you want to change.

2. Click the **Modify** menu, and then click **Page Properties**.

3. Click the **Title/Encoding** category.

4. Enter the title you want for the Web page title bar.

   TIMESAVER *Enter a title in the Title box on the Document toolbar.*

5. Select from the following options:

   ◆ **Document Type (DTD).** Select XHTML 1.0 Transitional or XHTML 1.0 Strict to make new Web pages XHTML-compliant.

   ◆ **Encoding.** Select the language you want. The default for HTML encoding is Unicode (UTF-8), which safely represents all characters.

   ◆ **Unicode Normalization Form.** If you select Unicode (UTF-8) for encoding, select the form option you want: C, D, KC, or KD. Form C is the most common one used for the Web in the Character Model. The others are provided by Adobe.

6. Click **OK**.

The Title/Encoding category in the Page Properties allows you to change the Web page title and specify the document encoding type you want. A Web page title is the text that visitors see on the title bar of their Web browser when they display the Web page. The document type and encoding options in the Page and Properties dialog box allow you to specify the language you want to use for a Web page. File encoding makes sure your Web browser and Dreamweaver use the right character set for the selected language. The standard settings for a simple HTML page are: Document Type (DTD) XHTML 1.0 Transitional, Encoding Unicode 4.0 UTF-8, and Unicode Normalization None.

Changing Page Properties for a Tracing Image

 DW 3.10

A **tracing image** is a JPEG, GIF, or PNG formatted image that lays in the background to help you layout the page. For example, you could comp your site in Fireworks and then bring it into Dreamweaver to use as a guide to align tables and layers. Tracing images are not saved with the final document and don't appear in a Web browser. It doesn't matter how big or complex the tracing images are because they are only used by Dreamweaver during the design phase. Once the file is saved and moved to the server, the tracing image goes away, and the file retains its original small size.

Change Page Properties for a Tracing Image

1. Open the Web page you want to change.

2. Click the **Modify** menu, and then click **Page Properties**.

3. Click the **Tracing Image** category.

4. Click **Browse**, locate the image you want to use, select it, and then click **OK**.

   TIMESAVER *Click the View menu, point to Tracing Image, and then click Load to insert a tracing image.*

5. Drag the **Transparency** slider to the percentage level you want for the image.

6. Click **OK**.

See Also

See "Using a Tracing Image" on page 212 for information on using a tracing image to create a Web page.

Using Visual Aids

When you're working in Design or Split view, you can use visual aids in Dreamweaver to make it easier to work with page elements, such as borders, backgrounds, and outlines that are normally invisible. Sometimes it's hard to adjust elements without being able to see the edge. For example, the Table Borders and Frame Borders commands on the Visual Aids submenu on the View menu make it easier to view and change the borders in tables and frames on a page. You can show or hide all the visual aids at once or select each item individually. The Visual Aid submenu highlights the menu icon or display a checkmark when a visual aid is turned on.

Show or Hide Visual Aids

◆ **All.** Click the **View** menu, point to **Visual Aids,** and then click **Hide All**.

TIMESAVER *Press Ctrl+Shift+I to show or hide all visual aids.*

◆ **Individual.** Click the **View** menu, point to **Visual Aids,** and then click each item you want to show or hide.

- ◆ CSS Layout Backgrounds.
- ◆ CSS Layout Box Model.
- ◆ CSS Layout Outlines.
- ◆ AP Element Outlines.
- ◆ Table Widths.
- ◆ Table Borders.
- ◆ Frame Borders.
- ◆ Image Maps.
- ◆ Invisible Elements.

Click to hide all visual aids

Click to show or hide individual visual aids

Working with Invisible Elements

Dreamweaver uses many styles of elements to create a Web page. Some of the elements are invisible, such as text and images, and some are not, such as anchors and line breaks. The invisible elements in a Web page are important to the structure and functionality of a page. However, they are not always necessary to view and make changes to a Web page unless you specifically want to work with an invisible element. You can use the Preferences dialog box to select the invisible elements you want to show or hide. After you set your invisible element preferences, you can use the Visual Aids submenu on the View menu to show (enable) or hide (disable) the Invisible Elements command. Showing invisible elements might slightly change the layout of a page, however, it's only temporary until you hide them.

Set Invisible Element Preferences

1 Click the **Dreamweaver** (Mac) or **Edit** (Win) menu, and then click **Preferences**.

2 Click the **Invisible Elements** category.

3 Select or clear the check box options you want to show or hide:

◆ **Named Anchors.** Displays an icon to mark anchor locations.

◆ **Scripts.** Displays an icon to mark JavaScript or VBScript.

◆ **Comments.** Displays an icon to mark the location of comments.

◆ **Line Breaks.** Displays an icon to mark the location of line breaks <br>.

◆ **Client-Side Image Maps.** Displays an icon to mark the location of client-side image maps.

◆ **Embedded Styles.** Displays an icon to mark the location of CSS styles embedded in the body section of a document.

◆ **Hidden Form Fields.** Displays an icon to mark the location of form fields that are set to "hidden."

- **Form Delimiter.** Displays the border of a form to make it easier to insert form fields.

- **Anchor Points For AP Elements.** Displays an icon to mark the location of code defining an AP Element, which is an element with an absolute position assigned to it. AP elements are not invisible, just the code defining it.

- **Anchor Points For Aligned Elements.** Displays an icon to mark the location of HTML code for elements that work with the align option, such as images, tables, ActiveX objects, plug-ins, and applets.

- **Visual Server Markup Tags.** Displays the location of visual server markup tags, such as Active Server Pages tags and ColdFusion tags, whose content cannot be displayed.

- **Nonvisual Server Markup Tags.** Displays the location of nonvisual server markup tags, such as Active Server Pages tags and ColdFusion tags, whose content cannot be displayed.

- **CSS Display: None.** Displays an icon to mark the location of hidden content using the display:none property.

- **Show Dynamic Text As.** Displays any dynamic text on your page in the format of {Recordset:Field} by default.

- **Server-Side Includes.** Displays the content of each server-side include file from the Web server.

4 Click **OK**.

Selecting Elements

Before you can work with an element, such as text or an image, you need to select the element first. If an element is invisible, you need to make it visible before you can select it. You can select an element in Design view by simply clicking the element. If you want to select the complete tag associated with an element, you can use the tag selector. The tag selector appears at the bottom of the Document window on the Status bar. The tag selector shows the tags within the current selection or insertion point. The leftmost tag in the tag selector is the outermost tag in the selection. Simply select the code or place the insertion point where you want to select a tag, and click the tag you want to select in the tag selector.

Select Elements

◆ **Visible Element**. In Design view, click the element or drag across it.

◆ **Invisible Element**. Click the **View** menu, point to **Visual Aids**, and then click **Invisible Elements**. You can select the invisible elements as a visible one.

◆ **Tags**. Select the code or place the insertion point where you want to select a tag, and then click the tag you want in the tag selector.

Tags selected

Table cell selected

Working with Web Page Text

5

Introduction

Now that you've created a Web page, it's time to throw in some text to get the message across. Text comes in many forms: from headings and paragraphs, bulleted points, and body text written especially for the Web. Your job as a Web designer is to make it all flow together in a logical, attractive, understandable fashion.

Many designers who come from the professional printing industry are surprised at the lack of typographic control on a normal Web page. Specific fonts are, suggested, not specified, sizes are relative, and line spacing seems to be imaginary. Designers of print-to-paper are used to exacting standards and control. For example, tell a print designer that although he specified the *Benguiat* font to be used in his brochure design, the readers might wind up with *Times New Roman*, or *Garamond*. That designer would be out the door and looking for a new print shop. Yet, that's what sometimes happens on the Internet.

Some Web designers to achieve the desired look, respond by converting their text into graphics, but don't. For one reason, text converted into graphics bloats the size of the page and increases download times; another reason is that text converted to graphics is not searchable.

Cascading Style Sheets (CSS) are more and more becoming a real option and give the Web designer almost as much control as the print designer.

In this chapter we're going to talk about text as it relates to standard Web page construction: Adding text to a page, modifying text, using text to attract attention, formatting text, checking text... text, text, text.

Adding Text to Web Pages

Working with text is not just about placing letters on a page; it's about using text as a page design element and it's also about readability. What's the use of adding text to a Web page if it's too small to read, or the font is not one that renders well on a pixel-based monitor? Remember, there are fonts that look good on paper, and fonts that look good on a computer monitor. Dreamweaver is going to help us out with the formatting part of the equation; it's up to you to make the words sound good. The cool thing about working with text in Dreamweaver is the choices you have; for example, you can choose to type text directly into a page, or copy and paste the text from a word processing document. Text is added to the Web page in several ways: you can open up a blank Web page and just start typing; however, you have very little control over text formatting. Another way is to create a table, and insert the text into the individual table cells. This gives you the ability to control your margins and paragraph formatting. The newest way is through the use of individual layers. Layers not only give you the ability to control your paragraph formatting; in addition, they give you the ability to move the layers, even stacking one layer on another.

Add Text to a Web Page

1. Open the Web page you want to add text.

   In this example we use a Web page with an inserted table.

2. Click with your mouse in the table cell that you want to add text.

3. Begin typing the text that you want to add.

4. Press the Enter key to start a new paragraph.

   Dreamweaver adds text based on its default formatting parameters, and automatically wraps the text when it comes to the end of the table cell.

Importing Tabular Data

If you have data in tabular form, such as a database or spreadsheet, you can import the data as delimited text files. Before you can import the data, you need to export or save the data in the database or spreadsheet as a delimited text file, which is a file format with the data separated by tabs, commas, colons, or semicolons. From here, you can import the data file to your page in Dreamweaver and format it as a data table. When you import the data, you can specify the table layout and formatting options you want.

Import Tabular Data

1. Open the Web page you want to import content.

2. Click in the location where you want to insert content.

3. Click the **File** menu, point to **Import**, and then click **Tabular Data**.

4. Click **Browse**, navigate to the location with the file you want to import, select the delimited file, and then click **Open**.

5. Click the **Delimiter** popup, and then select the delimiter type you used when you exported or saved the file.

6. Click the **Fit To Data** or **Set To** option. If you selected the Set to option, enter a specific width or a percentage of the browsers window width you want (in pixels).

7. Enter the cell padding and cell spacing you want (in pixels).

8. Click the **Format Top Row** popup, select the formatting option you want, and then enter the table border width you want (in pixels).

9. Click **OK**.

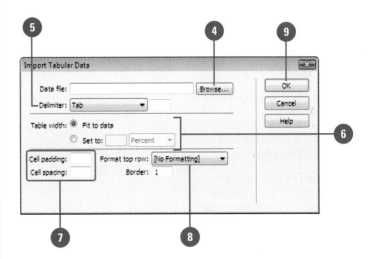

Importing Content from Microsoft Documents

If you're a Windows user you can import Microsoft documents directly onto your Web pages. You can use the Import submenu on the File menu to import content from Microsoft Word or Microsoft Excel documents into your Web pages. If you want to create a link to a Microsoft Word or Excel document, you can simply drag the document file to where you want the link in your page. If the document files is not located inside the local root folder, Dreamweaver prompts you to copy the file to the root to maintain proper site organization. In addition, when you upload your page to your Web server, you need to make sure you also upload the Microsoft Word or Excel document, so the link works properly.

Import Content from Microsoft Word or Excel

1. Open the Web page you want to import Microsoft content.

2. Click in the location where you want to insert content.

3. Click the **File** menu, point to **Import**, and then click **Word Document** or **Excel Document**.

4. Navigate to the location with the Microsoft document you want to import.

5. Select the document.

6. Click **Open**.

See Also

See "Cleaning Up Word HTML" on page 468 for information on cleaning HTML in a Word document.

Create a Link to a Microsoft Word or Excel Document

1 Open the Web page where you want to create a link to Microsoft content.

2 Drag the Word or Excel file from its current location to your page and position the link where you want it.

◆ You can use the Files panel to drag a file to the Document window. Click the Window menu, and then click Files.

3 Click the **Create A Link** option.

4 Click **OK**.

5 If the document is not located inside your root folder, click **Yes** to copy the document to the site root.

The Copy File As dialog box opens.

6 Click **Save**.

The name of the linked file appears as the link text, which you can change.

Drag here

Inserting Special Characters and the Date

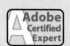 DW 3.12

In word processing you have all the letters of the alphabet, and you have special characters. Special characters help to further define what you're saying. For example, you could say that your Web site has a copyright date of 2007, or you could use a special character, and say it this way: ©2007. HTML only allows one space between characters. If you want to add more, you can use the Non-Breaking Space command on the Special Characters submenu. The Special Characters submenu also allows you to insert other characters, such as character with accents and other international characters. However, the visitor's browser must support the "other" character inserted for it to be visible to the user; therefore testing is essential. In addition to special characters, you have the ability to add things like the current date and even the time, and have the date/time items automatically update with the passage of time. When you use the Insert Date option your pages will always reflect the correct date.

Insert a Special Character

1. Open the Web page you want to insert special characters.

2. Click to place the insertion point where you want to insert text.

3. Choose one of the following options:

   ◆ Click the **Insert** menu, point to **HTML**, point to **Special Characters**, and then select a special character from the available options.

   ◆ Select the **Text** tab on the Insert bar, click the **Characters** button, and then select from the available special character options.

   Dreamweaver places the special character at the insertion point.

Did You Know?

You can add space between characters. Press Control+Shift+Spacebar (Win) or Option+Spacebar (Mac).

For Your Information

Special Characters vs Decorative Fonts

Special characters are not to be confused with decorative fonts. Some fonts, like Zaph Dingbats, and Symbols, are designed to give you small graphics (like a pointing finger, or smile face) in place of the letters of the alphabet. Special characters are actually coded into the HTML document, so that they produce exactly the symbol requested.

Insert Other Characters

1. Open the Web page you want to insert other characters.

2. Click to place the insertion point where you want to insert text.

3. Click the **Insert** menu, point to **HTML**, point to **Special Characters**, and then click **Other**.

4. Select a character from the available list. A copy of the HTML code used to display the character appears in the input window in the upper left.

5. Click **OK**.

Add the Date and Time

1. Open Dreamweaver, and then open a Web document.

2. Click to place the insertion point where you want to insert text.

3. Choose from the following options:

   ◆ Click the **Insert** menu, and then click **Date**.

   ◆ Select the **Common** tab on the Insert bar, and then click the **Date** button.

   The Insert Date dialog box opens.

4. Select the format you want the day and date to display.

5. Select a format for the time (optional).

6. Select the **Update Automatically On Save** check box to update the date/time every time the page is saved.

7. Click **OK**.

Selecting Text

Like any other application that process text, Dreamweaver needs a que from you as to what you want to do. If you plan to make a change to the current text, you need to inform Dreamweaver of that fact by making a selection. There are several ways that you can select text in Dreamweaver. The first thing to notice is that Dreamweaver does not have a specific text tool. That's because the cursor is sensitive to the area it's hovering over. For example, if you hover over an image, and click your mouse, Dreamweaver selects the image; however, if you're hovering over a section of text and click your mouse, Dreamweaver turns into a text tool, and create an insertion point into the text. That's why Dreamweaver doesn't have that old familiar Toolbox, like you see in applications such as: Photoshop, Illustrator, and Flash because it's the position of the cursor in the document that automatically determines what happens. Of course, once the text is selected, it can be modified, deleted, even copied.

Standard Selection Techniques

◆ **Single Click.** Creates an insertion point within the body of text.

◆ **Double Click.** Selects a single word (separated by spaces or a paragraph return).

NOTE *If the word ends with punctuation (period, comma, etc), they will not be selected.*

◆ **Triple Click.** Selects one paragraph (all text between two paragraph returns; including any punctuation).

◆ **Click and Drag.** Click within a body of text and drag the mouse to select a group of text. Release the mouse and the dragged text remains selected.

◆ **Click release Shift Click.** Click once within the body of text and release. Then move to another area, hold the shift key and click once. All the text between the two mouse clicks is selected.

Selected text

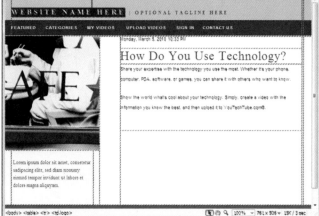

Select Using the Status Bar

1 Click to place the insertion point where you want to select text, and then look at the Status bar.

The tags for the area you've selected appear on the left side of the Status bar.

2 Click the specific tag you want in the Status bar to select the tag within the code.

For example, when you click the <p> (paragraph) tag, all the text associated with that tag appears selected.

Did You Know?

The tag selector is not just for text. For example, if you choose an image <alt> tag, the corresponding image within the document will be selected. This is a quick and easy way to make selections within complex Web documents.

You can use the Select All command to select all of the text within the selected body. Click once within the text body, click the Edit menu, and then click Select All, or press Ctrl+A (Win) or ⌘+A (Mac).

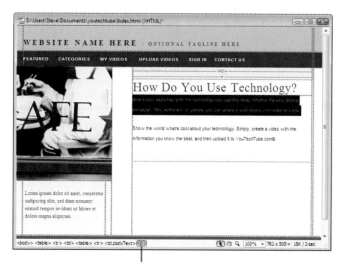

Text selected using tags on the Status bar

Copying and Pasting Text

If you cut or copy text from a file in any other application (word processor, spreadsheet, or database), Dreamweaver inserts the copied text at the insertion point of the cursor. Understand that the default Paste command has limited control over the formatting of text: It can only paste plain, unformatted text; bold, italic, or other formatting options are not carried over with the text… unless you're using Microsoft Word. By default performing a copy/paste command from MS Word retains most font formatting. Unfortunately, unless you change the Preferences of the Paste option, the Copy/Paste commands have limited control over text. For example, you have a heavily formatted section of text in Microsoft Word and you want to bring the text into Dreamweaver without any formatting because you plan to use a Style Sheet to do all the document formatting. That's where the Paste Special command comes into play. With Paste Special, you can control what formatting options are used when pasting the text.

Copy and Paste

1 Open a text document within your word processor (i.e. Microsoft Word).

2 Select the text that you want to paste into Dreamweaver.

3 Click the **Edit** menu, and then click **Copy**, or click the **Copy** button on the Standard toolbar or Home tab (Vista).

4 Open Dreamweaver, and the Web page you want to add the text.

5 Click to place the insertion point where you want to insert text.

6 Click the **Edit** menu, and then click **Paste**.

Dreamweaver pastes the copied text at the insertion point.

> **Did You Know?**
>
> *You can access the copy/paste preferences directly from the Paste Special dialog box.* When you select the Paste Special command, simply click the Paste Preferences button, and you can make your changes permanent.

Copy and Paste Special

1. Open a text document within Microsoft Word.

2. Select the text that you want to paste into Dreamweaver.

3. Click the **Edit** menu, and then click **Copy**, or click the **Copy** button on the Standard toolbar or Home tab (Vista).

4. Open Dreamweaver, and the Web page you want to add the text.

5. Click to place the insertion point where you want to insert text.

6. Click the **Edit** menu, and then click **Paste Special**.

7. Select from the following options:

   ◆ **Text Only.** Pastes text without formatting.

   ◆ **Text With Structure (paragraphs, lists, tables, etc.).** Pastes structured text without formatting.

   ◆ **Text With Structure Plus Basic Formatting (bold, italic).** Pastes structured text and simple HTML formatting.

   ◆ **Text With Structure Plus Full Formatting (bold, italic, styles).** Pastes structured text, HTML formatting, and CSS styles.

   ◆ **Retain Line Breaks.** Select this option to keep line breaks.

   ◆ **Clean Up Word Paragraph Spacing.** Select this option if you've chosen Text With Structure, or Text With Structure Plus Basic Formatting, and want to eliminate extra spacing between paragraphs.

8. Click **OK**.

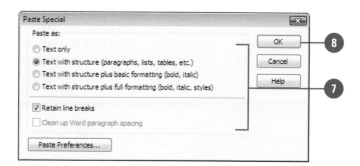

For Your Information

Working with Word Processing Programs

To assist in generating text on my Web pages, I work with Microsoft Word and Adobe Dreamweaver open at the same time. This way I'm able to type text in an application I'm comfortable with (MS Word), and quickly drag from my word processor directly into my Dreamweaver Web page. If you're copying text that contains multiple paragraphs, make sure your paragraphs are separated by two returns. When pasted into Dreamweaver, the paragraph breaks are preserved. If you just have a single return between paragraphs, Dreamweaver converts the paragraphs to line breaks.

Setting Copy/Paste Preferences

You can use the Copy/Paste section of the Preferences dialog box to customize how the Paste command inserts text into a Web page. You can set special paste preferences as default options to paste text from other programs. You can set options to paste text only, text with structure, such as paragraphs, list and tables, and text with structure and formatting, including HTML and CSS styles.

Set Copy/Paste Preferences

① Click the **Dreamweaver** (Mac) or **Edit** (Win) menu, and then click **Preferences**.

② Click the **Copy/Paste** category.

③ Select from the following check boxes:

◆ **Text Only.** Pastes unformatted text.

◆ **Text With Structure (paragraphs, lists, tables, etc.).** Pastes structured text without formatting.

◆ **Text With Structure Plus Basic Formatting (bold, italic).** Pastes structured text and simple HTML formatting.

◆ **Text With Structure Plus Full Formatting (bold, italic, styles).** Pastes structured text, HTML formatting, and CSS styles.

④ Select the **Retain Line Breaks** check box to keep line breaks in pasted text.

⑤ Select the **Clean Up Word Paragraph Spacing** check box if you selected the Text with Structure or Text with Structure Plus Basic Formatting option, and want to eliminate extra space between paragraphs when you paste your text.

⑥ Click **OK**.

Modifying Font Combinations

When you select one of Dreamweaver's default fonts, you'll notice that they come in groups of three: A primary font, secondary font, and general font. This is known as a **font combination**. Font combinations determine how a browser displays text in your Web page. A browser uses the first font in the combination that is installed on the user's system. For example, if you choose the Arial and the visitor does not have Arial, the browser attempts to find Helvetica, if it can't find Helvetica, it substitutes a sans-serif font. If none of the fonts in the combination are installed, the browser displays the text as specified by the user's browser preferences. You can use the Edit Font List command to set the font combinations that appear in the Properties panel and the Font submenu on the Text menu.

Modify Font Combinations

1 Click the **Text** menu, point to **Font**, and then click **Edit Font List**.

2 Select the font combination you want to edit.

3 Use any of the following to add, modify, or remove the selected font combination.

◆ **New Combination.** Click the Add button (Plus), select a font from the Available fonts list, and then click Left Arrow button to add it to the font list.

◆ **Delete Combination.** Select the font combination you want to remove, and then click the Subtract button (Minus).

◆ **Add Fonts.** Select a font from the Available fonts list, and then click Left Arrow button to add it to the font list.

◆ **Remove fonts.** Select a font from the Chosen fonts list, and then click Right Arrow button to remove it from the font list.

◆ **Change Combination Order.** Select the font combination you want to arrange, and then click the Up or Down arrows.

4 Click **OK**.

Formatting Characters

Selecting text is one thing; knowing what to do with it once it's been selected is another. Dreamweaver has a set of character formatting tags that allows you to change the size, color and style of the text, and then generate the specific HTML tags. Remember, formatting text is not just about changing the text; you also have you ask yourself the question of why you're changing it. Does that heading text really need to be THAT big… Is it OK to change the color of text to red? Many a good Web site has gone down the tubes because of bad design. Remember, do not change the text just because you can; change it because it reflects the overall design of the site.

Format Text Characters

1 Open the Web page you want to format.

2 Select a word inside the text that you want to modify.

> **TIMESAVER** *Press Ctrl+A (Win) or* ⌘*+A (Mac) to select all of the text within the selected body.*

3 Click the **Window** menu, and then click **Properties** to open the Properties panel.

4 Choose from the following type of formatting options:

◆ **Format.** Click the button and choose from the predefined styles. Leave this option at its default value.

◆ **Style.** Displays the class style currently applied to the text. If no styles have been applied the option displays No CSS. Leave this option at its default value.

◆ **Bold.** Click to **bold** the selected text.

◆ **Italic.** Click to *italicize* the selected text.

◆ **Font.** Click to change the font type of the selected text.

- ◆ **Size.** Click the **Size** button, and then first choose how you want to measure font sizes (percent, pixels, points, etc), and then change the size in the input field. For example, if you're fonts by percentage (default), and you change the size to 50 percent, the selected text will be half the size of the standard font; 200 percent, twice the size, etc.

- ◆ **Text Color.** Click the **Text Color** button, and then choose a new color for the selected text, or click in the coding box and type in the hexadecimal code value for the desired color.

NOTE *Hexadecimal codes are preceded by a pound sign (#), and are three sets of double-digit number values representing the percentages of red, green, and blue, respectively.*

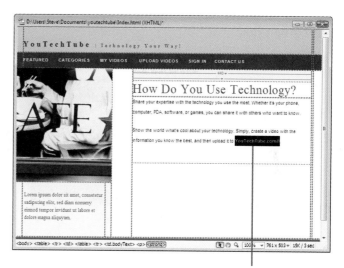

Formatted text
characters

Did You Know?

You can make multiple formatting changes at once. After you select the text you want to change, if you click the Page Properties button on the Properties panel, you can perform all of your formatting changes to the text, and change options to the Page Properties at the same time.

Formatting Paragraph Text

Paragraph text formatting differs from standard text formatting in one way: The changes made impact the entire paragraph, not just the individual words. For this reason, paragraph formatting does not require you to select the paragraph; you just have to click inside the paragraph you want to change. Once the paragraph is selected you can work with Dreamweaver's paragraph style options.

Format Paragraph Text

1. Open the Web page you want to format.

2. Select a word inside the text that you want to modify.

3. Click the **Window** menu, and then click **Properties** to open the Properties panel.

4. Choose from the following type formatting options:

   ◆ **Format.** Click the **Format** button and select one of the available options.

   NOTE *The paragraph style applies the default style for an <p> HTML tag, as do the H1 thru H6 Heading styles.*

   ◆ **Align.** Select one of the justification buttons: **Align Left**, **Align Right**, **Align Center**, or **Justify** to change the justification of the active paragraph.

   ◆ **Indent.** Click the **Text Indent** or **Text Outdent** button to indent (in or out) the left margin of the text paragraph.

   ◆ **Ordered/Unordered.** Click the **Ordered List** or **Unordered List** button to convert the select paragraph into a list.

   The formatting options are applied to the selected text.

Controlling Line Spacing

 DW 3.12

One of the problems with formatting text on a Web page is the problem of controlling line spacing. For example, when you press the Enter key to create a new paragraph, HTML create a <p> or paragraph tag, jumps you down to the next line, and leaves a bit of extra space between the lines; however, what if you don't want the extra space. HTML takes care of this pesky problem by giving us another obscure HTML code called a line break, or the <br> tag.

Control Line Spacing

1. Open the Web page you want to change.

2. Click your mouse inside the document and begin typing.

3. Use either of the following to control line spacing:

   ◆ **Paragraph.** Press the Enter key.

   Dreamweaver inserts the paragraph tag <p> into the text and adds extra line spacing between the two lines.

   ◆ **Line Break.** Press the Shift + Enter keys.

   Dreamweaver inserts the line break tag <br> into the text and does not add any extra space between the lines.

Inserting Horizontal Rules

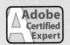 DW 3.12

Insert a Horizontal Line

1. Open and display the Web page you want to use.

2. Click where you want to insert a horizontal line.

3. Click the **Insert** menu, point to **HTML**, and then click **Horizontal Rule**.

Horizontal lines have a variety of uses in the construction of a Web page. Whether they're used to separate sections of a page or to underline an important piece of text, you have several decisions to make. Inserting a horizontal line provides a simple, yet effective way to highlight the information you want visitors to see. Lines have a variety of properties that you can modify, including width, height, alignment, and color.

Inserted horizontal line

Modify a Horizontal Line

1. Open and display the Web page with the horizontal line you want to change.

2. Select the horizontal line you want to modify.

3. Select the formatting options you want in the Properties panel:

   ◆ **W.** Width of the line. Specified in pixels or as a percentage of the window width.

   ◆ **H.** Height of the line in pixels.

   ◆ **Align.** Alignment of the line on the page.

   ◆ **Shading.** Select the check box to create a shaded line.

Creating Ordered and Unordered Lists

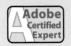

DW 3.12

Most word processors have the ability to create bulleted or numbered lists of information. A bulleted list can itemize a topic's points or catalog the properties of an object. A numbered list is helpful for giving step-by-step instructions. A list can break up the page and simultaneously draw the viewer's eye to key details. Lists are an important alternative to the basic textual tools of paragraphs and headings. In this chapter, you can study Dreamweaver's tools for designing and working with each of the three basic types of lists available in HTML: ordered lists, unordered lists, and definition lists. An ordered list is used when it's important that the listed items appear in a sequential order. As a professional chef, I use ordered lists all the time for the steps to a specific recipe. An unordered list is used when the sequence of the listed items is of no great concern. Again, as a chef, I use unordered lists to display my list of ingredients to a recipe.

Create an Ordered List

1. Open the Web page you want to format.

2. Click within the document where you want to insert the ordered list, or select a group of text that you want to convert into a list.

3. Click the **Window** menu, and then click **Properties** to display the Properties panel.

4. Click the **Ordered List** button in the Properties panel.

    Dreamweaver inserts the Roman numeral 1 into the document.

5. To add items to the list, type an item, and then press Enter (Win) or Return (Mac).

Did You Know?

You can create a nested or indented list. A nested list is a list that contains another list. Select the items you want to nest, click the Indent button in the Properties panel, or click the Text menu, and then click Indent.

Create an Unordered List

1. Open the Web page you want to format.

2. Click within the document where you want to insert the ordered list, or select a group of text that you want to convert into a list.

3. Click the **Window** menu, and then click **Properties** to display the Properties panel.

4. Click the **Unordered List** button in the Properties panel.

   Dreamweaver inserts a default round bullet into the document.

5. To add items to the list, type an item, and then press Enter (Win) or Return (Mac).

Create a List Using Existing Text

1. Open the Web page you want to format.

2. Select the paragraphs you want to make into a list.

3. Click the **Unordered List** or **Ordered List** button in the Properties panel, or click the **Text** menu, point to **List**, and then select the type of list you want: **Unorder List, Ordered List**, or **Definition List**.

2 List changed to bullets

Creating Definition Lists

 DW 3.12

A definition list doesn't use leading characters (bullets or numbers) to map the items; instead, definition lists are used in areas like glossaries. I might create a definition list explaining cooking terminology. A definition list does not use bullets to identify the items, and it's composed of two lines: the first line is for the name of the item, and the second line is indented and describes the item; hence the name, definition list. If you happen to have a very long definition, and you want to separate it into two or more paragraphs, don't press the Enter key; that will take you to a new definition term. Simply press the Shift plus Enter key to create a soft return, and then type the second paragraph.

Create an Definition List

1. Open the Web page you want to format.

2. Click within the document where you want to insert the definition list.

3. Click the **Text** menu, point to List, and then click and then click **Definition List**.

4. Type a definition term and press the Enter key. The new line is automatically indented.

5. Type in a definition description.

6. Press the Enter key to add another definition term, and press Enter again to add the corresponding definition description.

   The Definition list can be continued for as long as you want.

7. Press the Enter key twice to end the list and return to the normal paragraph style type.

Modifying Lists

After you create a list, you can use the List Properties dialog box to make changes to it. Some of the list options you can change include number style, number reset, or bullet style. You can make changes to the entire list or to a specific item in the list.

Modify a List

1 Click anywhere within the ordered list you want to modify, or click on a specific item that you want to change.

2 Click the **Text** menu, point to **List**, and then click **Properties**.

3 To modify the list use the following options:

◆ Click the **List Type** popup, and then click **Bulleted List**, **Numbered List**, **Directory List**, or **Menu List**.

◆ Click the **Style** popup, and then select the style you want.

NOTE *You'll see different options based on the list type chosen.*

◆ Enter the starting number you want to use by the list (available only when creating a numbered list).

4 To modify an individual item:

◆ Click the **New Style** popup to change the style of the active list item.

◆ Enter the reset count number you want to use by the active list item (available only when creating a numbered list).

5 Click **OK**.

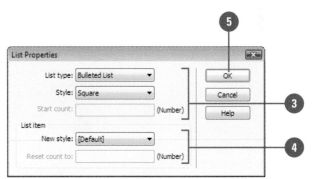

Applying Text Styles

Dreamweaver gives us the ability to change the style of text. A **style** is a collection of formatting settings saved with a Web site or template that you can apply to text, graphics, and tables at any time. Changing the style of text is useful when you want to draw the reader's eyes to a particular phrase or word. For example, using a bold font might indicate that the word is very important. Dreamweaver accomplishes this by using two types of tags: physical tags and logical styles. **Physical tags** change how the text looks (bold, italic, underline, etc). **Logical styles** define a certain look or style. For example, a paragraph style, or a heading style changes the text, based on pre-defined values. In addition, when you use logical styles for HTML text, it becomes easier to find what you're looking. For example, you could conduct a search to find all paragraphs defined as citation text. Dreamweaver provides you with built-in styles, or you can create your own user-defined styles.

Apply a Built-In Text Style

1. Open the Web page you want to apply a text style.

2. Select the character, word, or words that you want to apply the text style.

   If you select a word or words and apply a style, the style will only affect the selected text. If you click inside a paragraph and apply a style, the style will change the entire paragraph.

3. Click the **Text** menu, point to **Style**, and then select from the following options:

   ◆ Bold, Italic, Underline

   TIMESAVER *You can also change the font style in the Properties panel. Click the Bold, Italic, or Underline buttons you want to apply.*

   ◆ Strikethrough, Teletype, Emphasis, Strong

   ◆ Code, Variable, Sample, Keyboard

   ◆ Citation, Definition, Deleted, Inserted

Apply a Built-In Font and Size Style

1. Open the Web page you want to apply a text style.

2. Select the character, word, or words that you want to apply the text style.

   If you select a word or words and apply a style, the style will only affect the selected text. If you click inside a paragraph and apply a style, the style will change the entire paragraph.

3. Choose from any of the following style options:

   ◆ **Font.** Click the **Text** menu, point to **Font**, and then select the font style you want.

   ◆ **Size.** Click the **Text** menu, point to **Size**, and then select the point size you want.

   ◆ **Size Change.** Click the **Text** menu, point to **Size Change**, and then select the point size change you want.

   TIMESAVER *You can also change the font and size in the Properties panel. Click the Font or Size popup, and then select the style or size you want to apply.*

For Your Information

Using the <strong> and <em> Tags

The two style tags <b> bold and <I> italic are common use tags in Dreamweaver; however, it is better to use the, <strong> for bold and <em> for italic. Dreamweaver allows you to specify which tags to use. Click the Edit (Win) or Dreamweaver (Mac) menu, click Preferences, click the General category, select the Use <strong> and <em> in place of <b> check box, and then click OK.

Creating Text Styles

While embedding physical tags or logical styles into a document is a very common way to change the look of text, the Web design community is moving to Cascading Style Sheets. Cascading Style Sheets can be used in conjunction with logical styles to define how that style works when viewed by the visitor, and give you more control over what your visitors will see. It's also important to understand that the visual look of standard HTML styles and tags are defined by the browser application, and may appear different when viewed on different browsers. If you modify a style, you make the change once, but all text tagged with that style changes to reflect the new format.

Create a CSS Text Style

1. Open the Web page you want to create a customized style.

2. Click the **Text** menu, point to **CSS Styles**, and then click **New**.

3. Choose from the following options:

   ◆ **Selector Type.** Select the **Class (can apply to any tag)** option.

   ◆ **Selector.** Enter a name for the style.

   NOTE *Class names should begin with a period (if you don't add it, Dreamweaver will), and have no spaces or additional punctuation.*

   ◆ **Define In.** Select the **This Document Only** option or select an existing external style sheet.

4. Click **OK**.

5. Click the **Type** category.

6. Format the font based on the available options.

7. Click **OK**.

Apply a CSS Text Style

1 Open the Web page you want to apply a CSS text style.

2 Select in the paragraph that you want to apply the custom style.

Remember the style you created can only be used within the original document. If you open another document, you will not be able to use this new style.

3 Click the **Text** menu, point to **CSS Styles**, and then click on the name of the new style.

TIMESAVER *You can also change the Style in the Properties panel. Click the Style popup, and then select the style you want to apply.*

The new style is applied to the selected text.

Renaming Styles

If you no longer like the name you specified for a style or the name doesn't adequately describe the formatting style, you can rename it using the Style popup in the Properties panel. The Style popup provides access to the Rename command where you can change the name of a style.

Rename a Style

① Open the Web page you want to rename a style.

② Click the **Window** menu, and then click **Properties** to open the Properties panel.

③ Click the **Style** popup, and then click **Rename**.

④ Click the **Rename Style** popup, and then select the style you want to rename.

⑤ Type a new name for the style.

⑥ Click **OK** to close the dialog box and save your changes.

The Results panel appears, displaying the selected style.

Click style popup

Finding Text

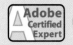 DW 3.2

If you need to quickly find another instance of a word or phrase in a Web page, you can use the Find Selection command instead of the Find and Replace command. All you need to do is select an instance of the text or phrase you want to find, and then select the Find Selection command on the Edit menu, or press Shift+F3. After you find the selection, you can use the Find Next command to locate the next occurrence of the selection.

Find Text by Selection

1 Open the Web page you want to find text.

2 Select a word or phrase.

3 Click the **Edit** menu, and then click **Find Selection**.

TIMESAVER *Press Shift+F3 to find the current selection.*

Dreamweaver goes through the document, finds and highlights the next occurrence of the selected word.

4 To locate the next occurrence of the word, click the **Edit** menu, and then click **Find Next**.

TIMESAVER *Press F3 to find the next occurrence of the current selection.*

Locates the next instance of "Upload"

Finding and Replacing Text or Code

 DW 3.2

Suppose that you discover you need to change a word throughout a Web page or entire site. You do not need to read through the document to find every instance of the word and manually change it. The Find and Replace command can do that for you. Dreamweaver can find every instance for you, and walk you through the Web site from page to page until all the corrections have been made. In addition to text, you can also find and replace code. You can search one or more Web page or an entire Web site. The results of performing a Find All and Replace All appear within the Results window under the Search tab, and results remain there until the next time you perform a Find All or Replace All. If you select a word or group of words before opening the Find and Replace dialog box, the words automatically are added to the Find box.

Find and Replace Text or Code

1 Open the Web page you want to find and replace text.

2 Click the **Edit** menu, and then click **Find and Replace**.

3 Choose from the following Find and Replace options:

- ◆ **Find In.** Click to determine what documents you want to search; everything from the current document to the entire site.

- ◆ **Search.** Click to determine what logical parts (Text or Source Code) of the document you want searched.

- ◆ **Find.** Enter the text that you want to find.

- ◆ **Replace.** Enter the text (optional) that you want to use to replace the text entered in the Find input box.

- ◆ **Load Query.** Click Load Query button to load a previously saved Find and Replace query.

- ◆ **Save Query.** Click Save Query button to save the current Find and Replace query.

3

Finds text

4 Choose from the following Find and Replace options:

◆ **Match Case.** Select to make the Find text case sensitive (charlie, as opposed to Charlie).

◆ **Match Whole Word.** Select to match whole words.

◆ **Ignore Whitespace.** Select to treat all whitespace as a single space for the purpose of matching.

◆ **Use Regular Expression.** Select to use string expressions to help locate information.

5 Choose from the following controls to find what you want:

◆ **Find Next.** Find the next occurrence of the Find input field, based on the current position of the cursor.

◆ **Find All.** Find all occurrences of the Find input field.

◆ **Replace.** Find the next occurrence of the Find input field and replace it with the text in the Replace field.

◆ **Replace All.** Find all occurrences of the Find input field and replace with the text in the Replace field.

6 Click **Close** to exit the Find and Replace dialog box.

The Results panel appears for the Find All and Replace All.

TIMESAVER *Press F3 (Win) or* ⌘+G *(Mac) to perform a search again without display the Find and Replace dialog box.*

Finds all the instances of the word "video" in the Results Panel

Using the Results Panel

 DW 3.2

Use the Results Panel

1 Open the Web page you want to find and replace text.

2 Click the **Window** menu, and then click **Results** to open the Results panel.

The list of pages containing the previous search results opens in the Results panel at the bottom of the Dreamweaver window.

3 Click the **Search** tab if necessary.

4 Choose from the following Find and Replace options:

◆ **Highlight Selection.** Double-click a selection from the Results panel to open the file if necessary and highlight the selection in the document.

◆ **Find and Replace.** Click to open the Find and Replace dialog box.

◆ **Stop.** Click to stop a search in progress.

◆ **Save Report.** Click to save the search results as a report in the XML file format.

5 Click the **Window** menu, and then click **Results** to close the Results panel.

The results of performing a Find All and Replace All search in the Find and Replace dialog box appear within the Results window under the Search tab. The search results remain there until the next time you perform a Find All or Replace All. You can access the search result by opening the Results panel. Within the Results panel, you can quickly highlight a specific result, open the Find and Replace dialog box, stop a search in progress, and save the search results in the XML.

2

Find and Replace

3

Stop   Save Report   Highlight selection

Defining Acronyms and Abbreviations

If your Web page contains acronyms, such as MADD for Mother's Against Drunk Drivers, and abbreviations, such as CE for Copy Editor, you can define them using HTML tags for use with search engines, spell checkers, language translation programs, or speech synthesizers.

Define Acronyms and Abbreviations

1. Open the Web page you want to define an acronym or abbreviation.

2. Select the acronym or abbreviation in the text.

3. Click the **Insert** menu, point to **HTML**, point to **Text Objects**, and then click **Acronym** or **Abbreviation**.

4. Enter the full text of the acronym or abbreviation.

5. Enter the language you want, such as en for English, it for Italian, or de for German.

6. Click **OK**.

Checking Spelling

One of the worst things that you can do (well, almost one of the worst), is to have misspelled words on your Web page. Not only do they distract the reader, they distract from the overall impression of professionalism that you're trying to imply. Besides, since everyone on the planet knows there's something called a spellchecker there's simply no excuse for misspelled words. Fortunately, Dreamweaver includes an simple spellchecker to help avoid such awkward moments. You should always spell check a Web page before it's moved online. One other fine point: Using a spellchecker does not mean that the words are used correctly. For example, to, too, and two, are all spelled correctly; however, they have very different meanings. So, the order of events follows: Spell Check first; then read the text (called type editing), and be sure that it makes sense.

Check Spelling

1 Open the Web page you want to spell check.

2 Click the **Text** menu, and then click **Check Spelling**.

   TIMESAVER *Press Shift+F7 to check spelling.*

   Dreamweaver begins the spell check process and stops on the first problem word.

3 Use the following options to work with the problem word:

   ◆ **Word Not Found In Dictionary.** Displays the offending word, and highlights the word in the Web page document.

   ◆ **Change To.** Type in the word you want to use to substitute for the offending word.

   ◆ **Suggestions.** Choose an option from the listed suggestions.

   ◆ **Add To Personal.** Click to add the offending word to Dreamweaver's personal dictionary. Excellent for names or technical terms that are spelled correctly, but keep coming up as misspelled.

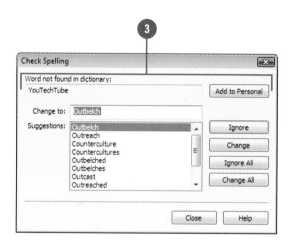

4 Choose from the following controls to change the selection:

◆ **Ignore.** Ignore the word, proceed to the next offending word, and don't add the word to the personal dictionary.

◆ **Change.** Change the word; based on the text in the Change To dialog box, or the appropriate selected suggestion.

◆ **Ignore All.** Ignore all occurrences of the offending word, but don't add to the personal dictionary.

◆ **Change All.** Change all occurrences of the offending word.

5 Click **Close** to close the Check Spelling dialog box, or click **OK** when the spell check is completed.

Did You Know?

You can spell check in more than English. Click the Edit (Win) or Dreamweaver (Mac) menu, click Preferences, click the General category, click the Spelling dictionary popup, select the dictionary language you want, and then click OK. You can download dictionaries for additional languages from the Dreamweaver Support Center. Click the Help menu, and then click Dreamweaver Support Center.

Using Undo and Redo

Probably one of the greatest inventions of the computer industry is the ability to Undo, and Redo. Now, if we could just figure out how to give real life an undo feature... that would be something. Dreamweaver gives us the ability to undo our past mistakes, and redo something we wished we had not removed. The History panel shows the actions you've just taken in Dreamweaver, and enables you to undo or repeat any number of steps. History gives us the ability to control our working environment, and allows us to try creative ideas; knowing full well, that if we make a mistake, it's a simple matter to go back in time. The History panel is Dreamweaver's time machine.

Undo or Redo One Action at a Time

◆ Click the **Edit** menu, and then click **Undo**, or click the **Undo** button on the Standard toolbar to reverse your most recent action, such as typing a word or formatting a paragraph.

   TIMESAVER *Press Ctrl+Z (Win) or ⌘+Z (Mac) to undo.*

◆ Click the **Edit** menu, and then click **Redo**, or click the **Redo** button on the Standard toolbar to restore the last action you reversed.

   TIMESAVER *Press Ctrl+Y to redo your undo.*

Click to Undo or Redo the previous command or action.

Undo and Redo buttons on the Standard toolbar

Undo or Redo Actions Using the History Panel

① Open a Web document, and perform several actions (i.e. create text, insert an image, etc).

② Click the **Window** menu, and then click **History** to open the History panel.

> **TIMESAVER** *Press Shift+F10 to open the History panel.*

You'll see a line-by-line listing of all the steps performed to the current Web document.

③ To perform a multiple undo, click the arrow located to the left History panel, and then drag it up the list.

Every item listed under the arrow will be undone.

> **NOTE** *To perform a multiple redo, click the arrow, and drag it down the list. All items above the arrow (including the item the arrow is pointing) will be restored.*

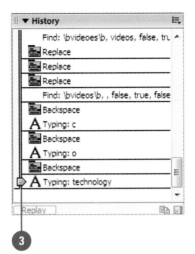

Did You Know?

You can change the number of History Steps. The default number of History steps is 50; while that may seem enough for most folks, you can change the number of steps in Preferences. Click the Edit (Win) or Dreamweaver (Mac) menu, click Preferences, click the General category, and then change the number of steps. The maximum value for history steps is 9,999… that's a lot of steps. When you're done, click OK.

Working with Web Page Images

6

Introduction

Is it true that a picture is worth a thousand words? Is it also true that every time a writer begins talking about images they use that same timeworn phrase? Am I ever going to get to the point? To be honest, a picture can be worth much more than a thousand words; in fact, a well-placed image can articulate more than words can ever convey. For example, ever try to verbally describe a sunset? Go ahead, I'll wait; give it a try.

Communication comes in three forms Visual, Vocal, and Verbal, and on a Web page the right visual image can be very powerful. On the other hand, placing images on a Web page can produce the opposite effect. I call it the why-did-they-use-that-image syndrome.

Good designers don't use images just because they can, but because they are needed to convey a specific message. Images should be used to drive your message home; they should blend seamlessly with the Web page, and the text on the pages. Don't' use images because you can, use them because you need them to convey your message.

Dreamweaver makes the insertion of images a snap; in fact, it's as simple as a drag and a drop. In turn, Dreamweaver creates the compliant HTML tags within the document to make the image display correctly on a variety of browsers. Once the images have been inserted, Dreamweaver's graphical user interface allows you to modify the images in terms of size and position. You can even set up external editing applications, such as: Adobe Photoshop, and Fireworks to revise the images on the fly.

In addition to adding simple images to a Web page, you can use graphics for navigational aids, rollover buttons; even image maps.

What You'll Do

Use Web Friendly Graphics

Define an Image Folder

Insert Images

Insert Images from Photoshop and Fireworks

Optimize Images Using Fireworks

Use Low Source Images

Modify Images

Align Images

Edit Images

Change Image Brightness and Contrast

Change Image Sharpness

Crop an Image

Use an External Editor

Set File Types/Editors Preferences

Create Rollover Images

Insert an Image Placeholder

Using Web Friendly Graphics

The Internet did not always support the use of graphics. As a matter of fact, its original use was for sharing of textual data among scientists and the U.S. Military. That was yesterday... Today the Internet supports static graphics, animations, video, and audio, along with all that textual data.

Preparing images for the Internet involves knowing what file formats are best to use for the Internet. Web friendly formats are designed to help the image appear good, load as quickly as possible, be compatible with all the major browsers on the market, and work seamlessly on any operating system (Macintosh, Windows, etc).

The formats that meet those requirements are then submitted to the World Wide Web Consortium, the international organization that controls and organizes the Internet. If they put their blessing on the format, it becomes a Web standard, and then all the browser manufacturers scramble to make their browsers compatible with that format. Eventually, the new browsers find their way into the marketplace, and designers begin using the formats in their Web pages.

The three major file formats that are considered the standard for static images are: GIF, JPEG, and PNG.

Depending on the type of image, and how you're using it, each one of these formats has their advantages and disadvantages.

The GIF Format

Short for Graphics Interchange Format, the GIF format (pronounced, jiff) is a unique Web compression technique that supports 8-bit images with a maximum of 256 colors. GIF is for images with distinct colors, such as line drawings, black and white images and small text groups that are only a few pixels high. With an animation editor, such as Adobe Fireworks, GIF images can be put together for animated images. GIF also supports transparency, where a color or colors can be set to transparent in order to let the color on the underlying Web page to show through. The compression algorithm used in the GIF format is called RLE (Run Length Encoding). This compression algorithm works best with solid colors; like you would encounter in clipart, or text; and since most clipart does not include many colors, the 256 maximum color restriction works just fine.

The GIF format is also considered lossless. In other words, images saved in the GIF format will be compressed without the removal of any color information. Therefore, when they're displayed on the visitor's browser, the image will be exactly what you saved, in terms of quality.

The JPEG Format

Short for Joint Photographic Experts Group, the JPEG (pronounced j-peg), is a Web format designed primarily for the compression and display of photographs. JPEGs allow for 24-bit images using millions of colors. To make JPEGs usable, the large amount of color information must be compressed, which is accomplished by removing what the compression algorithm considers unneeded information. JPEG compression is "lossy," meaning that the compression scheme sacrifices some image quality, in exchange for a reduction in the file's size. JPEG files can range from small amounts of lossless compression to large amounts of lossy compression. This is a common standard on the Web, but the data loss generated in its compression makes it undesirable for printing purposes. JPEG images do not support any level of transparency, and will fill transparent areas of the image with a user-defined matte color.

Once an image has been compressed using the JPEG format and saved, the color information that was removed can never be recovered. Therefore, it's best when editing an image to save a copy as the JPEG, so as to retain the original image information.

The PNG Format

Short for Portable Network Graphic, (pronounced ping) the PNG format was designed to be a patent-free successor to the GIF format. Though not designed specifically for the Web, PNG offers particular benefits in this environment such as improved image compression (10 to 30 percent smaller than the GIF format), two dimensional interlacing, storage of text with the image making it possible for search engines to gather information and offer subject searching for images in a standard way. In addition, the PNG format is used for lossless compression and displaying images on the web.

The PNG format comes in two sizes, the PNG-8 (used in place of the GIF format), and the PNG-24 (used in place of the JPEG format).

The advantages of PNG are that it supports images with millions of colors and produces background transparency without jagged edges. The disadvantages are that PNG images will not show up on older browsers (pre 4.0), and when using the full PNG-24 format with transparency, they can be comparatively larger in file size than JPEG images.

One other interesting feature of the PNG format is its ability to adjust the gamma of an image across operating systems. Typically, an image will display differently on a Mac or Windows monitor. The PNG format adjusts the image so that it appears the same... regardless of operating system.

Adobe Fireworks, and Adobe Flash use the PNG as their native format, so that means all the power of the format, including transparency, and opacity settings are fully supported.

Defining an Image Folder

It's important to set up a folder within your site folder that holds all of the images for a specific Web project. Creating this folder can be accomplished when you set up the site, or it can be made later. There are several advantages to setting up an image folder: it helps Dreamweaver in the organization of your site, and helps you locate images when you need to work on them. Since we're about to start adding images to our site, it's a good idea to stop and define this folder. Once the folder is created, you should copy all of your Web images into this folder. In addition, when you attempt to add an image to a Web page that is outside the site folder, Dreamweaver prompts you to copy the file to your site, and when you do, it adds the new images into the defined folder. All things considered, creating an image folder is a smart, efficient thing to do.

Define an Image Folder

1. Open your site folder, and create a new folder.

   In this example, we'll use the obvious and call the new folder, Images.

2. Click the **Site** menu, and then click **Manage Sites**.

3. Select your site from the available options.

4. Click **Edit**.

5. Click the **Advanced** tab.

6. Click the **Local Info** category.

7. Select the folder icon located to the right of the Default Images Folder Input box.

8 Navigate to the Local root folder, and then select the Images folder you want to use.

9 Click **Select** (Win) or **Choose** (Mac) to record the folder's location, and exit the Search dialog box.

10 Click **OK** to close the Site Definition dialog box.

11 Click **Done** to save your changes.

Inserting Images

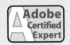

DW 2.13

The three basic elements of any static Web page are text, images, and links. Adding a static image to a Web page can be as simple as a drag and a drop. By the way, the term "static" simply refers to any non-moving Web image. A static image is not video; it does not dance, move, or sing… it just sits there. You can also add dynamic images, which are images that changes. For example, an advertising banner cycles through different images. Images can be added directly to a Web page or they can be added within a section of text: called an inline image. Dreamweaver gives you several ways to add images to your Web pages. The method you choose to add images depends on how you like to work with Dreamweaver. Any time you add an image to a Web page, Dreamweaver (by default) asks you to type in a description, and alternate text. This information is used by screen reader applications (i.e. JAWS) for visually impaired users; therefore it's important that this information is added to the image.

Insert an Image

1 Open the Web page you want to insert an image.

2 Click to place the insertion point where you want to place the image.

3 Using one of the following methods to insert an image:

◆ **Assets Panel.** Open the Assets panel, select the image you want to add to the page, and then drag the thumbnail, or filename of the image into the Web page.

◆ **Folder.** Open a folder on your desktop that contains Web friendly images, and then click and drag from the folder directly into the Web page.

◆ **Insert Panel.** Click the **Common** tab on the Insert panel, click the **Image** button arrow, click **Image**, select the image from the available options, and then click **OK**.

◆ **Insert Menu.** Click the **Image** menu, click **Image**, select the image from the available options, and then click **OK**.

Select Image Source dialog box

Insert Menu option

Select the image you want to insert.

136

4 If the image you selected is not contained within the site folder, click **Yes** to the alert asking for permission to make a copy of the image, and place it within the site folder, and then click **Save** in the Copy File As dialog box.

The Image Tag Accessibility Attributes dialog box opens.

5 Click in the Alternate Text Input field and type a very short description for the image.

For example, if the image is of a cell phone, you might enter the words, Image of a cell phone, or just, cell phone.

NOTE *If you prefer to leave this field blank, click the arrow to the right of the input box, and select the empty option.*

6 Click the file folder icon, located to the right of the Long Description input box, and then select the file that contains a longer description of the image.

NOTE *The Long Description option is a plain text document, which contains a longer description of the image. For example, if the image is of a sunset, you could describe the place and time the image was captured. Remember, the alternate text and long description are primarily used by the visually impaired. This file should be created in a text processor, saved as plain text, and placed inside the site folder.*

7 Click **OK** to add the image to the Web page.

Inserted image

Inserting Images from Photoshop and Fireworks

Adobe Certified Expert

DW 2.13

After you create or modify images in Adobe Photoshop CS3 in the PSD format or Adobe Fireworks CS3 in the PNG format, you can quickly copy and paste or insert them directly into Dreamweaver CS3 (New!). Dreamweaver handles the integration and optimizes them as Web-ready images in the selected format (GIF, JPEG, or PNG formats). In Photoshop, you can also paste all or part of a multi-layered or multi-sliced image into a Web page. After you insert these images into a Web page, you can edit the source image in Photoshop or Fireworks and update the image in Dreamweaver.

Copy and Paste Images from Photoshop or Fireworks

1. Open the image you want to copy in Photoshop CS3 (PSD format) or Fireworks CS3 (PNG format).

2. Select the image, layer, or slice.

3. Click the **Edit** menu, and then click **Copy**.

4. Exit Photoshop or Fireworks.

5. Open a Web page in Dreamweaver that you want to insert an image.

6. Click within the document where you want the image inserted.

7. Click the **Edit** menu, and then click **Paste**.

   The Image Preview dialog box opens.

8. Click the **Options** tab, and then specify the format, quality, and smoothing options you want.

9. Click the **File** tab, and then specify the scale options you want.

10. Click **OK**.

11. If prompted, locate the Images folder on your local root site, and save the image, and then specify Input Accessibility options.

    The image is inserted into the document with the specified format and settings.

Insert Images from Photoshop or Fireworks

1. Open a Web page you want to insert an image.

2. Click within the document where you want the image inserted.

3. Click the **Insert** menu, and then click **Image**.

4. Navigate to and select the image you want (.PSD or .PNG), and then click **OK** (Win) or **Open** (Mac).

5. Click the **Options** tab, and then specify the format, quality, and smoothing options you want.

6. Click the **File** tab, and then specify the scale options you want.

7. Click **OK**.

8. If prompted, locate the Images folder on your local root site, and save the image, and then specify Input Accessibility options.

Update Images from Photoshop or Fireworks

1. Open a Web page in Dreamweaver that contains text.

2. Select the image derived from a Photoshop PSD file.

3. Click **Edit Image** in the Properties panel.

   Dreamweaver opens the source PSD files in Photoshop.

4. In Photoshop, make the changes you want, and then save the file.

5. Select all or part of the image, copy it to the Clipboard, and then exit Photoshop or Fireworks.

   The image is optimized and updated.

Optimizing Images Using Fireworks

If you have Adobe Fireworks installed on your computer, you can use the program to optimize an image in a Web page from within Dreamweaver. When you select an image, you can use the Optimize In Fireworks button in the Properties panel or the Fireworks command on the Image submenu on the Modify menu.

Optimize an Image Using Fireworks

① Open a Web page with the image you want to optimize.

② Select the image you want.

③ Click the **Window** menu, and then click **Properties** to display the Properties panel.

④ Click the **Optimize In Fireworks** button in the Properties panel, or click the **Modify** menu, point to **Image**, and then click **Fireworks**.

⑤ Confirm whether to optimize as a PNG file or use the open image file.

⑥ Edit the image file.

⑦ Click **Done**.

⑧ Click **Update**.

⑨ Click the **File** menu, and then click **Save**.

Using Low Source Images

Loading graphics onto a Web page have a good and a bad side. The good side is that images spice up an otherwise dull and drab Web site. The bad side is that images take up file space and increase download times. It's a catch-22 situation; your visitors expect lots of graphics and cool stuff and, at the same time, expect the page to load fast. The current rule on the Internet is called the 8-second rule (it used to be the 10-second rule). In other words if your page doesn't load within 8 seconds, many of your visitors will go elsewhere. One way to make a page load quicker is to specify low source images for your graphics. **Low source** images are copies of the original image, but severely compressed. For example, you have an image on your Web site of the Colorado Rocky Mountains and it's 150 k. You really want to use the image; however, you know on the average browser it takes 20 seconds to download the image. So, you open a copy of the photograph in an image-editing application like Adobe Photoshop or Fireworks, and you compress the copy to the max, and you save it. In Dreamweaver, you use the image for the low-source. When the page opens in the visitor's browser, the low source image, quickly loads first, and then after the page opens, the higher-quality image loads over the other image.

Use a Low Source Image

1. Open the Web page that contains the image you want to apply the low source.

2. Select the image.

3. Click the **Window** menu, and then click **Properties** to display the Properties panel.

4. Click in the **Low Src** box, and use one of the following options:

   ◆ Enter the name and path of the low source image.

   ◆ Click the **Browse For File** button, and locate the file in the Select Image Source dialog box.

   ◆ Click the **Point To File** button, and drag over to the Assets panel. Release the mouse when you're hovering over the low source image file name.

Modifying Images

Once an image is placed into a Web page, Dreamweaver gives you the ability to modify the document in two ways: temporary and permanent. For example, you can adjust the size of the image temporarily by adjusting the width and height statements in the Properties panel or by directly accessing the <img> tab. You can even select the image, and click and drag the image at a selection handle to change its relative size. Unfortunately, while the size of the file on the page might change, an image saved on the hard drive does not. This causes problems with the download of the image to the visitor's site, as well as displaying the image within the visitor's browser. The best way to modify an image is to plan out what you need ahead of time, and then place the image into the Web page. That's a nice plan; however, many times, designs change during the course of the creation process, and what worked for an image yesterday, might not work today. With that in mind, Dreamweaver gives you the ability to modify the image whenever necessary. After you resize an image, you can reset the size or resample it to add and subtract pixels to match the appearance of the resized image.

Resize an Image

1. Open a Web page, and then select the image you want to modify.

2. Click the **Window** menu, and then click **Properties** to display the Properties panel.

3. Use any of the following resize methods:

   ◆ **Width or Height.** Drag a selection handle.

   ◆ **Proportions.** Shift-drag a corner selection handle.

   ◆ **Specific Size.** Click in the **W** and **H** boxes to change the size of the image width and height (in pixels).

4. To resample a resized image, click the **Resample** button in the Properties panel.

5. To return a resize image to its original size, click the **Reset Size** button in the Properties panel or delete the values in the W and H boxes in the Properties panel.

Drag to resize

Modify an Image Using the Properties panel

1. Open a Web page, and then select the image you want to modify.

2. Click the **Window** menu, and then click **Properties** to display the Properties panel.

3. Click in the **Border** box to add a border to the active image, as measured in pixels.

4. Click in the **V Space**, and **H Space** boxes to offset your images by adding vertical or horizontal white space (in pixels).

5. Click in the **Image Name** box to give the image a specific name. This is useful when calling the image using JavaScript.

6. Click in the **Alt** box to give the image the alternate text used by reader applications for the visually impaired.

    NOTE *In some browsers the Alt text is displayed in the empty box defined by the browser as the image loads.*

Did You Know?

You can edit image accessibility options. Edit the appropriate image attributes in Code view, edit the Alt box in the Properties panel, or right-click (Win) or control-click (Mac), the image, and then click Edit Tag.

Aligning Images

When you place an image into a Dreamweaver document, the default placement of the image is to the left and middle of the container area, which is a blank Web page, a table cell, or layer. Not only is alignment performed on images isolated within a container; they're also aligned according to adjacent images, or text.

Align an Image Using the Properties panel

 Open a Web page, and then select the image you want to modify.

 Click the **Window** menu, and then click **Properties** to display the Properties panel.

 Click the **Align** popup, and then select one of the following align options:

- ◆ **Browser Default.** No alignment attribute is included in the <img> tag. Most browsers use the baseline as the alignment default.

- ◆ **Baseline.** The bottom of the image is aligned with the baseline of the surrounding text.

- ◆ **Top.** The top of the image is aligned with the top of the tallest object in the current line.

- ◆ **Middle.** The middle of the image is aligned with the baseline of the current line.

- ◆ **Bottom.** The bottom of the image is aligned with the baseline of the surrounding text.

- ◆ **Text Top.** The top of the image is aligned with the tallest letter or object in the current line.

- ◆ **Absolute Middle.** The middle of the image is aligned with the middle of the tallest text or object in the current line.

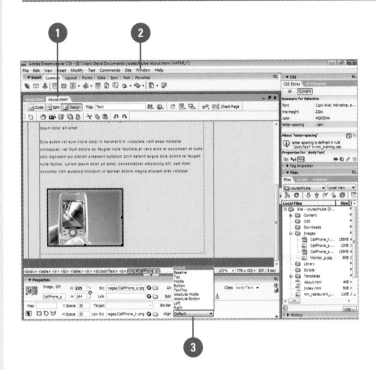

- ◆ **Absolute Bottom.** The bottom of the image is aligned with the descenders (as in y, g, p, and so forth) that fall below the current baseline.

- ◆ **Left.** The image is aligned to the left edge of the browser or table cell, and all text in the current line flows around the right side of the image.

- ◆ **Right.** The image is aligned to the right edge of the browser or table cell, and all text in the current line flows around the left side of the image.

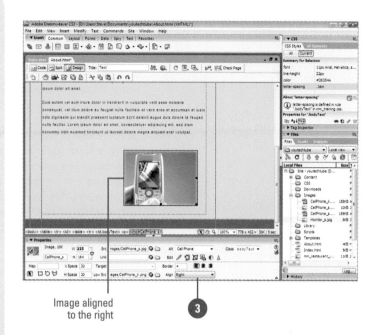

Image aligned to the right

3

Editing Images

When you place an image into a Dreamweaver document, there's a good chance that the image was first processed in another application. For example, you might use Adobe Fireworks or Photoshop to prep photographs. If you planned out the Web project, you'll be able to drop that image into the Web page, and it will fit like the proverbial glove. Unfortunately, you might not be the one creating the images; or its possible that you need to make a change. While it's always desirable to edit an image in the originating application, Dreamweaver gives you the ability to make minor changes to the image. For example, you can use Dreamweaver's new optimize feature (Hint: If you've ever used Photoshop's and Illustrator's Save For Web feature, you're halfway there). In addition, you can resize the image to fit a specific width and height. When you edit an image in Dreamweaver, you're actually making permanent changes to the original, and Dreamweaver lets you know as you work.

Use Optimize

1. Open the Web page with the image you want to edit.

2. Select the image you want to modify.

3. Click the **Modify** menu, point to **Image**, and then click **Optimize**.

4. Click the **Options** tab to utilize the following options:

   - **Format.** Click the **Format** popup, and then select a format from the available options.

   - **Palette.** Click the **Palette** popup, and then select a color palette from the available options.

   - **Loss.** Set to zero by default (not applicable PNG-8 images).

   - **Dither.** Select the **Dither** check box, and then set the dither percentage you want from zero to 100 percent. The dither option helps to visually approximate colors that are not in the original image.

- **Color Value.** Enter a value that represents the maximum number of colors in the image (2-256), and then adjust the colors (optional) in the color box.

- **Transparency.** Click the **Transparency** popup, and then click **No Transparency**, **Index Transparency** (based on available colors), or **Alpha Transparency** (based on an alpha mask).

- **Eyedropper.** Click the **Select Transparent Color** button, and then click in the Index Color box to choose the image colors to be made transparent. You can also use the other eyedropper buttons to add or remove a color from the transparency.

- **Remove Unused Colors.** Select the **Remove Unused Colors** check box to remove any unused colors from the color box.

- **Interlaced Browser Display.** Select the **Interlaced Browser Display** check box to display (loads) images in the client browser at low resolution and then progressively increases to full resolution.

- **Optimize To Size.** Click the **Optimize To Size** button to specify the desired size of the image. In turn, Dreamweaver attempts to optimize the image to the selected size.

Continue Next Page

For Your Information

Preparing Images for the Web

There are several differences between preparing image for the Web and for print documents. The major differences include: (1) Web images are typically saved at 72 dpi (dots per inch), while print images are generally saved at 300 dpi, (2) Web images are saved using the RGB (Red, Green, Blue) color system, while print images are CMYK (Cyan, Magenta, Yellow, Black) color mode, and (3) Web images are save to JPEG, GIF, or PNG format (which you can create or modify in Photoshop, Illustrator, and Fireworks), while print images are typically saved in the TIFF format.

Continue from Previous Page

5 Click the **File** tab to utilize the following options:

  ◆ **%.** Enter a value from 2 to 200 percent, or drag the slider to change the size of the image, based on a percentage value.

  ◆ **W and H.** Enter a value (in pixels) to change the width and height of the image.

  ◆ **Constrain.** Select the **Constrain** check box to keep the width and height in proportion.

  ◆ **Export Area.** Select the **Export Area** check box to crop the image using x and y, or w (width) and h (height) values. Alternately, you can click on the image in the Preview window, and use the corner and side anchor points to the manually adjust the image.

6 Select from the following Preview options:

  ◆ **Preview.** Select the **Preview** check box to toggle the preview of the image.

  ◆ **Saved Settings.** Click the **Saved Settings** popup, and then select from the preset optimization options.

  ◆ **Select.** Click the **Pointer** button to select and move a cropped image in the Preview window.

  ◆ **Crop.** Click the **Export Area** button to crop the active image. Use the Hand cursor to specify the area you want.

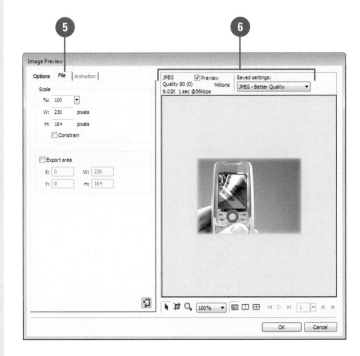

◆ **Zoom.** Click the **Zoom in/out** button to zoom the preview of the active image in (plus sign in magnifying glass) or out (press Alt (Win) or Option (Mac) minus sign in magnifying glass), or click the **Zoom** popup, and then select a preset zoom value.

◆ **Preview Display.** Click a button to change the view to display 1, 2 or 4 images.

◆ **Image display.** Click a button to control the view of multiple images used in animations.

NOTE *When you click the Options tab and select a different format, you see new options based on the selected format. In this example, the options displayed reflected the modification of a GIF image.*

7 Click **OK**.

Changing Image Brightness and Contrast

And if that were not all, you can change the brightness and contrast of the image, and increase its sharpness. Once you have inserted an image into a Web page, you can adapt them to meet your needs. Perhaps you don't quite like the colors it uses. You can increase or decrease the brightness of the image, as well as the color contrast. The Brightness/Contrast adjustment changes an image by an overall lightning or darkening of the image pixels. While good for special effects, its linear way of changing an image's brightness and contrast do not lend themselves to photo restoration.

Change Image Brightness and Contrast

1. Open the Web page with the image you want to modify.

2. Select the image you want to modify.

3. Click the **Modify** menu, point to **Image**, and then click **Brightness/Contrast**.

   TIMESAVER *Click the Brightness and Contrast button in the Properties panel.*

4. Select from the following options:

   ◆ **Brightness.** Click and drag the slider to change the overall brightness of the selected image (-100 - 100).

   ◆ **Contrast.** Click and drag the slider to change the overall contrast of the selected image (-100 - 100).

   ◆ **Preview.** Select to toggle the preview of the image in the display window.

5. Click **OK**.

Brightness and Contrast button

Select to preview the results

Changing Image Sharpness

If you have an image that looks a little fuzzy in spots, you can use the Sharpen command to create more image definition. Sharpening increases the contrast of pixels around the edges of objects in an image to increase the image's definition or sharpness. If you don't like the sharpening effect applied to an image, you can use the Undo command on the Edit menu before you save the image to revert the image back to the original.

Change Image Sharpness

1. Open the Web page with the image you want to modify.

2. Select the image you want to modify.

3. Click the **Modify** menu, point to **Image**, and then click **Sharpness**.

   TIMESAVER *Click the Sharpness button in the Properties panel.*

   NOTE *An alert may appear warning you that the changes you are about to make are permanent. Click OK to continue.*

4. Select from the following options:

   ◆ **Sharpness.** Click and drag the slider to increase the sharpness of the active image (0-10).

   ◆ **Preview.** Select to toggle the preview of the image in the display window.

5. Click **OK**.

Sharpness button

Select to preview the results

Cropping an Image

Cropping is the process of framing a portion of a photo and eliminating any unnecessary visual elements. If, for example, you have a photo that is not centered properly, you can crop out the side to center it. You can use the Crop button in the Properties panel to drag a resize handle on a graphic to crop out part of the image. The graphic remains unchanged and you can uncrop it at any time.

Crop an Image

1. Open the Web page with the image you want to modify.

2. Select the image you want to modify.

3. Click the **Modify** menu, point to **Image**, and then click **Crop**.

   TIMESAVER *Click the Crop button in the Properties panel.*

   NOTE *An alert may appear warning you that the changes you are about to make are permanent. Click OK to continue.*

4. Crop the image by clicking and dragging any of the 4 corners, or 4 side control points.

5. Click in the middle of the image and drag to move the crop window.

6. Double-click the image or press Enter (Win) or Return (Mac) to set the crop, or press the Esc (Escape) key to cancel.

   NOTE *Although the cropping function is permanent, you can always click the Edit menu, and then click Undo to return the image back to its original state.*

Crop button

Using an External Editor

Dreamweaver may give you some new and improved ways to edit an image; however, there's no substitute for the real thing. The two most powerful image-editing applications for raster-based (resolution dependent) images are: Adobe Photoshop, and Fireworks. You might recall an application that came bundled with Photoshop called, ImageReady... well, that application is no longer part of the Adobe family; being replaced by Fireworks. While Adobe would prefer that you use one of these two applications to edit your images, they know full well that there are other fish in the sea, so they not only give you the ability to edit images in Photoshop or Fireworks, they give you the ability to choose any application you want.

Edit an Image in an External Editor

1. Open the Web page with the image you want to edit.

2. Select the image you want to edit.

3. Click the **Modify** menu, point to **Image**, and then select one of the following options:

   ◆ **Photoshop.** Opens the selected image in Adobe Photoshop.

   ◆ **Fireworks.** Opens the selected image in Adobe Fireworks.

   ◆ **Browse.** Opens a Explorer (Win) or Finder (Mac) window and allows you to select the application to use.

   TIMESAVER *Double-click the image you want to edit using the default external image editor.*

4. Make the changes to the image, based on the selected application.

5. Click the **File** menu, and then click **Save**.

6. Click the **Close** button in the editing program and return to Dreamweaver.

   The changes are permanently applied to the image in Dreamweaver, which cannot be undone.

Setting File Types/ Editors Preferences

You can use the File Types/Editors section of the Preferences dialog box to choose the external image editor you want to use for specific file types. Setting specific external image editors for specific file types makes it quick and easy to edit images. All you need to do is double-click the image and the external image editor automatically opens. Any changes you make and save in an external image editor are displayed when you return to Dreamweaver. You can set different file types to open in different external editors, including Dreamweaver for script files. In addition, you can set Fireworks as your primary external editor for those extensions not specified.

Set File Type and Editor Preferences

1 Click the **Dreamweaver** (Mac) or **Edit** (Win) menu, and then click **Preferences**.

2 Click the **File Types / Editors** category.

3 Select the file extension you want to set an external editor, or add new extensions.

◆ **Add Extension**. Click the **Add** (+) button above the Extensions list, type an extension, and then press Enter (Win) or Return (Mac).

4 Select from the following options:

◆ **Remove Editor**. Select an editor, and then click the **Delete** (-) button above the Editors list.

◆ **Add Editor**. Click the **Add** (+) button above the Editors list, select the editor you want, and then click **Open**.

5 To make the editor the primary editor for the selected files, click **Make Primary**.

6 Click **OK**.

Set Other File Type and Editor Preferences

1. Click the **Dreamweaver** (Mac) or **Edit** (Win) menu, and then click **Preferences**.

2. Click the **File Types / Editors** category.

3. Click the **Reload Modified Files** popup, and then select the option you want: **Always**, **Never**, or **Prompt**.

4. Click the **Save On Launch** popup, and then select the option you want: **Always**, **Never**, or **Prompt**.

5. To set the primary external editor for file types not specified, click **Browse** next to the Fireworks box, select the Fireworks program, and then click **Open**.

6. To open script related files in Code view in Dreamweaver, enter the file types (separated by a space) in the Open In Code View box.

7. To open script related files in an external editor, click **Browse** next to the External Code Editor box, select the program you want, and then click **Open**.

8. Click **OK**.

Creating Rollover Images

Dreamweaver makes the insertion and creation of rollover images a snap. A rollover is an image that—when viewed in a browser—changes when the pointer moves across or hovers over it. You need two separate images to create the rollover: a primary (the image that displays when the page first loads) and a secondary (the image that appears when the pointer moves over the primary). Both images in a rollover should be the same size; if the images are not the same size, Dreamweaver resizes the secondary image to match the width and height properties of the primary image. In reality, rollover images are set to respond to a onMouseOver event; although you can change what event triggers the action (for example, a mouse click). Rollover images are used extensively in the creation of user-friendly navigation buttons. For example, you have a button that returns the user to the site's home page; when they roll over the image, it changes from a gray button with the word, HOME, in white, to a gray button with the word, HOME, in yellow.

Create a Rollover Image

1. Open the Web page you want to insert a rollover image.

2. Click to place the insertion point where you want to create a rollover image.

3. Click the **Insert** menu, point to **Image Objects**, and then click **Rollover Image**.

    TIMESAVER *Click the Image button arrow on the Common tab on the Insert bar, and then click Rollover Image.*

4. Select from the following options:

    ◆ **Image Name.** The name of the rollover image. This is the image's JavaScript call name.

    ◆ **Original Image.** The image you want to display when the page loads. Enter the path in the text box, or click **Browse** to select the image.

◆ **Rollover Image.** The image you want to display when the pointer rolls over the original image. Enter the path or click **Browse** to select the image.

◆ **Preload Rollover Image.** Select to preload the images in the browser's cache so no delay occurs when the user rolls the pointer over the image (recommended).

◆ **Alternate Text.** Text to describe the image for viewers using a text-only browser, or for the visually impaired (optional).

◆ **When Clicked Go to URL.** The file that you want to open when a user clicks the rollover image. Enter the path or click **Browse** and select the file.

5️⃣ Click **OK** to add the button to the active document.

NOTE *If you don't set a link for the image, Dreamweaver inserts a null link (#) in the HTML source code to which the rollover behavior is attached. If you remove the null link, the rollover image will not work.*

NOTE *You cannot see the effect of a rollover image in Design view.*

6️⃣ To see the effect in a browser, click the **File** menu, point to **Preview In Browser**, and then select the browser you to use.

Rollover button

Preview in browser

Inserting an Image Placeholder

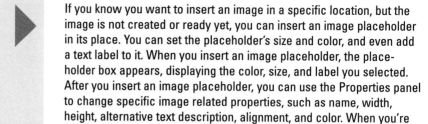

If you know you want to insert an image in a specific location, but the image is not created or ready yet, you can insert an image placeholder in its place. You can set the placeholder's size and color, and even add a text label to it. When you insert an image placeholder, the placeholder box appears, displaying the color, size, and label you selected. After you insert an image placeholder, you can use the Properties panel to change specific image related properties, such as name, width, height, alternative text description, alignment, and color. When you're ready to replace the image placeholder with an actual image, you can double-click the placeholder or use the Src box in the Properties panel to select the image.

Insert an Image Placeholder

1 Open the Web page you want to insert an image placeholder.

2 Click to place the insertion point where you want to place the image.

3 Click the **Insert** menu, point to **Image Objects,** and then click **Image Placeholder.**

The Image Placeholder dialog box opens.

4 Specify the image placeholder options you want:

◆ **Name.** Enter the text you want to appear as a label (optional). Leave blank if you don't want a label.

◆ **Width and Height.** Enter the width and height (in pixels) to set the image size.

◆ **Color.** Click the **Color** box to select a color, or enter the hexadecimal value for the color.

◆ **Alternate Text.** Enter text to describe the image for viewers using a text-only browser or for the visually impaired who use speech synthesizers (optional).

5 Click **OK.**

Set Image Placeholder Properties

① Open a Web page, and then select the image you want to modify.

② Click the **Window** menu, and then click **Properties** to display the Properties panel.

③ Specify the image placeholder related options you want:

◆ **Name.** Enter the text you want to appear as a label (optional). Leave blank if you don't want a label.

◆ **W and H.** Enter the width and height (in pixels) to set the image size.

◆ **Src.** Specify the source file for the image. Drag the **Point To File** button to a file in the Files panel or click the **Browser For Files** button to select a file.

◆ **Link.** Specify a hyperlink for the image placeholder. Drag the **Point To File** button to a file in the Files panel or click the **Browser For Files** button to select a file.

◆ **Color.** Click the **Color** box to select a color, or enter the hexadecimal value for the color.

◆ **Alt.** Enter text to describe the image for viewers using a text-only browser or for the visually impaired who use speech synthesizers (optional).

◆ **Create.** Click the **Create** button to start Fireworks to create a replacement image. The button is disabled if Fireworks is not installed on your computer.

Image placeholder

Click to create an image in Fireworks.

Linking Web Pages

7

Introduction

Static Web pages are composed of three basic elements: text, images, and links. Dynamic Web pages incorporate additional elements such as: video, animation, and/or audio. Of all of these elements, links are the primary building blocks of any Web page. If there were no links there would be no way for a visitor to control their journey through the maze of pages and sites that make up the World Wide Web. However, links are not just for moving a visitor from page to page, or site to site; in addition, links are used for transmitting emails, transferring data via FTP (file transfer protocol), and provide the ability to download data.

This chapter is devoted to creating links, modifying links, and attaching links to various outputs and URLs. Links are all about how you begin the process of making a Web page come alive.

Links come in all sizes and shapes; for example, a link can be as simple as an underlined section of text; for example, click here to go there, or it can be incorporated into a simple graphic, or even into a sophisticated JavaScript rollover. If your links are created using Flash, they can even include animation and sound.

The creation of a link is fairly straightforward... making that link intuitive to your visitor is the key to Web success. You don't want your visitors looking at a link and wondering if it is a link, or wondering what will happen if they click it.

Understanding Link Types

Links come in all sizes and shapes; however, what they link to is more important than what they look like. Link types refer to the function of the link; for example, the most popular (and common) link is the standard http or HyperText Transfer Protocol. With this link you can access Web pages, images, animations, just about anything that a wandering Web visitor would like to see and experience. However, there is more to the World Wide Web then a simple jump from page to page. The following list illustrates the more common types of Web links and their usage.

telnet:// The telnet link allows a user to log onto a remote computer (called the host), and take over control. For example, computer troubleshooters, could take over control of your computer from a remote location, and fix the problem, using the telnet link.

mailto: The mailto link allows a user to click and send email from a Web page. Basically, the mailto link opens a specified email application and automatically adds in the proper recipients address.

news:// The news link connects the user to a specific newsgroup. Newsgroups are basically electronic bulletin boards; on various subjects... a newsgroup can be found for virtually any subject under the sun, and then some.

http:// The http, or HyperText Protocol is the most common link type, and allows the user to connect to any page on the Internet.

ftp:// The ftp, or File Transfer Protocol is used primarily for uploading or downloading large amounts of data. This is performed typically using a FTP server, and requires the user have the correct username and password.

Use the Hyperlink dialog box to create a link.

Understanding Paths

When you create a link from one document to another, you need to specify the file path, or link path, to the linked document to make sure it works properly. There are three different ways to specify a link path: absolute, document-relative, and site root-relative.

An **absolute path** provides a complete URL (Uniform Resource Location) to the linked document, including the protocol. For example, *http://www.perspection.com/books/ od_books.htm.*

An absolute path is best used for linking to a document on another server. Think of an absolute path as a fixed location that doesn't change.

A **document-relative path** provides a partial path (the part not the same in URLs) to the linked document within the Web site. If you want to link to a document in the same folder, you only need to provide the file name of the linked document. You omit the part of the absolute path for both documents that are the same. For example, if you want to create a link from *http://www.perspection.com/books/ od_books.htm* to *http://www.perspection.com/ books/dwcs3.htm*, you can use the document-relative path *dwcs3.htm*.

If you want to create a link from the file *od_books.htm* to *http://www.perspection.com/ books/download/download_dwcs3.htm*, you can use the document-relative path *download/download_dwcs3.htm*. Each slash (/..) indicates that you move down one folder level.

If you want to create a link from the file *od_books.htm* to *http://www.perspection.com/ index.htm*, you can use the document-relative path ../index.htm. Each slash (../) indicates that you move up one folder level.

A document-relative path is best used for linking to a document in the same folder or one relatively close and you don't plan on moving the documents.

A **site root-relative path** provides a path from the site's root folder to a document. A site root-relative folder starts with a forward slash (/), which indicates the root folder. For example, if you want to link to *od_books.htm*, you can use the site root-relative path */books/od_books.htm.*

A site root-relative path is best used for linking to a document on a large Web site that uses several servers or one server that hosts several sites, where the local root folder is equivalent to another remote root folder.

Setting the Relative Path

When you create a new link, you can specify the default relative path setting you want to use, either document or site root. If you already have links, setting this option doesn't convert existing links, it only applies to new links. By default, Dreamweaver sets links to use document-relative paths, which sets the path of a link relative to the current document. A site root-relative path sets links to use the complete HTTP address. If you select the Site Root option, you need to also specify the complete URL in the HTTP Address box to the site root folder on the remote site. For example, if the local root location is C:\Web Site\ and the site root location is http://www.website.com/Pub_Docs/, then the local root folder Web site is set to be equivalent to the remote root folder Pub_Docs. Content linked with a site root-relative path doesn't display when you preview pages in a browser unless you specify a testing server, or use the Preview Using Temporary File option in Preferences.

Set the Relative Path for New Links

1. Click the **Site** menu, and then click **Manage Sites**.

2. Click the site you want to change, and then click **Edit**.

3. Click the **Advanced** tab.

4. Click the **Local Info** category.

5. Click the **Document** or **Site Root** option.

6. For site root-relative paths, enter the Web site URL in the HTTP Address box with the equivalent root address on a remote server.

   Dreamweaver uses this address to make sure links work on a remote server.

7. Click **OK**.

8. Click **Done**.

Set Preview in Browser to Use a Temporary File

① Click the **Dreamweaver** (Mac) or **Edit** (Win) menu, and then click **Preferences**.

② Click the **Preview In Browser** category.

③ Select the **Preview Using Temporary File** check box.

④ Click **OK**.

Adding a Link

Adding an http link to a Web page is a relatively simple and painless operation. You will need to decide what to use for the link (text, graphic, animation), what you are linking to (Web page, site, etc), and the correct path to the destination (URL or Uniform Resource Locator). Once you've answered those questions, it's a simple matter of opening Dreamweaver and getting to work. In this example, you're creating a simple text link that will connect the active Web page to the index page on another site.

Add a Text Link

1. Open the Web page that you want to add the link.

2. Enter or select the text that you want converted into a link, or click to place the insertion point where you want the link established.

3. Click the **Insert** menu, and then click **Hyperlink**.

4. Use the following options to convert the text into a link:

   ◆ **Text.** If you previously selected the text, it appears in this window. If you clicked in the document to add an insertion point, you need to add the text for the link.

   ◆ **Link.** Add the path and link document in the Link Input window, or click the **Browse** button to locate and add the link.

   ◆ **Target.** Click the **Target** popup, and then select from the following options:

      ◆ **_blank.** Opens the linked page in a new window.

   NOTE *Be careful of this option because some spam blockers prevent the opening of additional windows.*

- ◆ **_parent.** Loads the linked document in the immediate frameset of the active document.

- ◆ **_self.** Loads the linked document in the same browser window (default).

- ◆ **_top.** Loads the linked document in the topmost window of a frameset.

- ◆ **Title.** Insert the title for the link.

- ◆ **Access Key.** Enter a keyboard stroke (one letter), to select the link in the browser (optional shortcut).

- ◆ **Tab Index.** Enter a numerical value to indicate the tab order of this link, as it relates to all other links on the page (optional).

⑤ Click **OK** to add the link to the page.

In Code view the link would look like this:

<a href="http://sitename.com" tabindex="3" title="Title Text" accesskey="f" target"_self">This is the link text<a/>

Use to select the link file

Linked text

Link address appears here

See Also

See "Viewing a Site Map" on page 488 for information on linking documents using the site map.

See "Modifying a Link" on page 178 for information on changing link settings in the Properties panel.

Adding an Email Link

Where would we be without email... or at least that's a question that was posed to me by one of my students while I was teaching a class on communications. I will have to admit, e-mail is a big part of our communications structure. You see it everywhere you go: a patron in a restaurant, emailing their spouse on the quality of the roast beef, kids emailing their friends, who happen to be sitting right next to them in class. Email is all around us, and Dreamweaver makes the creation of an email link a veritable piece of baklava, cake. Remember, clicking an email link requires that the person doing the clicking has a valid email application, and a connection to the Internet.

Add an Email Link

1. Open the Web page that you want to add an email link.

2. Enter or select the text that you want converted into an email link, or click to place the insertion point where you want the link established. In this example, the appropriate text is selected.

3. Click the **Insert** menu, and then click **Email Link**.

4. Create the link using the following options:

   - **Text.** If you previously selected the text, it will appear in this window. If you clicked in the document to add an insertion point, you will be required to add the text for the link.

   - **E-Mail.** Enter a valid email address.

5. Click **OK** to add the email link to the page.

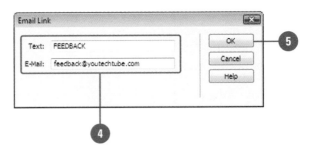

Modify an Email Link

1 Select the email link in Design view.

2 Click the **Window** menu, and then click **Properties** to display the Properties panel.

3 Modify the link using the following options:

◆ **Link.** Modify the name or path of the link by changing the link information, located within the Link box.

NOTE *If you remove the information in the Link box, you remove the link from the selected text.*

◆ **Target.** Since an email link opens another application; leave this field blank.

Linking within a Web Page

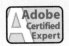 DW 2.3, 3.18

So far, the Web links created simply jump you from one page to another. When the selected document loads, it places you at the very top of the page. In most circumstances that's exactly what you want to happen; however, there are times when you want the page to load, and then start the visitor in the middle, or somewhere other than the very top. That's where named anchors come into play. **Named anchors** are internal navigation tools that let you select what part of the page you want the visitor to start. This is extremely helpful in long scrolling documents where you can have the page stop at a particular chapter or paragraph. Named anchors are an HTML anchor tag pair (<a></a>) that includes a name attribute. The named anchor serves as a target for links. To create a named anchor, you first place a named anchor on your Web page, and then create a link that directs the browser to the specific tag. Named anchors are represented by a small book icon that appears in the position of the anchor. You can have as many named anchors as you need in your document and, of course, the corresponding links that direct the browser to the correct anchor.

Add a Named Anchor

1. Open the Web page that you want to add named anchors.

2. Click to place the insertion point where you want the named anchor established. This is where the named anchor is coded in HTML.

3. Select the **Insert** menu, and then click **Named Anchor**.

4. Enter the name for this specific anchor (i.e. chapter1, TOC, etc).

   IMPORTANT *Named anchors are case sensitive, and must be used only once within the document.*

5. Click **OK** to add the named anchor to the document.

6. Repeat this process to add as many named anchors as needed.

   NOTE *To change the name of an established anchor, simply click on the book icon and change the name using the Properties panel.*

Anchor icon   Anchor name

Add Links to Named Anchors

1. Select the text (or graphic) that you want to use as the link to a previously created named anchor.

2. Click the **Window** menu, and then click **Properties** to display the Properties panel.

3. Click in the **Link** box.

4. Add the pound sign (#), followed by the name of the anchor (no spacing between the pound sign and the name of the anchor).

5. To test the links, click the **File** menu, point to **Preview In Browser**, and then select the browser you want to use.

> **TIMESAVER** *If you're using a lot of anchors, it's not a bad idea to make a list of the anchors, and the order in which they appear within the document. That way you don't have to hunt for the name or, worse yet, guess.*

Did You Know?

You can use the Point To File button to create a link to an name anchor. You can use the Point To File button that appears to the right of the Link box to select an anchor (if it appears in Design view). Simply click the Point To File button, and then drag it over the book icon for the name anchor and release.

Inserting a Navigation Bar

A navigation bar provides an easy-to-use way to get around a Web site. When you click a button on a navigation bar, it links you to another site page. When you incorporate the same navigation bar on every page in your Web site, visitor's can always access buttons to go to the pages they want on your site. Before you can insert a navigation bar into a Web page, you need to create a set of images for the display status of each navigation element.

Insert a Navigation Bar

1. Open the Web page you want to insert a navigation bar.

2. Click to place the insertion point where you want to create a navigation bar.

3. Click the **Insert** menu, point to **Image Objects**, and then click **Navigation Bar**.

   TIMESAVER *Click the Image button arrow on the Common tab on the Insert bar, and then click Navigation Bar.*

4. Select from the following options:

   - **Nav Bar Elements.** Click the **Plus** sign (+) to insert an element or select an element, and then click the **Minus** sign (-) to remove an element.

   - **Element Name.** Enter a name for the navigation bar element, which appear in the Nav Bar Elements list. Use the arrow buttons to arrange elements in the navigation bar.

   - **Up, Over, Down, and Over While Down Image.** Click **Browse** to select an image for each states. Only the Up image is required. The others are optional.

   - **Alternate Text.** Enter text to describe the element image for viewers using a text-only browser, or for the visually impaired (optional).

◆ **When Clicked Go To URL.** The file that you want to open when a user clicks the rollover image. Enter the path or click **Browse**, and then select the file.

◆ **Preload Images.** Select this option to download images as the page is downloaded.

◆ **Show Down Image Initially.** Select this option for elements that you want to display initially in the Down state instead of the Up state, the default.

◆ **Insert Elements.** Click the **Insert** popup, and then click **Horizontally** or **Vertically**.

◆ **Use Tables.** Select this option to insert elements as a table.

5 Click **OK** to add the navigation bar to the active document.

6 To see the effect in a browser, click the **File** menu, point to **Preview In Browser**, and then select the browser you want to use.

Did You Know?

You can modify a navigation bar.
Select the navigation bar you want to modify, click the Modify menu, and then click Navigation Bar. In the element list, select the element you want to edit, make any changes you want, and then click OK.

See Also

See "Modifying a Navigation Bar" on page 380 for information on using the Set Nav Bar behavior.

Creating Image Map Hotspots

Image maps are an image that has been sub-divided into regions (hotspots); when a user hovers and clicks within a hotspot, a predefined action occurs. For example, you could create a map of the United States with each State as a hot spot; clicking on a specific State would open another Web page and give you the current weather conditions. Dreamweaver allows you to create a client-side map, or a server-side map. Basically, client-side maps store the link information in the HTML document. Therefore, when a visitor clicks a hotspot in the image, the command is sent directly to the server. Server-side maps store the information on the server; while this allows the designer to modify a server-side map; in reality they're much slower, because every time the visitor clicks on a hot spot, the browser must go back to the originating server to map the response. Client-side maps are faster, because the server does not need to interpret where the visitor clicked. Since, in most cases, client-side maps are faster, easier for the visitor, and are supported by almost every browser your visitors are likely to have; it makes sense to include them into your Web pages.

Create a Client-Side Image Map

1. Open the Web page with the image you want to use to create an image map.

2. Place the image into the document that you want to use to create your image map.

3. Click the **Window** menu, and then click **Properties** to display the Properties panel.

4. Create an image map using the following tools:

   ◆ **Hotspot Tools.** Select the **Rectangular**, **Oval**, or **Polygon** hotspot tool, and draw an area on the selected image (this area represents the clickable link area for the visitor).

   ◆ **Pointer Tool.** Select the **Pointer** tool to select, move, or modify the hotspot.

5. Click **OK** to continue.

   Hotspot properties appear in the Properties panel.

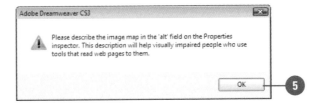

6 Enter the link for the active hotspot into the link box. Alternately, you can click the **Browse For File** button to select the link, or you can click the **Point To File** button, and drag to the link in the Files or Assets panel.

7 Click the **Target** popup, and then select from the following options:

◆ **_blank.** Opens the linked page in a new window.

◆ **_parent.** Loads the linked document in the immediate frameset of the active document.

◆ **_self.** Loads the linked document in the same browser window (default).

◆ **_top.** Loads the linked document in the topmost window of a frameset.

8 Enter the alternate text. Used by reader applications for the visually impaired, and for text-only browsers.

9 Continue using the hotspot tools until you have completed the client-side image map.

Hotspot

Modifying Image Map Hotspots

After you create some hotspots in an image map, you can modify them to create the links you want. Using the Pointer tool in the Properties panel, you can select one or more hotspots, move a hotspot area to a new location, resize a hotspot shape, or arrange the stacking order for overlapping hotspots in an absolutely-positioned element (AP element). If you want to duplicate a hotspot for use in the same image map or another one, you can copy and paste it. When you copy an image with one or more hotspots, the hotspots are copied along with the image.

Modify Image Map Hotspots

1. Open the Web page with the image map you want to change.

2. Click the **Window** menu, and then click **Properties** to display the Properties panel.

3. Click the **Pointer** tool.

4. Edit an image map using the following tools:

   ◆ **Select Multiple Hotspots.** Press and hold the Shift key, and then click each hotspot you want to select.

   TIMESAVER *Press Ctrl+A (Win) or ⌘+A (Mac) to select all the hotspots.*

   ◆ **Move Hotspots.** Drag the hotspot to a new location.

   TIMESAVER *Use the arrow keys to move a hotspot by 1 pixel. Use the Shift + arrow keys to move a hotspot by 10 pixels.*

   ◆ **Resize Hotspots.** Drag a hotspot selector handle.

   ◆ **Arrange Hotspots.** Select a hotspot, click the **Modify** menu, point to **Arrange**, and then click **Bring To Front** or **Bring To Back**.

   ◆ **Copy Hotspots.** Select the hotspot you want to copy, click the **Edit** menu, click **Copy**, click the **Edit** menu, and then click **Paste**.

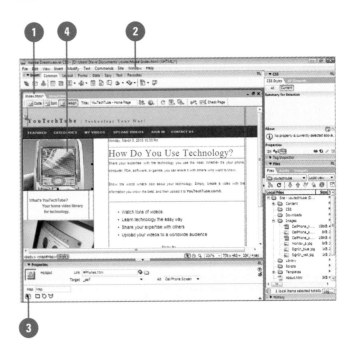

Creating a Null or Script Link

A **null link** is an undesignated link, while a **script link** executes JavaScript code or a call to a JavaScript function. A null link is a useful way to activate a link without specifying a target. You can also use a null link to attach behaviors to objects or text on a page. A script link is useful for performing an action, such as performing calculations, without leaving the current Web page.

Create a Null or Script Link

1 Open the Web page that you want to create a link.

2 Select the text, an image, or an object you want to use to create a null or script link.

3 Click the **Window** menu, and then click **Properties** to display the Properties panel.

4 Use the following options to create a link:

◆ **Null.** Type **javascript:;** (the word javascript followed by a colon, followed by a semicolon) in the Link box.

◆ **Script.** Type **javascript:** (the word javascript followed by a colon) followed by JavaScript code or a function call. Do not type a space between the colon and the code or call.

For Your Information

Attaching JavaScript Behaviors to Links

There are several commonly used behaviors you can attach to any link in a Web page. These include Set Text Of Status Bar, Open Browser Window, Jump Menu, and Set Nav Bar Image. **Set Text Of Status Bar** allows you to display a text message in the status bar, which is useful for describing a link destination. **Open Browser Window** lets you to open a URL in a separate new window. **Jump Menu** provides a way to edit a jump menu. **Set Nav Bar Image** allows you to customize the display of images in a navigation bar.

Modifying a Link

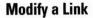

As with any design application, things can change; including links. Say for example, you create a link to a specific site, and the original site owner changes its address. It's even possible that you created the link and mistyped the link... surely that could never happen. The good news is that just like any other computer application, mistakes are relatively easy to correct, and modifying a link is no exception.

Modify a Link

① Select the link you want to change in the Design window.

② Click the **Window** menu, and then click **Properties** to display the Properties panel.

③ Modify the link using the following options:

◆ Link. Modify the name or path of the link by changing the link information, located within the Link input box. Alternately, you can click the **Browse For File** button, and then locate the file, or you can click the **Point To File** button, and then drag over to the Files or Assets panel.

TIMESAVER *Right-click the link, click Change Link, select the file you want to link to, and then click OK.*

◆ Target. Click the **Target** popup, and then select from the following options:

 ◆ **_blank.** Opens the linked page in a new window.

 ◆ **_parent.** Loads the linked document in the immediate frameset of the active document.

 ◆ **_self.** Loads the linked document in the same browser window (default).

 ◆ **_top.** Loads the linked document in the topmost window of a frameset.

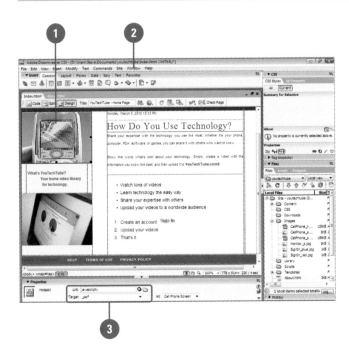

Removing a Link

Removing a link is a lot easier than creating one. As a matter of fact, it only takes a second or two of your precious time. There are several different ways to remove a link. You can delete the contents of the Link box in the Properties panel, use the Remove Link command, or delete the image or text and the link. Removing an entire link is simple, just select the graphic, or text that represents the link, and then press the Backspace (Win) or Delete (Mac) key.

Remove a Link

1. Select the text or graphic that contains the link.

   TIMESAVER *Right-click the link, and then click Remove Link.*

2. Click the **Window** menu, and then click **Properties** to display the Properties panel.

3. Click in the link box, and then erase all the text.

   The link is now removed.

   ◆ To prevent a link error, enter the # (null) symbol in the Link box

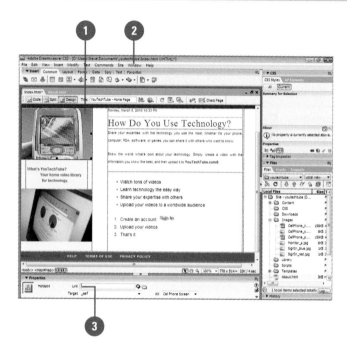

Updating Links

You can use the General section of the Preferences dialog box to specify how you want to update links in your Web pages. You can have Dreamweaver always update links, never update links, or prompt you when links change. Dreamweaver only updates links in your local root site. The remote site doesn't change until you update the files on the site. If the updating processing is taking too long, you can create a cache file to store information about all the links to speed up the process. The cache file is managed and maintained by Dreamweaver in the background while you work.

Set Preferences to Update Links Automatically

1 Click the **Dreamweaver** (Mac) or **Edit** (Win) menu, and then click **Preferences**.

2 Click the **General** category.

3 Click the **Update Links When Moving Files** popup, and then select one of the following:

♦ **Always.** Automatically updates all links when you move or rename a linked document.

♦ **Never.** Doesn't update any links when you move or rename a linked document.

♦ **Prompt.** Displays a dialog box listing all the linked documents you have changed. Click **Update** or **Don't Update** to update or leave the file unchanged.

4 Click **OK**.

Create a Cache File

① Click the **Site** menu, and then click **Manage Sites**.

② Click the site you want to change, and then click **Edit**.

③ Click the **Advanced** tab.

④ Click the **Local Info** category.

⑤ Select the **Enable Cache** check box.

⑥ Click **OK**.

The first time you change or delete links to files, Dreamweaver prompts you to load the cache.

⑦ Click **Yes** to load the cache and update all links to the file you changed, or click **No** to note the change for the future and not make any changes to the links.

⑧ Click **Done**.

> **Did You Know?**
>
> *You can re-create the cache.* Click the Site menu, point to Advanced, and then click Recreate Site Cache.

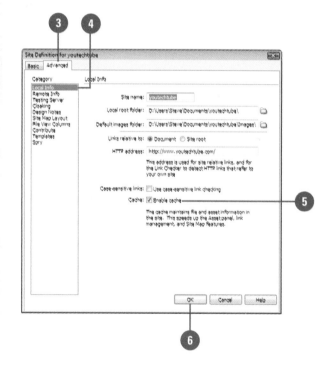

Changing Links Sitewide

If you need to change a link across the entire site, you can use the Change Link Sitewide command to manually make the change you want. This command is useful when you want to delete a file other documents are linked to and redirect the link to another document. After you change a link sitewide, the selected file become an **orphan** (no documents link to it), which you can safely delete without breaking links.

Change a Link Sitewide

① Open the Files panel, and then select the file you want to change in the Local view.

NOTE *If you are changing an e-mail, FTP, null, or script link, you don't need to select a file.*

② Click the **Site** menu, and then click **Change Link Sitewide**.

③ Select the options you want:

◆ **Change All Links To.** Click the **Browser For File** button to select the target file you want to unlink. If you are changing an e-mail, FTP, null, or script link, type the full text of the link you are changing.

◆ **Into Links.** Click the **Browser For File** button to select the new file to link to. If you are changing an e-mail, FTP, null, or script link, type the full text of the replacement link.

④ Click **OK**.

See Also

See "Finding Broken Links" on page 456 for information on finding broken links or "Fixing Broken Links" on page 456-458 for information on changing links sitewide.

Testing a Link

After you create or change a link, it's important to test the link to make sure it works the way you want. You can test a link by previewing the Web page with a link in a browser, or by opening the linked page. When you want to test a link of any kind, the best way is to preview the page in a browser and click the link you want to test. If you want to test a link to another page and open the linked page, the best way is to open the linked page from within Dreamweaver.

Test a Link

1. Click the **File** menu, point to **Preview In Browser**, and then select a browser to test the link.

   The link appears as blue underlined text.

2. Move your mouse over the link (the cursor changes to a hand icon with extended index finger).

3. Click the link to open it.

Open a Linked Page

◆ Select the link, click the **Modify** menu, and then click **Open Linked Page**.

◆ Press Ctrl (Win) or Command (Mac), and double-click the link.

> ### See Also
>
> See "Finding Broken Links" on page 456 for information on finding broken links or "Fixing Broken Links" on page 456-458 for information on changing links sitewide.

Click to open the linked page

Creating Page Layouts Using Tables

8

Introduction

Tables serve an important place in design; they allow you to precisely position text graphics, and objects on a Web page. Without tables, information would simply stack up on the page, and based on the width and height of the visitor's browser window, would reformat on the fly.

Although tables give designers control over the positioning of images and text on the page, tables were originally intended for displaying tabular data, not for use in page layout. However, never underestimate the creative brainpower of Web designers. Designers saw tables and thought that if they can hold, position and control tabular data, maybe they can hold other information. That started the use of tables for layout and design.

In Dreamweaver, you can easily add punch to your page by using a table to display a background image, in a row within a table, or in individual cells within a table. Table cells can be used to hold site navigation, as well as specific areas devoted to text, graphics, even animation and video.

Although tables are not the only way to format a Web page (you have frames and layers) they are still one of the most popular and stable ways to contain and control the layout of a web page. That's the good news...

In truth, tables will eventually be phased out as design elements and return to their original position of displaying tabular data. What will replace them is strict coding use elements such as layers. However, until that happens, tables will remain a valuable tool in the Web designer's arsenal.

This chapter will not only show you how to create and modify tables in Dreamweaver; in addition, you will learn how they fit into the overall design scheme of a Web page, and why they are necessary.

What You'll Do

Work with Tables

Switch Between Table Modes

Draw a Table in Layout Mode

Modify a Table in Layout Mode

Change Layout Table Properties

Add Spacer Images

Remove Spacer Images

Set Column Widths

Insert a Table in Standard Mode

Create a Nested Table

Add Columns or Rows to Tables

Split and Merge Cells

Add Content into a Table

Format Tables

Format Cells

Use a Tracing Image

Set Layout Mode Preferences

Working with Tables

Tables are basically grids that allow the designer to precisely control the content of a Web page. The three main mechanisms of a table are rows, columns, and cells. A row extends across the entire table from left to right. Columns extend vertically from the top to the bottom of the table. A cell is the area where a row and column intersect. By default, table cells will expand to fit the content inserted into them.

If you're working in the design window, Dreamweaver will visually display the table, and allow you to expand or contract the table or individual rows or columns with a simple click and a drag.

Creating a table in Dreamweaver is basically a three-step process: Step one: insert the table, Step two: modify the table to fit the specific design requirements of the current page, and Step three: add the content (text, graphics, etc) to the individual cells. Be advised, that since tables can display differently in different and older browsers, it's important to test your table-driven pages to make sure what you see is what you're visitors are seeing. The following examples illustrate how a table-driven Web page might appear in different browser windows.

Table

Switching Between Table Modes

You can create tables using three different modes: Standard, Expanded Tables, and Layout. Each mode has its strengths and weaknesses. Layout mode is best for creating a table, while Standard mode is best for displaying a table as it will appear in a Web browser and adding and editing content. Expanded Tables mode adds cell padding and spacing to all the tables in a document and increases borders to make editing easier. For example, you might use Expanded Tables mode to position the insertion point to the left or right of an image, without inadvertently selecting the image or table cell, and then switch back to Standard mode to make your changes. By default, Dreamweaver starts you out in Standard mode.

Switch Between Table Modes

1. Create a new Web page or open the Web page you want to view.

2. Click the **View** menu, and then click **Design** or click the **Design** button to display the page in Design mode.

3. Click the **View** menu, point to **Table Mode**, and then select from the following modes:

   ◆ **Standard.** Use to display a table as it will appear in a Web browser and edit it.

   TIMESAVER *To quickly return to Standard mode, click the [Exit] link in Expanded Tables or Layout mode, located at the top center of the Document window.*

   ◆ **Expanded Tables.** Use to edit a table. This mode adds cell padding and spacing, and increases border.

   TIMESAVER *Press F6 to switch to Expanded Tables mode.*

   ◆ **Layout.** Use to create a table. If the Getting Started in Layout Mode dialog box opens, click OK to continue.

   TIMESAVER *Press Alt (Win) or Option +F6 (Mac) to switch to Layout mode.*

Drawing a Table in Layout Mode

Creating tables using Dreamweaver's Layout mode gives you the ability to create a table by drawing boxes directly into the Design window. This method of table design is superior to designing in Standard mode because it gives you complete control over the design of the overall table, and the individual cells. In Layout mode you can draw tables and cells and even tables nested in other tables. It's a good idea to activate the ruler bars to help design the dimensions of the table. When you draw cells in a table, grid lines appear to help you align them. Standard mode gives you a better visual display of how the table will appear in a Web browser. It's a good idea to switch back to Standard mode before you add content or edit your tables.

Draw a Table in Layout Mode

1. Create a new page or open the existing page you want to add a table.

2. Click the **Design** button to display the page in Design mode.

3. Click the **View** menu, point to **Table Mode**, and then click **Layout**.

   ◆ If prompted, read the Getting Started in Layout Mode dialog box, and then click **OK**.

4. Click the **Layout** tab on the Insert panel.

5. Click the **Draw Layout Table** button on the Insert bar.

6. Click in the page and drag to create the initial table.

   NOTE *By default, the table is drawn from the upper-left portion of the active Web page.*

Add Cells in Layout Mode

① Create a new page or open the existing page you want to add a table.

② Click the **Design** button to display the page in Design mode.

③ Click the **View** menu, point to **Table Mode**, and then click **Layout**.

④ Click the **Layout** tab on the Insert panel.

⑤ Click the **Draw Layout Cell** button.

⑥ Click inside the table and drag to create an initial table cell using the light grid of lines as a guide.

NOTE *Dreamweaver creates the table cell, and adds other cell structures within the table to hold the new cell in place.*

⑦ Continue drawing cells until you have completed your layout of the table.

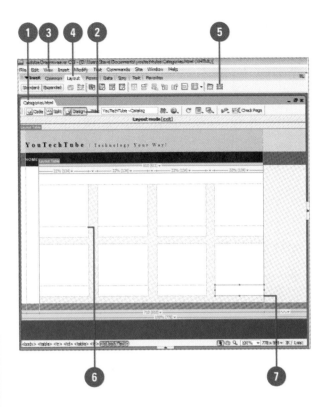

Modifying a Table in Layout Mode

After you create the initial layout table and cells, you can select, resize, move, or even delete the table and cells to fine tune it. When you move or resize a cell in a layout table, there are a few things you need to avoid. These include overlapping cells, crossing the boundaries of the layout table, and making the cell smaller than its contents. Before you can resize, move, or delete a table or cell, you need to select it first. You can select the table by clicking the tab at the top or an outside table edge, or select a cell by clicking a cell edge. When you select the table or place the insertion point in the table, the widths of layout tables and cells appear at the top or bottom of the table in pixels or as a percentage of the page width. Next to the widths are arrows for the table and column headers you can use to display a menu with related commands. When you point to a cell in Layout mode, Dreamweaver highlights it to make it easier to see.

Modify the Table and Cells

1. Open the Web page containing the table you want to modify.

2. Click the **Design** button to display the page in Design mode.

3. Click the **View** menu, point to **Table Mode**, and then click **Layout Mode**.

4. To modify the table:

   ◆ **Select Table.** Click the **Layout** tab, and then click in the table, but outside the cells, or click on the outside edge of the table.

   TIMESAVER *Click in the table, and then press Ctrl+A (Win) or* ⌘+A *(Mac) to select it.*

   ◆ **Resize Table.** Select the table, and then drag the control points on the right table edge to expand or contract the table.

   NOTE *You cannot make a table smaller than the internal cell structure.*

- ◆ **Move Table.** Select the table, and then drag to another location or use the arrow keys to move the table 1 pixel at a time.

  TIMESAVER *Hold down the Shift key, and then use the arrow keys to move the table 10 pixels at a time.*

- ◆ **Delete Table.** Select the table, and then press the Backspace (Win) or Delete (Mac) key to remove the table.

5 To modify the individual cells:

- ◆ **Select Cell.** Click on the edge of an active table cell, or Ctrl-click (Win) or ⌘-click (Mac) anywhere in the cell.

- ◆ **Resize Cell.** Select the cell, and then drag any of the control points on the cell edges to expand or contract the size of the selected cell.

- ◆ **Move Cell.** Select the cell, and then drag to another location or use the arrow keys to move the cell 1 pixel at a time.

  TIMESAVER *Hold down the Shift key, and then use the arrow keys to move the cell 10 pixels at a time.*

- ◆ **Delete Cell.** Select the cell, and then press the Backspace (Win) or Delete (Mac) key to remove the selected cell.

Changing Layout Table Properties

All tables have properties assigned to them. These properties give the table its structure and form, and help browsers displaying the table to be consistent in their view. The properties for a table are located in the Properties panel. Although most designers prefer to insert data or modify properties using the Standard mode, you can modify the properties of a table in either Standard or Layout mode. Tables are initially sized by their contents. However, once you move a table border, the new sizes will be written directly into the HTML code, and the column width or row height is adjusted accordingly.

Change the Properties of a Table

1. Open the Web page containing the table you want to modify.

2. Click the **Design** button to display the page in Design mode.

3. Click the **View** menu, point to **Table Mode**, and then click **Standard**.

4. Select the table you want to change.

   ◆ Click in the table, click the **Modify** menu, point to **Table**, and then click **Select Table**.

5. In the Properties panel, click the expander arrow.

6. Choose from the following options:

   ◆ **Table ID.** Enter an ID for the table (used when calling from JavaScript). In this example, leave it blank.

   ◆ **Rows.** Displays the number of rows in the selected table. Click to enter a new value.

   ◆ **Columns.** Displays the number of columns in the selected table. Click to enter a new value.

   ◆ **Cell Pad.** The number of pixels between a cell's content and the cell boundaries.

   ◆ **Cell Space.** The number of pixels between adjacent table cells.

◆ **Align.** Determines where the table appears relative to other elements in the same paragraph, such as text or images. Click to change alignment from Left (default), Center, or Right.

◆ **Border.** Enter the number of pixels for the table border.

◆ **Class.** Used with CSS to help define the properties of the table.

◆ **Clear Column Widths** and **Clear Row Heights.** Deletes all specified row height or column width values from the table.

◆ **Convert Table Widths To Pixels** and **Convert Table Heights To Pixels.** Sets the width or height of each table column to its current width in pixels and sets the width of the whole table to its current width in pixels.

◆ **Convert Table Widths to Percent** and **Convert Table Heights to Percent.** Sets the width or height of each column in the table to its current width expressed as a percentage of the Document window's width.

◆ **Bg Color.** Click to change the table's background color.

◆ **Brdr Color.** Click to change the color for the table's borders.

◆ **Bg Image** Enter a path and file to a background image for the table, or click the **Point To File** or **Browse For File** button to select the file.

Table selected

6

Expanded Properties panel

Adding Spacer Images

A **spacer image**, sometimes called a spacer GIF, is simply a transparent image that's used to control spacing when utilizing autostretch tables. The spacer image is simply a single-pixel transparent GIF, stretched out to be a specified number of pixels wide. Since a browser can't draw a table column narrower than the widest image contained in a cell in that column, placing a spacer image in a table column requires browsers to keep the column at least as wide as the image. It's an old trick used in Web design; however, it continues to be a solid and reliable way to force the size of table cells. In Dreamweaver, when you set a column to autostretch, the program automatically adds spacer images, (you can specify that no spacer image be used, if necessary). You can quickly identify columns that contain spacer images because they have a double-bar where the column width appears. In this example, a table is created and you don't want the far left and right columns to collapse when the visitor changes the width of the browser window. To accomplish this, you add spacer images to the edge columns. That way the blank columns always give your Web page some spacing, regardless of the width of the browser window. It's a neat trick that adds a degree of professionalism to a Web page.

Add a Spacer Image

1. Create a new page or open the existing page you want to add a table.

2. Click the **Design** button to display the page in Design mode.

3. Click the **View** menu, point to **Table Mode**, and then click **Layout**.

4. Select the table cell that you want to autostretch.

5. Click the **Autostretch** option in the Properties panel.

    TIMESAVER *Click the column header arrow, and then click Add Space Image.*

6. If you have not set a spacer image for this site, click one of the following options:

    ◆ **Create A Spacer Image File.** Creates a GIF spacer image and allows you to select a folder to store the file. (Default).

◆ **Use An Existing Spacer Image File.** Displays a dialog box to select a spacer image file.

◆ **Don't Use Spacer Images For Autostretch Tables.** Doesn't automatically add spacer images. This causes fixed-width columns to possibly change size or even disappear without any content in Design view.

7 Click **OK**.

Dreamweaver prompts you that it is creating the file and places a copy within the current site.

8 Click **Save**.

Dreamweaver adds the spacer cells to the adjacent columns.

Removing Spacer Images

If you no longer need a spacer image, you can easily remove spacer images in individual columns or remove all spacer images in the table. Removing a spacer image from a column may cause the column to collapse. You can avoid this by adding some content (even some text) to the column before removing the spacer image.

Remove an Individual Spacer Image

1. Open the Web page with the layout table you want to remove a spacer image.

2. Click the **View** menu, point to **Table Mode**, and then click **Layout**.

3. Select the column containing the spacer image you want to remove.

   NOTE *A double line, directly underneath the table, identifies the column.*

4. Click the **Column Header Arrow**, and then click **Remove Spacer Image**.

Remove All Spacers

1. Open the Web page with the layout table you want to remove a spacer image.

2. Click the **View** menu, point to **Table Mode**, and then click **Layout**.

3. Select the table you want to modify.

4. Click the **Table Header Arrow**, located at the top center of the table, and then click **Remove All Spacer Images**.

   TIMESAVER *Click the Remove All Spacers button in the Properties panel.*

Setting Column Widths

You can set a column to a fixed width or make it stretch to fill as much of a browser window as possible, known as autostretch. To prevent columns from growing wider or narrow, create your complete layout before making a column autostretch, and use spacer images when making a column autostretch. If you see two numbers for a column's width, then the column width set in the HTML code doesn't match the columns width on the screen. You can make the width specified in the code match the visual width. When you draw a layout cell, the width and height of the cell is automatically set by Dreamweaver even though the cell is empty. After you insert content into the cell, you can clear the excess width and height of the cell.

Set a Column to a Fixed Width

1. Open the Web page with the layout table you want to set column widths.

2. Click the **View** menu, point to **Table Mode**, and then click **Layout**.

3. Select the column containing the spacer image you want to remove.

   NOTE *A double line, directly underneath the table, identifies the column.*

4. Click the **Column Header Arrow**, and then click **Make Column Fixed Width**, or click the **Fixed** option in the Properties panel.

5. In the Properties panel, enter the fixed width or height you want.

Did You Know?

You can show or hide column widths. Right-click the table, point to Table, and then click Table Widths to enable or disable. You can also click the Table Header Arrow in a table, and then click Hide Table Widths.

Make a Column Autostretch

1. Open the Web page with the layout table you want to make a column autostretch.

2. Click the **View** menu, point to **Table Mode**, and then click **Layout**.

3. Select the column you want to modify.

4. Click the **Column Header Arrow**, and then click **Make Column Autostretch**.

   IMPORTANT *You can make only one column in a table autostretch.*

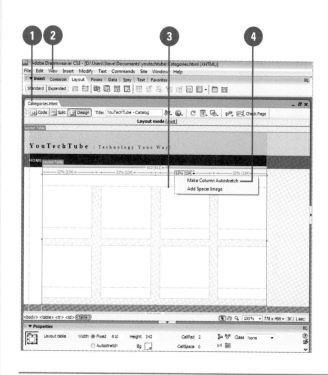

Modify Column Widths or Heights

1. Open the Web page with the layout table you want to modify.

2. Click the **Standard Mode** or **Expanded Tables Mode** button on the Layout tab on the Insert bar.

3. Select the table you want to modify.

4. Click the **Table Header Arrow**, and then select any of the following options:

   ◆ **Clear All Heights** or **Clear All Widths.** Removes the excess empty space in a cell.

   ◆ **Make All Widths Consistent.** Makes all the column widths the same.

5. To clear column width, click the **Column Header Arrow**, and then click **Clear Column Width**.

Inserting a Table in Standard Mode

Although inserting tables using the layout mode is the preferred way to create a table, some tables have such a logical form to them, that drawing individual cells seems a waste of valuable time. When you insert a table using Standard mode, you get a very ordered table... think spreadsheet and you've got a pretty good idea of what I'm talking about. And once the table is created, you can, if you choose, return to Layout mode, and continue the editing of the table. Tables created in Standard mode have all the rights and privileges of a table created in Layout mode. For example, you can add or subtract cells from the table design, add any type of information needed; even make an autostretch table. So remember, for creative tables, design them in Layout mode; however, for your basic run-of-the-mill utilitarian table, use the Standard mode.

Insert a Table in Standard Mode

1. Open a Web page where you want to insert a table.

2. Click to place the insertion point for the new table.

3. Click the **Standard Mode** button on the Layout tab on the Insert bar.

4. Click the **Insert** menu, and then click **Table**.

5. Create a table using the following options:

   ◆ **Rows.** Enter a value for the number of rows in the table.

   ◆ **Columns.** Enter a value for the number of columns in the table.

   ◆ **Table Width.** Enter a value (pixels or percent), for the initial width of the table.

   ◆ **Border Thickness.** Enter a value for the border width of the table.

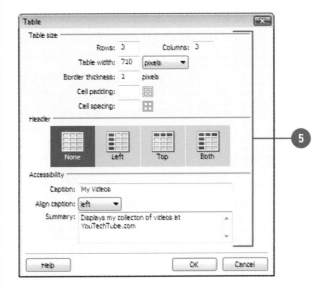

NOTE *If you create a table in Standard mode, then switch into Layout mode, the resulting layout table might contain empty layout cells. You might need to delete these empty layout cells before you can create new layout cells or move layout cells around.*

◆ **Cell Padding.** Enter a value for the number of pixels between a cell's content and the cell boundaries.

◆ **Cell Spacing.** Enter a value for the number of pixels between adjacent table cells.

◆ **Header.** Select a position for a header area in the table: None, Left, Top, Both.

◆ **Caption.** Enter a table caption (displays outside of the table).

◆ **Align Caption.** Click to align where the table caption appears in relation to the table: default, top, bottom, left, right.

◆ **Summary.** Enter a table description. Screen readers read the summary text, but the text does not appear in the user's browser.

6 Click **OK**.

Table in Standard Mode

Creating a Nested Table

A **nested table** is a table inside a cell of another table. You can format a nested table as you would any other table; however, its width is limited by the width of the cell in which it appears. For purposes of control, the Draw Layout Table command is the best tool for creating nested tables. The cells inside a nested table are isolated from changes made to the outer table; for example, when you change the size of a row or column in the outer table, the cells in the inner table don't change size. The question arises as to why you might want to do something like this, and there are several answers to that. You might want to use a table to add design elements to a page, and at the same time use one of the cells for tabular data, or you have a picture and a related caption and you want them to remain stationary in relation to one another while text on the page flows according to the size of the browser window. In older browsers (pre 5.0) creating nested tables can slow down the load of the page. In Web design one of the things we have to do is balance page content to load speed. Make sure you keep things in balance.

Nest a Table in Layout Mode

1. Open the Web page containing a table, or create a new table.

2. Click the **Design** button to display the page in Design mode.

3. Click the **View** menu, point to **Table Mode**, and then click **Layout Mode**.

4. Click the **Layout** tab on the Insert bar.

5. Click the **Draw Layout Table** button on the Layout tab, and then draw a table inside the existing table.

6. Click the **Draw Layout Cell** button on the Layout tab, and then draw new cells within the nested table.

   You can now place any elements you choose into the nested table cells.

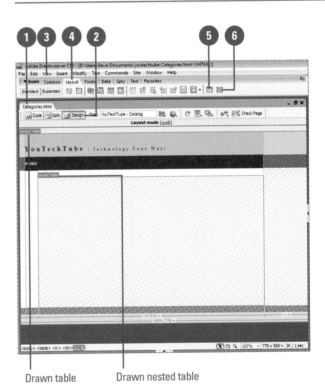

Drawn table   Drawn nested table

Nest a Table in Standard Mode

1. Open the Web page containing a table, or create a new table.

2. Click the **Design** button to display the page in Design mode.

3. Click the **Standard Mode** button on the Layout tab on the Insert bar.

4. Select the cell you want to insert the nested table.

5. Click the **Insert** menu, and then click **Table**.

6. Choose the properties for the nested table you want from the Table dialog box.

7. Click **OK**.

The nested table is inserted into the selected cell.

NOTE By default, the nested table is left justified and centered vertically within the cell. If you want to change the position of the nested table, select the cell that contains the table, and make your changes using the Properties panel. Remember you're making these changes to the cell containing the nested table, not the nested table.

See Also

See "Inserting a Table in Standard Mode" on page 200 for information on specific table properties.

Nested table in Standard Mode

Adding Columns or Rows to Tables

As you begin to work on a table, you might need to modify its structure by adding more rows and columns to accommodate new text, graphics, or other tables. The table realigns as needed to accommodate the new structure. When you insert rows or columns, the existing rows shift down, the existing columns shift right, and you choose what direction the existing cells shift. Similarly, when you delete unneeded rows, columns, or cells from a table, the table realigns itself.

Add a Column or Row to a Table

1. Open the Web page with the table you want to modify.

2. Click the **Standard Mode** or **Expanded Tables Mode** button on the Layout tab on the Insert bar.

3. Click to place the insertion point where you want to add a row or column.

4. To add a row or column, click the **Insert** menu, point to **Table Objects**, and then click **Insert Columns to The Left, Insert Column to The Right, Insert Row Above**, or **Insert Row Below**.

   TIMESAVER *Use buttons on the Layout tab on the Insert bar.*

5. To add multiple rows or columns, click the **Modify** menu, point to **Table**, and then click **Insert Rows Or Columns**, enter the number of columns or rows you want to add to the table, and the related options, and then click **OK**.

Did You Know?

You can delete rows and columns in a table. Select the rows or columns you want to delete, click the Modify menu, point to Table, and then click Delete Row or Delete Column.

Splitting and Merging Cells

Cells can also be split or combined (also known as merged). Often there is more to modifying a table than adding or deleting rows or columns; you need to make cells just the right size to accommodate the text you are entering in the table. For example, a title in the first row of a table might be longer than the first cell in that row. To spread the title across the top of the table, you can merge (combine) the cells to form one long cell. Sometimes to indicate a division in a topic, you need to split (or divide) a cell into two.

Split a Cell into Two Cells

1. Open the Web page with the table you want to modify.

2. Click the **Standard Mode** or **Expanded Tables Mode** button on the Layout tab on the Insert bar.

3. Select the cell or cells you want to split.

4. Click the **Modify** menu, point to **Table**, and then click **Split Cell**.

5. Click the **Columns** option or the **Rows** option.

6. Type the number of columns or rows you want.

7. Click **OK**.

Merge Cells Together

1. Open the Web page with the table you want to modify.

2. Click the **Standard Mode** or **Expanded Tables Mode** button on the Layout tab on the Insert bar.

3. Click a column, row, or group of adjacent cells, and then drag to select them.

4. Click the **Modify** menu, point to **Table**, and then click **Merge Cells**.

   The cells merge into a single, larger cell.

Adding Content into a Table

After you finishing creating the table layout and cells, you can insert content. You can add text, images, and other data in Standard or Layout modes. Simply click in the cell where you want to add material, and then type, paste, or insert the content you want. If you have content available in the Assets or Files panel, you can drag it into the table; releasing your mouse when you're hovering over the right cell. You can only add content to layout cells; the empty grey area in a layout table is not available for content. When you add content to a cell, it automatically expands to accommodate the incoming content, which changes the size of the column and table.

Add Text or an Image to a Table

1. Open the Web page that contains the table you want to add content.

2. Click to place the insertion point in the layout cell where you want to add content.

3. To add text, type or paste the text you want.

   ◆ Press Enter (Win) or Return (Mac) to add a paragraph return.

   ◆ Press Shift+Enter (Win) or Shift+Return (Mac) to add a soft return.

   NOTE *By default, the text is left justified and centered within the cell, and soft wraps at the end of the table cell.*

4. To add an image, click the **Insert** menu, click **Image**, select the image file you want, and then click **OK**.

   The table expands to accommodate the text or image content.

> ### See Also
>
> *See "Importing Tabular Data" on page 95 for information on importing data and creating a layout table.*

Modify Table Text

1. Select the table text you want to modify.

2. In the Properties panel, modify the text using the following options:

   - **Format.** Click to change the basic HTML format of the text (heading and paragraph styles).

   - **Style.** Click to work with CSS style sheets.

   - **Alignment.** Click to change the justification of the text (Align Left, Align Center, Align Right, or Justify).

   - **Bold/Italic.** Click to **bold** or *italicize* the selected text.

   - **Font.** Click to change the default font of the selected table text.

   - **Size.** Click to change the default size of the selected table text.

   - **Color.** Click to change the color of the selected table text (black, default).

Did You Know?

You can sort rows in a table. If you don't have any merged cells in a table, you can sort the table. Select the table or click in any cell, click the Commands menu, and then click Sort Table. In the Sort dialog box, set the options you want, and then click OK. Some of the sort options include Sort By, Order, Sort Includes The First Row, Sort Header Rows, Sort Footer Rows, and Keep All Row Colors The Same After The Sort Has Been Completed.

Formatting Tables

When you create a table, it's not just about what you place into the individual table cells; it's how you format the table and the individual cells. When formatting tables, you can set properties for the entire table or for individual rows, columns, or cells in the table. You can set table properties to specify the number of rows and columns you want as well as the number of pixels between cells, either CellPad or CellSpace. When a property is set to one value for the whole table and another value for individual cells, cell formatting takes precedence over row formatting, which in turn takes precedence over table formatting. For example, if you set the alignment for a single cell to center align, then set the alignment of the entire table to left align, the center align cell does not change to left align, since cell formatting takes precedence over table formatting. It's all about priority.

Format a Table

1. Open the Web page with the table you want to format.

2. Click the **Standard Mode** or **Expanded Tables Mode** button on the Layout tab on the Insert bar.

3. Select the table you want to format.

4. In the Properties panel, modify the table using the following options:

   ◆ **Table ID.** Enter an ID for the table (used when calling from JavaScript).

   ◆ **Rows.** Sets the number of rows in the selected table. Click to enter a new value.

   ◆ **Cols.** Sets the number of columns in the selected table. Click to enter a new value.

   ◆ **CellPad.** Sets the number of pixels between a cell's content and the cell boundaries.

   ◆ **CellSpace.** Sets the number of pixels between adjacent table cells.

Click to expand
Properties panel

- ◆ **Align.** Determines where the table appears, relative to other elements in the same paragraph, such as text or images. Click to change alignment from Left (default), Center, or Right.

- ◆ **Border.** Sets the number of pixels for the border of the table. Click to enter a new value.

- ◆ **Class.** Used with CSS (Cascading Style Sheets) to help define the properties of the table. In this example, leave the box at None.

- ◆ **Clear Column Widths and Clear Row Heights.** Deletes all specified row height or column width values from the table.

- ◆ **Convert Table Widths To Pixels and Convert Table Heights To Pixels.** Sets the width or height of each column in the table to its current width in pixels (also sets the width of the whole table to its current width in pixels).

- ◆ **Convert Table Widths To Percent and Convert Table Heights To Percent.** Sets the width or height of each column in the table to its current width expressed as a percentage of the Document window's width.

- ◆ **Bg Color.** Sets the table's background color.

- ◆ **Brdr Color.** Sets the color for the table's borders.

- ◆ **Bg Image.** Specifies the source and path to a table background image. You can click the **Browse For File** or **Point To File** button to select the file.

Formatting Cells

Cells can contain colors or image backgrounds, and when placing text and graphics, you decide how the information appears within the table cells; however, there is a priority to how the cells are formatted. When a property, such as background color or alignment, is set to one value for the whole table and another value for individual cells, cell formatting takes precedence over row formatting, which in turn takes precedence over table formatting. It's all about priority. For example, if you set the background color for a single cell to green, then set the background color of the entire table to blue, the green cell does not change to blue, since cell formatting takes precedence over table formatting.

Format Cells

① Open the Web page with the table you want to format.

② Click the **Standard Mode** or **Expanded Tables Mode** button on the Layout tab on the Insert bar.

③ Select the cell or cells you want to format.

④ In the Properties panel, modify the selection using the following options:

◆ **Horz.** Click to change the default (left) horizontal placement of items placed within the cell (Left, Center, Right).

◆ **Vert.** Click to change the default (middle) vertical placement of items placed within the cell (Default, Top, Middle, Bottom, Baseline).

◆ **W & H.** Enter a value for the width and height of selected cells in pixels, or as a percentage of the entire table's width or height. To specify a percentage, follow the value with a percent symbol (%).

NOTE *To let the browser determine the proper width or height based on the contents of the cell and the widths and heights of the other columns and rows, leave the box blank (default).*

- ◆ **No Wrap.** Select if you do not want text to wrap between the left and right borders of the selected cell.

- ◆ **Header.** Select to format the selected cells as table header cells. The contents of table header cells are bold and centered by default.

- ◆ **Bg Image.** Enter the filename for the background image. You can click the **Browse For File** or **Point To File** button to select the file.

- ◆ **Bg Color.** Click to choose a background color for the selected cells (background color is independent of text color).

- ◆ **Brdr Color.** Click to choose a border color for the selected cells.

- ◆ **Merge Cells.** Click to combine selected cells, rows, or columns into one cell.

NOTE *Merging cells can only be accomplished if they form a rectangular or linear block.*

- ◆ **Split Cells.** Click to divide a cell, creating two or more cells. This option is disabled if you have more than one cell selected.

4

Split button

Merge button

Using a Tracing Image

You can use a tracing image as a guide to create a page design in Dreamweaver. For example, you can use Adobe Photoshop to create an exact replica of what you want your Web page to look like (i.e. headings, body text areas, navigation, etc), and then use that image as a tracing image to help design the actual Web page. A tracing image is a JPEG, GIF, or PNG formatted image that appears in the background of the Document window. In addition, a tracing image is visible only in Dreamweaver, not visible when you view the page in a browser. When the tracing image is visible, the page's real background image and color are not visible in the Document window; however, the background image and color is visible when the page is viewed in a browser.

Insert a Tracing Image

1. Open a Web page that you want to insert the tracing image.

2. Click the **View** menu, point to **Tracing Image**, and then click **Load**.

3. Navigate to the image you want to use, select it, and then click **OK**.

4. Drag the **Transparency** slider to adjust the transparency of the tracing image.

   NOTE *If the chosen graphic file is not located in the current Site, Dreamweaver prompts you to save a copy within the active Site folder (recommended).*

5. Click **OK**.

   The tracing image now appears in the background of the current Web document.

Modify a Tracing Image

① Click the **View** menu, and then point to **Tracing Image**.

② Select from the following options:

◆ **Show.** Select to show or hide the tracing image.

◆ **Align With Selection.** Select an element in the document window, and then use this option to align the upper-left corner of the tracing image with the upper left corner of the selected element (i.e. a table cell).

◆ **Adjust Position.** Select to open a dialog box where you can precisely specify the position of the tracing image by entering coordinate values in the X and Y text boxes.

◆ **Reset Position.** Select to return the tracing image to its default position, the upper-left corner of the Web document.

Tracing image aligned to selection

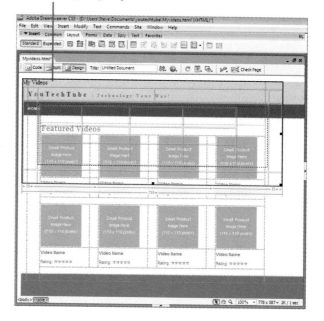

Setting Layout Mode Preferences

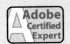

DW 2.11

You can use the Layout Mode section of the Preferences dialog box to specify the way Layout Mode works. You can set preferences to automatically add spacer images, and specify colors for different parts of a layout table, including the cell outline and highlight, and table outline and background. If you decide not to add spacer images when you use autostretch, then fixed-width columns may change size or even disappear without any content in Design view.

Set Layout Mode Preferences

1. Click the **Dreamweaver** (Mac) or **Edit** (Win) menu, and then click **Preferences**.

2. Click the **Layout Mode** category.

3. Select from the following options:

   ◆ **Autoinsert Spacers.** Select to automatically or never insert spacer images when you set a column to autostretch.

   ◆ **Spacer Image For Site.** Specify the site and then set the spacer image for the site. Click **Browse** to select an existing image file, or click **Create** to develop a new one.

   ◆ **Cell Outline.** Select a color for the cell outline.

   ◆ **Cell Highlight.** Select a color for the cell highlight; when you move the pointer to point to a cell (Mac).

   ◆ **Table Outline.** Select a color for the table outline.

   ◆ **Table Background.** Select a color for the table background.

4. Click **OK**.

Working with Cascading Style Sheets

9

Introduction

Cascading Style Sheets are one of the greatest things to come along since the creation of the World Wide Web. A hard definition of CSS might go something like this: Cascading Style Sheets (CSS) are a collection of formatting rules that control the appearance of the content in a Web page.

Using CSS styles to format a page, separates content from presentation. This gives you greater flexibility and control over the exact appearance of your Web pages. With CSS you can control text properties including specific fonts and font sizes; bold, italics, underlining, and text shadows; text color and background color, link color and underlining. With CSS controlling fonts, it ensures a more consistent treatment of your page layout and appearance in multiple browsers.

In this chapter you'll get an introduction to Cascading Style Sheets: what they are, and how to use them efficiently to create great Web content. You'll also learn how CSS functions, and how it's used to control multiple Web pages.

With Dreamweaver and Cascading Style Sheets we're getting closer and closer to the goal of What You See Is What You Get, and I can't wait.

Introducing Cascading Style Sheets

Cascading Style Sheets (CSS) are a revolution in the world of web design. Some of the benefits include:

◆ The layout of many documents from one single style sheet

◆ Precise control of layout

◆ Application of different layout to different media-types (screen, print, etc.)

◆ Many advanced and sophisticated techniques

Many of the CSS properties are similar to those of HTML. Therefore, if you are comfortable designing Web pages using HTML code, you will most likely recognize many of the codes.

CSS Versus HTML

If you wanted to change the color of the background of a Web page, the HTML code would look like this:

```
<body bgcolor="#0000FF">
```

To write the same thing using CSS, would look like this:

```
body {background-color: #0000FF;}
```

Incidentally, the code, in both cases, is instructing the browser to paint the background in pure blue.

CSS Breakdown

Cascading Style Sheets are broken down into three sections: a selector, property, and a value. In our example, body is the selector, background-color is the property, and #0000FF is the value.

Create CSS Styles

There are three ways you can apply CSS to an HTML document: Attributes, Tags, and External Style Sheets.

Attribute Styles

One way to apply CSS to HTML is by using the HTML attribute style. CSS used in this way is coded directly into the HTML document. For example, you can create your own named tags, and use them throughout the active document. Building on the above example, it can be applied like this:

```
<html>
 <head>
  <title>Attribute Style Example<title>
 </head>
 <body style="background-color: #0000FF;">
  <p>This page has a blue background</p>
 </body>
</html>
```

> **NOTE** *Attribute styles are a one-shot deal. That is, they are applied to single areas of an HTML document such as a background color, or a specific portion of text.*

Tag Styles

A second way to include CSS into an HTML document is to use the Tag Style method. In this method you control the formatting of standard HTML tags. For example, you could redefine the <H1> heading tag to always use a specific font, size and justification or, in this example, use the <body> tag to paint the background blue.

```
<html>
 <head>
  <title>Tag Style Example<title>
  <style type="text/css">
```

```
body {background-color: #0000FF;}

  </style>

 </head>

 <body>

  <p>This page has a blue background</p>

 </body>

</html>
```

> **NOTE** *A Tag style changes all instances of an HTML tag throughout the active document, but will not impact other Web documents.*

External Styles

This is the recommended way to create styles. Using this method you create a text document (called a style sheet). This document contains all of the formatting information necessary to drive your Web page. This document is then attached to one of more Web pages, and when the page loads, it gets its formatting information from the external style sheet.

The line of code must be inserted in the header section of the HTML code between the <head> and </head> tags. Like this:

```
<html>

 <head>

  <title>My document</title>

  <link rel="stylesheet" type="text/css"
href="style/style.css" />

 </head>

 <body>

<p>This page has a blue background</p>

 </body>

</html>
```

In the example, and external style sheet (basically, a text document) called style.css is used to format the active Web document.

Back to Basics

With all this talk of selectors, attributes, and values, you might assume that we're about to leave the Design mode of Dreamweaver and go back to the basics of straight HTML coding. Well, you can do that, if you choose; however, as you're about to find out, creating Cascading Styles Sheets is not difficult at all. As a matter of fact, Dreamweaver does most of the work for you. Now, isn't that nice of Adobe to provide us with so much help.

Style Types

There are three types of styles, and as you might guess, each one performs a specific function when using Cascading Style Sheets. The three types of Styles are as follows:

◆ **Class.** Creates a custom style that can be applied as a class attribute to a range or block of text.

> **NOTE** *Class names must begin with a period and can contain any combination of letters and numbers. If you don't enter a beginning period, Dreamweaver will enter it for you.*

◆ **Tag.** Creates a new style and attaches it to a current HTML tag. For example, changing the <body> tag so that each time it's applied the text is red.

◆ **Advanced.** Defines specific formatting for a particular combination of tags or for all tags that contain a specific ID attribute. The selectors available from the pop-up menu are a:active, a:hover, a:link, and a:visited.

Creating a Web Page with a CSS Layout

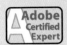 DW 2.9, 3.4, 3.9

If you're not sure where to start, you can create a Web page that already contains a CSS Layout. Dreamweaver includes over 30 different CSS layouts (**New!**). The CSS layouts are divided into 4 categories based on the page's column width: Fixed, Elastic, Liquid, or Hybrid. Each of the built-in CSS layouts includes extensive comments that explain the layout, so beginning and intermediate designers can learn quickly. After you select a CSS layout, you need to select the location (add to HTML head, create new file, or link to existing file) for the layout's CSS style sheet. A CSS layout can also be a starting point to create your own custom template, which you can add to the list of layouts in the New Document dialog box.

Create a Web Page with a CSS Layout

1. Click the **File** menu, and then click **New**.

   The New Document dialog box opens.

2. Click the **Blank Page** category.

3. Select the Page Type you want.

4. Select from the following CSS Layouts:

   ◆ **Fixed.** Column width is fixed (in pixels) and remains the same in a browser.

   ◆ **Elastic.** Column width is set relative to the size of the text in a browser (in ems).

   ◆ **Liquid.** Column width is set based on the percentage of the browser's width.

   ◆ **Hybrid.** Columns are set to a combination of Fixed, Elastic, and Liquid.

5. Click the **DocType** popup, and select the option you want.

6. Click the **Layout CSS** popup, and select the option you want:

   ◆ **Add To Head.** Adds CSS for the layout to the head of the new page.

For Your Information

Using Custom Layouts to Create New Documents

If you create a custom CSS layout, you can add it to the list of layouts in the New Document dialog box. When you create an HTML page with a CSS layout, the file needs to be saved with the .htm extension and the CSS for the layout needs to reside in the head of the HTML page. Move the saved HTML page to the following folder: Adobe Dreamweaver CS3\Configuration\Built-in\Layouts. On Windows the Adobe Dreamweaver CS3 folder is located in the Program Files folder and on the Macintosh, the folder is located in the Applications folder.

- ◆ **Create New File.** Add CSS for the layout to a new external CSS style sheet that attaches to the new page.

- ◆ **Link To Existing File.** Attaches an existing CSS file to the new page.

7 If you selected the Link To Existing File option in the Layout CSS popup menu, click the **Attach Style Sheet** icon, select the CSS file you want in the Attach External Style Sheet dialog box, and then click **OK**.

8 Click **Create**.

9 If you selected the Create New File option in the Layout CSS popup menu, enter a name for the new external file in the Save Style Sheet File As dialog box.

Create a CSS File

1 Click the **File** menu, and then click **New**.

The New Document dialog box opens.

2 Select from the following methods:

- ◆ **Blank.** Click the **Blank Page** category, and then click **CSS**.

- ◆ **Sample.** Click the **Page from Sample** category, click **CSS Style Sheet**, and then select the sample you want.

3 Click **Create**.

Creating CSS Styles

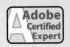 DW 3.4

As mentioned in the last section, CSS can be applied to an HTML document in one of three ways: Attributes, Tags, or Externally. Although we will cover all three methods in this section, it's important to understand that the external method gives you the most control over the styles, once they've been created. In the other two methods, the CSS styles created only apply to that one specific page, and changes to the styles must be performed by reopening the page. The external method is like creating a text document of how you want a page or pages to display. Any changes to the formatting are performed to the text document. When the Web page opens, and any changes made to the external document are immediately reflected in the active page... now that's what I call control.

Create an Attribute or Tag Style

1. Open the Web page you want to create a CSS style.

2. Click the **Text** menu, point to **CSS Styles**, and then click **New**.

3. Select the options for the type of style you want to create:

   - **Attribute Style.** Click the **Class** option, click the **Name** arrow, and then select a name for your style, or type one in. Attribute style tags must begin with a period.

   - **Tag Style.** Click the **Tag** option, click the **Name** arrow, and then select an HTML tag (in this example, body).

4. Click the **This Document Only** option.

5. Click **OK**.

6. Select a category, and then set the properties you want for the CSS style.

7. Click **OK**.

Create an External Style

1 Open the Web page you want to create an external CSS style.

2 Click the **Text** menu, point to **CSS Styles**, and then click **New**.

3 Click the **Class** or **Tag** option (in this example, tag).

4 Click the **Name** arrow, and then select an HTML tag (in this example, body.)

5 Click the **Define In** popup, and then click **New Style Sheet File**.

6 Click **OK**.

7 Enter the file name for the CSS style in the Save As input box.

8 Leave the other options at their default values, and then click **Save**.

> **NOTE** *Dreamweaver creates a folder in the active site called, CSS, and this is where all style sheets should be saved.*

9 Select a category, and then set the properties you want for the CSS style.

10 Click **OK**.

See Also

See "Setting CSS Properties" on page 228 for information on setting CSS properties for a rule.

Applying Internal CSS Styles

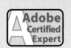 DW 3.4

Cascading Style Sheets function and perform just like their counterparts in word-processing applications. For example, you could create a character style in Microsoft Word that specifies text be Garamond, 12 point, bold, and the color black. When the style is applied to the text it will immediately take on those characteristics. If you access the style and change it (for example, change the color to red), all text associated with that style would change. CSS works the same way: You create a style for the text and apply the style to the Web document. Changing the style would subsequently change all text associated with that particular style. However, the difference between word-processing styles and CSS styles is that paragraph and character styles are one in the same. For example, if you select a word or group of words and apply a CSS style, the style is applied only to the selected text (also called an inline style). However, if you click within a paragraph (add an insertion point), the CSS style is applied to the entire paragraph. Generally, inline styles are frowned upon because of the amount of effort it takes to apply and modify the items on an item-by-item basis. Instead, you can convert an inline style to a CSS rule (**New!**) located in the head of the page or in an external style sheet, which is cleaner and easier to use.

Apply a Paragraph Style

1. Open the Web page you want to apply a paragraph style.

2. Click within a specific paragraph, to create an insertion point.

    NOTE *Do not select any text.*

3. Click the **Text** menu, point to **CSS Styles**, and then select a user-defined CSS style.

    TIMESAVER *In the Properties panel, click the Styles popup, and then select the CSS style you want.*

    The CSS style is applied to the entire paragraph.

    NOTE *A paragraph is defined as the information contained between two carriage returns.*

Apply a Character (Inline) Style

① Open the Web page you want to apply a character style.

② Select a word or words within the text document.

③ Click the **Text** menu, point to **CSS Styles**, and then select a user-defined CSS style.

The CSS style is applied to the selected text.

See Also

See "Moving CSS Rules" on page 232 for information on moving CSS rules to a style sheet.

Convert Inline CSS to a CSS Rule

① Open the Web page with the style you want to change.

② Click the **View** menu, and then click **Code**.

③ Select the entire <style> tag that contains the inline CSS you want to convert.

④ Right-click the selection, point to **CSS Style**, and then click **Convert Inline CSS To Rule**.

⑤ Click the Convert to popup, select a convert type, and then enter a class name for the new rule.

⑥ Specify a style sheet or select the head of the document as to where you want the new CSS rule.

⑦ Click **OK**.

Applying and Modifying External CSS Styles

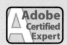 DW 3.4

When you start to modify an external style sheet, you really begin to see the awesome power of using CSS. An external style sheet normally contains all of the formatting options for one or more Web pages. When you attach the style sheet to the document, the style sheet controls the formatting of the document. For example, if you had a style sheet that modified the <body> tag to use the Helvetica font, centered, and 12 point, when the style sheet was attached to the HTML document, all text defined by the <body> tag would change, according to the rules set up by the style sheet. Since the style sheet is only a text document it's easy to make changes (they can even be made in a text editor). For example, you could access the style sheet and change the formatting of the text from centered to left, and then save the style sheet. The next time the Web page opens, all the <body> tag text will be left justified. In addition to this power, you can use more than one style sheet within a Web page. For example, you can have a style sheet that defines all your headings, one that defines the look of the page, and another that defines body text. Cascading Style Sheets separate the page content from the formatting, and give you total control over your designs.

Attach an External Style Sheet

1. Open the Web page you want to attach an external style sheet.

2. Click the **Text** menu, point to **CSS Styles**, and then click **Attach Style Sheet**.

3. Select from the following options:

   ◆ **File/URL.** Enter the path and file name of the external style sheet, or click **Browse** to select a file.

   ◆ **Add As.** Click the **Link** option to create a link from the page to the external style sheet (recommended), or click the **Import** option to write the style sheet directly into the page.

   ◆ **Media.** Click the **Media** arrow to select the media type associated with this particular page (Default: All).

   ◆ **Preview.** Click **Preview** to view the effects of the external style sheet on your page.

4. Click **OK**.

Modify an External Style Sheet

1 Open the Web page you want to modify an external style sheet.

2 Click the **File** menu, and then click **Open**.

3 Select the external style sheet file that you want to modify.

4 Click **Open**.

5 Modify the document to reflect the changes required.

6 Click the **File** menu, and then click **Save**.

When you reopen the Web document, the formatting reflects the changes made to the attached style sheet.

Did You Know?

You can quickly access any style sheet in Code view. Click the View menu, click Code view, right-click on the name of the external style sheet (Hint: it's located in the header section of the HTML document), and then click the Open command for the selected CSS style sheet.

You can use a Dreamweaver sample style sheet. Dreamweaver provides sample style sheets you can apply to your Web pages or use it as a starting point to create your own style sheet. Click the Window menu, click CSS Styles, click the Attach Style Sheet button, click the Sample Style Sheets link, select the sample style sheet you want, click Preview to apply it to the current Web page, and then click OK.

Removing Internal Styles

DW 3.4

You can remove a style from any tag, you can delete the redefined tag, or you can even edit the existing style to reflect different formatting. Once again this reflects the versatility of using style sheets over standard HTML coding. When you remove a style from a Web document the item or text will revert back to its original formatting. For example, if you remove a style from a section of body text, the text will revert back to the default for that particular tag. If, however, you have an external style sheet attached to a document, and you have applied a local class or attribute (internal) style to the text, when you remove the localized style, the text will revert back to the rules supplied by the external style sheet.

Remove an Internal Style

1. Open the Web page you want to remove an internal style.

2. Select the stylized text, or place the insertion point in a paragraph containing stylized text.

3. Click the **Text** menu, point to **CSS Styles**, and then click **None**.

   TIMESAVER *In the Properties panel, click the Styles popup, and then click None.*

   The CSS style is removed from the selected text.

Did You Know?

You can rename a CSS class style. Click the Window menu, click CSS Styles, right-click the CSS class style you want to rename in the CSS Styles panel, click Rename Class, enter a new name, and then click OK.

Using the CSS Styles Panel

 Adobe Certified Expert DW 3.4

Use the CSS Styles Panel

1. Open the Web page that contains the stylized text you want to view.

2. Click the **Window** menu, and then click **CSS Styles** or click the **CSS** button in the Properties panel.

3. The following options are available on the CSS Styles panel:

   ◆ **All or Current.** Shows all of the active document's style rules, or just the currently selected rule.

   ◆ **Rules Window.** Displays a list of the active document's rules.

   ◆ **Properties Window.** Displays a list of the properties for the rule selected in the Rules window.

   ◆ **Show Category View.** Displays the properties for the selected rule by categories.

   ◆ **Show List View.** Displays the properties for the selected rule in List view (color, font, etc).

   ◆ **Show Only Set Properties.** Displays only set properties.

   ◆ **Attach Style Sheet.** Attaches an external style sheet.

   ◆ **New CSS Rule.** Creates a new CSS rule.

   ◆ **Edit Style Sheet.** Opens a dialog box to edit styles.

   ◆ **Unlink CSS Style Sheet.** Deletes the selected rule or property.

Dreamweaver gives you complete control over internal and external styles with the CSS Styles panel. The CSS Styles panel lists all the internal and external styles attached to the active Web page. In addition to displaying the styles, known as rules, the CSS Styles panel gives you the ability to attach style sheets, modify existing styles (internal or external), and even remove styles.

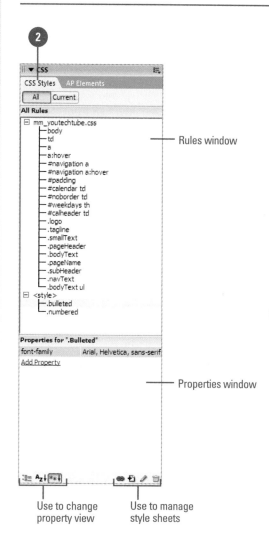

Rules window

Properties window

Use to change property view

Use to manage style sheets

Setting CSS Properties

 DW 3.4

After you create a new CSS rule, you can alter properties for it. The CSS Rule Definition dialog box lets you select the CSS properties you want to define a CSS rule. You can set CSS properties for any of the following categories: Type, Background (image and color), Block (spacing and alignment), Box (placement), Border (width, color, and style), Lists (bullets or numbers), Positioning (on page), and Extensions (filters, page breaks, and pointers).

Set CSS Properties

1. Open the Web page that contains CSS styles (internal or external) you want apply properties.

2. Open the CSS Styles panel.

3. Double-click the rule or property you want to define.

    TIMESAVER *Select the rule or property, and then make changes to the available attributes in the lower panel in the CSS Styles panel. Use the Show buttons at the bottom of the CSS Styles panel to display different attributes.*

4. Specify the options you want in the CSS Rule Definition dialog box:

    ◆ **Type and Font.** Click the **Type** category, and then specify the following options: Font, Size, Style, Line Height, Decoration (underline, overline, line-through, or blink), Weight (boldface), Variant (small caps), Case (first letter, uppercase or lowercase), or Color.

    ◆ **Background Image and Color.** Click the **Background** category, and then specify the following options: Background Color, Background Image, Repeat, Attachment, or Horizontal Position and Vertical Position.

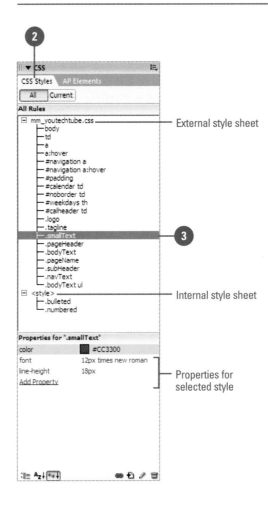

External style sheet

Internal style sheet

Properties for selected style

- ◆ **Spacing and Alignment.** Click the **Block** category, and then specify the following options: Word Spacing, Letter Spacing, Vertical Alignment, Text Align, Text Indent, Whitespace (*Normal* collapses white space, *Pre* works like the pre tag, or *Nowrap* only with br tag), or Display.

- ◆ **Placement.** Click the **Box** category, and then specify the following options: Width and Height, Float, Clear, Padding, Same For All (padding), Margin, or Same For All (margins).

- ◆ **Border Width, Color, and Style.** Click the **Border** category, and then specify the following options: Style, Same For All (style), Width, Same For All (width), Color, or Same For All (color).

- ◆ **Bulleted and Numbered Lists.** Click the **List** category, and then specify the following options: Type, Bullet Image, or Position.

- ◆ **Page Positioning.** Click the **Positioning** category, and then specify the following options: Type (*Absolute, Relative, Fixed,* or *Static*), Visibility (*Inherit, Visible,* or *Hidden*), Z-Index, Overflow, Placement, or Clip.

- ◆ **Filters, Page Breaks, and Pointers.** Click the **Extensions** category, and then specify the following options: Pagebreak, Cursor, or Filter.

5 Click **OK**.

Working with CSS Rules

  DW 3.4

A CSS rule consists of two parts: selector and declaration. The **selector** identifies the formatted elements (such as p, body, or h1), while the **declaration** defines the style properties. The declaration is a collection, known as a block, of properties and values. For example, font-family: Arial; defines the text style as the Arial font. The declaration is everything between the braces ({}). After you create a CSS rule, you can use the CSS Styles panel to modify and customize it to better suit your needs. If you no longer need a CSS rule, you can remove it.

Modify an Existing Rule

1 Open the Web page that contains CSS styles with the rule you want to apply a property.

2 Open the CSS Styles panel.

3 Select a rule from the available options in the All Rules pane (All mode) or select a property in the Summary for Selection pane (Current mode).

4 Use any of the following methods:

◆ Double-click a rule or property to open the CSS Rule Definition dialog box. Make changes to the rule, and then click **OK** to save the changes.

◆ Click the **Show Only Set Properties** button, click the **Add Properties** link, and then fill in a value for the property in the Properties panel.

◆ Click the **Show Category View** or **Show List View** button, and then fill in a value for the property in the Properties panel.

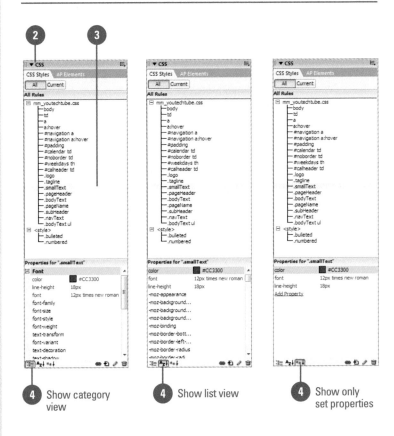

4 Show category view

4 Show list view

4 Show only set properties

Delete an Existing Rule

1 Open the Web page that contains CSS styles with the rule you want to delete.

2 Open the CSS Styles panel.

3 Select a rule from the available options.

4 Click the **Delete** button in the CSS Styles panel.

> **NOTE** *The rule will be deleted and all text the rule was attached to will revert back to their default format.*

Did You Know?

You can edit a CSS style sheet. Instead of editing individual rules, you can edit the entire style sheet. Click the Window menu, click CSS Styles to open the CSS Styles panel, click the All button, double-click the name of the style sheet you want to edit, modify the style sheet in the Document window, and then save your changes.

You can change the name of a CSS selector. Open the CSS Styles panel, click the All button, click the selector you want to change, click it again to make the name editable, change the name, and then click Enter (Win) or Return (Mac).

Moving CSS Rules

DW 3.4

After you create a set of CSS rules that you like, you can move them (**New!**) from one document to another, from the head of a document to an external style sheet, and between different external CSS files. If a conflict arises when you move a CSS rule from one place to another, you can specify how you want Dreamweaver to handle it.

Move CSS Rules to a New Style Sheet

1. Open the document with the CSS rules you want to move.

2. Open the CSS Styles panel or display Code view.

3. Select the rule or rules you want to move.

 ◆ To select multiple rules, Ctrl-click (Win) or ⌘-click (Mac) the rules you want to select.

4. Right-click the selection, point to **CSS Styles**, and then click **Move CSS Rules**.

5. Select the **A New Style Sheet** option.

6. Click **OK**.

7. Enter a name for the new style sheet.

8. Click **Save**.

> ### Did You Know?
>
> ***You can move a rule in the CSS panel.*** Left-click the rule you want to move, and then drag it to a new position in the CSS panel.

Move CSS Rules to an Existing Style Sheet

1. Open the document with the CSS rules you want to move.

2. Open the CSS Styles panel or display Code view.

3. Select the rule or rules you want to move.

   ◆ To select multiple rules, Ctrl-click (Win) or ⌘-click (Mac) the rules you want to select.

4. Right-click the selection, point to **CSS Styles**, and then click **Move CSS Rules**.

5. Click the **Style Sheet** option, and then select an existing style sheet already linked to the document from the popup or click **Browse** to select an existing style sheet.

6. Click **OK**.

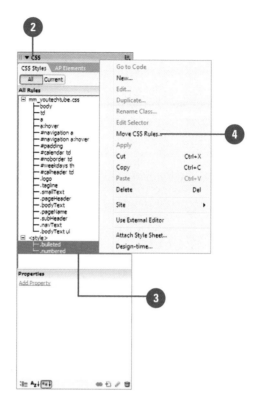

Did You Know?

You can rearrange or move CSS rules by dragging. Open the Styles panel, click the All button, select the rules you want to move, and then drag them to the new location. You can move a rule to another style sheet or the document head or rearrange rules within a style sheet.

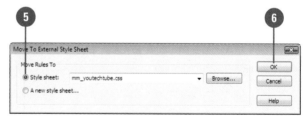

Using the Relevant CSS Tab

The Relevant CSS tab lets you track the CSS rules affecting the currently selected text element as well as modifying the rule's properties. The Relevant tab is located in the Tag Inspector. Click the Window menu, and then click Tag Inspector. The Relevant CSS tab consists of two sections:

◆ The upper portion of the Relevant CSS tab shows the rules affecting the current selection and the tags that they affect.

◆ The lower portion of the Relevant CSS tab displays the properties of the currently selected element in an editable grid.

The properties are arranged alphabetically, with the set properties sorted to the top of the tab. Set properties are displayed in blue; properties irrelevant to the selection are displayed with a red strike through line. Hovering over a rule that is irrelevant displays a message explaining why the property is irrelevant. Typically, a property is irrelevant because it is overridden or not an inherited property.

You can also use the lower panel of the Relevant CSS tab to modify the properties of a selection. The editable grid lets you change the values for any of the displayed properties. Any changes you make to a selection are applied immediately, letting you preview your work as you go.

Working with ID Selectors

 DW 1.2

CSS Advanced styles redefine the formatting for a particular combination of elements, or for other selector forms as allowed by CSS (for example, the selector td h2 applies whenever an h2 header appears inside a table cell).

This is accomplished through the association of styles to HTML tags through ID attributes and ID selectors. ID attributes in HTML tags uniquely identify that tag with a name. Styles can be linked to that ID just like they can with classes. The big difference is that ids cannot be used on more than one tag. This also means that style definitions for ids only relate to one tag per page. You should never run into the need to apply an ID selector more than once. Should you need to use an ID selector on more then one occasion in any given page, you will need to re-plan your CSS.

For example, an ID can be applied to the h1 tag of a document containing heading text. The tag will be given the ID "master-heading" indicating that it is the sole and primary heading of the page. As such it will also receive a unique style.

Advanced styles can also redefine the formatting for tags that contain a specific id attribute (for example, the styles defined by #myStyle (user defined) apply to all tags that contain the attribute-value pair id="myStyle").

The following example is an ID selector:

```
#MyID {
   color: #0033ff;
}
```

The primary difference between a Class and ID selector is that the first character is a hash or pound sign (#).

Creating advanced styles also helps when Web pages are converted into text documents. For example, if ID's are selected for various heading, body, and sub text, these unique names can be used to help convert the Web text to print text.

In addition to ID selectors, CSS specifications refer to link styles as Pseudo-classes. These are special classes that describe styles for elements that only apply under certain circumstances. For example, the four default pseudo-classes you will find in the Advanced menu are:

◆ **a:link.** Describes any hyperlink that has not been visited by the user's browser. In other words, the page linked to is not present in the browser's local memory.

◆ **a:visited.** Describes any hyperlink that has been visited and is present in the browser's local memory.

◆ **a:hover.** Describes a hyperlink while the user's mouse happens to be hovering over it. This class is recognized by all version 4 and higher browsers, except Netscape 4.

◆ **a:active.** Describes a hyperlink that has been clicked but not yet released.

   NOTE *The hover class is recognized by all version 4 and higher browsers, except Netscape.*

Creating and Applying an ID Selector

If you want to define the formatting for a combination of tags, you can use the Advanced option to create an ID selector. You can specify one or more HTML tags to create an ID selector or select one from the popup menu, which includes a:active, a:hover, a:link, and a:visited. After you specify the tags you want to use, you can define the formatting associated with it. When you're done, you can apply the ID selector to other elements.

Create an ID Selector

1 Open the Web page you want to create an ID selector.

2 Click the **Text** menu, point to **CSS Styles**, and then click **New**.

3 Click the **Advanced** option.

4 Enter an Advanced style name in the Selector box (in this example #mainBody), or select one from the list.

5 Click the **Define In** popup, and then select a new or existing external style sheet or click the **This Document Only** option.

6 Click **OK**.

7 Click the **Type** category, and make the modifications you want. Some include the following:

◆ **Font.** Click the arrow button, and then select a font (in this example, click Verdana, Arial, Helvetica, sans-serif).

◆ **Size.** Click the arrow button, and then select a size (in this example, enter 24 pixels).

◆ **Variant.** Click the arrow button, and then select an option (in this example, click small-caps).

◆ **Color.** Click the arrow button and then select a color (in this example, click Blue (#0000FF)).

8 Click **OK**.

Apply an ID Selector

1. Click to place the insertion point into a portion of the text that you want to apply the ID selector.

2. Right-click one of the tags in the quick tag selector (in this example the <p> tag).

3. Point to **Set ID**, and then select from the available ID selector options (in this example, paragraphText).

   The selected paragraph now changes to the modifications made to the #paragraphText ID selector.

Checking for CSS Browser Compatibility

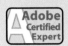 DW 2.6, 3.13

The Browser Compatibility Check (BCC) (New!) analyzes the HTML and CSS on the open page and determines whether it has problems in certain browsers. Browser targeting checks your pages for all popular platforms and browsers, including Firefox, Internet Explorer (Mac and Win), and Safari. When you run the BCC, it scans the open page and reports any potential CSS problems in the Results panel. Each potential problem is given a confidence rating, a circle. The amount of the circle filled in—quarter, half, three-quarter, or full—determines the occurrence probability level of the problem. Browser problems fall into three categories: serious (visible problem), warning (not supported), and informational (no visible effect). A direct link to documentation and solutions related to the problem is also provided on the Adobe CSS Advisor Web site (New!).

Check for CSS Browser Compatibility Issues

1. Click the **File** menu, point to **Check Page**, and then click **Browser Compatibility**.

   The Results panel appears with the Browser Compatibility Check tab, indicating any problems.

2. Double-click an issue to select it.

   Information about the potential problem appears to the right in the Results panel.

3. To display the issue in the code, click the **Check Page** button on the Document window, and then click **Next Issue** or **Previous Issue**.

4. To open the Adobe CSS Advisor Web site, click the link at the bottom right of the Results panel.

5. To exclude an issue from future checking, right-click the issue in the Results panel, and then click **Ignore Issue**.

   ◆ To edit the Ignore Issues list, click the green arrow in the Results panel, click **Edit Ignored Issues List**, delete the issue from the Exceptions.xml file, and then save and close the file.

Select Browsers to Check

1. Click the **Check Page** button on the Document window, and then click **Settings**.

   The Target Browsers dialog box opens.

2. Select the check boxes next to the browsers you want to check and clear the ones you don't want to check.

3. Click the **Version** popup for each browser to select the version you want.

4. Click **OK**.

View and Save a BCC Report

1. Click the **File** menu, point to **Check Page**, and then click **Browser Compatibility**.

   ◆ You can also click Window, click Results, and then click the Browser Compatibility Check tab.

   The Results panel appears with the Browser Compatibility Check tab, indicating any potential problems.

2. To view the report, click the **Browse Report** button in the Results panel.

3. To save the report, click the **Save Report** button in the Results panel.

Formatting CSS Code

You can use the Code Format section of the Preferences dialog box to access CSS source formatting options. You can set options to indent properties, and insert separator lines to make it easier to work with CSS code. As you make formatting option changes, a preview of the CSS code appears in the dialog box. If you like the preview results, you can accept the options. Otherwise, you can continue to make option changes. After you set CSS code formatting preferences, you can apply them to an entire document (in a CSS style sheet) or the head of the document only (embedded CSS code).

Set CSS Code Formatting Preferences

1. Click the **Dreamweaver** (Mac) or **Edit** (Win) menu, and then click **Preferences**.

2. Click the **Code Format** category.

3. Click the **CSS** button.

4. Select from the following CSS source code format options:

   ◆ **Indent Properties With.** Sets the indent number and type (Tabs or Spaces) for properties within a rule.

   ◆ **Each Property On Separate Line.** Places each property within a rule on a separate line.

   ◆ **Opening Brace On Separate Line.** Places the opening brace for a rule on a separate line from the selector.

   ◆ **Only If More Than One Property.** Places the single-property rules on the same line as the selector.

   ◆ **All Selectors For A Rule On Same Line.** Places all selectors for the rule on the same line.

   ◆ **Blank Line Between Rules.** Inserts a blank line between each rule.

5. Click **OK**.

6. Click **OK**.

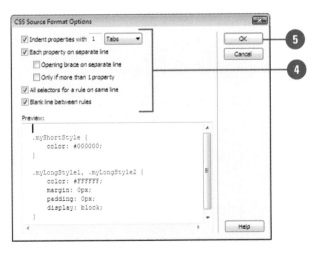

Format CSS Code in a CSS Style Sheet Manually

1. Open the CSS style sheet you want to format.

2. Click the **Commands** menu, and then click **Apply Source Formatting**.

   The formatting options set in CSS code formatting preferences are applied to the entire document.

Format Embedded CSS Code Manually

1. Open the HTML page that contains CSS embedded in the head of the document.

2. Select any part of the CSS code.

3. Click the **Commands** menu, and then click **Apply Source Formatting To Selection**.

   The formatting options set in CSS code formatting preferences are applied to all CSS rules in the head of the document only.

Setting CSS Styles Preferences

You can use the CSS Styles section of the Preferences dialog box to control the way Dreamweaver writes the code that defines CSS styles. You can specify the properties—including font, background, margin and padding, border and border width, or list-style—you want Dreamweaver to write in shorthand, determine whether Dreamweaver edits existing styles in shorthand, and select the editing tool you want to use to modify CSS rules. Shorthand CSS is an abbreviated syntax that allows you to create styles.

Set CSS Styles Preferences

1. Click the **Dreamweaver** (Mac) or **Edit** (Win) menu, and then click **Preferences**.

2. Click the **CSS Styles** category.

3. Select from the following CSS style options:

   ◆ **When Creating CSS Rules Use Shorthand For.** Select the check boxes for the properties you want Dreamweaver to write in shorthand.

   ◆ **When Editing CSS Rules Use Shorthand.** Select the font and size you want to use to display text within pre, code, and tt tags.

   ◆ **When Double-clicking In CSS Panel.** Select the option with the editing preference you want to use: CSS dialog, Properties panel, or Code view.

4. Click **OK**.

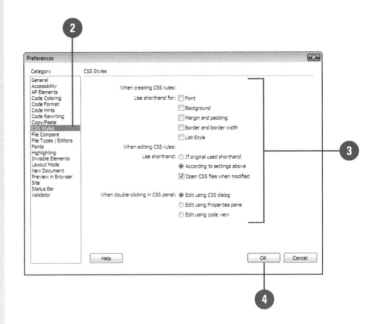

Using Design-Time Style Sheets

In Dreamweaver, you can use design-time style sheets to show or hide designs applied by a CSS style sheet as you work on a Web page. This is useful when you want to include or exclude the effect of a style sheet as you design a page. Design-Time style sheets only apply while you are working on a page. When the page display the page in a browser, only the styles that are actually attached to or embedded in the page appear.

Use Design-Time Style Sheets

① Open the Web page you want to create a CSS style.

② Click the **Text** menu, point to **CSS Styles**, and then click **Design-Time.**

③ Select from the following CSS style options:

◆ **Show.** Click the **Plus** (+) button above Show Only At Design-Time, select the CSS style sheet you want to show, and then click **OK**.

◆ **Hide.** Click the **Plus** (+) button above Hide At Design-Time, select the CSS style sheet you want to hide, and then click **OK**.

◆ **Remove.** Click the style sheet you want to remove, and then click the appropriate **Minus** (-) button.

④ Click **OK**.

The CSS Styles panel displays an indicator, either "hidden" or "design" that reflects the current status of the style sheet.

Show in design-time

Hide in design-time

Creating Page Layouts Using CSS-P

10

Introduction

Cascading Style Sheets-Positioning (CSS-P) is more than the perfect positioning of words and objects on a Web page, in addition, layers technology lets you create movable containers (called **AP elements**, formally known as layers) that allow you to precisely position Web text and objects, even going so far as to stack one AP element on top of another, or to use JavaScript to show or hide AP elements. For example, you could have several AP elements containing thumbnails of images and when you hover over a particular AP element, a JavaScript would show a previously hidden AP element with information about the image. The incorporation of AP elements into a Web page gives the designer, for the first time, the use of all three dimensions: width, height, and even depth (stackable AP elements).

There is, of course, in all things a good news/bad news scenario. The good news is that AP elements and CSS-P are awesome tools for the creative designer to use. The bad news is that they do not work in earlier browsers (pre 4.0). Fortunately, Dreamweaver turns that bad news on its head by giving you the ability to convert AP elements into a more compatible tables document and vise versa.

This chapter covers the use of AP elements and CSS-P for the creation and implementation and total control of the design of Web pages. We'll focus in on how to create CSS-P design, and why you might want to use it.

Introducing CSS Layouts and AP Elements

In the beginning, support for Cascading Style Sheets (CSS) was a bit sketchy; however, as time when on, and CSS caught on, more and more browsers came on board. In response, Dreamweaver began giving Cascading Style Sheets complete support.

Cascading Style Sheets is all about the control of the Web page, and are a designer's dream come true. Not only do you have the ability to specify and apply specific font characteristics; in addition you can precisely place elements on the page. Basically CSS are a set of rules encased within a style sheet. The rules are customized styles, or modified HTML tags that define the look, position, and feel of the Web page. In the previous chapter, you learned about the syntax of CSS. In this chapter you'll learn how to use CSS to control and format Web pages, using AP elements (**New!**), formally known as layers. An AP element is a movable container that allows you to precisely position Web text and objects

Web designers have always wanted the type of control over text and graphic elements that page designers have had, and with the advent of CSS, and in incorporation of AP elements, that day has finally arrived.

CSS and AP elements give you the ability to precisely position elements on a Web page, and let you stack AP elements over each other. This addition of the third dimension is not only a new concept in Web design, but is exactly why CSS absolute position is called, AP elements. Not only can Web designers position elements using x and y (width and height) positioning, they now have z indexing (depth)… and that's what I call control.

The Code

When you use Dreamweaver to create an AP element, the HTML code looks something like the following:

```
<div id="Layer4" style="position:absolute; visibility:inherit; width:200px; height:175 px; z-index:6">
</div>
```

Although it's not the only way to create the code, AP elements are usually placed between <div> …</div> or … tags.

Creating AP elements in Dreamweaver's design window (the most common method) is as simple as a drag and release. The visible result is the creation of a square or rectangle, which becomes a floating element on the Web page. This element can be populated with text, images or any combination thereof. Think of an AP element as a floating, independent table cell, and you have the picture. To move an AP element to a different position on the Web page, the designer has only to click and drag.

In addition to creating and moving the AP elements about the Web page, you have the ability to stack AP elements in the third dimension. By default every AP element is assigned a z-index, or stacking order. The first AP element is assigned the stacking order of 1, and each new AP element follows the progression 2, 3, 4, etc. Therefore, when two AP elements interact, they can actually slide over each other; creating Web designs that would have been impossible in straight HTML.

If you've ever used AP element-intensive applications, such as: Adobe Photoshop, Illustrator, or InDesign, you're ready to get started designing CSS AP elements in Dreamweaver.

Creating AP Elements

An AP element is an HTML page element that has absolute position assigned to it. An AP element can contain text, images, or other HTML body content. You can create AP elements by using styles and rules, or by drawing them on the page manually using the Draw AP Div tool. When you manually create AP elements, they are not attached to any particular style, and therefore stand on their own. If you want to change all the AP elements attached to a style, all you need to do is change the style. If you want to change all the manually created AP elements, you need to modify each one independently. While this does not impair the display of the AP element in the browser window, it does mean that creating AP elements with styles (discussed later in this chapter) helps to make modifications quick and easy.

Create an AP Element Manually

1. Open the page you want to add an AP element.

2. Click the **Layout** tab on the Insert bar, and then click the **Draw AP Div** button.

3. Click in the Document window in Design view, and then use one of the following methods:

    ◆ **Draw An AP Element.** Drag to create the AP element the size you want. You can also use Ctrl+drag or ⌘+drag to draw multiple AP elements. Release the Ctrl or Command key when you finished drawing.

    ◆ **Insert An AP Element.** Click the **Insert** menu, point to **Layout Objects**, and then click **AP Div**.

4. Click the edge of the AP element to select it.

    Selection handles appear around the edges of the AP element.

5. To adjust the width and height of the new AP element, drag one of the selection handles.

6. To adjust the position of the AP element, drag the AP element handle (tab in the upper-left corner) or the edge of the AP element.

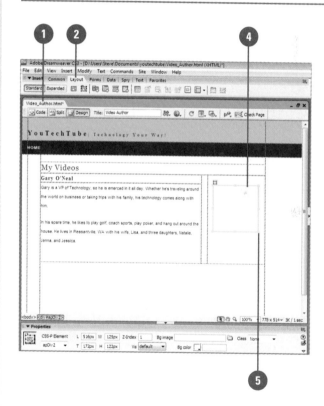

Nesting AP Elements

If you thought that creating an AP element was the greatest thing since sliced bread, then you're going to love that fact that you can nest AP elements. When you nest an AP element, you're placing an AP element within an AP element. Each AP element has its own formatting controls and gives you precise control over its position, for example, of text and graphics. Since the nested AP elements will be positioned based on the current position of the parent AP element, it's considered to have relative positioning concerning the page, and absolute or relative positioning within the nest.

Nest an AP Element

1. Open the page you want to add an AP element.

2. Click the **Layout** tab on the Insert bar, and then click the **Draw AP Div** button (formally called the Layer button).

3. Create an AP element in the Design view window of the current document.

4. Click the **Draw AP Div** button a second time; hold down Alt (Win) or Option (Mac) and drag to create another AP element within the first AP element.

5. Drag the parent AP element and the nested AP element moves at the same time.

6. To reposition the nested AP element relative to the parent AP element, drag the nested AP element.

Setting AP Element Preferences

You can use the AP Element section of the Preferences dialog box to specify the default settings you want for new AP elements. Whether you create a new AP element using the Draw AP Div button on the Layout tab on the Insert bar or the AP Div command on the Layout Objects submenu on the Insert menu, Dreamweaver uses the default options you set in the Preferences dialog box for visibility, width and height, and background color options to create a new AP element.

Set AP Element Preferences

1. Click the **Dreamweaver** (Mac) or **Edit** (Win) menu, and then click **Preferences**.

2. Click the **AP Elements** category.

3. Select from the following CSS style options:

   ◆ **Visibility.** Select the default option to show or hide AP elements: Default, Inherit, Visible, Hidden.

   ◆ **Width and Height.** Specifies the default width and height (in pixels) when you use Insert > Layout Objects > AP Div.

   ◆ **Background Color.** Specifics the default background color.

   ◆ **Nesting: Nest When Created Within An AP Div.** Select to create a nested AP Div when you draw within an existing AP Div.

   ◆ **Netscape 4 Compatibility: Add Resize Fix When Inserting AP Element.** Select to insert JavaScript code to fix a problem with Netscape 4 browsers.

   NOTE *You can add or remove JavaScript code manually by selecting the Commands menu, and then click Add/Remove Netscape Resize Fix.*

4. Click **OK**.

Using CSS Positioning

Cascading Style Sheets Positioning, or CSS-P, allows for specific positioning in HTML of Web elements. You can apply CSS-P to a block of text, a block element, an image, or an AP element. There are two ways to apply positioning: One is to create a style class and apply it to selections of text blocks on the page (this basically converts the object to an AP element, automatically), the second way is to create an AP element, and modify it independently of creating a style. In the end, you have a fully controllable CSS-P AP element. Once an AP element is established, it is controlled using absolute or relative positioning. **Relative positioning** means that AP elements are given a position relative to the top-left corner of the parent container, and is considered to be part of the flow of the page, such as a normal inline element within a text flow, or an AP element, nested with another AP element. **Absolute positioning** means that the AP element is positioned outside the flow of the Web page. In other words, nothing can make it move or change position. Setting the absolute positioning of the AP element does not impact the positioning of elements within the AP element. You can use the Properties panel to position and place AP elements where you want.

Change CSS-P Positioning Manually

1. Open the Web page that contains the AP elements you want to modify.

2. Select the AP element you want to change.

3. Open the Properties panel, and then modify the AP elements absolute position using the following options:

   ◆ **L.** Enter a value (in pixels) to position the AP element from the Left side of the Web page.

   ◆ **T.** Enter a value (in pixels) to position the AP element from the Top of the Web page.

   ◆ **Z-Index.** Enter a numerical value to indicate the AP element's stacking position when two or more AP elements overlap each other (higher numbers indicate a higher position within the stacking order of the active Web page).

L and T   Z-index

Create a CSS-P Style

1. Open the Web page you want to create an AP element style.

2. Click the **Text** menu, point to **CSS Styles**, and then click **New**.

3. Click the **Class** option.

4. Enter a name for your new class. The style name must begin with a period.

5. Click the **This Document Only** option or click the popup, and then select an attached style sheet.

6. Click **OK**.

7. Click the **Positioning** category.

8. Specify AP element positioning using the following options:

   ◆ **Type.** Click the **Type** arrow, and then select an option: Absolute, Relative, Fixed, or Static.

   The Static option is used when you do not wish to add content to an AP element.

   ◆ **Width.** Enter a Width (in pixels) for the new AP element.

   ◆ **Height.** Enter a Height (in pixels) for the new AP element.

   ◆ **Placement.** Enter a value (in pixels) for the absolute position of the AP element box in relation to the Web page.

   ◆ **Clip.** Enter a value (in pixels) for the absolute position of the AP element content in relation to the Web page.

   ◆ **Overflow.** Click the **Overflow** arrow, and then select an option when content exceeded the container.

9. Click **OK** to add the embedded style to the active Web page.

Applying a CSS-P Style

Once you've created one or more styles with AP elements, it's a simple matter to apply those styles to existing elements within a Web page. For example, you can create a navigational system, and then attach an AP element style that would control the elements position, width, height, and Z-index. You can apply AP element styles to text, groups of text, images, or virtually anything on a standard Web page. Not only can the dimensions and position of an AP element be controlled by CSS-P styles; in addition there are options for controlling fonts, sizing, styles; even the insertion of a color or background image into the AP element.

Apply a CCS-P Style

1. Open the Web page that contains text and/or graphics you want to apply an AP element style.

2. Select a group of text, or a graphic element on the page.

3. Click the **Text** menu, point to **CSS Styles**, and then select the appropriate style you want.

   The selected CSS-P style is applied to the selected Web object.

Did You Know?

You can create styles by using the ID of the AP element. You can name an AP element HeadLine (AP element's ID's are changed in the Properties panel), and then create a customized style named, #HeadLine (remember to begin the name of the style with the # sign). Any AP elements with the name HeadLine (case is important), takes on the style of the #HeadLine CSS-P style.

Apply a Z-Index to an AP Element

1. Open the Web page that contains multiple AP elements you want to modify.

2. Open the Properties panel.

3. Select one of the AP elements, and then enter a value of 1 into the Z-index box in the Properties panel.

4. Select another AP element, and then enter a value of 2 into the Z-index box in the Properties panel.

5. Drag one of the AP elements so that it overlaps the other AP element.

   The AP element with the higher Z-index is positioned on the top of the other AP element.

Did You Know?

The Z-index option works only when AP elements overlap. A single Web page can contain any number of AP elements. So long as the AP elements do not overlap, the Z-index is not utilized. However, when they overlap, the Z-index determines what AP element is on top of another.

Modifying CSS-P Properties

After you create a style, it's not locked in stone. For example, you might create a style using a particular font, and later change your mind. Or you might create a style using a color or background for the AP element, and later wish to change the style. Editing CSS-P styles is a snap in Dreamweaver, mainly because Adobe knows that sometimes you want to change your mind. The easiest way to change the properties of the style is through the CSS Styles panel, and that's exactly where we're headed. When you change a style, all elements currently assigned that style change to reflect the modifications.

Modify CSS-P Properties

1. Open the Web page that contains one or more styles you want to modify.

2. Open the CSS Styles panel.

3. Click the **All** button.

4. Select the style you want to modify.

5. Click the **Edit Style** button.

    TIMESAVER *Double-click the style you want to modify in the CSS Styles panel.*

6. Use the categories to change the following options:

    ◆ **Type.** Click the **Type** category to define basic font and type settings for a CSS style.

    ◆ **Background.** Click the **Background** category to define background settings for a CSS style.

    ◆ **Block.** Click the **Block** category to define spacing and alignment settings for tags and attributes.

    ◆ **Box.** Click the **Box** category to define settings for tags and attributes that control the placement of elements on the page.

- ◆ **Border.** Click the **Border** category to define settings, such as width, color, and style, for the borders around elements.

- ◆ **List.** Click the **List** category to modify list settings, such as bullet size and type, for list tags.

- ◆ **Positioning.** Click the **Positioning** category to modify the tag or block of selected text into a new AP element using the default tag for defining AP elements as set in the AP Elements preferences.

- ◆ **Extensions.** Click the **Extensions** category to modify filters, page break, and pointer options, most of which aren't supported in any browser or are supported only in Internet Explorer 4.0 and above.

7 Click **OK** to save the changes, or click **Apply** to view how the changes impact the style before saving.

Did You Know?

It's important to preview AP element positioning. Dreamweaver only previews relative positioning when you're working with a nested AP element or have not set any top or left attributes. Therefore, always preview your pages to visually verify that the positioning is accurate.

Working with AP Elements

After you create the AP elements you want, you can use the AP Elements panel and other commands to manage and work with AP elements. You can change the stacking order and place one AP element in front or behind another, hide some AP elements while showing others, move and align AP elements across the screen, and resize them individually or together.

Work with AP Elements in the AP Elements Panel

 Open the Web page that contains one or more AP elements you want to modify.

② Click the **Window** menu, and then click **AP Elements** to display the AP Elements panel.

③ Use the AP Elements panel to change the following options:

◆ **Show or Hide.** Click the Eye icon column to show (open eye) and hide (closed eye) elements.

TIMESAVER *Click the header Eye icon at the top of the column to show or hide all the elements.*

◆ **Stacking Order.** Drag an element up or down in the list. A line appears as you drag to indicate the position.

Show or hide

Stacking order

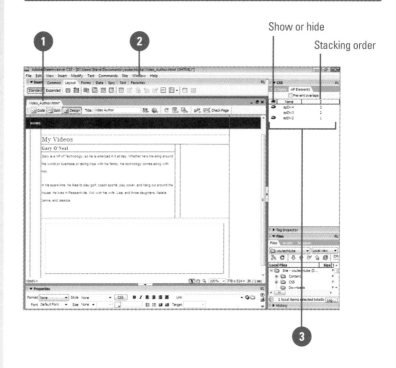

Move, Resize, and Arrange AP Elements

1 Open the Web page that contains one or more AP elements you want to modify.

2 Select the AP element you want.

3 Use the AP Elements panel to change the following options:

◆ **Move.** Drag the AP element handle (tab in the upper-left corner) or the edge of the AP element.

TIMESAVER *Use the arrow keys to move an AP element one pixel at a time.*

◆ **Resize.** Drag one of the selection handles or type values for width (W) and height (H) in the Properties panel.

TIMESAVER *Use Ctrl (Win) or Option (Mac) and the arrow keys to resize an AP element one pixel at a time. Use Shift+Ctrl (Win) or Shift+Option (Mac) and the arrow keys to resize by the grid snapping increment.*

◆ **Make Same Width or Height.** Select two or more AP elements, click the **Modify** menu, point to **Arrange**, and then click **Make Same Width** or **Make Same Height**.

◆ **Align.** Select two or more AP elements, click the **Modify** menu, point to **Arrange**, and then select an alignment option. All the AP elements align themselves to the last selected AP element.

◆ **Stacking Order.** Click the **Modify** menu, point to **Arrange**, and then **Bring To Front** or **Send To Back**.

Creating a Rollover Using AP Elements

AP Elements have several unique properties that let you design way beyond the static text and graphic Web pages of the past. You can show and hide AP elements to create effects. For example, you can create a drop-down menu, or you can display the larger version of an image when you point, or rollover, the small thumbnail version. In this example, Dreamweaver shows or hides the AP elements with the different images.

Create a Show/Hide Rollover

1. Create a new Web page.

2. Click the **Layout** tab on the Insert bar.

3. Click the **Draw AP Div** button, and then create two AP elements.

   ◆ An AP element 60 by 60 pixels, which contains a small thumbnail graphic. Name the AP element in the Properties panel, Thumb.

   ◆ An AP element 300 by 300 pixels, which contains the larger image. Name this AP element, Main.

4. Move the Thumb AP element to the left in the document window, and then move the Main AP element to the right.

5. Drag an image to the Thumb AP element, and an image to the Main AP element (the images should have the same width and height as the AP elements).

6. Open the Properties panel.

7. Select the **Main** AP element and change the Visibility of the AP element to **Hidden**.

8. Click the **Window** menu, and then click **Behaviors** to display the Behaviors panel.

9. Select the Thumb AP element.

10 Click the **Add Behavior** button, and then click **Show-Hide Elements**.

11 Select div "Main" from the available elements.

12 Click the **Show** button.

13 Click **OK**.

14 Click the **Event** list arrow, and then click **onMouseOver**.

15 Click the **Add Behavior** button, and then click **Show-Hide Elements**.

16 Select div "Main" from the available elements.

17 Click the **Hide** button.

18 Click **OK**.

19 Click the **Event** list arrow, and then click **onMouseOut**.

20 Click the **File** menu, point to **Preview In Browser**, and then select a browser.

When the Web page displays, rolling over the smaller thumbnail of the image causes the larger image to display. When you roll out of the thumbnail AP element, the larger image disappears... like magic.

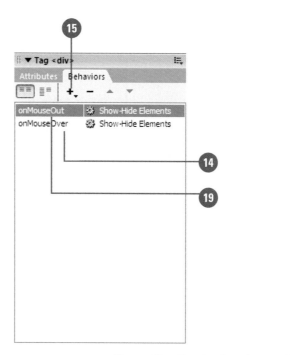

Converting AP Elements to Tables

While the advantage to designing with AP elements is the greater flexibility it affords, one of the greatest disadvantages of using AP elements is that they are viewable in only the most recent generation of browsers. Dreamweaver enables you to get the best of both worlds by making it possible for you to use AP elements to design complex page layouts, and then to transform those AP elements into tables that can be viewed in earlier browsers. For example, you might need to convert your AP elements to tables if you need to support browsers before version 4.0. Nevertheless, Dreamweaver's capability to convert AP elements to tables enables you to create complex layouts with ease. Designing this way has some limitations—you can't, for example, overlap AP element items on top of one another. If you have any overlapping AP elements within the document, Dreamweaver does its best to reposition the AP elements side by side. However, it's best if you make those corrections manually before performing the conversion. In addition, instead of using tables or Layout mode to create a document, some Web designers prefer to work with AP elements. If you need to convert a table back to AP elements, you can do it in Dreamweaver.

Convert AP Elements to a Table

1. Open the Web page that contains AP elements you want to convert to a table.

   ◆ Make sure you don't have any overlapping AP elements.

2. Click the **Modify** menu, point to **Convert**, and then select **AP Divs To Tables**.

3. Select from the following table layout options:

   ◆ **Most Accurate.** Attempts to convert the AP element document as close to the original as possible.

   ◆ **Smallest.** Choose to collapse smaller than a user-defined size.

   ◆ **Use Transparent GIFs.** Select this option to allow the use of transparent GIF files in empty cells.

   ◆ **Center On Page.** Select this option to center the table on the active Web page.

④ Select from the following layout tools options:

◆ **Prevent Overlaps.** Select to prevent cells from overlapping.

◆ **Show AP Elements Panel.** Select to show the AP Elements panel (displays when you click the OK button).

◆ **Show Grid.** Select to display a grid in the document window.

◆ **Snap To Grid.** Select to force the newly created table to snap to the existing grid.

⑤ Click **OK**.

Convert Table to AP Elements

① Open the Web page that contains a table you want to convert to AP elements.

② Click the **Modify** menu, point to **Convert**, and then click **Tables To AP Divs**.

③ Select from the following table layout options:

◆ **Prevent Overlaps.** Select to prevent AP elements from overlapping.

◆ **Show AP Elements Panel.** Select to show the AP Elements panel (displays when you click the OK button).

◆ **Show Grid.** Select to display a grid in the document window.

◆ **Snap To Grid.** Select to force the newly created table to snap to the existing grid.

④ Click **OK**.

Animating AP Elements Using the Timeline

A timeline is a visual representation of frames in an animation. A timeline in Dreamweaver is similar to the timeline in Flash. You can use the timeline to animate AP elements along a path. The process is similar to Flash. The timeline consists of frames, keyframes, Animation bar, Behaviors and Animation channels, playback head, playback controls (Rewind, Back, Play, AutoPlay, and Loop), and frame numbers. You can create an animation by inserting keyframes at animation points or dragging a path. If you want to create a complex animation, recording the path is easier. However, if you want more control, using keyframes is the way to go.

Animate an AP Element Using the Timeline

1. Open the Web page that contains AP elements you want to animate.

2. Click the **Window** menu, and then click **Timelines** to display the Timelines panel.

   TIMESAVER *Press Alt+F9 (Win) or Option+F9 (Mac) to open the Timelines panel.*

3. Select the AP element you want to animate.

4. Click the **Modify** menu, point to **Timeline**, and then click **Add Object To Timeline**.

   TIMESAVER *Drag the selected AP element into the Timelines panel.*

5. Click the keyframe marker at the end of the bar.

6. Move the AP element on the page to where you want the animation to end.

   A line appears showing the path of the animation in the Document window.

7. To move in a curve, select it in the animation bar and Ctrl-click (Win) or ⌘-click (Mac) a frame in the middle to add a keyframe. Repeat this step to add more keyframes.

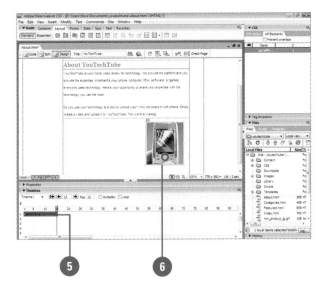

Record an AP Element Animation

1 Open the Web page that contains AP elements you want to animate.

2 Select the AP element, and then move it to where you want the animation to start.

3 Click the **Modify** menu, point to **Timeline**, and then click **Record Path Of AP Element**.

4 Drag the AP element on the screen to create an animation path.

5 Release the mouse at the point where you want the animation to stop.

Dreamweaver displays the animation bar in the timeline and adds the needed keyframes.

Did You Know?

You can play the animation using the playback controls. The timeline includes playback controls, like a DVD player, you can use to rewind and play an animation. Besides the rewind and play buttons, the playback controls also include the Back button, and the AutoPlay and Loop check boxes. The Back button moves the playback head one frame to the right. The AutoPlay check box makes the timeline automatically play when the page loads in a browser. The Loop check box makes the timeline loop indefinitely when the page loads and plays in a browser.

Creating Frames

11

Introduction

When it comes to Web design, frames have been around for quite a long time. In that time they have constantly fallen in and out of favor. Some Web designers can't live without them, and some designers would never in a million years use them. However, whether you love them or dislike them, frames are here to stay... at least for today.

Frames are an interesting way to design a Web document. Think of a window with separate panes of glass. Now, think of that window as a Web page, and each one of those separate panes of glass as a separate HTML document, and you've got a pretty good visualization of a Web page containing frames. For example, you can have a two-frame page with one frame containing the navigation for the site, and the other frame the contents. When you click on a link in the navigation frame, the content frame displays another HTML document, and the frame containing the navigation never changes.

There's a certain beauty in being able to change one area of a Web page, and leave another area static. Good Web designers with a good sense of how to utilize frame technology can create some pretty awesome Web sites.

A framed document is composed of a frameset page (called so because it uses the <frameset> tag), and two or more HTML documents. When the frameset page loads on the visitor's browser, it calls and loads the HTML documents, and displays the page.

Dreamweaver makes the coding and managing of frames easy with a point-and-click interface. You control the commands for modifying the properties of the overall frames, and each individual frame. This chapter will give you the essentials of creating frames, and information for inserting and modifying frames and framesets, as well as how you might apply them in your own Web designs.

Introducing Frames

Frame documents use a <frameset>... </frameset> tag set to create documents in multiple views. The multiple view nature of frame documents lets designers keep certain information visible, while other windows within the frame are scrolled or replaced. For example, within the same window, one frame might display a static banner, a second a navigation menu, and a third the main document that can be scrolled through or replaced by navigating in the second frame.

If you were to design a Frame page directly in HTML, it might look something like this:

```
<!DOCTYPE HTML PUBLIC "-//W3C//DTD HTML 4.01
Frameset//EN"
   "http://www.w3.org/TR/html4/frameset.dtd">
<html>
<head>
<title>A frameset </title>
</head>
<frameset cols="20%, 80%">
  < frameset rows="100, 200">
      <frame src="doc1.html">
      < frame src="doc2.gif">
  </ frameset >
  < frame src="doc3.html">
</ frameset >
</html>
```

Image

Frames divide a browser window into two or more document windows, each displaying a different document, or a different part of the same document. Frames in an HTML document cause a web page to look as if it's divided into multiple, scrollable regions. Each separate frame has a distinct name, which the frameset uses to load specific HTML documents.

Frames in HTML documents are created and controlled through three distinct element types: FRAMESET, FRAME and NOFRAMES.

The Frameset Element

A frameset divides the browser window into two or more rectangular regions. For example the following HTML code describes a basic frameset:

```
<frameset cols="30%,30%,40%">
```

This code describes a frame set divided vertically into three regions, and each region is a percentage of the width of the browser window (30%, 30%, and 40%). Since the rows attribute was not used this frameset does not include and rows.

The Frame Element

The Frame element defines a single frame in a frameset, and can include up to seven attributes: src, name, frameborder, marginwidth, marginheight, scrolling, and noresize. Since the frame tag is not defined as a container it has no matching end tag. The following is an example of a frame element:

```
<html>

<frameset rows="20%,80%">

        <frame src="http://www.power.com/">

        <frameset cols="60%,40%">

                <frame
src="http://www.andy.com/">

                <frame
src="http://www.steve.com/">

        </frameset>

</frameset>

</html>
```

The <noframes> Tag

The noframe element contains content that should only be rendered when frames are not displayed. Noframe is typically used in a Frameset document to provide alternate content for browsers that do not support frames or have frames disabled. The following is an example of the noframes tag.

```
<noframes>

    <p>The Frameset contains:

    <ul>

        <li><A href="contents_of_frame1.html">content_1</A>

        <li><img src="image.gif">

        <li><A href="noframes.html">Some other neat contents</A>

        </ul>

    </noframes>
```

Creating a New Frame

Most of the framesets on the Web today use two or three frames. For example, a common setup is to have one narrow frame spanning the top of the page to hold a banner and some site navigation; a lower-left frame to hold a table of contents or additional navigation; and a large lower-right frame to hold the content of the site. Or it can be as simple as two frames: one small frame for navigation, and a larger frame for the main body of information. You can create a new document with frames using samples from the New Document dialog box or add frames to an existing document using the Frames button or dragging a frame border. After you create a frameset, you can enter text, images, and other content in each of the frames, as you would for any normal HTML document, or you can instruct the frame to load a previously created HTML document.

Create a Frameset from a Sample

1. Click the **File** menu, and then click **New**.

2. Click the **Page from Sample** category.

3. Click **Frameset** in Sample Folder options.

4. Select a Sample Page.

    TIMESAVER *Click the Get more content link to add more templates to the New Document dialog box.*

5. Click **Create**.

    The Frame Tag Accessibility Attributes dialog box opens.

6. Click the **Frame** popup, select a frame, and then enter a name (one word, start with a letter, and case-sensitive) for each frame in the document.

7. Click **OK**.

Did You Know?

You can use a grid to help layout a frame document. Click the View menu, point to Grid, and then click Show Grid to show the grid.

Insert a Frameset

1. Create a new HTML document, or open an existing one.

2. Click the **Layout** tab on the Insert bar.

3. Click the **Frames** button, and select a frameset from the available options (in this example, Left Frame).

   The Frame Tag Accessibility Attributes dialog box opens.

6. Click the **Frame** popup, select a frame, and then enter a name (one word, start with a letter, and case-sensitive) for each frame in the document.

7. Click **OK**.

Create a Frameset with Click and Drag

1. Create a new HTML document, or open an existing one.

2. Click the **View** menu, point to **Visual Aids**, and then click **Frame Borders**.

   Dreamweaver creates a heavy outline around the edges of the document window.

3. Position the cursor over one of the borders until it turns into a double-headed arrow, and then drag to create a new frame.

4. Continue dragging from the vertical or horizontal border until you have the frames you want.

   TIMESAVER *Hold down Alt (Win) or Option (Mac) while you drag an existing frame border to create a new frame instead instead of moving it.*

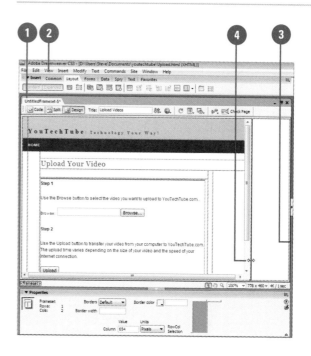

Opening a Web Page in a Frame

After you create a frame, you can specify the content you want to appear in it. You can insert new content in a frame the same way you insert other content, such as text or images, into Web page or open an existing HTML Web page in a frame. If you consistently use the same Web page in a frame, you can make the page the default document when the frameset appears in a browser.

Open an Existing Web Page in a Frame

1. Open the Web page with frames you want to modify, and then click to place the insertion point in the frame where you want to insert a Web page.

2. Click the **File** menu, and then click **Open in Frame**.

   TIMESAVER Press Ctrl+Shift+O (Win) or ⌘+Shift+O (Mac).

3. Navigate to the drive and folder location where you want to open the Web page.

4. Click the **Files of Type** list arrow (Win) or popup (Mac), and then select the type of file you want to open.

5. Select the page you want to open from the page list in the working folder, or type the URL of the page you want.

6. Click **OK**.

File opened in a frame

Providing Information for No Frame Support

If a browser doesn't support frames, you can provide information to visitors instead of leaving them hanging with no where to go. When a browser that doesn't support frames loads the frameset document, the browser displays the information you provide in a noframes tag. The Edit NoFrames Content command makes it easy to add the information you want without inserting HTML code. However, if you are comfortable entering code, you can certainly enter the information in the noframes tag.

Provide Information for Browsers with No Frame Support

1. Open the Web page with the frameset you want to modify.

2. Click the **Modify** menu, point to **Frameset**, and then click **Edit NoFrames Content**.

   The Design view clears, and the words "NoFrames Content" appears at the top of the Document window.

3. Type the information you want visitors to see when their browser's don't support frames.

   ◆ You can also click the **Window** menu, click **Code Inspector**, and the type the HTML code for the text you want to display in the body tags inside the noframes tags.

4. Click the **Modify** menu, point to **Frameset**, and then click **Edit NoFrames Content**.

   The normal view of the frameset document appears.

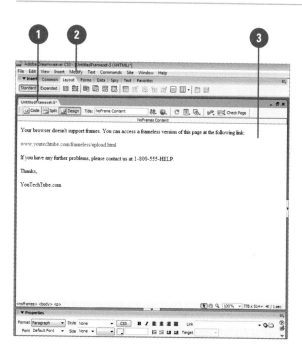

Selecting Frames and Framesets

Before you can make any changes to a frame or frameset, you need to select it first. You can select a frame or frameset directly in the Document window, by using keyboard shortcuts, or by using the Frames panel. The Frames panel shows you the frames within a frameset. A frameset appears with a thick border and each frame appears with a thin gray link along with a frame name, which makes them easier to view and select. When a frame is selected in the Document window, the frame border appears outlined with a dotted line. When a frameset is selected, all the frame borders appear with a light dotted line.

Select Frames and Framesets

◆ **Frames Panel**. Click the **Window** menu, click **Frames** to display the Frames panel, and then use any of the following:

◆ **Frame**. Click the frame.

◆ **Frameset**. Click the border around the frameset.

◆ **Document Window**. Display the Web page with frames in Design view, and then use any of the following:

◆ **Frame**. Alt-click (Win) or Option-Shift-click in a frame.

◆ **Frameset**. Click one of the frameset's internal borders.

◆ **Different Frames or Framesets**. Use the Arrow keys to select frames or framesets.

◆ **Next or Previous**. Press Alt+Left Arrow or Alt+Right Arrow (Win) or ⌘+Left Arrow or ⌘+Right Arrow (Mac).

◆ **Parent Frameset**. Press Alt+Up Arrow (Win) or ⌘+Up Arrow (Mac).

◆ **First Child Frame or Current Frameset**. Press Alt+Down Arrow (Win) or ⌘+Down Arrow (Mac).

Selected frame

272

Adding Frameset Information

A frameset document consists of separate frames. As a matter of fact, each one of the frames is simply a small HTML document. Frames can contain any normal HTML information, including text, tables, images, multimedia, objects, and even nested frames. When you create a Frameset document, you're actually creating several separate documents. You have the frameset HTML document, and a separate HTML document for each of the frames. For example, if you create a frameset with two frames, you're actually saving three separate documents: one for the frameset and one for each of the frames within the document.

Add Frameset Information

1. Create a new Web page with a frameset, or open an existing one.

2. Click in a frame where you want to add some information.

3. Add or insert the text and graphics you want until the frames are filled with the specified information (in this example, a graphic).

Drag graphic from Files panel

Saving a Frameset

When you create a frameset with two frames, you're actually saving three separate documents: one for the frameset and one for each of the frames within the document. You can save the frameset and each document in a frame individually or you can save them all at once. Before you can preview a frameset in a browser, you need to save the frameset and all frame document first. Once the frame documents have been saved, they can be opened independently of the frameset and modified just like regular HTML documents; any changes to the page will be reflected when it's reopened in the frameset. When you reopen the frameset document, it locates and reopens the associated pages and place them into the proper frames.

Save a Frameset as a New File

1. Select the frameset you want to save.

2. Click the **File** menu, and then click **Save Frameset As**.

    TIMESAVER Press Ctrl+Shift+S (Win) or ⌘+Shift+S (Mac).

    NOTE Dreamweaver prompts you to save your document in the active site folder (strongly recommended).

3. Navigate to the location where you want to save the frame document.

4. Enter a name for the frameset document.

5. Click **Save**.

Did You Know?

You can save the frameset and all frame documents at the same time. Click the File menu, and then click Save All.

Save a Frame as a New File

1. Click in the frame you want to save.

2. Click the **File** menu, and then select **Save Frame As**.

    TIMESAVER *Press Ctrl+Shift+S (Win) or* ⌘*+Shift+S.*

    NOTE *Dreamweaver prompts you to save your document in the active site folder (strongly recommended).*

3. Navigate to the location where you want to save the frame document.

4. Enter a name for the new frame document.

5. Click **Save**.

Modifying Frames

Once a frameset is created its possible, and quite likely that you will want to modify the dimensions of the frames to fit a specific design need. Remember that the frame within a frameset functions as a container for a specific HTML document. If this document is not set up correctly, you may experience problems with unwanted reformatting of the information when it displays in the browser window. Therefore, it's important to modify the frames to give your document the best look and feel for the visitor.

Resize a Frame

1. Open the Web page with the frameset you want to modify.

2. To display visual frame borders, click the **View** menu, point to **Visual Aids**, and then click **Frame Borders**.

3. Mouse over one of the borders until your cursor turns into a double-headed arrow.

4. Drag a frame border to modify its position and size.

Add a Frame

1. Open the Web page with the frameset you want to modify.

2. To display visual frame borders, click the **View** menu, point to **Visual Aids**, and then click **Frame Borders**.

3. Holding down Alt (Win) or Option (Mac) and drag one of the borders.

4. Release you mouse to add the new frame to the document.

Delete a Frame

1. Open the Web page with the frame you want to modify.

2. To display visual frame borders, click the **View** menu, point to **Visual Aids**, and then click **Frame Borders**.

3. Click the frame border and drag it into the border of the enclosing or parent frame.

   NOTE If no parent frame is present, drag the frame border to the edge of the page.

4. Release the mouse and the frame is removed.

   If the deleted frame contains unsaved content, Dreamweaver asks if you want to save the file before closing it.

Changing Frame Properties

As mentioned before, frameset documents are simply individual HTML documents, with all the rights and privileges of any other HTML document. They can have any content; including tables and layers, and they have the same properties of any other HTML document, such as: backgrounds, margins, headings, etc. You can change the properties of a HTML document destined to be displayed within a frameset in one of two ways. The first is to open the document directly in Dreamweaver, make any changes, and then save the document. When it's opened within the frameset, the changes to the properties will be displayed as ordered by you. The second way is to change their properties while viewing the document within the frameset (recommended). Since the procedure is basically the same, we'll examine the changing of page properties while viewing the document in the frameset.

Change Page Properties for a Frame Document

1. Open the Web page with the frameset you want to modify.

2. Right-click the HTML frame document that you want to modify, and then click **Page Properties**.

3. Select from the following Page Properties options:

   ◆ **Appearance.** Select to change the overall appearance of the page; including background, text and margins.

   ◆ **Links.** Select to change linking information; link colors and fonts and underlining.

   ◆ **Headings.** Select to modify the heading font, color and size.

   ◆ **Title/Encoding.** Select to modify the title and encoding of the page (this information is used by browsers to help properly display the page).

   ◆ **Tracing Image.** Select to add or modify a tracing image.

4. Click **OK**.

Change Frame Properties

1 Open the Web page with the frameset you want to modify.

2 Select the frame you want to modify in the Frames panel or Alt-click (Win) or Shift-Option-click (Mac) the frame in Design view.

3 Open the Properties panel.

4 Select from the following Page Properties options:

- **Frame Name.** Enter the name you want used by a link's target attribute or by a script to refer to a frame. A frame name must start with a letter and it's case-sensitive.

- **Scr.** Specifies the source document to display in the frame.

- **Scroll.** Click to select a scroll display option: No (hide), Yes (show), Auto (only when needed), or Default (dictated by browser).

- **No Resize.** Select to prevent visitors from dragging frame borders in a browser.

- **Borders.** Click to select a border display option: No (hide), Yes (show), or Default (dictated by browser).

- **Border Color.** Click to select a color for the frame borders.

- **Margin Width.** Specify the width in pixels of the left and right margins.

- **Margin Height.** Specify the height in pixels of the top and bottom margins.

Changing Frameset Properties

In addition to setting properties for the individual frames and frame documents, you can also set properties for the frameset. After you select the frameset, you can use the Properties panel to view and set frameset properties. The available options allow you to change border and frame sizes. You can show or hide borders, change border width and color, and set the frame sizes for rows and columns of the frameset. The RowCol Selection area in the Properties panel provides tabs on the left side and top to select a frame. After you select a frame, you can set the frame height and width you want in the Value box and how much space the browser allocates to each frame in the Units popup. You can set these options for each frame you select. In the Document window, you can also change the frameset title.

Modify Frameset Border Properties

1. Open the Web page with the frameset you want to modify.

2. Click the **View** menu, point to **Visual Aids**, and then click **Frame Borders** to display visual borders.

3. Open the Properties panel, and then expand it.

4. Click one of the frame borders to select the frameset.

5. Modify the frames using the options in the Properties panel:

   ◆ **Border Window.** Click to select the specific frame (row/column) you want to modify.

   ◆ **Borders.** Click to select border displays option you want: No (hide border), Yes (show border), or Default (dictated by browser).

   ◆ **Border Width.** Enter a value (in pixels) for the width of the borders.

   ◆ **Border Color.** Click to select a color for the borders.

280

Modify Frameset Size Properties

1. Open the Web page with the frameset you want to modify.

2. Click the **View** menu, point to **Visual Aids**, and then click **Frame Borders** to display visual borders.

3. Open the Properties panel, and then expand it.

4. Click one of the frame borders to select the frameset.

5. Click a tab on the left side or top of the Row/Col Selection area to select the frame you want to set the Value and Units below.

6. Enter a value to determine the height or width of the frame.

7. Click the **Units** popup, and then select the measurement units for the Row/Column value you want:

   ◆ **Pixels.** Sets the size of the column or row to an absolute value. Typically used with a left-side frame.

   ◆ **Percent.** Sets the column or row to be a percentage the total width or height of its frameset.

   ◆ **Relative.** Allocates the available space after Pixels to the selected column or row. Typically used with a right-side frame.

Did You Know?

You can set the title for a frameset page. Open the page, select the frameset in Design view, and then type a name for the frameset in the Title box on the Document toolbar. When a visitor opens the frameset page in a browser, the title appears in the browser's title bar.

Targeting Links

Thus far, this chapter has dealt with the creation of frameset documents, and the adding and saving of Web data on the individual HTML pages. However, the real power of frames is their ability to load new pages into selected frames, based on an available link. For example, you could be a photographer that wants people to see your images (and hopefully buy them). You create a two-framed Web document that has links to your images on the left. When you click on a link, the frame on the right changes to display a large example of your photographic talent. To use a link in one frame to open a document in another frame, you need to set a target for the link. The target instructs the browser into which frame to place the new document. When a visitor clicks the link, the specified content opens in the specified frame.

Create a Targeted Link

1 Open the Web page with the frameset you want to create a targeted link.

2 Select the object or text to be converted into a targeted link.

3 Open the Properties panel.

4 Create the link to the new document using one of the following methods:

◆ Click the **folder** icon, and then select the **link file**.

◆ Drag the **Point to File** icon to the Files panel to select the link file.

5 Click the **Target** button, and then select the target frame name (at the bottom of the list), or select from the following options.

◆ **_blank.** Opens the linked document in a new browser window, leaving the current window untouched.

◆ **_parent.** Opens the linked document in the parent frameset of the frame the link appears in, replacing the entire frameset.

- ◆ **_self.** Opens the link in the current frame, replacing the content in that frame.

- ◆ **_top.** Opens the linked document in the current browser window, replacing all frames.

IMPORTANT *Frame names appear when you're editing the document within a frameset. When you edit a document in its own window, frame names do not appear in the Target popup menu. If you're editing a document outside of the frameset, you can type the target frame's name in the Target text box.*

6 Click the **File** menu, point to **Preview In Browser**, and then select a browser of your choice to test the document.

Preview in a browser; click to test link

For Example

Inserting a Navigation Bar

Using a frameset document to hold a navigation bar in one frame, and then change the content in another frame is probably one of the most common reasons for the creation of a frame document. The advantage is obvious: when the visitor clicks on a link, they never lose site of the navigation system, because it's locked safely away in its own frame. In this example, we'll use a previously created navigational bar, and insert it into a two-framed frameset document. The top frame is named, navigation, and the bottom frame is named, content. When the links are clicked the navigation frame, the content frame will change and load the new HTML documents.

Creating Quick and Easy Frame Links

This method is great for those Web sites that contain a lot of links to a lot of boring text documents. To make this process work, the name of the HTML document should be the name you want for the link; for example, formatting.html, or frame_help.html. The documents are the standard HTML type: graphics, text… the whole nine yards. You just want to create a simple, almost file folder kind of page, where a visitor clicks on a link, and it loads the appropriate page in another frame.

Create Quick and Easy Frame Links

1. Create a frameset document with two frames: one for the links, and one for the documents. Name them links and documents.

2. Open the Files panel and display all the HTML documents that you want to use as links.

3. Drag and drop one of the files from the Files panel into the links frame (it appears as an underlined link).

    NOTE *If the original name of the HTML document is document_1.html, the linked text will be document_1, without the HTML extension.*

4. Select the linked text.

5. Open the Properties panel, click the **Target** popup, and then select the content frame name as the target for this file.

6. Repeat steps 3-5 until you have all your documents displayed as links.

7. Click the **File** menu, point to **Preview In Browser**, and then select a browser of your choice to test the document.

    NOTE *If you don't like the file name as the link name, you can always select the file name in the links frames and change it. The change in name will not affect the link to the file.*

Links frame

Working with Flash and Other Multimedia

12

Introduction

It almost seems that every page you visit on the Web uses Flash or other multimedia in some way or another. Whether it's an intro movie, or animated buttons, it's everywhere. However, if you don't have applications such as Flash, does that mean you can't create multimedia? If you have Dreamweaver it's a snap to quickly add Flash and other multimedia to your Web pages.

For example, Adobe Dreamweaver comes with two handy tools: Flash Text and Flash Buttons, both of which allow you to add Flash to your pages very easily. As you might expect from Adobe, the addition of Flash Text and Buttons to your Web page is very easy.

In addition to Flash elements such as text and buttons, Dreamweaver lets you add user-defined Flash movies, Java Applets (Java programs used on Web pages to operate animation, calculators, and other tasks), and ActiveX Controls (can be used to add specialized functionality, such as animation, pop-up menus, or Web pages). Most multimedia is controlled by specific plug-ins. For example, the Flash plug-in allows you to play flash movies, just as the QuickTime plug-in allows you to play QuickTime movies. plug-ins are a part of the open application architecture of Web browsers. Without the ability to use plug-ins, the only way you would be able to use some of the current multimedia would be if the players were actually coded into the browsers, which would be unreasonable and not very practical.

This chapter will introduce you to multimedia, and how to incorporate it into your Web design. As with anything in design, the important thing is that the multimedia support your message, and not just used because you can.

Introducing Flash File Types

Adobe Flash allows you to create a variety of file types—FLA, SWF, SWT, SWC, and FLV—for different purposes. The Flash file (.fla) is the source file format for the Adobe Flash program. This file format cannot be opened in Dreamweaver; you can only open this file format in Flash. You use the source Flash file (.fla) to create the other Flash file formats.

You can insert the following Flash file formats into a Web page in Dreamweaver:

- **Flash SWF (.swf).** This file format creates a compressed movie of the Flash (.fla) file.

- **Flash Template (.swt).** This file format creates a SWF file you can customize with your own text or links, such as a Flash button or Flash text.

- **Flash element file (.swc).** This file format creates a SWF file you can create Rich Internet applications with customizable parameters.

- **Flash Video file (.flv).** This file format creates a video file with audio and video encoding you can play in the Flash Player.

If you have Adobe FlashPaper 2 or later, you can convert printable files into Flash documents or Adobe PDF files, which you can insert into Dreamweaver.

You don't need to have Adobe Flash installed on your computer to insert these file formats into pages in Dreamweaver. However, when you do have Adobe Flash installed on your computer, you can make changes to the source Flash files (.fla), and then create the file format you want to use in Dreamweaver.

You can use the Media button on the Common tab on the Insert bar, or use the Media submenu on the Insert menu to add different Flash file types into a page in Dreamweaver.

Inserting a Flash or Shockwave Movie

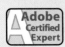

DW 2.13, 3.15

Flash can create all types of multimedia content. From a lead-in page (called a splash screen), to animated banners, to cool-looking, as well as functional menus, Flash is leading the way in Web based multimedia content. Flash utilizes resolution independent vector graphics, streaming audio, and even raster images to create fast-loading Web content. Flash is so popular that according to the World Wide Web Consortium, over 90 percent of people surfing the Web have browsers that can view Flash content. And since version 4, Flash has its own scripting language to help designers take designs into the Stratosphere. Dreamweaver does not create Flash movies; however, it makes it very easy to add them to your Web pages. Once inserted, the Properties panel will give you access to controls that instruct the browser exactly what to do when the movie loads.

Insert and Preview a Flash or Shockwave Movie

1. Open the Web page you want to insert a movie.

2. Click to place the insertion point where you want the movie.

3. Insert the movie using one of the following options:

   ◆ Click the **Common** tab on the Insert bar, click the **Media** arrow button, and then click **Flash**.

   ◆ Click the **Insert** menu, point to **Media**, and then click **Flash**.

4. Navigate to the location with the Flash file (extension .swf), and then select it.

5. Click **OK**.

6. Enter the accessibility attributes (title, access key, and tab index) you want.

7. Click **OK**.

8. To view the Flash content, click the Flash placeholder icon, and then click the **Play** button in the Properties panel to begin the preview. Click **Stop** to end the preview.

Changing Flash or Shockwave Movie Properties

After you insert a Flash or Shockwave movie into your page in Dreamweaver, you can use the Properties panel to set or change movie properties. You can use the Properties panel to adjust the movie size and scale, set loop and autoplay options, show or hide a border, align the movie on the page, and specify a background color for the movie area. If you have the Flash program installed on your computer, you can even edit the source Flash file (.fla) associated with the SWF file directly from the Properties panel.

Change Flash Movie Properties

1 Open the Web page with the movie you want to change properties.

2 Select the Flash SWF file or a Shockwave movie.

3 Click the **Window** menu, and then click **Properties** to display the Properties panel.

4 Click the expander arrow in the lower-right corner of the Properties panel to view all Flash options.

5 Set any of the following options to control a Flash or Shockwave movie:

◆ **Name.** Enter a name to identify the movie for scripting.

◆ **W and H.** Enter the width and height of the movie (in pixels).

◆ **File.** Enter the path to the Flash or Shockwave file. Or click the folder icon to browse to a file, or type a path.

◆ **Src.** Specifies the path to a Flash source document (FLA) (when Dreamweaver and Flash are both installed on your computer).

◆ **Edit.** Click to locate and update a FLA file; the option is grayed out if the Flash program is not installed on your computer.

◆ **Reset Size.** Click to return the selected movie to its original size.

- **Loop.** Select to make the movie play continuously.

- **Autoplay.** Select to automatically play the movie when the page loads.

- **V Space and H Space.** Specify the number of pixels of white space above, below, and on both sides of the movie.

- **Quality.** Controls anti-aliasing during playback of the movie.

- **Scale.** Controls how the movie fits into the dimensions set in the width and height text boxes.

- **No Border.** Select to fit the movie into the set dimensions so that no borders show and maintains the original aspect ratio.

- **Exact Fit.** Select to scale the movie to the set dimensions, regardless of the aspect ratio.

- **Align.** Controls how the movie is aligned on the page.

- **Bg.** Defines a background color for the movie area.

- **Parameters.** Opens a dialog box for entering additional parameters to pass to the movie.

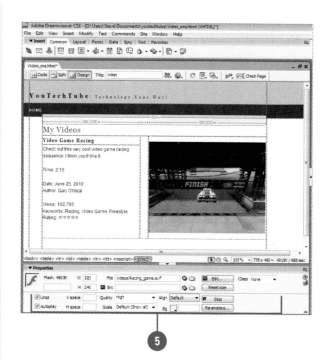

Did You Know?

You can preview all Flash content in a page. Press Ctrl+Alt+Shift+P (Win) or Shift+Option+⌘+P (Mac) to set all Flash objects and SWF files to play.

Creating a Flash Button

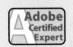

DW 3.15

Flash is one of those applications that started with humble beginnings, and then wound up changing much of how we view and interact with the Web. As a matter of fact, there are sites out there (for example, Coca Cola) that are all Flash sites. Flash is a dynamic application that lets you create everything from a simple set of animated buttons, to an interactive interface for an embedded video production. In this example, we're not even going to open Flash up, because Dreamweaver gives us the ability to create a series of predefined Flash buttons, and then load them directly into our Dreamweaver documents. It's important to know that you will not be able to see the button's animation effect in the display window of Dreamweaver; however, all you have to do is test the Web page by going to the File menu, and clicking the Preview In Browser option.

Insert and Create a Flash Button

1. Open the Web page you want to add a Flash button.

2. Click to place the insertion point where you want the Flash button.

3. Insert the Flash button using one of the following options:

   ◆ Click the **Common** tab on the Insert bar, click the **Media** arrow button, and then click **Flash Button**.

   ◆ Click the **Insert** menu, point to **Media**, and then click **Flash Button**.

4. Design the Flash button using the following options:

   ◆ **Style.** Select a Flash button style from the available options (the sample box shows you the selected button).

   ◆ **Button Text.** Enter the text you want displayed on the button.

   ◆ **Font.** Click the **Font** button, and select the font for the text.

   ◆ **Size.** Enter a size for the button text.

   ◆ **Link.** Enter the link for the button, or click **Browse** to select the proper link.

- ◆ **Target.** Click the **Target** button, and then select from the following options:

    - ◆ **_blank.** Opens the linked document in a new window.

    - ◆ **_parent.** Loads the linked document in the parent of the active document.

    - ◆ **_self.** Loads the linked document in the same browser window (default).

    - ◆ **_top.** Loads the linked document in the topmost window.

- ◆ **Bg Color.** Click the **Bg** color box, and then select a background color.

- ◆ **Save As.** Enter a name for the new button (the name should end with the extension of .swf), or click **Browse** to select one.

5 Click **Apply** to preview the button in the Design window.

6 Click **OK**.

7 Enter the accessibility attributes (title, access key, and tab index) you want.

8 Click **OK**.

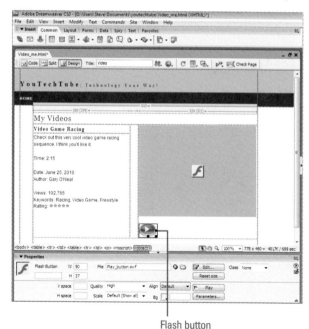

Flash button

Did You Know?

You can access more Flash button styles. In the Insert Flash Button dialog box, click the Get More Styles button. Dreamweaver opens the Adobe Exchange Web site, where you can find more buttons (and many other things).

Creating Flash Text

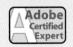 DW 3.15

Flash has more tricks up its sleeve than just adding a button or two, and Dreamweaver gives you access to all of these cool features. For example, you can add Flash text objects to a Web document. Flash text objects let you create and insert a Flash SWF file that contains just text. This allows you to create a small, vector-graphic movie with the designer fonts and text of your choice, and they will display exactly as you intended them. In addition, you can add something called a Flash Paper document. Flash Paper documents are documents designed in Flash; which means you will have to have the Flash application, or get a Flash Paper document from another designer. The advantage to Flash Paper documents is that they will maintain their formatting on any compliant browser. Finally, you can insert Flash video directly into your documents. Again, as with Flash Paper, you will first need to edit the video in Flash, and then save it as a Flash FLV file.

Insert a Flash Text Object

1. Open the Web page you want to add Flash text.

2. Click to place the insertion point where you want the Flash text object.

3. Insert the Flash Text Object using one of the following options:

   ◆ Click the **Common** tab on the Insert bar, click the **Media** arrow button, and then click **Flash Text**.

   ◆ Click the **Insert** menu, point to **Media**, and then click **Flash Text**.

4. Design the Flash text using the following options:

   ◆ Font. Click the **Font** button, and then select the font for the text.

   ◆ Size. Enter a size for the text.

   ◆ Color. Click the color box, and then select a color for the normal state of the text.

   ◆ Rollover color. Click the color box, and then select a color for the rollover state of the text.

   ◆ Text. Enter the text to be used for the Flash object.

- ◆ **Link.** Enter the link for the text, or click **Browse** to select the proper link.

- ◆ **Target.** Click the **Target** button, and then select from the following options:

  - ◆ **_blank.** Opens the linked document in a new window.

  - ◆ **_parent.** Loads the linked document in the parent of the active document.

  - ◆ **_self.** Loads the linked document in the same browser window (default).

  - ◆ **_top.** Loads the linked document in the topmost window.

- ◆ **Bg Color.** Click the Bg color box, and then select a background color.

- ◆ **Save As.** Enter a name for the new button (the name should end with the extension of .swf), or click **Browse** to select one.

5 Click **Apply** to preview the button in the Design window.

6 Click **OK.**

7 Enter the accessibility attributes (title, access key, and tab index) you want.

8 Click **OK.**

Flash text

Did You Know?

You can insert FlashPaper documents.
Click to place the insertion point, click the Insert menu, point to Media, click FlashPaper, enter or browse to select the file, click OK, enter accessibility information, and then click OK.

Inserting a Flash Video

DW 2.13, 3.15

When you create a Flash video (.flv) file using Adobe Flash, you insert the Flash video component in Dreamweaver. When you view the page in a browser, the component displays the Flash video and playback controls. You can deliver the Flash video in two delivery formats: Progressive Download Video or Streaming Video. **Progressive Download Video** downloads the FLV file to the visitor's computer and then plays it. The video starts to play before the download is complete to speed up the process. On the other hand, **streaming video** buffers the video on the Web server with Adobe Flash Media Server, and then plays it.

Insert a Flash Video

1. Open the Web page you want to insert a Flash video.

2. Click to place the insertion point where you want the Flash video.

3. Insert the Flash video using one of the following options:

   ◆ Click the **Common** tab on the Insert bar, click the **Media** arrow button, and then click **Flash Video**.

   ◆ Click the **Insert** menu, point to **Media**, and then click **Flash Video**.

4. Click the **Video Type** popup, and then click **Progressive Download Video** or **Streaming Video**.

5. Select from the following Flash video options:

   ◆ **URL (Progressive).** Specifies a relative or absolute path to the FLV file.

   ◆ **Server URI (Streaming).** Specifies the server name, program name, and instance name.

   ◆ **Stream Name (Streaming).** Specifies the name of the FLV file; .flv extension is optional.

   ◆ **Skin.** Click the **Skin** popup, and then select the appearance of the Flask Video component.

- ◆ **Width and Height.** Specifies the width and height of the FLV video (in pixels).

- ◆ **Constrain.** Select to maintain the same aspect ratio between the width and height.

- ◆ **Live Video Feed (Streaming).** Select to play the streaming live video content from the Flash Media Server.

- ◆ **AutoPlay.** Select to play the video when the page opens.

- ◆ **Auto Rewind.** Select to return the playback to the beginning.

- ◆ **Buffer Time (Streaming).** Specifies the time (in seconds) needed to buffer before the video starts to play.

- ◆ **Prompt Users To Download Flash Player If Necessary.** Select to insert code to detect the required Flash Player version and prompts the user to download the latest version.

- ◆ **Message.** Enter the message you want to display when a user needs to download the latest version of Flash Player.

6️⃣ Click **OK**.

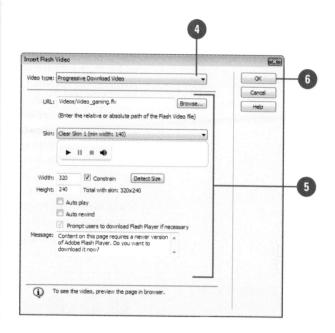

Did You Know?

You can remove the code that detects the Flash Player version. Click the Commands menu, and then click Remove Flash Video Detection.

You can delete the Flash Video component. Select the Flash Video component, and then press Delete.

You can edit the Flash Video component. Select the Flash Video component placeholder, open the Properties panel, and then make your changes.

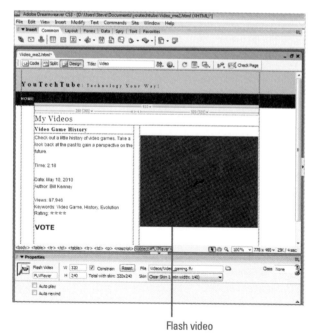

Flash video

Using Flash Elements

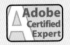 DW 3.15

Flash elements allow you to easily build Rich Internet Applications using pre-built elements. In Dreamweaver, you can insert Flash elements into your documents. Adobe is working hard to make your job a lot easier. A big part of this is to increase integration between Adobe applications: such as Dreamweaver and Flash. Flash elements are .swf files created in Flash, and are directly inserted and customized in a page you are creating with Dreamweaver. Inserting Flash into Dreamweaver is not new; however, you can now configure the Flash element directly within Dreamweaver using the Tag inspector, without the need to return to Flash to edit the source code. This improves workflow and reduces the time spent passing the elements back and forth between the Dreamweaver and Flash developer for simple edits. The Image Viewer (Dreamweaver's built-in Flash element) is a resizable application for loading and viewing a series of unprogressive JPEG or SWF images. You define a list of images, along with a link and caption for each image.

Insert the Image Viewer Flash Element

1. Open the Web page you want to insert the Flash element.

2. Click to place the insertion point where you want the Flash element.

3. Click the **Insert** menu, point to **Media**, and then click **Image Viewer**.

   NOTE *Web site visitors must have Flash Player 7 installed to see any Image Viewers in your pages.*

   The Save Flash Element dialog box opens.

4. Navigate to an appropriate location within your site.

   NOTE *Save the Flash element in the active Dreamweaver site.*

5. Enter a filename for the Flash element.

6. Click **OK**.

   Dreamweaver saves the Flash element, and inserts it into the page.

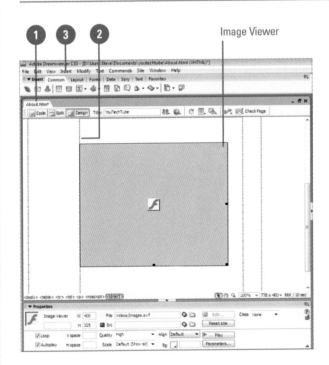

Image Viewer

Use the Image Viewer Flash Element

1. Open the Web page with the Image Viewer Flash element you want to play.

2. Select the Image Viewer placeholder.

3. Click the **Window** menu, and then click **Tag Inspector** to display the Tag Inspector panel.

4. Click the field next to imageURLs, and then click **Edit Array Values** icon.

5. Click the **Plus** (+) sign and click the folder icon to select images you want to use, or click the **Minus** (-) to remove images.

6. Click **OK**.

7. Click the **Play** button in the Properties panel to preview the Image Viewer.

8. Use the following Image Viewer controls to view images:

   ◆ Click the **Next** or **Previous** button to view sequential images.

   ◆ Enter a number in the text box to skip to a specific image.

   ◆ Click the **Play** button to view the images as a slide show; click the **Stop** button to stop the slide show format.

   ◆ Click the **Stop** button in the expanded Properties panel to stop playing the Image Viewer.

For Your Information

Downloading and Installing Flash Elements

In addition to the Flash elements already installed with Dreamweaver, you can also download and install additional elements using the Adobe Extension Manager. The Extension Manager is a stand-alone programs that comes with Dreamweaver that allows you to install and manage extensions in Adobe programs. You can find the latest Flash elements for Dreamweaver on the Adobe Exchange Web site. Click the Help menu, and then click Dreamweaver Exchange. For instructions to use the Adobe Extension Manager program, see "Using Adobe Extension Manager," on page 544.

Modifying Flash Elements

The Tag Inspector and the Properties panel allow you to view and edit a Flash element attributes. The Tag inspector enables you to view and edit every attribute associated with a given tag, on the other hand, the Properties panel shows common attributes.

Modify the Image Viewer Flash Element

① Open the Web page with the Image Viewer Flash element you want to modify.

② Select the Image Viewer placeholder.

③ Click the **Window** menu, and then click **Tag Inspector** to display the Tag Inspector panel.

④ Click in the field beside the image URLs parameter, and then click the **Edit Array Values** icon.

⑤ Select a value, and then click the **Minus** (-) button to remove images or click the **Plus** (+) button to add images.

⑥ Select a value, enter in the URL of the image file, or click the **Browse** button (folder icon) and select the file from the search list; use files that are located in the active site (Images can be non-progressive JPG or SWF files).

⑦ Click **OK**

⑧ Additional options in the Tag Inspector include:

 ◆ **BgColor.** Controls the Flash element background color.

 ◆ **FrameColor.** Controls the color of the border for the images.

 ◆ **FrameShow.** Select to display a frame around each image.

 ◆ **FrameThickness.** Controls the size in pixels for the border around each image.

- **CaptionColor.** Controls the color of the image captions.

- **CaptionFont.** Controls the font for the image captions.

- **CaptionSize.** Controls the point size of the image captions (point size measures in pixels).

- **ImageCaptions.** Contains the captions for each image specified in imageURLs. Captions can be used for some, all, or none of the images.

- **ImageLinks.** Contains a URL for each image specified in imageURLs.

- **ImageURLs.** Contains the location of the images to appear in the Image Viewer.

- **ImgLinkTarget.** Indicates the browser window in which to load the URLs.

- **ShowControls.** Displays the Image Viewer controls.

- **SlideAutoPlay.** Controls whether to play the images in a slide show (yes or no).

- **SlideDelay.** Determines the amount of time (in seconds) in between each image.

- **SlideLoop.** Sets the image slide show to continually play.

- **Title.** Defines the title at the top of the Image Viewer.

- **TitleColor.** Controls the color of the title contained in title.

- **TitleFont.** Controls the font for the Image Viewer.

- **TitleSize.** Controls the point size of the Image Viewer title.

- **TransitionsType.** Controls how images appear in the Image Viewer (from None to Random).

Creating a Web Photo Album

If you have Adobe Fireworks 4 or later installed on your computer, you can create a complete Web photo album in Dreamweaver within minutes. The Web photo album contains thumbnails that when clicked show the larger size of the pictures with navigation to go forward or backward to view the entire album. A Web photo album can be used to showcase products, portfolios, art and photography galleries and more... Dreamweaver thinks of everything.

Create a Web Photo Album

1. Create a folder for your photo album on your hard drive (in this example, a folder was created named, PhotoAlbum).

2. Open Dreamweaver, and then open a blank page (only used to access the Create Web Photo Album command).

3. Click the **Commands** menu, and then click **Create Web Photo Album**.

4. In the Create Web Photo Album dialog box, specify any of the following options:

   ◆ **Photo Album Title.** Enter a title for the photo album (appears in the thumbnail page).

   ◆ **Subheading Info.** Enter subheading info (shows along with the enlarged pictures).

   ◆ **Other Info.** Enter any additional information (shows along with the enlarged pictures).

   ◆ **Source Images Folder.** Click **Browse** to select the folder containing the original images.

   NOTE *Keep the file names of your original images to the old 8.3 rule, and avoid special characters.*

   ◆ **Destination Folder.** Click **Browse** to select the folder you created in step 1 (this folder should be located within the working site folder).

- ◆ **Thumbnail Size.** Click the button to select a specific size for the thumbnails.

- ◆ **Show Filenames.** Select to display filenames along with the images.

- ◆ **Columns.** Enter the number of columns to use for displaying the thumbnails.

- ◆ **Thumbnail Format.** Select a thumbnail file format.

- ◆ **Photo Format.** Select a photo file format.

- ◆ **Create Navigation Page For Each Photo.** Select to create a navigation page for each image.

⑤ Click **OK** to create the album.

Dreamweaver prompts you with a popup box, and a message saying that the photo album has been created and you can view the album.

⑥ Click **OK**.

Dreamweaver creates three sub-folders inside your original folder, and an index page.

- ◆ **Thumbnails.** Contains all the thumbnails.

- ◆ **Images.** Contains all the images.

- ◆ **Pages.** Contains the larger images and navigation between pictures and go back to home.

- ◆ **Index.htm.** The page which will have all the thumbnails with links to the larger images.

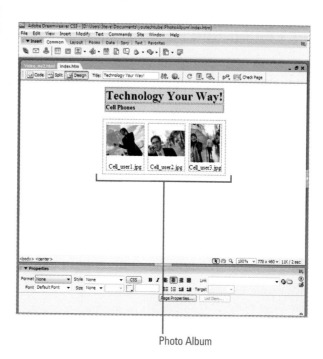

Photo Album

For Your Information

Using CSS Styles with the Index Page

Once the index page is created you can modify it to fit the style of your site. Open the index page and apply a template to format the page or use CSS Styles to format the text you want to change.

Linking or Embedding Sound

If you want to add some life to a Web page, you can add sound to it. Dreamweaver allows you to add a variety of sounds formats, including WAV, MIDI, MP3 (MPG), AIF, RA (Real Audio), MOV (QuickTime). Some audio formats require visitors to download and install a plug-in to play the sound. Some plug-ins include QuickTime, Windows Media Player or RealPlayer. You can add a sound to a page by linking the audio file to text or an image or by embedding the audio file directly into the page. When you link an audio file, the visitor needs to click the link to play the sound. When you embed an audio file, the sound plays when you load a page with a background sound, or when you trigger an event. When you add sounds to one or more pages, use careful judgement and discernment. The old adage "less is more" seems to be a good rule of thumb. It's always a good practice to provide a way for visitors to turn off the sound.

Link to a Sound File

1. Open the Web page you want to create a link to an audio file.

2. Select the text or image you want to use as the link to the audio file.

3. Open the Properties panel.

4. Click the **Browse For File** button next to the Link box to select the audio file, or enter the file's path and name.

Did You Know?

You can link to or embed other videos (AVI or MPEG). Instead of using a sound file, you can use the same steps to link to a video file or embed a video file.

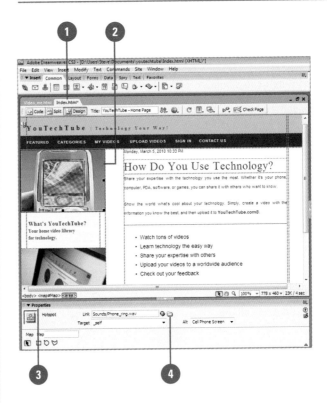

Embed a Sound File

1. Open the Web page you want to embed a sound file.

2. Click to place the insertion point where you want to embed a sound file.

3. Embed a sound file using one of the following options:

   ◆ Click the **Common** tab on the Insert bar, click the **Media** arrow button, and then click **Plugin**.

   ◆ Click the **Insert** menu, point to **Media**, and then click **Plugin**.

4. Open the Properties panel.

5. Click the **Browse For File** button next to the Link box to select the audio file, or enter the file's path and name.

6. Enter the width and height for the placeholder, or drag to resize it.

Using Java Applets

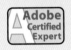

DW 2.10

You can insert a Java applet into an HTML document using Dreamweaver. Java is a programming language that allows the development of lightweight applications (applets) that can be embedded in web pages. Java applets are executed in a secure area (called a sandbox) by most Web browsers, preventing them from accessing local data. The code of the applet is downloaded from a Web server and the browser embeds the applet into a Web page. In order for an applet to run, it requires the Java plug-in, which isn't available by default on all browsers, and is considered more difficult to build and design a good user interface than other technologies such as DHTML and Flash. It is, however, still a very popular system for the design of Web navigational systems, games, and audio and text effects.

Insert a Java Applet

1 Open the Web page you want to insert a Java applet.

2 Click in the Document window to place the insertion point.

3 Insert the Java applet using one of the following options:

◆ Click the **Common** tab on the Insert bar, click the **Media** arrow button, and then click **Applet**.

◆ Click the **Insert** menu, point to **Media**, and then click **Applet**.

4 Navigate to the location with the file containing a Java applet.

5 Select a file containing a Java applet.

6 Click **OK**.

7 Enter the accessibility attributes (title, access key, and tab index) you want.

8 Click **OK**.

Java Applet file

Modify Java Applet Preferences

1 Open the Web page you want to modify settings for a Java applet.

2 Open the Properties panel, and then click the expander arrow to display all properties.

3 Select the Java applet you want to modify settings.

4 Select from the following Java Applet options:

◆ **Name.** Enter a name to identify the applet for scripting.

◆ **W and H.** Enter the width and height of the applet, in pixels.

◆ **Code.** Enter the file containing the applet's Java code, or click the folder icon to browse to a file.

◆ **Base.** Displays the folder containing the selected applet (this text box is filled automatically, when you select an applet).

◆ **Align.** Controls is aligned of the applet on the page.

◆ **Alt.** Specifies alternative content (usually an image) to be displayed if the user's browser doesn't support Java applets or has Java disabled.

◆ **V Space and H Space.** Specify the amount of white space in pixels above, below, and on both sides of the applet.

◆ **Parameters.** Opens a dialog box for entering additional parameters to pass to the applet.

Java Applet attributes

Expander arrow

Using ActiveX Controls

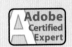 **DW 2.10**

You can insert an ActiveX control in your page. ActiveX controls (formerly known as OLE controls) are reusable components, somewhat like miniature applications, that can act like browser plug-ins. They run in Internet Explorer with Windows, but they don't run on the Macintosh or in Netscape Navigator. The ActiveX object in Dreamweaver lets you supply attributes and parameters for an ActiveX control in your visitor's browser.

Insert an ActiveX Control

1. Open the Web page you want to insert an ActiveX control.

2. Click to place the insertion point where you want to insert an ActiveX control.

3. Insert the ActiveX control using one of the following options:

   ◆ Click the **Common** tab on the Insert bar, click the **Media** arrow button, and then click **ActiveX**.

   ◆ Click the **Insert** menu, point to **Media**, and then click **ActiveX**.

4. Enter the accessibility attributes (title, access key, and tab index) you want.

5. Click **OK**.

   An icon marks where the ActiveX control appears on the page in Internet Explorer.

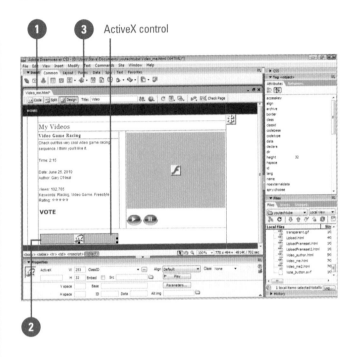

ActiveX control

Modify ActiveX Properties

1. Open the Web page you want to modify ActiveX control properties.

2. Select the ActiveX icon in the Document window.

3. Open the Properties panel, and then click the expander arrow to display all properties.

4. Select from the following options:

   ◆ **Name.** Enter a name to identify the ActiveX object for scripting.

   ◆ **W and H.** Enter the width and height of the object (in pixels).

   ◆ **Class ID.** Identifies the ActiveX control to the browser (enter a value or select one).

   ◆ **Embed.** Inserts an embed tag within the object tag for the ActiveX control.

   ◆ **Align.** Aligns the object.

   ◆ **Parameters.** Select to enter additional parameters to pass to the ActiveX object.

   ◆ **Src.** Defines the data file used for a Netscape Navigator plug-in if the Embed option is on.

   ◆ **V Space and H Space.** Enter the amount of white space (in pixels) above, below, and on both sides of the object.

   ◆ **Base.** Displays the URL containing the ActiveX control.

   ◆ **Alt Img.** Enter an image to be displayed if the browser doesn't support the object tag.

   ◆ **Data.** Enter a data file for the ActiveX control to load.

5. Click the **File** menu, point to **Preview In Browser**, and then select a browser to preview the ActiveX control.

Expander arrow

Using Plug-ins

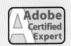
You can include content on a page that runs in a Netscape Navigator plug-in, such as a QuickTime or RealPlayer movie, in the user's browser. After you insert content for a Netscape Navigator plug-in, you can use the Properties panel to set options and parameters for the selected element. When you're ready to preview the content, you can play all the plug-in elements at once or play them individually. If you want to play movies in Design view, the proper plug-ins must be installed on your computer.

Insert Plug-in Content

1. Open the Web page you want to insert a plug-in content.

2. Click to place the insertion point where you want to insert Plug-in content.

3. Insert the Plug-in using one of the following options:

   ◆ Click the **Common** tab on the Insert bar, click the **Media** arrow button, and then click **Plugin**.

   ◆ Click the **Insert** menu, point to **Media**, and then click **Plugin**.

4. Navigate to the location with the Plug-in file, and then select it.

5. Click **OK**.

   An icon marks where the Plug-in control appears on the page in Netscape Navigator.

QuickTime movie

Play the Plug-in

1. Open the Web page with the plug-in you want to play.

2. Use any of the following options to play a Plug-in:

   ◆ **Selected Elements.** Select the media elements, click the **View** menu, point to **Plugins**, and then click **Play**, or click the **Play** button in the Properties panel.

   ◆ **All Elements.** Click the **View** menu, point to **Plugins**, and then click **Play All**.

3. Use any of the following options to stop a Plug-in:

   ◆ **Selected Elements.** Click the **View** menu, point to **Plugins**, and then click **Stop**, or click the **Stop** button in the Properties panel.

   ◆ **All Elements.** Click the **View** menu, point to **Plugins**, and then click **Stop All**.

Use button to play and stop the plug-in movie

Use to play or stop the plug-in movie

Checking for Plug-ins ▶

Use the Check Plugin action to send visitors to different pages depending on whether they have the specified plug-in installed. For example, you might want visitors to go to one page if they have Shockwave and another page if they do not. The Check Plugins action is an excellent tool for making your visitor's experience a pleasant one.

Use the Check Plug-in Action

1 Open the Web page you want to use.

2 Select an object (for an element) or click the <body> tag in the tag selector (for an entire page).

3 Open the Behaviors panel.

4 Click the **Plus** (+) button, and then click **Check Plugin** from the Actions menu.

5 Select a plug-in from the **Plugin** popup, or type the exact name of the plug-in in the adjacent text box.

6 Configure Check Plug-in using the following options:

◆ **If Found, Go To URL.** Enter a URL for visitors who have the plug-in.

NOTE *To cause visitors with the plug-in stay on the same page, leave this field blank.*

◆ **Otherwise, Go To URL.** Enter an alternative URL for visitors who don't have the plug-in.

NOTE *To cause visitors without the plug-in stay on the same page, leave this field blank.*

◆ **Always Go To First URL If Detection Is Not Possible.** In general, if the plug-in content is integral to your page, select this option; visitors without the plug-in will often be prompted by the browser to download the plug-in. If the plug-in content is not essential to your page, leave this option deselected.

NOTE *This option applies only to Internet Explorer; Netscape Navigator can always detect plug-ins.*

⑦ Click **OK**.

⑧ Select an event from the popup menu.

⑨ Click the **File** menu, point to **Preview In Browser**, and then select a browser to test the page from the available options.

IMPORTANT *Plug-in detection is not possible in Internet Explorer on the Macintosh, and most plug-ins cannot be detected in Internet Explorer on Windows.*

Plug-in movie

Creating Forms

13

Introduction

Forms are all around us... You fill out forms to get your driver's license, apply for a job; even to get married. A simple definition of a form would be some method for extracting information on a particular subject. For example, to fill out a job application form, you would have to enter your pertinent information on who you are (name, address), recent jobs, why you're experienced enough to apply for the job, and government stuff, like your social security number. An even simpler definition would be to say that forms collect information... it's how you collect that information that makes all the difference.

For example, you might design your form on paper, and the person filling out the form is required to write the information down with a pen or pencil. The information is collected by another person, and along with other forms, compiled (by hand) into a final readable product. Not very efficient; however, that's the way it was done, many long years ago.

Today forms are filled out on a computer screen; the data is validated and compiled into a readable final product, along with relevant statistics and averages. What I'm describing is creating electronic forms, designed, implemented, and finished, all with the help of Adobe Dreamweaver.

Adobe Dreamweaver simplifies the process of creating and implementing forms of any size and complexity. In this chapter you learn how to create basic forms, and populate the forms with all the goodies, such as: check boxes, radio buttons, text input fields; even drop-down menus.

Once a form is created, it can deposit that information into an appended database, where other statistical applications can massage the data into any structure desired by the final user.

What You'll Do

Understand Forms

Create a Form

Insert Form Objects

Modify Text Fields and Text Areas

Modify Radio Buttons and Check Boxes

Modify Lists and Menus

Modify Buttons

Insert an Image Button

Make Form Objects Dynamic

Use Tables to Control Forms

Validate Forms

Create and Edit a Jump Menu

View Example Code for Forms

Understanding Forms

As mentioned in the previous section, forms are all about the collection and eventual processing of information. Considering the information-based society that we live and work in, without forms the entire world would probably fall apart in a matter of days. Well, maybe that's a bit exaggerated; however, forms collect information, information drives our lives, and Dreamweaver makes the creation of those forms a virtual snap.

Beyond Dreamweaver

It's important to understand that although Dreamweaver will make the overall creation of a form easy (buttons, check boxes, input fields, etc), it does not include the backend tools that make the form functional. For that you will need to install a form handler on your server. In many cases someone in the IT department performs this function. Understand that until the form handler is installed, your visitors will not be able to send you any data; no matter how many times they click the Submit button.

While the scope of the book is not to teach you how to write form handler code, there are many sites that offer free form-handler scripts. These sites typically provide scripts for collecting simple and predictable form data; for more complex scripts the services of an engineer might be required.

Form Elements

Forms can be populated with any number of elements. For example, you could create a simple bio form that asks for information such as name, address, phone number, sex, age, social security number, etc. Because of all this information, it's a good idea to sketch out the general look and feel of the form on a piece of paper, and then use that as a visual guide to the creation of the form in Dreamweaver. When you create a interactive field, Dreamweaver inserts the code necessary to display the field in the browser.

Dynamic Form Elements

A dynamic form element is a form object that gets its initial value by the Web server where the Web site is stored. When a visitor opens a form page in a browser, the dynamic form objects get information directly from the Web server before the page appears on the screen. When form objects are dynamic, it makes updating a snap. In order to use dynamic form objects, you need to have a data source set up and available on your Web server.

Form Validation

Once the various form elements are ironed out, you can look at the possibility of validating some of the fields. For example, it might be difficult to create a validation for a name field; however, you at least check to see that the field is not blank. In addition, you could check to see if all zip code fields contain five numbers and not alphabetic characters. Options that require specific answers, such as sex (male/female) could be placed as a pop-up with the correct choices, and other options could be designed using check boxes or radio buttons. In most cases using check boxes allows the user to choose more than one option (check all that apply), and radio button typically allow for a single choice from a group (choose only one). When you choose form validation, Dreamweaver creates a script that instructs the browser how to handle the input.

Form tab with form related buttons

Form elements

Creating a Form

Just because Dreamweaver makes the initial creation of the form easy for you, it doesn't mean that you shouldn't think about its construction. One of the rules in creating forms is that you're designing the form for the person who is filling it out... not for you. The form should be as simplistic as possible with easy to understand instructions. When they make a mistake (not filling in a field), there should be a way to tell that person a mistake was made, and what to do to correct it. Studies show that the more difficult the form, the less likely that people are going to spend the time to fill it out. There are two stages in the creation of a form: The initial insertion of the form, and then populating the form with text and form objects.

Create a Form

1. Create a new HTML document, or open an existing one.

2. Click to place the insertion point where you want to insert a form.

3. Insert the form using one of the following options:

   ◆ Click the **Forms** tab on the Insert bar, and then click the **Form** button.

   ◆ Click the **Insert** menu, point to **Form**, and then click **Form**.

   An empty form appears with a dotted red outline.

   TROUBLE? *If you don't see the outline, click the View menu, point to Visual Aids, and then click Invisible Elements.*

4. Open the Properties panel.

5. Click the red form outline to select the form.

6. Type a name to identify the form for reference purposes with a scripting language.

7 Enter the path to the page or script that processes the form data, or click the **Browse For File** button to select a file (if you don't have this information, you can add it later).

8 Click the **Method** popup, and then select one of the following options:

◆ **Default.** Uses the browser's default setting to send the form data to the server. Typically the default is the GET method.

◆ **GET.** Appends the value to the URL requesting the page.

◆ **POST.** Embeds the form data in the HTTP request.

9 Insert the form objects you want and specify the information in the Input Tag Accessibility Attributes dialog box. When you create form objects, follow these guidelines:

◆ **Unique Names.** Use a unique name that identifies the object for scripting purposes. Avoid using spaces or special characters.

◆ **Layout.** Use line and paragraph breaks, formatted text, and tables to design the form layout.

Form with text element

See Also

See "Inserting Form Objects" on page 318 for information on inserting form objects.

See "Inserting Form Objects" on page 318 for information on inserting form objects.

For Your Information

Starting a Form from a Sample

Instead of creating a form from scratch, you can start a form from a sample, and then make the changes you want to suit your own needs. Click the File menu, click New, click the Page from Sample category, click Starter Page (Basic), click the sample page you want, such as Survey, Multiple Choice or Register (Basic), and then click Create.

Inserting Form Objects

After you create a form, you can starting inserting form objects. Form objects are the individual elements—such as text field, text area, button, check box, radio button, or menu—that make up the form and visitors fill out. The form objects allow you to create a form that makes it easy for visitor's to use, yet still provide you with the important information you need. Each form object is designed to gather a specific types of information. For example, if you have a list of categories and you can select more than one category, you should use the check box form object. If you can only select one category, you should use the radio button form object instead.

Insert Form Objects

1. Open a page that contains a form, or create a new document and insert a form.

2. Click to place the insertion point to where you want to insert a form object.

3. Click the **Insert** menu, point to **Form**, and then select from the following commonly used form objects:

   ◆ **Text Field.** Select to create a text field that consists of one line or multiple lines. In addition, text fields are used to create a password field that hides the text the user enters.

   ◆ **Text Area.** Select to create a large text area that is commonly used by a visitor to enter large amounts of data; for example, a comment field.

   ◆ **Button.** Select to create a button object. Buttons are used to submit form data to the server or to reset the form. Standard form buttons are typically labeled Submit, Reset, or Send. You can also assign other processing tasks that you've defined in a script.

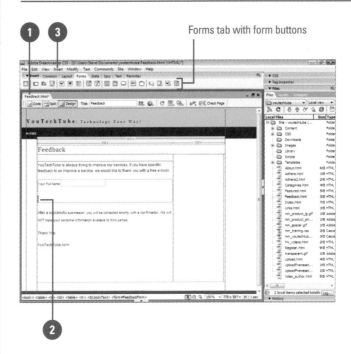

Forms tab with form buttons

◆ **Checkbox.** Select to let users select more than one option from a set of options.

◆ **Radio Button.** Select to let users select only one choice from a set of options. Radio buttons are typically used in groups.

◆ **List/Menu.** Select to let users select one or more items from a list.

4 In the Input Tag Accessibility Attributes dialog box, specify the following options:

◆ **ID.** Enter a unique ID for the form object.

◆ **Label.** Enter a label for the form object.

◆ **Style.** Select a style for the form object.

◆ **Position.** Select a position for the label in relation to the form object.

◆ **Access Key.** Enter a keyboard equivalent (single letter) in the Access Key text box. For example, if you entered the letter N into the field, pressing Alt+N (Win) or Control+N (Mac) in the browser automatically selects that field.

◆ **Tab Index.** Enter a numerical value for the tab order of the form object in the Tab Index text box. For example, if you entered the number 3 into the field, pressing the tab key three times would cause the field to be selected.

5 Click **OK**.

Form

Modifying Text Fields and Text Areas ▶

A text field consists of one line or multiple lines used to enter small distinct amounts of data or information, such as your name or address. You can also use a text field to create a password field that hides the text the user enters. A text area is a large text field commonly used to enter large amounts of data or information, such as comments. After you create a text field or text area, you can use the Properties panel to set or change options for the form objects.

Work with Text Field and Text Area Properties

1 Select a text input field or text area within a form document.

2 Open the Properties panel.

3 Select from the following text field or text area options:

◆ **Char Width.** Enter the maximum number of characters that can be displayed in the field.

◆ **Max Chars.** Enter the maximum number of characters that can be entered in the field for single-line text fields.

◆ **Num Lines.** Enter the height of the field for multiple-line text fields.

◆ **Wrap.** Determines how the user's input will be displayed when the user enters more information than can be displayed within the defined text area.

  ◆ **Off.** Prevents text from wrapping to the next line.

  ◆ **Virtual.** Sets word wrap in the text area.

  ◆ **Physical.** Sets word wrap in the text area, as well as to the data when it is submitted for processing.

3 Text field

◆ **Type.** Designates the field as a single-line, multiple-line, or password field.

   ◆ **Single-line.** Selecting to cause the Char Width and Max Chars settings to map to a single line with defined boundaries.

   ◆ **Password.** Select to create a password field (information typed into the field appears as asterisks or dots).

   ◆ **Multi-line.** Select to create a multi-line field.

NOTE *The default for text area fields is multi-line.*

◆ **Init Value.** Enter an initial value that displays when the field first loads.

◆ **Class.** Click to apply CSS rules to the object directly or through a CSS Style sheet.

Text area selected

③ Text area

Modifying Radio Buttons and Check Boxes

Radio buttons and check boxes allows you to create options for users to select. A radio button allows a user to select only one choice from a set of options, while a check box allows a user to select more than one option from a set of options. Radio buttons are typically used in groups. Both form objects are very used for when you want to create a survey. After you create a radio button or check box, you can use the Properties panel to set or change options for the form objects.

Work with Radio Button and Checkbox Properties

1. Select a radio button or checkbox within a form document.

2. Open the Properties panel.

3. Select from the following radio button options:

   ◆ **Radio Button/Checkbox.** Enter a name for the Radio Button or Checkbox object.

   NOTE *If the name of a group of radio buttons is the same, then the user will only be able to select one button (i.e. male or female). The name cannot contain spaces or special characters.*

   NOTE *Unlike radio buttons, every checkbox must have a unique name.*

   ◆ **Checked Value.** Enter in a value to be sent to the server when the button is selected. For example, male or female.

   ◆ **Initial State.** Select whether to have the button selected or not when the form first loads.

   ◆ **Class.** Click to apply CSS rules to the object directly or through a CSS Style Sheet.

Radio button

Radio button

Modifying Lists and Menus

Lists and menus perform similar tasks; each allows you to select an item from a list of related items. However, there are some differences. A list allows you to scroll through the items as well as select multiple items, while a menu doesn't. When you select an item from a list or menu, you can execute an action using a script or behavior. After you create a list or menu, you can use the Properties panel to set or change options for the form objects.

Work with List/Menu Properties

1. Select a list/menu field within a form document.

2. Open the Properties panel.

3. Select from the following list/menu options:

   ◆ **List/Menu.** Enter a unique name for the menu.

   ◆ **Menu.** Select to have the menu drop down when clicked.

   ◆ **List.** Select to display a scrollable list of items when clicked.

   ◆ **Height.** Enter a value to determine the number of items displayed in the menu (List type only).

   ◆ **Selections.** Select to allow the user to select multiple items from the list (List type only).

   ◆ **List Values.** Click to add items to the menu.

   ◆ **Class.** Click to apply CSS rules to the object directly or through a CSS Style Sheet.

   ◆ **Initially Selected.** Select from the available items to make the item initially selected when the browser loads the form.

Use to add items to the menu

Click to select initial menu selection

Click to add items to the menu

Modifying Buttons

Buttons are used to execute an action. Form buttons are generally used to submit form data to the server or to reset the form. Standard form buttons are typically labeled Submit, Reset, or Send. In addition to the standard form buttons, you can assign other processing tasks that you've defined in a script or behavior to create a custom button. After you create a button, you can use the Properties panel to set or change options for the form objects.

Work with Button Properties

1. Select a button field within a form document.

2. Open the Properties panel.

3. Select from the following button options:

   ◆ **Label.** To label the text field, check box, or radio button option, click next to the object, and then type the label.

   ◆ **Value.** Enter the name of the button (appears directly on the button).

   ◆ **Action.** Determines what happens when the button is clicked.

      ◆ **Submit Form.** Select to submit the form data for processing when the button is clicked.

      ◆ **Reset Form.** Select to clear the contents of the form when the button is clicked.

      ◆ **None.** Select if you want to add a JavaScript behavior for the button.

   ◆ **Class.** Click to apply CSS rules to the object directly or through a CSS Style Sheet.

Inserting an Image Button

Instead of using one of the built-in buttons provided by Dreamweaver, you can insert an image and use it as a button. This allows you to create a custom look for your form, yet still provide the functionality you want. After you insert an Image button, you can use the Properties panel to set or change options for the form object.

Insert an Image Button

1. Create a new HTML document, or open an existing page.

2. Click to place the insertion point where you want to insert an image button.

3. Insert the image using one of the following options:

   ◆ Click the **Forms** tab on the Insert bar, and then click the **Image Field** button.

   ◆ Click the **Insert** menu, point to **Form**, and then click **Image Field**.

4. Locate and select the image you want to use as a button.

5. Click **OK**.

6. In th Properties panel, select from the following options:

   ◆ **Image Field.** Enter a unique name for the image.

   ◆ **Scr.** Enter the path and name for the image or click the **Browse For File** button to select the image file.

   ◆ **Alt.** Enter a description of the image.

   ◆ **Align.** Click to select an alignment option.

   ◆ **Edit Image.** Click to edit the image in your default editor.

   ◆ **Class.** Click to apply CSS rules to the object directly or through a CSS Style Sheet.

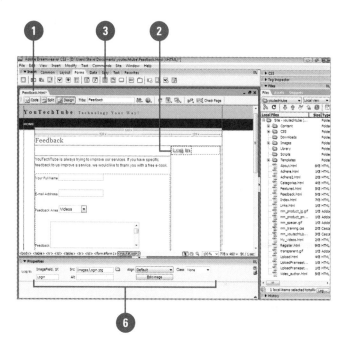

Making Form Objects Dynamic

Instead of setting static form options in Dreamweaver, you can set form options dynamically (on the fly) from your Web server, known as a dynamic form object. For example, you can dynamically set a form menu or list menu with entries from a database, display content in text fields when viewed in a browser, or preset a radio button or check box when viewed in a browser.

When a page with a dynamic form object is displayed from a Web server, the initial state is determined by the server. Making form objects dynamic makes updating and maintaining a Web site much easier. Instead of manually changing a menu item, you can simply change an entry in a database table where the information is stored.

In order to use dynamic form objects, you need to have a data source set up, such as a MySQL database, and available on your Web server. The set up and connection of a data source is outside the scope of this book, so you should see your ISP or Web administrator for more details.

Make Form Objects Dynamic

1 Select the form object you want to make dynamic within a form document.

2 Open the Properties panel.

3 Click the **Dynamic** button or click the **Lighting Bolt** icon.

4 Select the options you want to make the form object dynamic; the options vary depending on the form object.

   ◆ Select an existing data source, or click the **Plus** (+) button to define a new data source.

5 Click **OK**.

Using Tables to Control Forms

When you create a table, it's a simple matter to add form elements on a line-by-line basis. However, in many cases this simplistic method may not suit your particular form layout. In that case it's tables to the rescue. A smart form designer can use a table within the form (just like in standard design), to control the look and positioning of all the form elements. Once the table is inserted into the form it's a simple matter to use the individual table cells to insert the various elements (for more information on the creation of a table, turn to Chapter 8). The only requirement for the table is that it must be placed with red dotted lines defining the form.

Control the Form with Tables

1 Create a new document or open an existing page.

2 Click to place the insertion point to where you want to insert a form.

3 Insert the form using one of the following options:

 ◆ Click the **Forms** tab on the Insert bar, and then click the **Form** button.

 ◆ Click the **Insert** menu, point to **Form**, and then click **Form**.

An empty form appears with a dotted red outline.

4 Select the form.

5 Click the **Insert** menu, and then click **Table**.

6 Click into an individual cell.

7 Click the **Insert** menu, point to **Form,** and then select from the available form objects.

The table cells control the placement and design of the form.

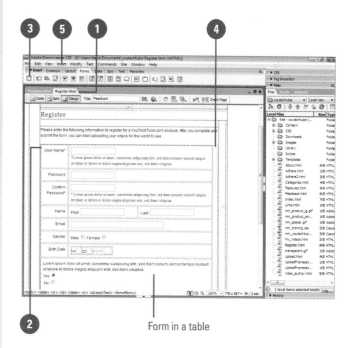

Form in a table

Validating Forms

The Validate Form action checks the contents of specified text fields to ensure that the user has entered the correct type of data. You can attach this action to individual text fields using an onBlur event to validate the fields as the user is filling out the form, or attach it to the form with the onSubmit event to evaluate several text fields at once when the user clicks the Submit button. Attaching this action to a form prevents the form from being submitted to the server if any of the specified text fields contains invalid data. In addition, Dreamweaver can add JavaScript code that checks the contents of specified text fields to ensure that the user has entered the correct type of data.

Validate HTML Form Data

1 Open a form document, or create a new form document.

> **IMPORTANT** *The form document must contain at least one text field and a Submit button. In addition, all text fields must have unique names.*

2 Select the **Submit** button inside the form that you want to validate.

3 Click the **Window** menu, and then click **Behaviors** to display the Behaviors panel.

4 Click the **Add Behavior** button (the Plus (+) sign), and then click **Validate Form**.

5 Select the form input fields one at a time, and then validate the form using the following options:

- ◆ **Required.** Select to make the form object required.

- ◆ **Anything.** Accepts any input entered by the user.

- ◆ **Number.** Restricts input to numeric.

- ◆ **Email address.** Looks for an e-mail address with the @ sign.

- ◆ **Number from.** Enables you to enter a minimum and maximum range for numeric values.

6 Click **OK** to add the validation information (in script) to the HTML form document.

7 Click the **Action** button in the Behaviors panel, and then select one of the following options:

◆ **OnSubmit**. Select if you are validating multiple fields when the user submits the form.

◆ **OnBlur or OnChange**. Select if you are validating individual fields.

8 Click the **File** menu, point to **Preview In Browser**, and then check the current validation actions.

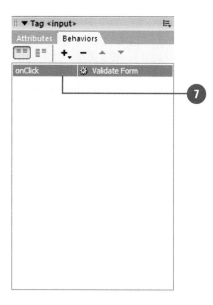

Creating and Editing a Jump Menu

Most Web sites employ buttons to helps the visitor navigate through the various pages; however, it's possible to create a jump menu, using a simple form element. A jump menu utilizes a form object to create a list of menu options. When the visitor clicks on the list, a drop-down menu displays a listing of all the available page options. Displaying a listing of all available page options within a single drop-down menu is a creative use of form objects that makes navigation through a complex site much easier for your visitors. After you create a jump menu, you can make changes to it as needed. You can add, delete, rename or change the order of items in the menu. In addition, you can modify the file an item links to. If you want to change the location in which a linked file opens, or to add or change a menu selection prompt, you need to apply the Jump Menu behavior from the Behaviors panel.

Create a Jump Menu

1 Create a new Web page or Open the Web page where you want to insert a jump menu.

2 Click to place the insertion point to where you want to insert a jump menu.

   NOTE *Dreamweaver inserts a form at the insertion point (if you haven't already created one).*

3 Click the **Insert** menu, point to **Forms**, and then click **Jump Menu**.

4 Create the jump menu using the following options:

   ◆ **Menu Items.** Click the **Plus** (+) sign to add more "unnamed" menu items to the list. Click the **Minus** (-) sign to remove "unnamed" items from the list. Use the up and down arrows buttons to move selected items within the list.

   ◆ **Text.** Select an "unnamed" menu item in the Menu Items box, and then enter a name in the text field. Continue selecting "unnamed" items until all have been properly named.

Jump menu

- **When Selected Go To URL.**
  Select a menu item in the Menu Items box, and then enter the path and filename of the page you want opened for the selected item or click **Browse** to select the file.

- **Open URLs In.** If you're not working within a frameset, you have only one option: Main Window.

- **Menu ID.** Enter a unique name for the menu in the input field (optional).

- **Insert Go Button After Menu.** Select to add a button that activates the jump menu.

- **Select First Item After URL Change.** Select to reset the menu selection to the top item after each jump.

⑤ Click **OK**.

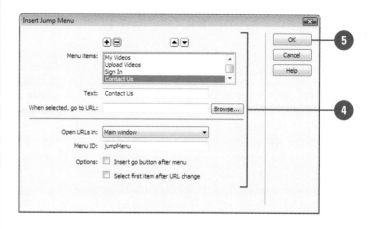

Edit a Jump Menu

① Open the Web page where you want to edit a jump menu.

② Open the Properties panel.

③ Select a jump menu object.

④ Click the **List Values** button.

⑤ Make the changes you want.

- Click the **Plus** (+) sign to add more "unnamed" menu items to the list. Click the **Minus** (-) sign to remove "unnamed: items from the list. Use the up and down arrows buttons to move selected items within the list.

⑥ Click **OK**.

Viewing Example Code for Forms

The <form></form> Tags

The first step in the creation of a form is to place the HTML <form></form> tags on your page. The form tags, when inserted into the document will be delineated by a red line, which will be invisible when the page loads into a standard browser. The red line is a visible design element that lets you know you're working on a form. All items defining the form must be placed within those lines.

```
head>
<meta http-equiv="Content-Type"
content="text/html; charset=ISO-8859-1" />
<title>Untitled Document</title>
</head>
<body>
<form id="form1" name="form1" method="post"
action="">
</form>
</body>
</html>
```

Form Elements

Forms can be populated with any number of elements. For example, you could create a simple bio form that asks for information such as name, address, phone number, sex, age, social security number, etc. Because of all this information, it's a good idea to sketch out the general look and feel of the form on a piece of paper, and then use that as a visual guide to the creation of the form in Dreamweaver. When you create a interactive field, Dreamweaver inserts the code necessary to display the field in the browser. The following is an example of the HTML code necessary to display a text input field for a person's name, address, city, state, and zip code.

```
<body>
<form id="form1" name="form1" method="post"
action="">
  <label>Name
  <input type="text" name="textfield" />
  </label>
<label>Address
    <input type="text" name="textfield2" />
    </label>
<label>City
    <input type="text" name="textfield3" />
    </label>
<label>State
    <input type="text" name="textfield4" />
    </label>
<label>Zip
    <input type="text" name="textfield5" />
    </label>
</form>
```

Form Validation

Once the various form elements are ironed out, you can look at the possibility of validating some of the fields. For example, it might be difficult to create a validation for a name field; however, you at least check to see that the field is not blank. In addition, you could check to see if all zip code fields contain five numbers and not alphabetic characters. Options that require specific answers, such as sex (male/female) could be placed as a pop-up with the correct choices, and other options could be designed using check boxes or radio buttons. In most cases using check boxes allows the user to choose more than one option (check all that apply), and radio button typically allow for a single choice from a group (choose only one).

When you choose form validation, Dreamweaver creates a script that instructs the browser how to handle the input. The following is an example of a form validation script that validates an email address input field.

```
function MM_validateForm() { //v4.0
  var
i,p,q,nm,test,num,min,max,errors='',args=MM_valida
teForm.arguments;
  for (i=0; i<(args.length-2); i+=3) { test=args[i+2];
val=MM_findObj(args[i]);
    if (val) { nm=val.name; if ((val=val.value)!="") {
      if (test.indexOf('isEmail')!=-1) {
p=val.indexOf('@');
        if (p<1 || p==(val.length-1)) errors+='- '+nm+'
must contain an e-mail address.\n';
      } else if (test!='R') { num = parseFloat(val);
        if (isNaN(val)) errors+='- '+nm+' must contain
a number.\n';
        if (test.indexOf('inRange') != -1) {
p=test.indexOf(':');
          min=test.substring(8,p); max=test.sub-
string(p+1);
          if (num<min || max<num) errors+='- '+nm+'
must contain a number between '+min+' and
'+max+'.\n';
    } } } else if (test.charAt(0) == 'R') errors += '-
'+nm+' is required.\n'; }
  } if (errors) alert('The following error(s)
occurred:\n'+errors);
  document.MM_returnValue = (errors == '');
```

Viewing the HTML Behind the Page

14

Introduction

In the world of the Internet, the graphics, text, animation, and all the "stuff" that the visitor sees displayed in their browser is the front end of a Web page, and the power behind the page is the HTML code. The HTML code sits quietly behind the scenes, letting the front end get all the credit; however, without the code the Internet would fall apart. It's the cosmic glue that holds the whole thing together.

Designers, like myself, remember when there were no graphical design interfaces (like Dreamweaver), and all Web pages were designed code line, by tedious code line. I remember working by candlelight into the wee hours of the morning, until I thought my head was going to burst... okay, so maybe I didn't use candles, but it was a lot of painstaking work. Although Dreamweaver changed all of that with its intuitive graphical design interface, the code is still there. However, we're not the ones doing the coding, Dreamweaver is... and isn't that nice.

What You'll Do

Understand HTML

Use Code View

Set Code View Options

Enter HTML Code

Work with HTML Head Tags

Insert HTML Comments

Use the Coding Toolbar

Use Quick Tag Editor

Use the Tag Inspector

Use the Tag Chooser

Use the Reference Panel

Set Code Format Preferences

Set Code Hint Preferences

Set Code Rewriting Preferences

Set Code Color Preferences

Understanding HTML

HTML stands for the HyperText Markup Language. HTML code is the major language of the Internet's World Wide Web. Web sites and Web pages are written in HTML code. With HTML code and the World Wide Web, you have the ability to bring together text, pictures, sounds, and links... all in one place! HTML code files are plain text files, so they can be composed and edited on any type of computer... Windows, Mac, UNIX, whatever.

HTML documents look a lot like word processing documents. You can have text that's bold and italicized, larger and smaller, or it can look typewritten. The HTML code might look something like this:

You can have <b>bold</b> and <i>italicized</i>, <font size=+2>Larger</font> and <font size=-2>Smaller</font>, or it could look <tt>typewritten</tt>.

Most HTML code is enclosed within braces < >, and when you place the code between the braces it's said to be a tag. An HTML **tag** is code inserted in a document that specifies how the document, or a portion of the document, should be formatted. For example, the <b> tag is saying to start bold text, and the </b> tag is saying to stop bold text. The tag with the slash (/) is known as the closing tag. Many opening tags require a following closing tag, but not all do. Tags make up the entire structure of an HTML document.

HTML files are just normal text files; they usually have the extension of .htm, .html, or .shtml. HTML documents have two parts, the head and the body. The body is the larger part of the document, as the body of a letter you would write to a friend. The head of the document contains the document's title and similar information, and the body contains most everything else.

Common Tags

Symbol	Defines
<html>	Start of the HTML document
<head>	The document heading
<body>	The body of the document
<title>	The document title
<div>	A section in a document
<span>	A section in a document
<h1>	Text heading
<p>	A paragraph
<style>	Format of text
<img>	An image placeholder
<a>	A hyperlink
<iframe>	An inline frame
<!-- comment -->	A comment

Here's an example of a basic HTML document:

```
<html>

<head><title>Title goes
here</title></head><body>Body goes here</body>

</html>
```

You may find it easier to read if you add extra blank lines such as follows...

```
<html>
<head>
<title>Title goes here</title>
</head>
<body>
Body goes here
</body>
</html>
```

Extra spaces and line breaks (blank lines) are ignored when the HTML is interpreted (displayed) by a Web browser, such as Microsoft Explorer or Apple Safari... so add them if you wish.

When working with HTML code it's all about the tags. The HTML tags instruct the text how to look and how it's formatted. In addition, tags control graphics, animation, in short... everything. For example the following uses the <b> or bold tag:

The cow jumped <b>OVER</b> the moon.

When displayed within a browser it would look like this:

The cow jumped **OVER** the moon.

The start tag <b> instructs the text following the tag to use boldface; the end tag </b> instructs the text to stop boldface and return to normal.

HTML page in Code view

HTML page in Design mode

Using Code View

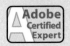 DW 3.17

Dreamweaver utilizes three document views: Design, Split, and Code. The Design view gives you a real-time view of your design, the Split view gives you a look at the visual and the code, and the Code view gives you a straight look at the HTML code of your Web page. When you work in the Code view you're going back to the basics of Web design… the actual code that makes it all happen. Some designers never look at the code, and some designers claim that you can't be good at creating Web pages without knowing the code. To be honest, I'm in the second camp. I believe that to really understand the design of a Web page, you need to know how the code makes a page function. Only then do you have complete control over the design of the page. Of course, I could be wrong…

Access the Code View

1 Open the Web page you want to view code.

2 Access the Code view using one of the following methods:

◆ Click the **View** menu, and then click **Code**.

◆ Click the **Code View** button on the document window.

◆ Click the **View** menu, and then click **Split**.

◆ Click the **Split View** button on the document window.

Dreamweaver's document changes to display the code of the current page.

Did You Know?

You can adjust the size of the panes in Split view. Drag the splitter bar located between the two panes. When you adjust the pane, Code view updates automatically.

Code view

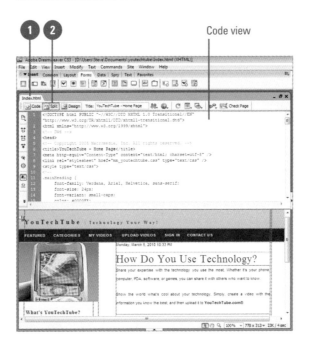

View Code in a Separate Window Using Code Inspector

1. Open the Web page you want to view code.

2. Click the **Window** menu, and then click **Code Inspector**.

3. Use the toolbar to select from the following options:

   ◆ **File Management.** Get, put, check in or check out a file.

   ◆ **Preview/Debug In Browser.** Preview or debug the file in a browser or Device Central.

   ◆ **Refresh Design View.** Refreshes Design view to reflect code changes in Code view.

   ◆ **Reference.** Opens the Reference panel.

   ◆ **Code Navigation.** Allows you to move quickly in the code.

   ◆ **View Options.** Allows you to change the way code appears in Code view.

4. When you're done, click the **Close** button.

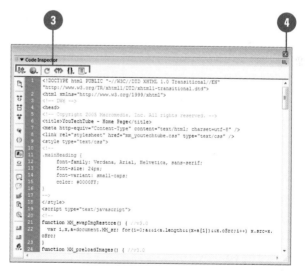

Did You Know?

You can use the coder-oriented workspace (Win). In Windows, you can display a workspace design for coding. The workspace displays the panel groups docked on the left side of the main window, and the Document window appears in Code view. The Properties panel is collapsed. Click the Window menu, point to Workspace Layout, and then click Coder.

Setting Code View Options

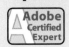 DW 3.17

You can select Code view options to change the way code appears in Code view. When you select the Code View Options command on the View menu or click the View Options button on the Code toolbar, you can set options to set word wrapping, display line numbers, hide characters, highlight invalid code, color code, and indent code automatically.

Use Code View Options

1. Open the Web page you want to view code.

2. Switch to the Code view.

3. Click the **View Options** button on the document toolbar, and then select from the following options:

    ◆ **Word Wrap.** Forces the HTML code to wrap, based on the width of the Code view window.

    ◆ **Line Numbers.** Displays line numbers to the left of the HTML code.

    ◆ **Hidden Characters.** Displays hidden code elements, such as tabs and character returns.

    ◆ **Highlight Invalid Code.** Highlights any code that Dreamweaver considers incorrect.

    ◆ **Syntax Coloring.** Colorizes the HTML code, to visibly separate it from the text.

    ◆ **Auto Indent.** Automatically indents the HTML code to aid in readability.

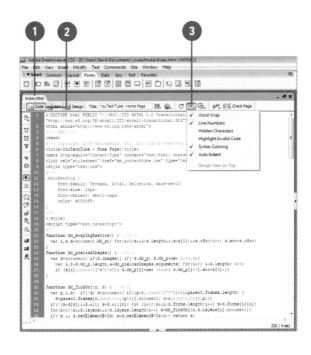

Did You Know?

You can print code. Open the Web page you want to print in Code view, click the File menu, click Print Code, specify the options you want, and then click OK (Win) or Print (Mac).

Entering HTML Code

You can enter HTML code in Code view like you are typing text into a word processor. However, when you type HTML code, it uses a specific structure and layout. As you type, the Code Hints popup menu appears to help you enter correct HTML code tag names, attributes, and values as you type code in Code view or the Quick Tag Editor. For example, when a tag requires the selection of a color, Dreamweaver displays a color palette. When a font is required, a font list is automatically displayed, and when a file is required a browse button magically appears allowing you to select and insert the file. If a page does contain invalid code, it appears in Design view and optionally highlights in Code view. When you select the invalid code, the Properties panel displays information as to why the code is invalid and steps to fix it.

Enter HTML in Code View

1. Open the Web page you want to view code.

2. Switch to the Code view.

3. Click to the right of a tag and press Enter to create a space between the opening and closing body tag.

4. Enter the HTML code you want on the new line.

   ◆ **Code Hints**. When you type the left brace "<" the Code Hints popup menu appears, listing all possible HTML codes. Begin entering in the code name, and Code Hints will display the correct code. Double-click it or select it and press Enter (Win) or Return (Mac) to add the tag.

   TIMESAVER *Press Control+Spacebar to display a Code Hints menu or press Esc to close the Code Hints menu.*

5. To indent the selected code, press Tab; to outdent the selected code, press Shift+Tab.

6. To add a closing tag, type a left brace and forward slash "</", and Dreamweaver will automatically insert the correct closing tag.

7. To remove a tag, right-click in the tag, and then click **Remove Tag**.

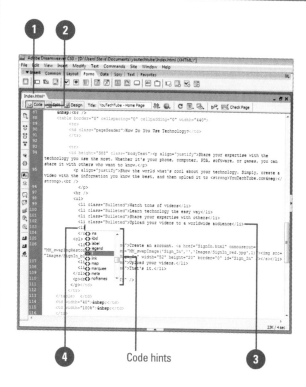

Code hints

Working with HTML Head Tags

DW 3.17

Each page contains information about the document in the head section. You can set the properties of head elements to control how your pages are identified on the Web by search browsers. You can insert the following head tags: meta, keywords, description, refresh, base, or link. A **meta** tag records information about the current page, such as encoding, author, copyright, or keywords. The **keywords** and **description** tags record information many search engines, such as Google or Yahoo, look for to create an index for your page for use in their search results databases. For the best results, specify a few descriptive keywords and a short description for a page. The **refresh** tag specifies the amount of time before the page is refreshed in a browser. The **base** tag sets the base URL that all document-relative paths in the page use. The **link** tag defines a relationship between the current page and another file. After you insert a head tag, you can always make changes and adjustments by using the head content, selecting the head element, and making changes in the Properties panel.

View and Insert Head Tags

1. Open the Web page you want to view and change head properties.

2. To insert head tags, click the **Insert** menu, point to **HTML**, point to **Head Tags**, and then select the tag you want: Meta, Keywords, Description, Refresh, Base, or Link.

3. Enter the information or specify the options you want, and then click **OK**.

4. Click the **View** menu, and then click **Head Content**.

5. To edit an element, click one of the icons in the head section to select it, and then change the properties you want in the Properties panel.

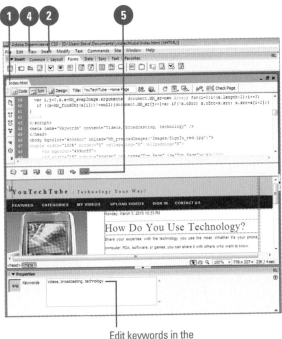

Edit keywords in the Properties panel

Did You Know?

You can check for balanced tags and braces. In Code view, click to place the insertion point where you want to check, click the Edit menu, and then click Select Parent Tag or Balance Braces. You can select the commands again to check the next level out.

Inserting HTML Comments

DW 3.19

Insert HTML Comments

1. Open the Web page you want to insert comments.

2. Click to place the insertion point where you want to insert a comment (in Code or Design view).

3. Click the **Insert** menu, and then click **Comment**.

4. Type the comment you want.

5. Click **OK** (in Design view).

Did You Know?

You can change the code using the Selection submenu. Select the code you want in Code view, right-click (Win) or control-click (Mac) it, point to Selection, and then click the selection command you want.

You can copy and paste code. Copy the code from Code view or from another program, click to place the insertion point in Code view where you want to paste the code, click the Edit menu, and then click Paste.

See Also

See "Working with Invisible Elements" on page 90 for information on displaying comment markers in Design view.

If you're writing large sections of code or working with other people to develop a site, it's important to insert comments into your HTML code. An HTML comment is descriptive text that explains the purpose and process for the page's code. The comment text only appears in Code view; the information is for internal development purposes only. You can insert comments in Code view or Design view. After you insert a comment, you can edit it directly in Code view, or select the comment marker and make changes in the Properties panel.

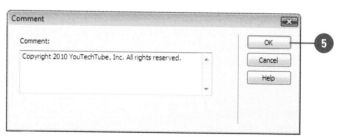

Using the Coding Toolbar

 Adobe Certified Expert DW 3.17

When you switch to Code or Split view, the Coding toolbar appears along the left side of the Code view pane. The toolbar provides easy access to the most common coding related commands. If the Code view pane is not large enough, an expander arrow appears, which you click to access additional buttons. Some of the tools allow you to collapse and expand the content between a set of opening and closing tags, select tags, insert and remove comments, format code, and highlight invalid code.

Use the Coding Toolbar

1 Open the Web page you want to view code.

2 Switch to the Code view.

3 Click to place the insertion point in the code or select a block of code.

4 Click the button you want on the Coding toolbar:

- **Open Documents.** Displays a list of open documents. Click the one you want to open it.

- **Collapse Full Tag.** Collapses the content between a set of opening and closing tags. You need to place the insertion point in the opening or closing tag.

- **Collapse Selection.** Collapses the selected code.

- **Expand All.** Restores all collapsed code.

- **Select Parent Tag.** Selects the code tag immediately outside of the line with the insertion point.

- **Balance Braces.** Selects the code tag and surrounding parentheses, braces, or square brackets of the line with the insertion point.

- **Line Numbers.** Shows or hides the numbers at the beginning of each line of code.

- **Highlight Invalid Code.** Highlights invalid code in yellow.

- **Apply Comment.** Inserts comment tags around the selected code, or opens new comment tags.

- **Remove Comment.** Deletes comment tags from the selected code.

- **Wrap Tag.** Wraps selected code with the selected tag from the Quick Tag Editor.

- **Recent Snippets.** Inserts a recently used code snippet from the Snippets panel.

- **Move or Convert CSS.** Moves CSS to another location or convert inline CSS to CSS rules.

- **Indent Code.** Shifts the selection to the right.

- **Outdent Code.** Shifts the selection to the left.

- **Format Source Code.** Displays options to apply source code formatting to selected code, or to the entire page if no code is selected. You can also access Code Format Settings Preferences dialog box or the Tag Library Editor.

TIMESAVER *You can perform many of these same commands on the Insert bar.*

See Also

See "Moving CSS Rules" on page 232 for information on moving CSS rules to a style sheet.

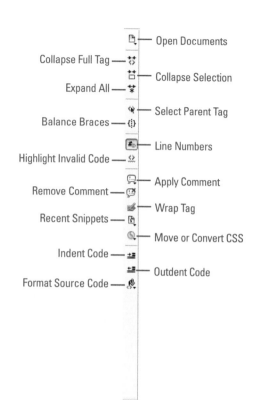

Open Documents
Collapse Full Tag
Collapse Selection
Expand All
Select Parent Tag
Balance Braces
Line Numbers
Highlight Invalid Code
Apply Comment
Remove Comment
Wrap Tag
Recent Snippets
Move or Convert CSS
Indent Code
Outdent Code
Format Source Code

Using Quick Tag Editor

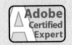

DW 3.17

Creating Web documents in the Design view is a beautiful and elegant way to design Web pages; however, sometimes you just need to get under the hood and make changes directly to the code. Dreamweaver gives you a way to make alterations to the code using the Quick Tag Editor. When activated, the Quick Tag Editor displays as a small pop-up window and allows you to edit a tag, add a tag, or enclose the current selection within a tag. In addition, you can use a list of tags and attributes to help jog your HTML memory, and save you some typing. Dreamweaver's Quick Tag Editor can be used in three ways: Insert HTML (used for adding new tags and code at the current cursor position), Wrap Tag (wrap one tag around one or more other tags and content) and Edit HTML (displays the entire selected tag with all the attributes), and is a great time saver for making those small tweaks to the code of any Web document. While most designers will perform most of the creative process using the Design view, it's nice to know that you have a powerful tool like the Quick Tag Editor when you need to get back to coding basics.

Open the Quick Tag Editor

1. Open the Web page you want to view code.

2. Open the Quick Tag Editor using any of the following methods:

   ◆ Click the **Modify** menu, and then click **Quick Tag Editor**.

   ◆ Use the keyboard shortcut Ctrl+T (Win) or ⌘+T (Mac).

   ◆ Click the **Quick Tag Editor** icon in the Properties panel.

Did You Know?

Dreamweaver helps you with the syntax of the code. If you fail to add the quotation marks around a parameters value, the Quick Tag Editor will do it for you. If you want to add more than one tag, you can use the right arrow key to move beyond the first set of braces, in the Quick Tag Editor. Then simply enter in a left brace and add the additional tag.

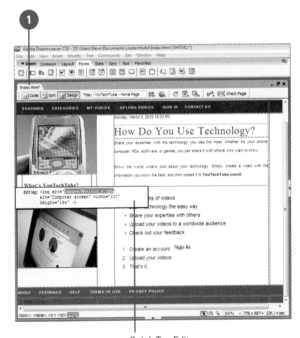

Quick Tag Editor

Use Quick Tag Editor in Wrap Tag or Insert HTML Mode

1. Open the Web page you want to view code.

2. Select a portion of text within the document (for Wrap Tag mode) or click in the text area (do not select any text) to place an insertion point (for Insert HTML mode).

3. Open the Quick Tag Editor.

4. Use the HTML tags in the pop-up hint list to insert a tag, or manually enter a customized XML tag.

5. Press Enter to wrap the selected text with the tag.

Use Quick Tag Editor in Edit Tag Mode

1. Open the Web page you want to view code.

2. Select a complete tag in Code view (i.e. img), or select an object, such as an image, in Design view.

3. Open the Quick Tag Editor.

   The tag with all its attributes will be displayed within the Quick Tag Editor window.

4. Manually enter any changes to the tag and attributes.

5. Press Enter to add the tag to the document.

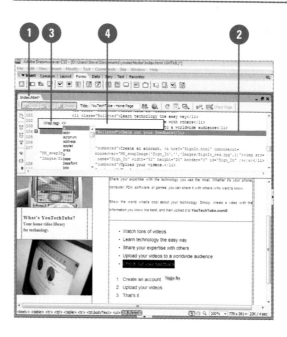

Using the Tag Inspector

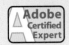

DW 3.17

Dreamweaver's Tag Inspector gives you control over your code by displaying a collapsible outline of the tags used on the current page. This feature allow you to quickly determine if tags are correctly nested, and to view and change tag attributes. For example, you may want to change the attributes of the <body> tag, or change the overall color and size of the default font; both these and many more options are available using the Tag Inspector. When selected, the Tag Inspector displays a collapsible structure of all the attributes within the selected Web element. This view gives you an overall view of the code and how it's laid out. When you select a tag all the attributes for that tag are displayed for you to view and edit.

Access the Tag Inspector

1. Open the Web page you want to view in the Tag Inspector.

2. Make a selection using one of the following methods:

   ◆ **Code View.** Select a specific HTML tag or section of text.

   ◆ **Split View.** Select a HTML tag in the Code pane or select an object in the Design pane.

   ◆ **Design View.** Select an object in the window, or create a selection of text.

3. Click the **Window** menu, and then click **Tag Inspector** to display the Tag Inspector.

4. Select from the following views:

   ◆ **Category View.** Displays a list of general categories within collapsible headings. Click the plus (+) or minus (-) sign icon to display all available attributes.

   ◆ **List View.** Displays a list of all available attributes for the selected Web element.

5. Select the attribute that you want to add or modify, and enter the correct value in the input field.

6. Press the Enter key to record your changes.

Tag Inspector

Selected element

Using the Tag Chooser

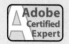

DW 3.17

The Tag Chooser allows you to insert any tag from the Dreamweaver tag libraries in your page. A tag library is a collection of tags for a certain type that contains tag information, code hints, target browser checks, and other features. You can insert tags from the following types: HTML, CFML, ASP.NET, JSP, JRun custom library, ASP, PHP, and WML. If you are looking for a specific tag in a specific category, the Tag Chooser can help you insert it into your code with the right syntax.

Insert Tags Using the Tag Chooser

1. Open the Web page you want to insert a tag using the Tag Chooser.

2. Click to place the insertion point in the code where you want to insert a tag.

3. Right-click (Win) or control-click (Mac) near the insertion point, and then click **Insert Tag**.

4. Select a category of tags from the tag library, or expand the category and select a subcategory.

5. Select a tag from the right pane.

6. To view syntax and usage information for the selected tag, click **Tag Info**.

7. To insert the selected tag into your code, click **Insert**.

8. If a tag requires more information, enter the required information in the tag editor, and then click **OK**.

9. Click **Close**.

Did You Know?

You can add or remove tags, attributes, and libraries from the Tag Library. Click the Edit menu, click Tag Libraries, click the Plus (+) or Minus (-) buttons to select commands to add or remove tags, attributes, and libraries.

Using the Reference Panel

It doesn't matter whether you're an experienced Web designer, or a newcomer to the field. Sooner or later you're going to need a bit of help, in the form of reference material. I'll admit that I'm a big reader... I love to read. I have a library full of books on creativity and design. Unfortunately, I can't carry all those books with me when I'm on a lecture tour. That's why one of my favorite features in Dreamweaver is the Reference panel. The Reference panel gives you instant (on screen) access to 10 O'Reilly reference manuals, 2 Adobe manuals, and a UseableNet Accessibility Reference. Now that's a lot of reading material, and instant information at your fingertips. For example, you're coding a page, and you need a bit more information on the HTML body tag... it's there, or you need a bit of help with the new syntax of XHTML... it's there. As a matter of fact, when you first open the Reference panel, the information displayed is based on the selected element on the active Web page.

Access the Reference Panel

1. Open Dreamweaver (do not open a document).

2. Click the **Window** menu, and then click **Reference**.

3. Select information based on the following options:

   - Click the **Book** popup to select from the list of available reference manuals.

   - Click the **Tag** popup to select from a list of available HTML tags.

   - Click the **Select Attribute** icon to choose from a list of available attributes, for the selected tag.

   The reader window displays the information based on your selections.

Reference information

Access Specific Information

1. Open the Web page you want to access specific information.

2. Perform one of the following:

   ◆ **Code View.** Select a specific HTML tag, CSS style rule, or other HTML text.

   ◆ **Split View.** Select an item in the Code pane or select an object or text in the Design pane.

   ◆ **Design View.** Select an object, graphic, or portion of text.

3. Select the element you want specific information.

4. Press Shift+F1 (Shortcut for accessing the Reference panel).

   The panel opens and displays information about the selected page element.

Reference information for the selected element

Did You Know?

You can search for tags, attributes, or text in code. Click the Edit menu, click Find And Replace, specify the Find in document, select Source Code in the Search popup, enter the text you want to find, enter the replace text (optional), specify any options, and then click the Find or Replace buttons you want.

You can save and reuse searches. Click the Edit menu, click Find And Replace, set the search criteria you want, click the Save Query button (the disk icon), navigate to the folder where you want to save the search, and then click Save. To reuse a search, click the Load Query button (the folder icon), navigate to the folder with the saved search query file, select it, click Open, and then use the Find or Replace buttons you want.

Setting Code Format Preferences

DW 2.11

You can use the Code Format section of the Preferences dialog box to change the way your code looks in Code view. The options you set in the Code Format section, except the Override Case Of option, are automatically applied only to new documents or additions to documents you create in the future. If you want to reformat an existing document, you can use the Apply Source Formatting on the Commands menu.

Set Code Format Preferences

1 Click the **Dreamweaver** (Mac) or **Edit** (Win) menu, and then click **Preferences**.

2 Click the **Code Format** category.

3 Select from the following options:

◆ **Indent.** Select to have Dreamweaver indent generated code, and then specify how many spaces or tabs to indent.

◆ **Tab Size.** Specify how many spaces for a tab character.

◆ **Automatic Wrapping.** Select to insert a line-break character at the end of the column width.

◆ **Line Break Type.** Select the type of remote hosting site.

◆ **Default Tag Case and Default Attribute Case.** Select <lowercase> or <uppercase>.

◆ **Override Case Of: Tags and Attributes.** Select whether to override your case settings.

◆ **TD Tag: Do Not Include A break Inside The TD Tag.** Select to prevent problems with white space and line breaks on older browsers.

◆ **Advanced Formatting.** Click to set formatting options for CSS code and individual tags and attributes in the Tag Library Editor.

4 Click **OK**.

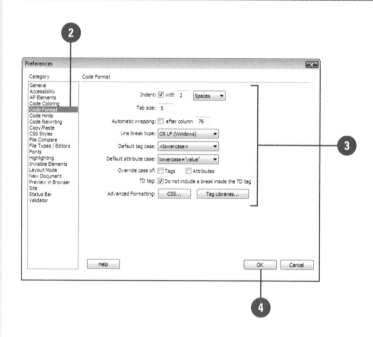

Setting Code Hint Preferences

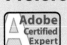 DW 2.11

You can use the Code Hint section of the Preferences dialog box to set options for the Code Hints popup menu. Code Hints does more than help you type in a simple HTML code tag. It helps you insert tag names, attributes, and values as you type code in Code view or the Quick Tag Editor. For example, when a tag requires the selection of a color, Dreamweaver displays a color palette. When a font is required, a font list is automatically displayed, and when a file is required a browse button magically appears allowing you to select and insert the file.

Set Code Hint Preferences

1. Click the **Dreamweaver** (Mac) or **Edit** (Win) menu, and then click **Preferences**.

2. Click the **Code Hint** category.

3. Select from the following check boxes:

   ◆ **Close Tags.** Select an option to specify how you want to insert closing tags. The default inserts tags automatically after you type the characters </. You can also insert it after a final bracket >, or not at all.

   ◆ **Options.** Select the **Enable Code Hints** check box to use code hints, and then drag the slider to set the code hints menu delay you want.

   ◆ **Menus.** Select the check boxes for the types of code hints you want to display, and clear the others you don't want.

   IMPORTANT *Even if you disable code hints, you can display a popup hint in Code view by pressing Control+Spacebar.*

4. To add or remove tags and attributes, click the **Tag Library Editor** link.

5. Click **OK**.

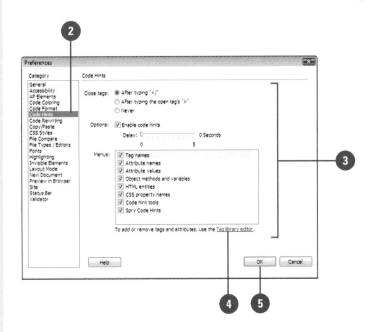

Setting Code Rewriting Preferences

 DW 2.11

You can use the Code Rewriting section of the Preferences dialog box to specify how and if Dreamweaver changes your code. Some of the rewriting options allows you to fix invalid nesting and unclosed tags, prevent duplicate names for form objects, ensure attributes values and URLs contain legal characters, and add the right JavaScript tags upon opening active content files. These options have no effect when you edit your code in Code view. If you disable the rewriting options, invalid HTML code that would have been rewritten is displayed in the Document window.

Set Code Rewriting Preferences

1. Click the **Dreamweaver** (Mac) or **Edit** (Win) menu, and then click **Preferences**.

2. Click the **Code Rewriting** category.

3. Select from the following options:

   ◆ **Fix Invalidly Nested and Unclosed Tags.** Select to rewrite overlapping or transposed tags and inserts closing quotation marks and closing brackets as needed.

   ◆ **Rename Form Items When Pasting.** Select to prevent duplicate names for form objects.

   ◆ **Remove Extra Closing Tags.** Select to delete closing tags that don't have an associated opening tag.

   ◆ **Warn When Fixing Or Removing Tags.** Select to display a summary of invalid HTML code Dreamweaver wants to fix.

   ◆ **Never Rewrite Code: In Files With Extensions.** Select to prevent code rewriting in files with specific file extensions, and then specify the files extensions you want separated by a space.

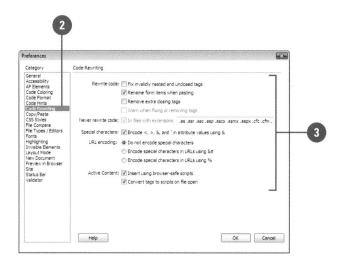

- ◆ **Encode <, >, &, And " In Attribute Values Using &.** Select to make sure attribute values you enter outside Code view contain legal characters.

- ◆ **Do Not Encode Special Characters.** Select to prevent Dreamweaver from changing URLs to use only legal characters.

- ◆ **Encode Special Characters In URL Using &#.** Select to make sure URLs you enter outside Code view contain legal characters (use the &# encoding method).

- ◆ **Encode Special Characters In URL Using %.** Select to make sure URLs you enter outside Code view contain legal characters (use the % encoding method).

- ◆ **Insert Using Browser-safe Scripts.** Select to make sure the active content you insert uses the right tags for use in browsers.

- ◆ **Convert Tags To Scripts On File Open.** Select to change <object>, <embed>, and <applet> tags null and add the needed JavaScript tags when you open a file with active content.

4 Click **OK**.

Setting Code Color Preferences

DW 2.11

You can use the Code Coloring section of the Preferences dialog box to specify colors for general categories of tags and code elements, such as HTML Image or style tags, Library items, or CSS properties. For a selected tag or code element, you can specify the text color, background color, and any formatting (Bold, Italic, or Underline) you want to make it easier to work with your code.

Set Code Color Preferences

1. Click the **Dreamweaver** (Mac) or **Edit** (Win) menu, and then click **Preferences**.

2. Click the **Code Coloring** category.

3. Click the **Default Background** color box, and then select a color.

4. Click the document type in which you want to set code colors.

5. Click **Edit Coloring Scheme**.

6. Select the style for the document type you want to change.

7. Specify the text color, background color, and any formatting (Bold, Italic, or Underline) you want.

   The sample code in the Preview pane displays the new styles and colors.

8. Click **OK**.

9. Click **OK**.

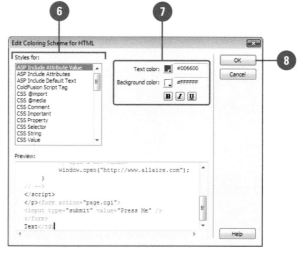

Working with Behaviors

15

Introduction

Everybody loves the versatility that JavaScript can bring to a Web page, yet not that many people love programming in JavaScript, to make it happen. Dreamweaver makes your life easier by allowing you to insert Behaviors, most of which directly translate into JavaScript. Using behaviors, you can do things like insert pop-up windows, create disjointed rollovers, check to see if users have a certain plug-in or what browser they're running.

The best thing about behaviors and commands is that they are extendable. Many third party companies and individuals write commands and behaviors for Dreamweaver. You can download these extensions from the Web, most often for free!

A **behavior** is a combination of an event with an action triggered by that event. In the Behaviors panel, you add a behavior to a page by specifying an action and then specifying the event that triggers that action. Adobe Dreamweaver behaviors insert JavaScript code in documents to allow users to interact with a Web page, change the page, or to produce certain tasks. Behaviors are attached to a specific element on your page, whether it's a text link, an image, and even certain HTML specific tags.

An action consists of pre-written JavaScript code that performs a specific task, such as opening a browser window, showing or hiding an AP element, playing a sound, or stopping a Flash movie. The actions provided with Dreamweaver are written by engineers to provide maximum cross-browser compatibility.

In this chapter you'll learn how to apply behaviors to Web elements, how to edit and modify behaviors; even how to create and maintain a library of all your important behaviors.

Introduce Behaviors

Apply Behaviors to Page Elements

Apply Behaviors to Entire Page

Edit Behaviors

Work with Behaviors

Add Behavior Effects

Go to Another Web Page

Open Another Browser Window

Display Text Messages

Preload and Swap Images

Change Element Properties

Drag an AP Element

Modify a Navigation Bar

Show and Hide Elements

Execute a JavaScript

Introducing Behaviors

Dreamweaver helps non-programmer types (you know who you are) use built-in JavaScript functions that are useful to any Web project. The code generated is well optimized so you do not have to worry about performance. A Dreamweaver behavior consists of two parts: An **action** that instructs the browser what to do, and an **event** that triggers the specific actions.

Dreamweaver comes supplied with dozens of behavior actions, the most useful being:

- **Check Browser.** The Check Browser action sends visitors to different pages depending on their specific browser.

- **Check Plug-in.** The Check Plug-in action sends visitors to different pages depending on whether they have the specified plug-in installed.

- **Go To URL.** The Go To URL action opens a new page in the current window or in the specified frame.

- **Open Browser Window.** The Open Browser Window action opens a URL in a new window.

- **Play Sound.** The Play Sound action plays a sound (requires the visitor have the ability to play sounds).

- **Popup Message.** The Popup Message action displays a JavaScript alert with the message you specify.

- **Preload Images.** The Preload Images action loads images that do not appear on the page right away (i.e. rollover images) into the browser cache.

- **Show Pop-Up Menu.** The Show Pop-Up Menu behavior creates a pop-up menu within a page.

- **Show/Hide Elements.** The Show/Hide Elements action causes specified layers to be shown or hidden.

- **Swap Image.** The Swap Image action creates button rollovers and other image effects (including swapping more than one image at a time).

- **Swap Image Restore.** The Swap Image Restore action restores the last set of swapped images to their previous source files (automatically added whenever you attach the Swap Image action).

- **Validate Form.** The Validate Form action checks the contents of selected text fields to ensure that the user has entered the correct type of data.

NOTE *Behavior code is client-side JavaScript code; that is, it runs in browsers, not on servers.*

Behaviors are attached to a specific element on your page, whether it's a text link, an image, and even certain HTML specific tags. After you attach a behavior to a page element, whenever the event you've specified occurs for that element, the browser calls the action (the JavaScript code) that you've associated with that event. (The events that you can use to trigger a given action varies from browser to browser.) For example, if you attach the Popup Message action to a link and specify that it will be triggered by the onMouseOver event, then whenever someone points to that link with the mouse pointer in the browser, your message pops up in a dialog box. A single event can trigger several different actions, and you can specify the order in which those actions occur.

In order to make a behavior work, an action is linked to an event. Events are, effectively, messages generated by browsers indicating that a visitor to your page has done something. For example, when a visitor moves the pointer over a link, the browser generates an onMouseOver event for that link; the browser then checks to see whether there's some JavaScript code that the browser is to call when the event is generated. Different events are defined for different page elements; for example, in most browsers onMouseOver and onClick are events associated with links, where onLoad is an event associated with images and with the body section of the document. Notice the specific way that JavaScript code is written. It's not only important to get the spelling of a code piece correct; in addition, case is important. For example onBlur is correct… onblur is not. The good news is that Dreamweaver inserts the correct code into the document through the use of the Behaviors panel.

The possible Events associated with an Action are:

- **onBlur.** Activates when a blur event occurs. A field gains focus when the user clicks inside the text box, and the focus is lost (onblur) when the user clicks outside the box, anywhere on the page.

- **onClick.** Activates when the user clicks the left mouse button on the object.

- **onDblClick.** Activates when the user double-clicks the object.

- **onError.** Activates when an error occurs during object loading.

- **onFocus.** Activates when the object receives focus. A field gains focus when the user clicks inside the object.

- **onKeyDown.** Activates when the user presses a key.

- **onKeyPress.** Activates when the user presses an alphanumeric key.

- **onKeyUp.** Activates when the user releases an alphanumeric key.

- **onLoad.** Activates after the browser loads the object.

- **onMouseDown.** Activates when the user clicks the object with either the mouse or a form button.

- **onMouseMove.** Activates when the user moves the mouse over the object.

- **onMouseOut.** Activates when the user moves the mouse pointer outside the boundaries of the object.

- **onMouseOver.** Activates when the user moves the mouse pointer into the object.

- **onMouseUp.** Activates when the user releases a mouse button while the mouse is over the object.

- **OnUnload.** Activates immediately before the object is unloaded.

The target browser you select determines which events are supported for a given element. Internet Explorer 4.0, for example, has a much wider array of events for each element than Netscape Navigator 4.0 or any 3.0 browsers.

The power of Behaviors lies in the fact that they use JavaScript code to create dynamic and interactive Web pages. Although JavaScript is not new to Web page design, it's quickly becoming more and more popular as the days roll by, and the World Wide Web Consortium (www.w3c.org) is working overtime to make all the code pieces work the same on all browsers. However, no matter how good the code is, there will always be times when the code warrior (you) decides that the code needs to be edited or completely eliminated. Thankfully, with Dreamweaver, this is no problem whatsoever.

Applying Behaviors to Page Elements

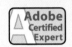

DW 3.14

Dreamweaver allows you to attach behaviors to links, images, form elements, or any of several other HTML elements. The Behaviors panel allows you to attach, modify, and manage behaviors embedded in a page. In the Behaviors panel, you can use options to show all events for a specific category, or only the ones currently attached to the page. The target browser you select determines which events are supported for a given element. Dreamweaver works well with current browsers. However older ones may be more limited. Internet Explorer 4.0, for example, has a much wider array of events for each element than Netscape Navigator 4.0 or any 3.0 browsers. If you need additional functionality, you can attach more than one event to a specific action; for example, when you user clicks on a specific image, the image changes, and a prerecorded sound plays. When you use multiple actions, they occur in the order in which they're listed in the Actions column of the Behaviors panel.

Apply One or More Behaviors to a Page Element

1. Open the Web page you want to apply a behavior to an element.

2. Click the **Window** menu, and then click **Behaviors** to display the Behaviors panel.

3. Select an element (image or link) on the page in Design view.

4. Click the **Add Behavior** button (plus sign), and then select a behavior action from the Actions menu.

   NOTE *Actions dimmed in the menu can't be chosen for that particular Web element.*

   IMPORTANT *The Deprecated submenu provides features for those who used them in Dreamweaver 8 or earlier. Dreamweaver CS3 provides new ways to perform the same tasks.*

5. Enter the parameters and options you want for the selected action; the parameters and options vary depending on the selected action.

6 Click **OK**.

The action is embedded into the HTML code, and appears in the Behaviors panel. The default event is onClick.

7 Click the default Event (onClick), and then click the **Event** list arrow to select the event you want to associate with this action (in this example, onMouseOver).

8 If you want to apply more than one behavior, repeat steps 4-7.

9 Click the **File** menu, point to **Preview In Browser**, and then select a browser to test your Web page.

10 In your browser, perform the event to trigger the action.

Did You Know?

You can show events for a specific browser. Open the Behaviors panel, click the Add Behavior button, point to Show Events For, and then select the browser that you want to show events.

You can show all events or only the ones currently attached to the page. Open the Behaviors panel, click the Show All Events button to show all available events, or click the Show Set Events button to show only the events currently attached behaviors.

See Also

See "Checking for CSS Browser Compatibility" on page 338 for information on using browser compatibility.

For Your Information

Testing Browser Compatibility

Unlike CGI scripts, the client interprets Behavior JavaScript code. The good news is that there are currently many early browsers that support JavaScript. Each browser supports different JavaScript features. Some bugs are platform-specific, while others are browser-specific. To ensure that your site will function correctly, Dreamweaver gives you the ability to check the site, and list any problems that might occur with earlier browsers. The two most important ways are to check the code live in various browsers, or let Dreamweaver check the page for browser incompatibility issues. To check the code live, click the File menu, point to Preview In Browser, and then select a browser. Dreamweaver opens the active page in the selected browser, and you can check the page for errors live. To check browser compatibility, click the File menu, point to Check Page, and then select Browser Compatibility. Dreamweaver checks the current page, and gives you a list of any possible errors by browser type and version.

Applying Behaviors to Entire Page

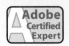

DW 3.14

In addition to attaching behaviors to links, images, form elements, or any of several other HTML elements, you can also attach behaviors to an entire document (using the <body> tag). The process to apply a behavior to an entire page is similar to the one you use to attach a behavior to an individual page element. The difference is what you select. For a page element, you select the element; for an entire page, you select the <body> tag, which applies the behavior to the document. For example, you can use the Check Plug-in behavior to check for the existence of media players, such as Adobe Flash, Apple QuickTime, and Microsoft Windows Media Player, and then redirect a visitor.

Apply a Behavior to a Web Page

1 Open the Web page you want to apply a behavior to an entire page.

2 Click the **Window** menu, and then click **Behaviors** to display the Behaviors panel.

3 Click the <body> tag in the tag selector at the bottom left of the Document window.

4 Click the **Add Behavior** button (plus sign), and then select a behavior action from the Actions menu.

5 Enter the parameters and options you want for the selected action; the parameters and options vary depending on the selected action.

6 Click **OK**.

Did You Know?

You can download and install third-party behaviors. If you don't find the behavior functionality you need, you can download and install behaviors created by third-party developers. Open the Behaviors panel, click the Plus (+) button, and then click Get More Behaviors from the Actions menu. In your browser, search for the behavior you want on the Exchange site, and then download and install it according to the site instructions.

Apply the Check Plugin Behavior to a Web Page

1. Open the Web page you want to apply a behavior to an entire page.

2. Click the **Window** menu, and then click **Behaviors** to display the Behaviors panel.

3. Click the <body> tag in the tag selector at the bottom left of the Document window.

4. Click the **Add Behavior** button (plus sign), and then click **Check Plugin**.

5. Select the following options from the Check Plugin dialog box.

   ◆ **Select.** Click the **Select** option, and then select a plugin from the popup menu (in this example, Flash).

   ◆ **Enter.** Click the **Enter** option, and then enter or browse for the name of the required plugin (use if your plugin is not displayed in the Select popup menu).

   ◆ **If Found Go To URL.** Enter or browse for the name of the URL to go to, if the required plugin is found on the visitor's computer.

   ◆ **Otherwise Go To URL.** Enter or browse for the name of the URL to go to, if the plugin is not found on the visitor's computer.

   ◆ **Always Go To First URL If Detection Is Not Possible.** Select if the visitor's computer does not allow for plugin checking, and the browser loads the first URL.

6. Click **OK**.

Editing Behaviors

After you create a behavior, you can quickly and easily change the parameters for the action or the event that triggers the action. When you complete your changes to a behavior, all occurrences of the behavior on the page are updated. If other pages use the same behavior, you need to update the behavior on each page.

Edit the Parameters for a Behavior

1. Open the Web page with the behavior you want to change.

2. Click the **Window** menu, and then click **Behaviors** to display the Behaviors panel.

3. Select an element on the Web page that contains an attached behavior, or if the behavior is attached to the document, click the <body> tag in the tag selector at the bottom left of the Document window.

   The behaviors attached to the element appear in the Behaviors panel.

4. Select the specific event for the action that you want to edit.

5. Click the **Behaviors Options** button, and then click **Edit Behavior**.

   TIMESAVER *Double-click the event to open the dialog box; you can also select it, and then press Enter (Win) or Return (Mac).*

6. In a behaviors dialog box, make the changes you want; the dialog box options differ depending on the behavior.

7. Click **OK**.

Change the Event for a Behavior

1. Open the Web page with the behavior you want to change.

2. Click the **Window** menu, and then click **Behaviors** to display the Behaviors panel.

3. Select an element on the Web page that contains an attached behavior, or if the behavior is attached to the document, click the <body> tag in the tag selector at the bottom left of the Document window.

   The behaviors attached to the element appear in the Behaviors panel.

4. Click the specific event that you want to edit.

5. Click the **Event** list arrow, and then select the event you want to trigger the action from the available options.

Working with Behaviors

Behaviors you have attached to a selected page element appear in the Behaviors panel in the behaviors list by event in alphabetical order. If you have multiple actions for a specific event, the behaviors are executed by the browser in the order in which they appear in the behavior list. You can use the Behaviors panel to change the order. If you no longer need a behavior, you can remove it from the list.

Change Multiple Behavior Order

① Open the Web page with the behavior you want to change.

② Click the **Window** menu, and then click **Behaviors** to display the Behaviors panel.

③ Select an element on the page that contains multiple behaviors.

The behaviors attached to the element appear in the Behaviors panel.

④ Select the behavior action you want to change.

⑤ Click the **Up** or **Down** buttons to move the action to a different stacking order.

TIMESAVER *Press the Up and Down arrow keys to move the selected action.*

Remove a Behavior

1. Open the Web page with the behavior you want to remove.

2. Click the **Window** menu, and then click **Behaviors** to display the Behaviors panel.

3. Select an element on the Web page that contains an attached behavior, or if the behavior is attached to the document, click the <body> tag in the tag selector at the bottom left of the Document window.

   The behaviors attached to the element appear in the Behaviors panel.

4. Select the behavior action you want to delete.

5. Click the **Remove Event** button (minus sign).

   The behavior is removed from the document.

Adding Behavior Effects

Dreamweaver Effects give you one more way to create dynamic Web pages. For example, you can use Behavior Effects to make a Web element shrink to half size, or to slowly fade away, there's even an event that lets you make objects shake. While these options are fun to use, remember that Web design is not about what you can do to a site to make it dynamic. You have to ask yourself this question: Are the special effects that I'm using helping me to keep my visitor's attention, and are they in line with the message that I'm trying to send. If the answer to those questions is yes, then by all means, use effects; however, if the answer is no, then stay away from using the effects.

Adding Effects

1. Open the Web page you want to apply a behavior effect to an element.

2. Click the **Window** menu, and then click **Behaviors** to display the Behaviors panel.

3. Select an element on the page that you want to attach an effect.

4. Click the **Add Behavior** button (plus sign), point to **Effects**, and then select an effect from the following options:

   ◆ **Appear/Fade.** Use this effect when you want the element to slowly appear or fade from the Web page.

   ◆ **Blind.** Use this effect when you want the element to slowly rise or lower on the page (like opening or closing a blind).

   ◆ **Grow/Shrink.** Use this effect when you want the element to increase or decrease in size.

   ◆ **Highlight.** Use this effect when you want the element (typically text) to change color.

   ◆ **Shake.** Use this effect when you want the element to shake side to side.

- **Slide.** Use this effect when you want the element to slide. Works by selecting the container tag of the content tag that you want to slide.

- **Squish.** Use this effect when you want the element to slowly reduce in size until gone (the anchor point for the squish effect is the upper-left corner of the Web object).

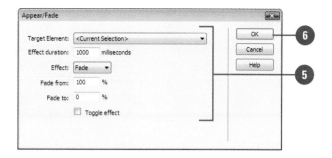

5 Specify the options you want in the dialog box for the specific effect; the options vary depending on the effect.

IMPORTANT *Not all the behavior effects work for all the elements in Dreamweaver; an error message may appear.*

6 Click **OK** to attach the effect to the Page, Document, or Tag.

Behavior effects

Going to Another Web Page

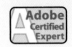

The Go To URL behavior gives you the ability to link an element on a Web page to a URL address. For example, you can create a Web page, and then use the Go To URL behavior to direct visitors to other sites and pages, or you could create a set of interactive buttons for use on a standard HTML driven Web site. Whichever option you choose, the ability to direct a visitor to other Web sites is essential to creating Internet-oriented documents.

Use the Go To URL Behavior

1. Open the Web page you want to apply a behavior.

2. Click the **Window** menu, and then click **Behaviors** to display the Behaviors panel.

3. Click the element you want to add the Go To URL behavior.

4. Click the **Add Behavior** button (plus sign), and then click **Go To URL**.

   A dialog box appears, allowing you to set the details of the action.

5. Type the URL or click **Browse**, select the URL from the Select File dialog box, and then click **OK**.

6. Click **OK**.

7. To change the trigger, click the event, click the **Event** list arrow, and then select the event you want.

Opening Another Browser Window

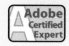
DW 3.14

The Open Browser behavior allows you to set a hyperlink to open in a new browser window. When you use the Open Browser behavior, you need to specify the URL you want to open in the new browser window and any window attributes, such as width, height, navigation and location toolbar, status bar, menu bar, scrollbar as needed and resize handles. If you want to use this behavior with text, you can also use the Change Property and Change Property Restore behaviors to change the pointer to a hand when visitors hover over your text link.

Open Another Browser Window

1. Open the Web page you want to apply a behavior.

2. Click the **Window** menu, and then click **Behaviors** to display the Behaviors panel.

3. Click the element you want to add the Open Browser Window behavior; typically link text or graphic.

4. Click the **Add Behavior** button (plus sign), and then click **Open Browser Window**.

   A dialog box appears, allowing you to set the details of the action.

5. Type the URL or click **Browse**, select the URL from the Select File dialog box, and then click **OK**.

6. Enter a window size (width and height in pixels).

7. Select the check boxes with the window attributes you want to use.

8. Enter a window name. The window name is used in the behavior script, so it cannot have any spaces or special characters.

9. Click **OK**.

10. To change the trigger, click the event, click the **Event** list arrow, and then select the event you want.

Displaying Text Messages

DW 3.14

Dreamweaver provides several behaviors to display user text messages, including Popup Message and Set Text. The Set Text behavior consists of four individual behaviors: Set Text of Container, Set Text of Frame, Set Text of Status Bar, and Set Text of Text Field. These behaviors allow you to display text in an alert dialog box, a container, specific frame, text field, or the Status bar.

Create a Popup Message Window

1. Open the Web page you want to apply a behavior.

2. Click the **Window** menu, and then click **Behaviors** to display the Behaviors panel.

3. Click the element you want to add the Popup Message behavior.

4. Click the **Add Behavior** button (plus sign), and then click **Popup Message**.

   A dialog box appears, allowing you to set the details of the action.

5. Type the message you want.

6. Click **OK**.

7. To change the trigger, click the event, click the **Event** list arrow, and then select the event you want.

372

Create a Status Bar Message

① Open the Web page you want to apply a behavior.

② Click the **Window** menu, and then click **Behaviors** to display the Behaviors panel.

③ Click the element you want to add a behavior.

④ Click the **Add Behavior** button (plus sign), point to **Set Text**, and then click **Set Text Of Status Bar**.

A dialog box appears, allowing you to set the details of the action.

⑤ Type the message you want.

⑥ Click **OK**.

⑦ To change the trigger, click the event, click the **Event** list arrow, and then select the event you want.

Preloading and Swapping Images

DW 3.14

The Preload Images behavior allows you to preload images when a Web page initially loads. This is useful when you want to swap images on mouse rollover buttons. The Preload Images behavior loads the rollover image when the page initially loads, so visitors will not experience a delay while the image loads the first time a visitor points to the button. The Swap Images behavior allows you to swap one image for another when an event occurs. The most common use of this behavior is to create rollover buttons. Along with the Swap Image behavior, you can also use the Swap Image Restore behavior, which restores the images that were swapped by the Swap Image behavior.

Preload Images

1. Open the Web page you want to apply a behavior.

2. Click the **Window** menu, and then click **Behaviors** to display the Behaviors panel.

3. Click the element or <body> tag in the tag selector for the entire page you want to add the Preload Images behavior.

4. Click the **Add Behavior** button (plus sign), and then click **Preload Images**.

    A dialog box appears, allowing you to set the details of the action.

5. Click **Browse**, locate and select the image you want to preload, and then click **OK**.

6. Click the **Add Items** button (plus sign).

7. To add more images, repeat steps 5 and 6.

8. Click **OK**.

9. To change the trigger, click the event, click the **Event** list arrow, and then select the event you want.

Swap Images

1. Open the Web page you want to apply a behavior.

2. Click the **Window** menu, and then click **Behaviors** to display the Behaviors panel.

3. Click the image you want to swap.

4. Click the **Add Behavior** button (plus sign), and then click **Swap Image**.

   The selected image appears highlighted in the Swap Image dialog box.

5. Click **Browse**, locate and select the image you want to swap it with, and then click **OK**.

6. To insert a Preload Images behavior, select the **Preload Images** check box.

7. To insert a Swap Image Restore behavior, select the **Restore Images onMouseOut** check box.

8. To remove a swap, select an image in the list, and then delete the file and path in the Set Source To box.

9. Click **OK**.

10. To change the trigger, click the event, click the **Event** list arrow, and then select the event you want.

Changing Element Properties

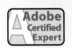 DW 3.14

The Change Property behavior allows you to change properties, such as font styles, borders or visibility, for an element on a Web page. The Change Property behavior is useful for adding interactivity to a Web page. For example, you can have the Change Property behavior display a text description or link address when a user points to a picture on a page. Along with the Change Property behavior, you can also use the Change Property Restore behavior, which restores the most recent property changes made by the Change Property behavior. When you use the Change Property Restore behavior, Dreamweaver displays a message dialog box acknowledging the use of the behavior. You can double-click the behavior to display a list of properties being restored.

Use the Change Property Behavior

1. Open the Web page you want to apply a behavior.

2. Click the **Window** menu, and then click **Behaviors** to display the Behaviors panel.

3. Click the element you want to add the Change Property behavior (in this example, select the cell phone image).

4. Click the **Add Behavior** button (plus sign), and then click **Change Property**.

   A dialog box appears, allowing you to set the details of the action.

5. Click the **Type Of Element** popup, and then select the type you want to change (in this example, select DIV).

6. Click the **Element ID** popup, and then select an ID (in this example, select div "apTextSign").

   The AP element to the right of the cell phone image contains text, which you'll change the font size to a larger size.

7 Click the **Select** option and select the property you want to change (in this example, select fontSize), or click the **Enter** option and enter the property you want to change.

8 Enter the new value you want (in this example, enter 24).

9 Click **OK**.

10 To change the trigger, click the event, click the **Event** list arrow, and then select the event you want.

Font size changes to 24 pt.

Point here to change property

Dragging an AP Element

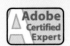 DW 3.14

The Drag AP Element behavior allows you let visitors on a Web page to drag an AP (Absolute Positioned) element. This behavior is useful for creating interactive training, games, and interface controls, such as a slider. The behavior allows you to specify how you want the AP element to move. You can constrain the movement in a specific direction, to a specific location or target, or to snap to another element. In order to use the Drag AP Element behavior, you need to call the behavior before the visitor can drag the element. To achieve this, you need to attach the Drag AP Element behavior to the body object with the onLoad event.

Use the Drag AP Element Behavior

1. Open the Web page you want to apply a behavior.

2. Click the **Window** menu, and then click **Behaviors** to display the Behaviors panel.

3. Create the AP Element you want to add the Drag AP Element behavior.

4. Click <body> in the tag selector in the Document window.

5. Click the **Add Behavior** button (plus sign), and then click **Drag AP Element**.

   A dialog box appears displaying the Basic tab.

6. Click the **Movement** popup, and then click **Constrained** or **Unconstrained**.

7. If you selected the Constrained option, enter values for Up, Down, Left, and Right (in pixels).

   The values are relative to the starting position of the AP element. To constrain movement, use the following methods:

   ◆ **Rectangle.** Enter positive values in all four boxes.

   ◆ **Vertical.** Enter positive values for Up and Down and 0 for Left and Right.

◆ **Horizontal.** Enter positive values for Left and Right and 0 for Up and Down.

8 Enter values for the Drop Target in the Up, Down, Left, and Right boxes (in pixels), or click **Get Current Position** to automatically insert the current position of the AP element.

The drop target is the spot where you want the visitor to drag the AP element. Values are relative to the top left corner of the browser window.

9 Enter a Snap If Within value (in pixels) to specify how close the visitor needs to be to the drop target before the AP element snaps to the target.

10 To define the drag handle, track movement, and trigger an action, click the **Advanced** tab.

◆ **Drag Handle.** Click the popup, and then select **Entire Element** or **Area Within Element**. For an area, enter values for the area you want within the element.

◆ **While Dragging.** Select the **Bring Element To Front, then** check box, select a position, and then enter the script code or function you want executed during the drag.

◆ **When Dropped.** Enter the script code or function you want executed when dropped, and then select the **Only If Snapped** check box to execute the code only if snapped.

11 Click **OK**.

12 To change the trigger, click the event, click the **Event** list arrow, and then select the event you want.

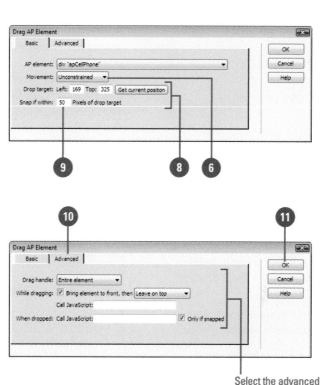

Select the advanced options you want

Modifying a
Navigation Bar

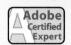 DW 3.14

The Set Nav Bar Image behavior allows you to change an image into a navigation bar image or modify an existing navigation bar. You can change images depending on the current state of the navigation bar (either Up image, Over image, or Down image), or change the URL or select a window when a visitor clicks a navigation bar button. By default, clicking a navigation bar image causes all other images to display the Up state. You can specify advanced settings to change the default Up state to something else.

Use the Set Nav Bar Behavior

1. Open the Web page with the navigation bar you want to change.

2. Click the **Window** menu, and then click **Behaviors** to display the Behaviors panel.

3. Select the image in the navigation bar you want to change.

4. Click the **Add Behavior** button (plus sign), and then click **Set Nav Bar Image**.

   A dialog box appears displaying the Basic tab.

5. Change the options you want for the navigation bar image.

6. Click **OK**.

See Also

See "Inserting a Navigation Bar" on page 172 for information on inserting a navigation bar and setting specific options in the Set Nav Bar Image dialog box.

Set Multiple Images for a Navigation Bar

1 Open the Web page with the navigation bar you want to change.

2 Click the **Window** menu, and then click **Behaviors** to display the Behaviors panel.

3 Select the image in the navigation bar you want to set.

4 In the Behaviors panel, double-click the Set Nav Bar Image action related with the event you want to change.

A dialog box appears displaying the Basic tab.

5 Click the **Advanced** tab.

6 Click the **When Element Is Displaying** popup, and then select one of the following options:

◆ **Over Image or Over While Down Image.** Select to change the display of another image when the pointer is over the selected image.

◆ **Down Image.** Select to change the display of another image after a visitor clicks the image.

7 Select another image on the page.

8 Enter the path and file name of the image or click **Browse** to select the image file.

9 If you selected Over Image or Over While Down Image, enter the path and file name of the image or click **Browse** to select the image file.

10 Click **OK**.

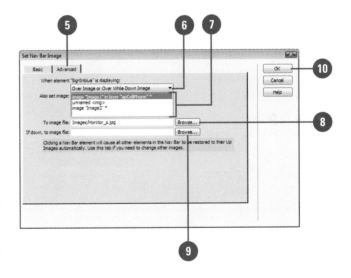

Showing and Hiding Elements

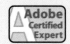

DW 3.14

Show or Hide Page Elements

1. Open the Web page you want to apply a behavior.

2. Click the **Window** menu, and then click **Behaviors** to display the Behaviors panel.

3. Click the element you want to add a behavior.

4. Click the **Add Behavior** button (plus sign), and then click **Show-Hide Elements**.

    A dialog box appears, allowing you to set the details of the action.

5. Click the element you want to show, hide, or restore.

6. Click **Show**, **Hide**, or **Default**, which restores the default visibility of the element.

7. Repeat steps 5 and 6 for each element you want.

8. Click **OK**.

9. To change the trigger, click the event, click the **Event** list arrow, and then select the event you want.

The Show-Hide Elements behavior allows you to show, hide, or restore the visibility of elements on a page. This behavior is useful for displaying information or providing interaction when a visitor points to an element. For example, when a visitor points to a picture or a text box, you can display information about the item to provide added value and some interactivity. When the visitor moves the pointer away, you can restore the element back to its original state.

Executing a JavaScript

The Call JavaScript behavior runs a line of script when an event occurs. The behavior only runs one line of script, which means you can execute a single line of code or a procedure that calls a section of code. To use the Call JavaScript behavior, you need JavaScript experience and coding knowledge, which is outside the scope of this book.

Use the Call JavaScript Behavior

① Open the Web page you want to apply a behavior.

② Click the **Window** menu, and then click **Behaviors** to display the Behaviors panel.

③ Click the element you want to add a behavior.

④ Click the **Add Behavior** button (plus sign), and then click **Call JavaScript**.

A dialog box appears, allowing you to set the details of the action.

⑤ Type the line of script you want to run.

⑥ Click **OK**.

⑦ To change the trigger, click the event, click the **Event** list arrow, and then select the event you want.

Using Spry Widgets and Effects

16

Introduction

The Spry framework is a JavaScript library that allows you to use built-in HTML, CSS, and JavaScript code to create widgets, add special effects, and integrate XML data in your Web pages.

A spry widget is a page element, such as a menu bar, tabbed or collapsible panels, or form validation, that provides added functionality without all the scripting. A widget consists of three different parts: structure, behavior, and styling. A widget structure is HTML code that defines the structure of the widget. A widget behavior is JavaScript that specifies what happens to a widget when an event occurs. Widget styling is CSS code that determines the look of the widget.

You can insert a built-in spry widget, Dreamweaver takes care of all three aspects of the widget. It provides the HTML, CSS, and JavaScript as well as the style of the widget, which you can modify to suit your own needs. For example, you can edit menu items, modify panels, and change the appearance of the page. The CSS and JavaScript files related with the widget are named with the same name as the spry widget, and stored in a SpryAssets folder in your site.

Dreamweaver also includes built-in spry effects that allow you to apply visual effects, such as highlighting information or creating transitions, to elements on a page. You can apply one or more effects, such as a fade, highlight, blind up and down, slide up and down, grow and shrink, shake, and squish, to create a dynamic user experience.

In this chapter you'll learn how to insert and work with spry widgets, and add spry effects to elements on your Web pages with minimal or not knowledge of JavaScript. If you have a strong knowledge of JavaScript you can create your own spry widgets or effects.

Inserting Spry Widgets

Dreamweaver provides a wide variety of spry widgets (**New!**) you can insert in your Web pages. Some of the widgets include page region definition, tables, menu bars, form validation, and panels to store data in a compact space. When you insert a spry widget, Dreamweaver creates a SpryAssets folder (on first use) in your local root site to store the widget, data, and any spry effects. The CSS and JavaScript files related with the widget are named with the same name as the spry widget, and also stored in a SpryAssets folder. If you want (which is not recommended), you can change the default folder location where Dreamweaver saves and stores your spry assets.

Insert a Spry Widget

1. Open the Web page you want to insert a spry widget.

2. Click to place the insertion point where you want to insert the spry widget.

3. Click the **Insert** menu, and then point to **Spry**.

   TIMESAVER *You can click the Spry tab on the Insert bar to use buttons to insert spry widgets.*

4. Click the spry widget on the submenu you want to insert:

   ◆ **Spry XML Data Set.** Identifies data for regions, tables, or lists.

   ◆ **Spry Region.** Creates an area to wrap around objects, such as tables and repeat lists.

   ◆ **Spry Repeat.** Creates a duplicate region.

   ◆ **Spry Repeat List.** Creates an ordered, unordered, definition list, or drop-down list.

   ◆ **Spry Table.** Creates a table for static or dynamic data.

   ◆ **Spry Validation.** Create form validation for a text field or area, drop-down, or check box.

   ◆ **Spry Menu Bar.** Creates a set of navigational menu buttons.

For Your Information

Downloading Spry Files Before You Begin

Before you add Spry widgets, you need to download and link the latest required Spry Framework files from the Adobe Labs Web site (http://labs.adobe.com/technologies/spry/). Unzip the Spry Framework files into the SpryAssets folder on your local root site. You can put all the files (includes **great samples**) to the SpryAssets to make sure you have everything. If space is tight, make sure you copy the includes and widgets folders, and the SpryData.js, SpryEffect.js, and xpath.js files. When you transfer files to your Web server for delivery on the Web, you need to transfer the files in the SpryAssets folder too.

- ◆ **Spry Tabbed Panels.** Creates a set of panels to store data in a compact space.

- ◆ **Spry Accordion.** Creates a set of collapsible panels to store large amounts of data in a compact space.

- ◆ **Spry Collapsible Panel.** Creates a set of collapsible panels to store data in a compact space.

⑤ If prompted, specify widget or input tag accessibility attribute options; the widget options vary depending on the widget.

⑥ Click **OK**. If prompted, click **Yes** or **No** to add a form tag.

Change the Default Spry Assets Folder

① Click the **Sites** menu, and then click **Manage Sites**.

② Select the site you want to change, and then click **Edit**.

③ Click the **Advanced** tab.

④ Click the **Spry** category.

⑤ Enter a path and folder name to the location where you want to store spry assets, or click **Browse** to select a folder location.

⑥ Click **OK**.

⑦ Click **Done**.

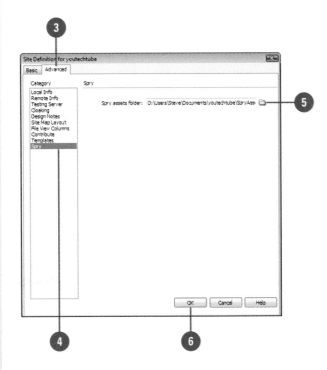

Selecting and Editing Spry Widgets

After you insert a spry widget, you can select and edit the widget to customize it for your specific needs (**New!**). You can edit the parameters and options for a spry widget or modify the style, or appearance, of a spry widget using CSS. Before you can edit a spry widget, you need to select it first by pointing to the widget until you see the widget's blue tabbed outline and then clicking the widget's tab in the upper left corner.

Select and Edit a Spry Widget

1. Open the Web page with the spry widget you want to edit.

2. Point to the widget until you see the blue tabbed outline, and then click the widget tab to select it.

3. Click the **Window** menu, and then click **Properties** to display the Properties panel.

4. Specify the options you want in the Properties panel for the selected widget; the options vary depending on the widget you select.

5. Make changes to the content of the widget in the Design window.

Did You Know?

You can edit the style of a spry widget in the related CSS file. You can open the CSS file located in the SpryAssets folder, make the changes you want, and then save it, or open the CSS panel and change the CSS styles for the spry widget.

Change the Appearance of a Spry Widget

1. Open the Web page with the spry widget you want to edit.

2. Click in the part of the spry widget you want to change.

3. Click the **Window** menu, and then click **Properties** to display the Properties panel.

4. Specify the options you want in the Properties panel for the selected widget.

   ◆ **Style**. Click the **Style** popup to change the current style.

   ◆ **CSS**. Click the **CSS** button to change cascading style sheet options in the CSS Styles panel.

   ◆ **Format**. Use the normal formatting options, such as: Format, Font, Size, Bold, Italic, and alignment and spacing buttons.

Working with Spry Panel Widgets

A spry panel widget allows you to store content in a compact space using tabs. Dreamweaver provides three different types of spry panels (**New!**): accordion, collapsible, and tabbed. Each spry panel type provides a tab-like interface that displays content when a visitor clicks a tab. The differences between the spry panel types lies in the display and style of the tabs. If you have a large amount of content, the accordion panel is your best bet. Try each one to see which one works best with the content you want to display.

Insert and Work with Spry Panel Widgets

1. Open the Web page you want to insert a spry widget, and then click to place the insertion point where you want it.

2. Click the **Insert** menu, point to **Spry**, and then select the spry panel element you want:

   ◆ **Spry Tabbed Panels.** Creates a set of panels to store data in a compact space.

   ◆ **Spry Accordion.** Creates a set of collapsible panels to store large amounts of data in a compact space.

   ◆ **Spry Collapsible Panel.** Creates a set of collapsible panels to store data in a compact space.

3. Select the panel widget.

4. Point to a tab, click the eye icon (if available) to edit the panel contents, or select the panel contents and edit it.

5. Click the **Window** menu, and then click **Properties** to display the Properties panel.

6 Specify the options you want in the Properties panel for the selected widget; the options vary depending on the widget. Some of the options include:

◆ **Panel Order.** Click the **Up** or **Down Arrow** buttons.

◆ **Default Panel.** Click the **Default Panel** popup, and then select the panel you want.

◆ **Delete Panel.** Select the panel, and then click the **Minus** button.

◆ **Animate Panel.** Select the panel, and then select or clear the **Enable Animation** check box.

Working with Spry Validation Widgets

A spry validation widget allows you to determine whether information or data in a form is valid or invalid. Dreamweaver provides several types of spry validation elements (**New!**): text field, text area, select (from a drop-down menu), and check box. When you insert a spry validation element, the Input Tag Accessibility Attributes dialog box opens, requesting information and options to make the form object accessible to the visually impaired. After you insert a spry validation element, you can use the Properties panel to specify the validation options you want; each element provides different validation options.

Insert and Work with Spry Validation Widgets

1. Open the Web page you want to insert a spry widget, and then click to place the insertion point where you want it.

2. Click the **Insert** menu, point to **Spry**, and then select the spry validation element you want:

   ◆ **Spry Validation Text Field.** Creates a text box that displays valid or invalid states when a visitor enters text or doesn't enter text as a required field.

   ◆ **Spry Validation Select.** Creates a drop-down menu with a list of options divided into sections that displays valid or invalid states when a visitor selects an element in the list.

   ◆ **Spry Validation Checkbox.** Creates a check box that displays valid or invalid states when a visitor selects or doesn't select a check box.

   ◆ **Spry Validation Text Area.** Creates a text area that displays valid or invalid states when a visitor enters text or doesn't enter text as a required field.

3. Specify the Input Tag Accessibility Attributes dialog box options you want.

4. Click **OK**.

5 Select the panel widget.

6 Click the **Window** menu, and then click **Properties** to display the Properties panel.

7 Specify the options you want in the Properties panel for the selected widget; the options vary depending on the widget. Some of the general options include:

◆ **Initial State.** Indicates the state when the page loads in the browser or when the form is reset.

◆ **Focus State.** Indicates the state with the insertion point.

◆ **Valid State.** Indicates the state when the visitor entered information correctly.

◆ **Required State.** Indicates the state when the visitor fails to enter information.

◆ **Minimum or Maximum Number Of Characters State.** Indicates the state when the visitor has not entered the minimum number of characters or entered more than the maximum number of characters.

◆ **Minimum or Maximum Value State.** Indicates the state when the visitor has entered a value that is less or greater than the allowed value.

See Also

See Chapter 13 "Creating Forms" on page 313 for information on specific options in the Input Tag Accessibility Attributes dialog box, and specific form element options in the Properties panel.

Working with Spry Menu Bar Widgets

A spry menu bar widget (**New!**) allows you to create a set of navigational menus that come with submenus. A menu bar makes it easy for visitors to navigate to different parts of your site in the same way they choose commands in a program, such as Dreamweaver. You can insert two types of menu bars: horizontal or vertical. You can link a menu item to a specific place or execute a script. In addition, you can add tool tips to provide a short description of menu items for visitors.

Insert and Work with Spry Menu Bar Widgets

1. Open the Web page you want to insert a spry widget, and then click to place the insertion point where you want it.

2. Click the **Insert** menu, point to **Spry**, and then click **Spry Menu Bar**.

   IMPORTANT *If your page contains Flash content, the DHTML layers used to create the menu bar may cause problems.*

3. Click the **Horizontal** or **Vertical** option.

4. Click **OK**.

5. Select the panel widget.

6. Click the **Window** menu, and then click **Properties** to display the Properties panel.

7. Specify the options you want in the Properties panel for the selected widget:

   ◆ **Add Main Menu.** Click the **Plus** (+) button above the first column, and then rename the menu in the Text box.

   ◆ **Add Submenu.** Select a main menu item, click the **Plus** (+) button above the second column, and then rename the menu in the Text box.

- ◆ **Delete Menu.** Select the main menu or submenu item you want to delete, and then click the **Minus** (-) button.

- ◆ **Change Menu Order.** Select the menu item you want to reorder, and then click the **Up** or **Down** buttons.

- ◆ **Link Menu.** Select the menu item you want to apply a link, and then type the link in the Link box or click the **Browse** button to select a file.

- ◆ **Add Tool Tip.** Select the menu item you want to create a tool tip, and then type the text for the tool tip in the Title text box.

- ◆ **Target.** Enter one of the following options:

  - ◆ **_blank.** Opens the linked page in a new window.

  - ◆ **_parent.** Loads the linked document in the immediate frameset of the active document.

  - ◆ **_self.** Loads the linked document in the same browser window (default).

  - ◆ **_top.** Loads the linked document in the topmost window of a frameset.

- ◆ **Styles.** Click the **Turn Styles Off** button to disable the styling of a menu bar, which is helpful to see the HTML structure of the widget. Click the **Turn Styles On** button to enable it again.

Identifying Spry Data Sets

A spry data set (**New!**) allows you to provide interactive data to visitors on your site. The data on the page changes based on the visitors selections. For example, you can select an option in one part of a page, and then display other content somewhere else on a page without requiring a full-page refresh. To use data sets to create a dynamic page, you need to take a few steps. First, you identify one or more data sets (XML source files) that contain the data you want to use. Next, you insert one or more spry data objects to display the data on a page. When a visitor opens the page in a browser, the data set loads like a normal table containing columns and rows.

Identify the Spry XML Data Set

1. Open the Web page you want to use.

2. Click the **Insert** menu, point to **Spry**, and then click **Spry XML Data Set**.

    TIMESAVER *If you don't have XML data set, you can get a sample at www.adobe.com/go/ learn_dw_spryframework.*

3. Enter a name for the spry data set or use the default one, ds1.

4. Click **Browse**, navigate to and select the XML data file, and then click **OK**.

5. To design the page using a sample feed on your test server, click the **Design Time Feed** link.

6. Click **Get Schema** to populate the Row Elements panel.

7. Select the element that contains the data you want to display. The element typically is a repeating node with one or more subfields.

    The XPath text box shows the data found in the data set.

8. To see how the data looks in a browser, click **Preview**.

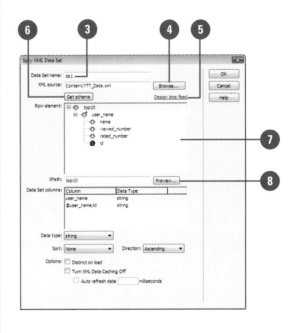

9 If you want to validate the data to make sure it's a specific type, click the **Data Type** popup, and then select a data type.

10 If you want to sort the data as it loads, click the **Sort** popup, select a sort option, click the **Direction** popup, and then select the direction you want.

11 Select the **Distinct On Load** check box to eliminate any duplicate columns.

12 Select the **Turn XML Caching Off** check box to load data directly from the server, otherwise it caches it on your local computer.

13 Select the **Auto Refresh Data** check box, and then enter a value in milliseconds to refresh the XML data from the server at the indicated interval.

14 Click **OK**.

View the Spry XML Data Set

1 Open the Web page with the spry XML data set you want to view.

2 Click the **Window** menu, and then click **Bindings** to display the Bindings panel.

The spry XML data set appears, displaying the structure of the data.

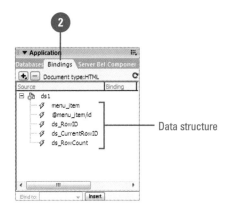

Data structure

Creating a Spry Region

After you identify the data sets (XML source files) you want to use, you can insert one or more spry data objects to display the data on a page. A spry data object is enclosed in a spry region on a page, so you need to insert one first or let Dreamweaver do it for you. You can create a region or a repeated region (**New!**). There are two types of regions: a region and a detail region. A spry region is a page section that wraps around data objects. A spry detail region updates data based on changes made in a master table object (also known as a spry table) some where else on a page. A repeat region is a data structure you can format to display your data. A repeat region is useful for elements you want to repeat within a page layout, such as a gallery of images.

Create a Spry Region

1. Open the Web page you want to insert a spry region, and then click to place the insertion point where you want it.

2. Click the **Insert** menu, point to **Spry**, and then click **Spry Region**.

   TIMESAVER *Click the Spry tab on the Insert bar, and then click the Spry Region button.*

3. Select the **DIV** or **SPAN** option.

4. Click the **Region** or **Detail Region** option to specify the type of region you want to insert.

5. Click the **Spry Data Set** popup, and then select the data set you want to use.

6. Click the **Wrap Selection** option to insert a new region around an object, or the **Replace Selection** option to replace an existing region for an object.

7. Click **OK**.

   Dreamweaver inserts a region placeholder on your page.

   You can replace the placeholder with spry data objects, such as a table or repeat list, or with dynamic data from the Bindings panel.

Spry region

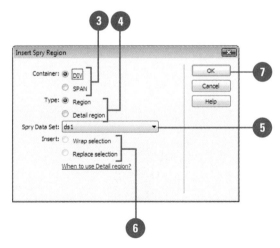

Create a Spry Repeat Region

1. Open the Web page you want to insert a spry region, and then click to place the insertion point where you want it.

2. Click the **Insert** menu, point to **Spry**, and then click **Spry Repeat**.

   TIMESAVER *Click the Spry tab on the Insert bar, and then click the Spry Repeat button.*

3. Select the **DIV** or **SPAN** option.

4. Click the **Repeat** or **Repeat Children** option to specify the type of region you want to insert.

   Use the Repeat Children option when data validation is done for each line in a list at the child level.

5. Click the **Spry Data Set** popup, and then select the data set you want to use.

6. Click the **Wrap Selection** option to insert a new region around an object, or the **Replace Selection** option to replace an existing region for an object.

7. Click **OK**.

   Dreamweaver inserts a region placeholder on your page.

   You can replace the placeholder with spry data objects, such as a table or repeat list, or with dynamic data from the Bindings panel.

Spry repeat region

Creating Spry Data Objects

A spry data object (**New!**), such as a table or repeated list, displays data from a spry data set. A spry data object is enclosed in a spry region on a page, so you need to insert one first. If you don't, Dreamweaver inserts one for you. The table data object allows you to display your data in a simple table or a dynamic master table. A dynamic master table uses a spry detail region to display data updates based on changes made by visitor interaction in a master table object. First, you insert a master table, and then you insert a detail region. The repeat list data object allows you to display your data as an ordered list, an unordered (bulleted) list, a definition list, or a drop-down list.

Create a Spry Table

1. Open the Web page you want to insert a spry region, and then click to place the insertion point in the spry region where you want it.

2. Click the **Insert** menu, point to **Spry**, and then click **Spry Table**.

   TIMESAVER *Click the Spry tab on the Insert bar, and then click the Spry Table button.*

3. Click the **Plus (+)**, **Minus (-)**, and **Up** or **Down** buttons to add, subtract, or arrange columns.

4. To specify a column to sort, select the column, and then select the **Sort Column When Header Is Clicked** check box.

5. If you have CSS associated with your page, use the popup menus (Odd Row, Even Row, Hover, or Select) to select a CSS class or attach a style sheet.

6. To create a dynamic master table for use with a detail region, select the **Update Detail Region When Row Is Clicked** check box.

7. Click **OK**.

   Dreamweaver inserts a spry table in your page. Data references appear in curly brackets ({}) for each of the included elements.

Spry table

Create a Spry Repeat List

1 Open the Web page you want to insert a spry region, and then click to place the insertion point where you want it.

2 Click the **Insert** menu, point to **Spry**, and then click **Spry Repeat List**.

   TIMESAVER *Click the Spry tab on the Insert bar, and then click the Spry Repeat List button.*

3 Click the **Container Tag** popup, and then select the tag you want to use: UL (Unordered List), OL (Ordered List, DL (Definition List), or SELECT (Drop-down List).

   ◆ If you choose the SELECT (Drop-down List) option, you also need to select a display column and value column (the value sent to the background server).

4 Click the **Spry Data Set** popup, and then select the data set you want to use.

5 Click the **Display Column** popup, and then select the columns you want to display.

6 Click **OK**.

   Dreamweaver inserts a repeated region in your page.

Adding and Removing Spry Effects ▶

Dreamweaver goes a step further with spry widgets that allows you to add special effects to page elements. A spry effect is useful for highlighting information or creating an animated transition. You can use the Behaviors panel to add a variety of spry effects (**New!**) including fades, highlights, blinds, slides, shakes, and squishes. You can combine more than one effect to an element to create a unique display. If you no longer want to use an effect, you can quickly remove it.

Apply a Spry Effect

① Open the Web page with the element you want to apply a spry effect.

② Select the element on the page you want to change.

③ Click the **Window** menu, and then click **Behaviors** to display the Behaviors panel.

④ Click the **Add Behavior** button (plus sign), point to **Effects**, and then select the effect you want:

◆ **Appear / Fade.** Makes the element appear or fade away.

◆ **Highlight.** Changes the element background color.

◆ **Blind.** Displays the element with a window blind effect.

◆ **Slide.** Moves the element up or down.

◆ **Grow / Shrink.** Makes the element increase or decrease in size.

◆ **Shake.** Makes the element shake from left to right.

◆ **Squish.** Makes the element disappear in the upper left corner.

⑤ Specify the options you want for the selected spry effect; the options for the effect vary depending on the one you select.

⑥ Click **OK**.

Add Behavior button

Remove a Spry Effect

1. Open the Web page with the effect you want to remove.

2. Select the element on the page with the spry effect.

3. Click the **Window** menu, and then click **Behaviors** to display the Behaviors panel.

4. Select the effect you want to remove in the Behaviors panel.

5. Click the **Remove Event** button in the subpanel title bar.

   ◆ You can also right-click (Win) or control-click (Mac) the behavior, and then click **Delete Behavior**.

Behaviors panel

Did You Know?

Applying a spry effect adds code to your Web page file. When you apply a spry effect, Dreamweaver adds code to the document that initiates and identifies the SpryEffects.js file, which provides the executable code to perform the effect. Do not remove or modify this code in Code view.

You can add multiple effects to an element. Select the element you want to apply multiple effects, open the Behaviors panel, click the Add Behavior button (plus sign), point to Effects, select the effect you want on the submenu, select the element's ID from the target element list, or select <Current Selection>, specify the other options you want, and then click OK.

Checking Out Spry Samples

Before you add Spry widgets, you need to download and link the latest required Spry Framework files from the Adobe Labs Web site (http://labs.adobe.com/technologies/spry/).

When you unzip the Spry Framework files, you also get some samples and demo files that show you by example how to use a spry widget.

Using Code Snippets and Libraries

17

Introduction

The Snippets panel is a collection of Scripts (called Snippets) that you can drop into your Web pages. Essentially, a snippet is a pre-built selection of code. The Snippets panel in turn acts like a code library, with sections or folders for different snippets. There are ten major folders, and some folders have subfolders to organize content.

Each folder has a small triangle, located to the right of the folder name. Clicking this icon expands or contracts the folders contents, revealing either more folders or snippets of code. For example, expanding the JavaScript folder reveals 16 more sub-folders, jam-packed with cool features to add to your Web site. There are thousands of JavaScript codes that can be executed within a Web browser, so Dreamweaver categorized JavaScript into sub-folders to help you better understand where to find the code you need. You will find a group of scripts for managing and controlling Browser functions, cookies, readable functions and a whole host of additional tools. All said and told, the JavaScript folder alone has over 80 individual snippets.

Most well designed Web sites have areas that are repeated from page to page. These would include header areas, navigation bars, information boxes, footers, etc. Occasionally, changes need to be made in these areas. There are wonderfully easy-to-use components in Dreamweaver to make those changes appear on multiple pages when the change is made at one location. Dreamweaver has two such components, Libraries and Templates. Library items are sections of a Web page that can be used over and over again. Dreamweaver Templates are really large Library items.

In this chapter you'll learn how to work with and add snippets to your Web pages, as well as modify and edit them. In addition, you'll learn how Library items can streamline your workflow in the creation of a complex Web site.

What You'll Do

Introduce Snippets

Insert a Snippet

Edit Existing Snippets

Create Snippets

Introduce Assets and Libraries

Use the Assets Panel

Insert an Asset

Work with Site Assets

Work with Color and URL Assets

Work with Favorite Assets

Create and Insert Library Items

Edit Library Items

Work with Library Items

Create an External JavaScript Library

Insert and Edit an External JavaScript

Use Server-Side Includes

Introducing Snippets

If you build a complex Web site, it's almost a certainty that you will use design elements over and over again, however each time you need them you either have to recall a particular command, or more likely copy and paste the code containing the content you want to reuse. Knowing that is not the most efficient way to work, Dreamweaver created a solution that most people don't know about called Code Snippets.

Similar in philosophy to Microsoft's macros or Adobe's actions, snippets are a incredible way to automate some of your repetitive tasks and make your job easier. They are composed of bits of code and/or content that you can save, edit, use, and reuse as often as you want on any Web site you happen to be working on.

Dreamweaver snippets allow you to save and reuse chunks of code over and over. This saves time and effort in maintaining a large Web site. Plus Dreamweaver has a lot of pre-written snippets to use. Use snippets to store things like, headers and footers, logos, and scripts.

Snippets offer a simple and convenient method of creating fragments of reusable code. Snippets can be a single line or a considerable sized chunk of code such as HTML, XHTML, CSS, CFML, PHP, JavaScript and other types of code. Since they are reusable, snippets save you hours of time because you don't have to recreate the same code over and over. You have the ability to create snippets in Dreamweaver, or in another application, and bring them into the Snippets panel, use the pre-designed snippets supplied by Dreamweaver, or use snippets created by other designers.

Snippet Example

The following is an example of snippet code, written in JavaScript that checks for the current location of the mouse.

```
/*
Example:
function test()
{
  if (document.layers) getMouseLoc;    //NS
  else if (document.all) getMouseLoc(); //IE
  alert(mouseLocation.x+","+mouseLocation.y);
}
in the BODY: <a href="#"
    onMouseOver="test()">test</a> */
function Point(x,y) { this.x = x; this.y = y; }
mouseLocation = new Point(-500,-500);
function getMouseLoc(e)
{
  if(!document.all)  //NS
  {
    mouseLocation.x = e.pageX;
    mouseLocation.y = e.pageY;
  }
  else            //IE
  {
    mouseLocation.x = event.x +
        document.body.scrollLeft;
    mouseLocation.y = event.y +
        document.body.scrollTop;
  }
  return true;
}
//NS init:
if(document.layers){
        document.captureEvents(Event.MOUSEMOVE);
        document.onMouseMove = getMouseLoc; }
```

DW 3.7

Information on the current location of the mouse can be used to trigger a variety of actions. For example, when the user hovers over an image, a dialog box could appear to describe the image.

Block and Wrap

Dreamweaver employs two types of snippets: a wrap snippet and a block snippet. Wrap snippets will insert code above and below any selected content on the page. Block snippets, by contrast, simply drop in the snippet content after the insertion point on the page.

To use a block snippet, place an insertion point inside an open document, select the snippet from the Snippets panel, and then click the Insert button at the bottom of the panel. You can also drag and drop the snippet from the panel into an open document, as you would an image or any other media file.

To use a wrap snippet, select the content in Design view that the snippet will wrap around, select the snippet in the Snippets panel, and then click the Insert button at the bottom of the panel.

Summary

Snippets are a great way to reduce the time spent reproducing repetitive tasks. They're easy to use and apply to the documents. However, they do require some experience in writing code in languages such as: HTML, XHTML, CSS, CFML, PHP and JavaScript.

While it's not the purpose of the chapter to teach you how to write snippet code, there are a lot of Web sites out there that offer free (and for cash) snippets, which you can download and use in the construction of your Web sites. Some of these sites include:

http://www.assonetriver.com/snippets/

http://www.luckychair.com/downloads.html

http://www.programmersheaven.com/search/ LinkDetail.asp?Typ=1&ID=13270

As a matter of fact, simply do a Web search using the words "free" and "snippets" and sort through the hundreds of hits. One word of caution: not all snippets are created equal, and may contain code that is not compatible with every browser, so checking and testing is the rule of the day, when it comes to downloading snippets. In addition, some sites might use the downloading of a snippet to also download a virus onto your computer, so know the sites that you're downloading the snippets.

Inserting a Snippet

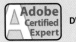 DW 3.7

As mentioned in the previous section, you can apply (add) a snippet to a Dreamweaver document in one of two ways: block or wrap. The blocking method requires that you click to create an insertion point in the document and then add the snippet; the wrapping method requires that you select (in Design mode) the selection of the page that you want to wrap the code around. Both methods have their advantages; for example, you could use the block method to insert a snippet into the HTML code that would pre-load rollover images, or you could use the wrap method to select a section of text, or an image, that turns the selection into a link, but is masked from appearing in the status window of the browser. Although Dreamweaver contains many pre-designed snippets, they may require a bit of editing before use.

Add a Block Snippet

1 Open the document you want to insert the block snippet.

2 Click the **Window** menu, and then click **Snippets** to display the Snippets panel.

   TIMESAVER *Press Shift+F9 to display the Snippets panel.*

3 Click in the page where you want to insert the snippet.

4 Click the **Plus** (+) icon next to the folder with the snippet you want to insert in the Snippets panel (in this example, click the (+) next to the Footers folder).

5 Select the snippet you want to insert.

6 Click the **Insert** button in the Snippets panel.

   TIMESAVER *You can also drag a snippet from the Snippets panel directly into the document at the insertion point of the cursor, or double-click the snippet in the Snippets panel.*

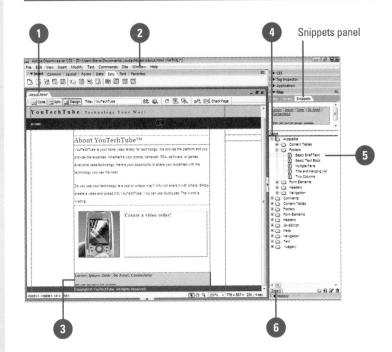

Snippets panel

Add a Wrap Snippet

1. Open the document you want to insert the Wrap snippet.

2. Click the **Window** menu, and then click **Snippets** to display the Snippets panel.

3. Select the text in Design view that you want to apply this snippet.

4. Click the **Plus** (+) or **Minus** (-) icon next to the folder to display the snippet you want to insert from the Snippets panel (in this example, click the (+) next to the Text folder).

5. Select the snippet you want to insert (in this example, click Service Mark).

6. Click the **Insert** button in the Snippets panel to wrap the snippet around the selected text.

   NOTE *The snippet will have to be edited to include the proper URL.*

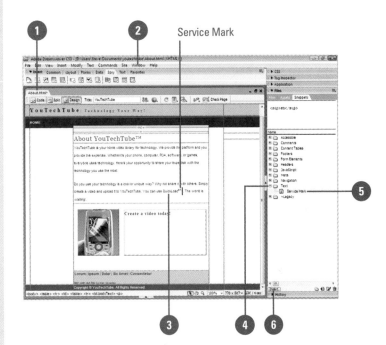

Service Mark

Did You Know?

You can insert a recent snippet. Click the Insert menu, point to Recent Snippet, and then select the recently used snippet you want.

You can add or edit a keyboard short-cuts for a snippet. Open the Snippets folder, right-click (Win) or control-click (Mac) in the Snippets panel, click Edit Keyboard Shortcuts, click the Commands popup, select Snippets (if necessary), select the snippet you want to change, enter a keyboard shortcut in the Press key box, and then click OK.

Editing Existing Snippets

In Dreamweaver, you can use one of the many pre-designed snippets, one you developed yourself or others you downloaded from the Web. If any of these snippets is not exactly what you need, you can edit the snippet code directly in Dreamweaver to create your own. In addition to editing snippet code, you can also change snippet options, including name, description, snippet type (either block or wrap), and preview type (either in Design or Code view). The blocking method requires that you click to create an insertion point in the document and then add the snippet; the wrapping method requires that you select (in Design view) the selection of the page that you want to wrap the code around.

Edit a Snippet

1. Click the **Window** menu, and then click **Snippets** to display the Snippets panel.

2. Click the **Plus** (+) or **Minus** (-) icon next to the folder to display the snippet you want to insert from the Snippets panel (in this example, click the (+) next to the Footers folder).

3. Select the snippet that you need to edit (in this example, click Title and Hanging List).

4. Click the **Edit Snippet** button in the Snippets panel.

   NOTE *If you don't want to change the original snippet, simply make a copy of the snippet you want to change, and perform the edit to the copy.*

5. Edit the snippet using the following options:

   ◆ **Name.** Change the name for the snippet, if desired.

   ◆ **Description.** Change the description of this snippet, if desired.

   NOTE *Name and Description appear in the Snippets panel.*

- ◆ **Snippet Type.** Select the **Wrap Selection** option for the wrap type or the **Insert Block** option for the block type.

- ◆ **Insert Code.** Modify the code to fit the particular situation (in this example, the copyright date, and links were updated to reflect the current project).

- ◆ **Preview Type.** Select the **Design** or **Code** option to specify how you want to preview the snippet in the Document window.

6 Click **OK**.

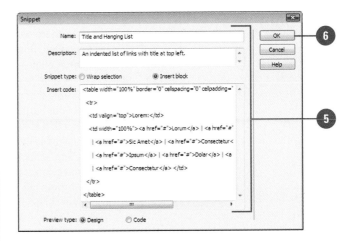

Did You Know?

You can delete a code snippet or snippet folder. Open the Snippets folder, click the snippet folder or code snippet you want to remove, click the Remove button, and then click Yes. When you delete a folder, all the snippets in the folder are also deleted.

You can share a snippet. Snippets are located in the Programs Files (Win) or Applications (Mac) folder in the following subfolders: Adobe/Adobe Dreamweaver CS3/Configuration /Snippets/*snippet type name*. You can copy and paste a snippet file into the same location to share it with others.

Creating Snippets

 DW 3.7

Although Dreamweaver supplies you with dozens of useful sections of snippet code, there will always be the time when you need something that isn't supplied. One method is to jump out onto the Web, go to your friendly search engine, and look for something that might fit the bill. Not only are there a lot of sites out there that have free code for you to use, it's very possible that you might be able to modify an existing piece of code to suit your purposes. And let's not forget Adobe; they've given us the exchange that is just jam packed with high end code snippets for just about any occasion; many of them free. Just point your browser to: *http://www.adobe.com/cfusion/exchange/* While this section is not designed to make you a snippet programmer, there are probably a lot of you code warriors out there (myself included), which have the ability to write our own snippets. And here's a bit of advice... if you design, what you think is a really cool snippet, you can post it on the Adobe Exchange and share it with others.

Create a New Snippet Folder

1. Click the **Window** menu, and then click **Snippets** to display the Snippets panel.

2. Select the folder where you want to create a new snippet folder.

3. Click the **New Snippet Folder** button.

    The new folder appears selected with the name, untitled.

4. Type a name for the folder, and then press Enter (Win) or Return (Mac).

Did You Know?

You can rename a snippet folder or a code snippet. Open the Snippets folder, click the snippet folder or code snippet you want to rename, click the item again, edit the name, and then press Enter (Win) or Return (Mac).

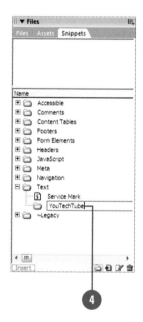

Create a Snippet

1 Click the **Window** menu, and then click **Snippets** to display the Snippets panel.

2 Select the folder that you want to add your new snippet.

3 Click the **New Snippet** button.

4 Use the following options to create the snippet:

◆ **Name.** Enter a name for the snippet.

◆ **Description.** Enter a description of the snippet.

◆ **Snippet Type.** Select the **Wrap Selection** option for the wrap type or the **Insert Block** option for the block type (in this example, Insert Block).

◆ **Insert Code.** Enter or paste the code for the snippet. For the Wrap Selection option, enter or paste the code in the Insert Before or Insert After box (in this example, JavaScript code was added to create a date last modified area to the page; the file is called Snippet.xml in the Scripts folder).

TIMESAVER *You can copy code from another text program (even Microsoft Word), and paste it using Ctrl+V (Win) or ⌘+V (Mac) into the Snippet dialog box.*

◆ **Preview Type.** Select the **Design** or **Code** option to specify how you want to preview the snippet in the Document window.

5 Click **OK**.

Dreamweaver saves the code and adds it to the Snippets panel.

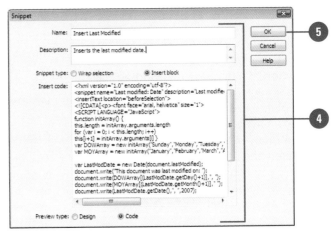

Introducing Assets and Libraries

 DW 4.5

Introducing Assets

Assets are individual elements, such as images, movies, colors, scripts, and URL links, you add to your Web site. You create assets when you insert elements from other programs, such as Adobe Photoshop or Adobe Flash. The assets are stored in the Assets panel, where you can insert and manage them for use in other parts of your Web site.

Introducing Libraries

Dreamweaver provides two special types of assets: libraries and templates. A library is a Dreamweaver file that contains individual assets or copies of assets, while a template is a Dreamweaver file that contains editable regions. The assets in a library are called **library items**.

Library items are sections of a Web page that can be used over and over again. You can create a library item from any element in the body section of a document, including navigation bars, images, text, tables, forms, Java applets, plug-ins, and ActiveX controls. For example, a navigation system that you want to use on many of the pages in your site is best created and saved as a library item. That way when you need it, all you have to do is add the navigation to the page by dragging it out of the Assets panel.

This gives you a tremendous savings in terms of time creating all those replicating items in Web design. And another benefit is the consistency factor. You know that if the original Library item works, they all work, because they are based on the original item.

Library items, also give you a grand advantage, when it comes to changes. Again,

let's say that you've created a catalog Web site with hundreds of pages that contain images, and descriptions of your products. However, they're not the only things on those pages; you've got a header, footer, navigation, background image or color. There's a lot of stuff going on... and then something happens. You make a modification to the site that requires you to add another button to the Navigation bar... OPS.

No problem. You created the navigation system for those pages as a library item, and then you inserted that item into a template (more about Templates in a later chapter). So all you have to do is open the original library item, make your changes, and instruct Dreamweaver to update the site. Sounds too good to be true, doesn't it?

Dreamweaver stores library items in a Library folder within the local root for each site. However, for linked items, such as images, the library stores only a reference to the item. When you insert a library item in a page, Dreamweaver creates a link to it instead of inserting it, so the item is able to be updated later.

Planning is the Key

The time to begin the creation of library items is at the very beginning stages of site development. As you are working out the natty details, look at sketches of your pages, and decide what items are worth creating library items and/or templates, and what are not. It's a bit late in the process (after the site is designed) to think back and wish that you had converted this item or that into a library item or template. Think up front... begin with the end in mind.

Using the Assets Panel

DW 4.5

While the Files panel gives you access to your Web site, and allows you to add, delete, and link files, quickly and efficiently, it doesn't help you in the actual placement of assets into the documents. That job is left to the Assets panel. The Assets panel holds all of the individual elements that make up your Web pages; they're the puzzle pieces that when properly assembled create awesome Web sites. The Assets panel includes a variety of elements that you store in a site, such as images, movie files, colors, and library elements.

Use the Assets Panel

1. Click the **Window** menu, and then click **Assets** to display the Assets panel.

2. Click the **Site** option to show all of the assets in your site, or click the **Favorites** option to show only the assets you set as a favorite.

3. Click any of the following category buttons to display the assets you want:

   ◆ **Images.** Displays images in the GIF, JPEG, or PNG formats.

   ◆ **Colors.** Displays the colors that are used in pages and style sheets in your site.

   ◆ **URL.** Displays any external links in your current site documents.

   ◆ **Flash.** Displays files in any version of the Flash format.

   ◆ **Shockwave.** Displays files in any version of the Shockwave format.

   ◆ **Movies.** Displays files in QuickTime or MPEG format.

   ◆ **Scripts.** Displays JavaScript or VBScript files.

   ◆ **Templates.** Displays a list of all the templates in the site.

   ◆ **Library.** Displays a list of all library items (elements used in multiple pages).

Inserting an Asset

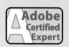
Insert an Asset

1. Open the Web page you want to insert an existing asset.

2. Click in the document to add an insertion point.

3. Click the **Window** menu, and then click **Assets** to display the Assets panel.

4. Click the **Site** option to show all of the assets in your site, or click the **Favorites** option to show only the assets you set as a favorite.

5. Select the category that contains the asset you want to insert.

   IMPORTANT *You cannot select the Templates category. Templates are applied to an entire document.*

6. Insert the asset using one of the following methods:

   ◆ Click the **Insert** button in the Assets panel. The asset appears at the insertion point.

   ◆ Click and drag the asset from the Assets panel directly into the active document. The asset appears where you release your mouse.

Did You Know?

You can view an asset in the preview area. Open the Assets panel, select the category that contains the asset you want to view, and then select the asset.

Once an asset is part of a Web site, you can insert it in another page using several different methods. You can drag the asset from the Assets panel directly into Design or Code view or click to place the insertion point where you want the asset and use the Insert button at the bottom of the Assets panel.

Working with Site Assets

 DW 4.5

The Assets panel does much more than let you look at assets of your site. As a matter of fact, it's a powerful tool to help you manage and edit all the elements that make up a Web site. You can use the Assets panel to edit an image, or even create a new image. Once an asset is edited, it will impact all Web pages that use that particular asset. For example, you use the Assets panel to reopen an image that's used on several Web pages, perform a bit of touchup, and then save the file. In response, all the pages that used that particular asset will update to reflect the changes. Now that's power.

Modify an Asset

1 Select the **Window** menu, and then click **Assets** to display the Assets panel.

2 Select the category that contains the asset you want to edit.

3 Double-click the asset you want to edit, or select the asset, and then click the **Edit** button.

Dreamweaver launches the program required to edit the image (default application is Fireworks).

4 Make changes to the image, save the file, and then close the edit program.

The image is resaved with the changes, and all Web pages that contact the image automatically reflect the changes when loaded.

Did You Know?

You can select multiple items in the Assets panel. Open the Assets panel, select an asset, and then use Shift-click to select a consecutive series of assets, or use Ctrl-click (Win) or ⌘-click (Mac) to include or exclude individual assets in the selection.

Working with Color and URL Assets

If you regularly use the same color or URL in a Web site, you can add it to the Assets panel in the Favorites list, so it's available whenever you need it. After you add a color or URL, you can apply it to selected text or images in Design view. For example, you can select text on a page and apply a color asset to change text color or select text or an image on a page and apply a URL link to it.

Add a New Color Asset

1. Open the Web page you want to insert an existing asset.

2. Click the **Window** menu, and then click **Assets** to display the Assets panel.

3. Click the **Favorites** option.

4. Click the **Color** category.

5. Click the **New Color** button.

6. Select the color from the color list.

Add a New URL Asset

1. Open the Web page you want to insert an existing asset.

2. Click the **Window** menu, and then click **Assets** to display the Assets panel.

3. Click the **Favorites** option.

4. Click the **URLs** category.

5. Click the **New URLs** button.

6. Enter the URL and nickname (optional) you want.

   A nickname helps you identify a URL; it doesn't affect the link.

7. Click **OK**.

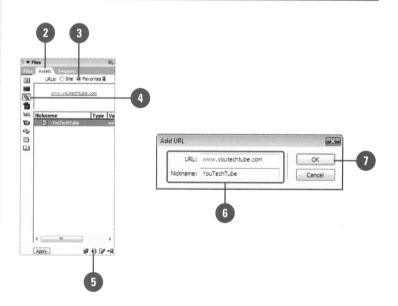

Apply a Color to Text

1. Open the Web page you want to apply a color to text.

2. Select the text you want to apply a color.

   If you click to place the insertion point, the color applies to the text appearing after the insertion point.

3. Click the **Window** menu, and then click **Assets** to display the Assets panel.

4. Click the **Color** category.

5. Select the color you want to apply.

6. Click the **Apply** button.

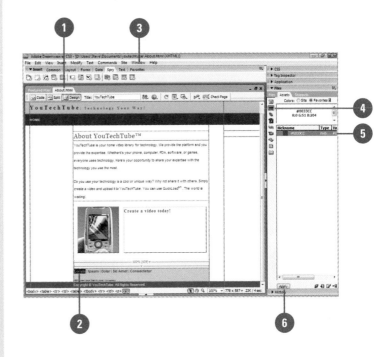

Apply a URL to an Image or Text

1. Open the Web page you want to apply a URL to an image or text.

2. Select the image or text you want to apply a URL.

3. Click the **Window** menu, and then click **Assets** to display the Assets panel.

4. Click the **URLs** category.

5. Select the URL you want to apply.

6. Click the **Apply** button.

   TIMESAVER *Drag the URL from the Assets panel to the selected image or text in Design view.*

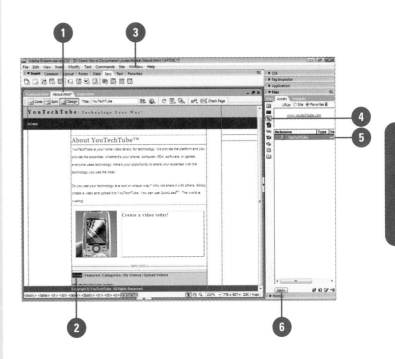

Working with Favorite Assets

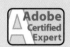

DW 4.5

When the list of assets for a Web site becomes long, it's difficult to find the assets you want to use. For the assets you frequently use, you can add them to a Favorites list to make them easier to find, and even group related ones together. If the name of the assets in your Favorites list are difficult to identify, you can give them nicknames to make them easier to locate and use. When you give a nickname to an asset, it doesn't effect the real filename of the asset.

Add or Delete a Favorite Asset

1. Select the **Window** menu, and then click **Assets** to display the Assets panel.

2. Select the category that contains the asset that you want to modify.

3. Select one or more assets you want to add from the Site list or remove from the Favorites list.

4. Use any of the following methods:

   ◆ **Add.** Click the **Add To Favorites** button in the Assets panel.

   ◆ **Delete.** Click the **Remove From Favorites** button in the Assets panel.

Add favorite

Remove favorite

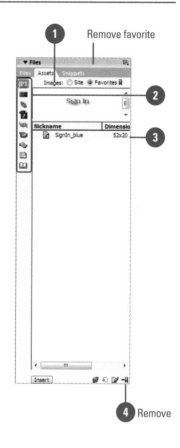

Remove

Group Assets in a Favorites Folder

1 Click the **Window** menu, and then click **Assets** to display the Assets panel.

2 Select the category that you want to create a group.

3 Click the **Favorites** option.

4 Click the **New Favorites Folder** button.

5 Type a name for the folder, and then press Enter (Win) or Return (Mac).

6 Drag assets into the folder.

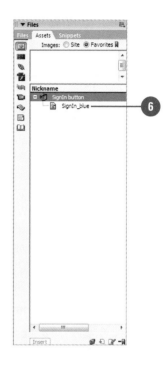

For Your Information

Creating a Nickname for a Favorite Asset

In order to help make assets easier to identify, you can give items placed into the favorites list a nickname, which doesn't impact the real file name. Nicknames can help you identify items that have boring file names like: DCSN0002.JPG, and change it to Sunrise_in_Paris.JPG (assuming, of course, that it actually is a sunrise in Paris). Right-click (Win) or control-click (Mac) the assets name or icon, click Edit Nickname, type a nickname, and the press Enter (Win) or Return (Mac).

Creating and Inserting Library Items

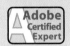

DW 3.5

Library items are elements in a Web page you store in a library that you can reuse to quickly create other pages. It can't be overstated just how valuable library items are; not only to increased speed in construction, but perfect consistency between pages. Creating and using library items is fairly straightforward; you create and select an element, such as a navigation bar, and then use the New Library Item button in the Library category to create a library item. After you create a library item, you can use it on any page with a simple click and a drag.

Create a Library Item

1. Open a page that contains information you want to convert to a library item.

2. Click the **Window** menu, and then click **Assets** to display the Assets panel.

3. Click the **Library** category.

4. Select the item or items that you want converted into a library item.

5. Click the **New Library Item** button.

   Dreamweaver adds the item to the Assets panel as an untitled library item.

6. Enter a name for the library item, and then press Enter (Win) or Return (Mac).

   NOTE *Dreamweaver creates all Library Items with the .lbl extension.*

   NOTE *If this is the first library item created, Dreamweaver creates a new subfolder called Library, and place it in the working site folder. All library items are placed within this folder.*

Use a Library Item

1. Open the Web page you want to insert a library item.

2. Click the **Window** menu, and then click **Assets** to display the Assets panel.

3. Click the **Library** category.

4. Use one of the following methods to add a library item to a page:

   ◆ Drag and drop the item from the Library in the Assets panel directly into the page.

   ◆ Click to place the insertion point in the active document, select the library item you want to insert, and then click the **Insert** button in the Assets panel.

Did You Know?

You can disconnect a library item from a library. If you to edit a library item on a specific page and not everywhere else it's used, you need to disconnect the library item from the library. Open the Assets panel, select the Library category, right-click the library item you want to disconnect, and then click Detach From Original.

Editing Library Items

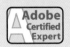

DW 3.5

Creating and using library items is fairly straightforward: You create an object, such as a navigation bar and instruct Dreamweaver that it is now a library item. That item can be used on any Web page with a simple click and a drag. Both the creation, saving, and subsequent use of library items, is discussed in the previous section. The fun part (and it's easy) is when you need to make a modification to a library item. When you think about it, that's the real power of library items,. When you make changes to a library item, Dreamweaver changes the item everywhere it was used.

Edit a Library Item

1. Click the **Window** menu, and then click **Assets** to display the Assets panel.

2. Click the **Library** category.

3. Open the library item using one of the following methods:

    ◆ Select the item, and then click the **Edit** button in the Assets panel.

    ◆ Double-click on the library item.

    ◆ In the Properties panel, click the **Open** button.

    Dreamweaver opens the document in a new window.

4. Make changes to the item using standard editing techniques.

5. Click the **File** menu, and then click **Save**.

    Dreamweaver opens the Update Library Items dialog box.

6. Choose from the following options:

    ◆ **Update Library Items In These Files.** Displays a list of all files associated with this library item.

    ◆ **Update.** Click the **Update** button to perform an update on all displayed files.

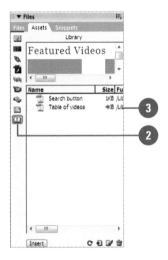

◆ **Don't Update.** Click the **Don't Update** button to cancel the update.

Dreamweaver opens the Update Pages dialog box.

7 Choose from the following options:

◆ **Look In.** Click the **Look In** option to update all files within a specific site, or click the **Entire Site** option to update all files within the working site.

◆ **Update.** Select to update Library Items, Templates (associated with the Library Item), or both.

◆ **Show Log.** Select to show a log of the update when finished.

8 Click **Start** to begin the update process, if necessary, and then click **Close**.

Did You Know?

You can display the filename and location of the source file for a library item. Select the item on one of your pages, open the Properties panel, and then view the filename and location in the Src box.

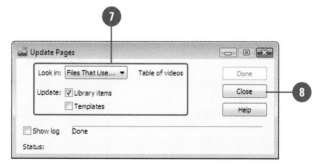

Working with Library Items

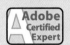 DW 3.5

If you choose not to update a library item when you edit it, you can still update it later using the Update Current Page or Update Pages commands. The Update Current Page allows you to update the active document in the Document window, while the Update Pages command allows you to update the entire Web site. In addition to updating library items, you can also rename individual items or delete the ones you no longer use.

Update Library Items on a Page or an Entire Site

1. Open the Web page with library items you want to update.

2. Update the library items using either of the following methods:

   ◆ **Update Current Page.** Click the **Modify** menu, point to **Library**, and then click **Update Current Page**.

   ◆ **Update Entire Site.** Click the **Modify** menu, point to **Library**, click **Update Pages**, specify what update in the **Look In** popup, select the **Library Items** check box, and then click **Start**.

Did You Know?

You can customize the highlight color of library items. Click the Dreamweaver (Mac) or Edit (Win) menu, click Preferences, select the Highlighting category, select the Library Items check box, select a highlighting color, select the Show check box, and then click OK.

You can show or hide highlighting. Click the View menu, point to Visual Aids, and then click Invisible Elements.

Rename or Delete a Library Item

1. Open the Web page with library items you want to rename or delete.

2. Click the **Window** menu, and then click **Assets** to display the Assets panel.

3. Click the **Library** category.

4. Select the library item you want to rename or delete.

5. Use any of the following methods:

   ◆ **Rename A Library.** Right-click the library item, click **Rename**, type a new name, and then press Enter (Win) or Return (Mac).

   ◆ **Delete A Library.** Right-click the library item, click **Delete**, or click the **Delete** button, and then click **Yes** to confirm the deletion.

Did You Know?

You can recreate a missing or deleted library item. Select the item on one of your pages, open the Properties panel, and then click the Recreate button.

Creating an External JavaScript Library

As you develop a site, you use some Dreamweaver behaviors and JavaScript code constantly. The basic rollover image, for example, is so useful for navigation bars, you may end up putting it on every page of your site. Unfortunately, each time you add a behavior to a page, Dreamweaver adds lines of JavaScript code as well and more code means slower downloads. You usually end up using the same behaviors repeatedly, so it makes sense to collect these functions and save them in an external JavaScript file. External JavaScript's help you speed up the download of your Web pages. When the scripts are downloaded, they are cached on the visitor's computer. Once your scripts are cached, each subsequent page that is downloaded only requires the browser to download the HTML... and not the scripts, which saves time. You can create a JavaScript file (.js) in Dreamweaver or an external editor, and then copy the JavaScript code that Dreamweaver produces or enter your own code in the JavaScript file (.js) and save it in your site folder (typically in a folder called Scripts) for easy access from the Assets panel.

Create a JavaScript File in Dreamweaver

1. Click the **File** menu, and then click **New**.

   The New Document dialog box opens.

2. Click the **Blank Page** category.

3. Click the **JavaScript** page type.

4. Click **Create**.

5. Enter your JavaScript code, or copy and paste Dreamweaver generated JavaScript code (located in Code view) in the JavaScript file.

6. Click the **File** menu, and then click **Save**.

7. Navigate to the folder location in your local root site folder where you want to store the script file, typically called Scripts folder.

8. Enter a name for the script file.

9. Click **Save**.

Create an External JavaScript Library Item by Dragging

1 Open the local root site folder for your Web site from the desktop.

2 Drag the user-created JavaScript file from the desktop into the internal folder named, Scripts.

3 Open Dreamweaver.

4 Click the **Site** menu, point to **Manage Sites**, select the site that you dragged the JavaScript code, and then click **Done**.

5 Click the **Window** menu, and then click **Assets** to display the Assets panel.

6 Click the **Scripts** category.

7 Click the **Refresh** button.

The new JavaScript code appears in the Assets panel.

Did You Know?

You can create an external JavaScript library item by dragging a JavaScript file directly to a page. Open a page in Dreamweaver, drag the user-created JavaScript file (.js) from the desktop directly to the page in Dreamweaver, and then click Yes to save the code in the active site folder (recommended). Open the Assets panel, click the Scripts category, and then click the Refresh button to display the JavaScript file.

Assets panel

Inserting and Editing an External JavaScript

After you create an external JavaScript file in Dreamweaver or another external editor and store it in a folder, typically called Scripts, in your local root site folder, you can insert the JavaScript into any page in your site and reduce page download times. If yo u need to make a change to an external JavaScript file, you can do it directly from Dreamweaver using the Assets panel. When you make a change to a JavaScript file, the new code is automatically used when the script is called.

Insert an External JavaScript

1. Open the Web page you want to insert an external script.

2. Click in the document where you want to insert the JavaScript code.

   NOTE *If the script is to be attached to the entire Web page, click the <body> tag in the tag selector at the bottom left of the Document window.*

3. Click the **Window** menu, and then click **Assets** to display the Assets panel.

4. Click the **Scripts** category.

5. Select the script you want attached to the page.

   TROUBLE? *If the script is not available in the list, click the Refresh button.*

6. Click the **Insert** button.

   Dreamweaver inserts the script into the page.

Did You Know?

You can get free javascripts on the Web. Check out the free scripts at www.java-script.net. You can also perform a search for free javascripts for additional Web sites.

Edit External Scripts

1. Click the **Window** menu, and then click **Assets** to display the Assets panel.

2. Click the **Scripts** category.

3. Select the script you want to edit.

4. Click the **Assets Options** button, and then click **Edit**.

   The script appears within a window, the same size as the current document window.

5. Make the necessary changes to the script.

6. Click the **File** menu, and then click **Save**.

7. Click the **Close** button to close the JavaScript document.

Using Server-Side Includes

 DW 1.3

A server-side include is a file that the Web server uses in your pages when a browser opens the page. In Dreamweaver, you can insert server-side includes in your pages, edit the includes, or preview pages containing includes.

When you insert a server-side include in a Web page, Dreamweaver places a reference to an external file; the actual contents of the server-side include are not placed in the file. However, Dreamweaver displays the contents of the server-side include in Design view to make it easier to create and layout your pages. In addition, you can preview your pages in your browser to display them as if they were on your Web server. When you display a page with a server-side include in your browser, the server creates a new page inserting the contents of the file and displays the result. This can make updating files more flexible, however it doesn't take a little longer to display the page.

There are two types of server-side includes: Virtual and File. The type you need depends on the Web server you use. Some servers can only use certain types of files for server-side includes, so check the documentation of your server software to determine which is the best type for you. Or, you can just try each type to see which one works for you.

Insert a Server-Side Include

1 Open the Web page where you want to place the server-side include.

2 Click the **Insert** menu, and then click **Server-Side Include**.

3 Locate and select the server-side include file you want to insert.

4 Click **OK**.

Modify a Server-Side Include

1 Open the Web page with the server-side include you want to modify.

2 Select the server-side include.

3 Open the Properties panel.

4 Use the options in the Properties panel to modify server-side settings or change/update the server-side include file.

◆ If your server is an Apache Web server, click Virtual. This works well for Apache Web server where File doesn't always.

◆ If you server is a Microsoft Internet Information Server (IIS), click File. This works well for IIS where Virtual only works in certain circumstances.

Creating Templates

18

Introduction

A template is a common structure of a Web site design. Usually Web sites follow a standard structure, such as a header, a navigation bar and a footer that are common to all your pages. Now, imagine that your site has 50 pages. If you need to make one small change, for example adding a new link, you would need to go to each of those pages and change it manually. But using a template you only need to change it in the template and all the pages will be updated automatically.

Think of Dreamweaver templates as really large library items. Instead of occupying a small part of a page, templates control all areas of a page that are to be kept consistent throughout the majority of a Web site. Once created, areas within the template are then made editable so new content can be inserted from page to page.

If nothing else, templates are a fantastic timesaving tool. They allow you to create pages that share the same design but contain different content, and if you modify a template document, you immediately update the design of all pages that were created from that template.

In this chapter, you'll learn how templates can streamline your workflow.

Introducing Templates

 DW 2.8

Think of templates as really big library items. For example, an entire Web page can be saved as a template. You could have the navigation built into the page; along with editable areas for text or graphics. Let's face it; large and complex Web sites have many pages that have a similar look and feel. Think of a catalog Web site where you would click to view items in the catalog. Let's say that the site has hundreds of items, and the only difference between the pages is the description of the item and an image. Instead of creating hundreds of pages from scratch, you need only create one template and have editable areas for the description and image.

Templates can be comprised of virtually any Web design components. They can include graphics, images, CSS, Flash, just about anything that you would place on a normal Web page. Since a template will contain areas that are editable, and areas that are locked, most templates are designed using a series of tables, or AP elements. As the designer of the template, you decide what areas of the template are editable and what areas are locked out. Of course, this means little to your visitors; locked and editable areas only define to the Web designer what areas can be changed and what areas remain the same.

For example, you create a Web page that emulates a newsletter. The navigation, footers, and the e-newspaper flag remain the same; however, there are areas of the page that you want to update with the latest news. When you design the template, the navigation, footers, and flag are locked, and the areas for the news are editable.

Templates don't control what visitors do with the page; they control how other designers edit the page. When the template is used, the designer assigned to change the data, can only access and change the areas you mark as editable. This prevents the accidental (or purposeful) changing of the page, except where you as the Template designer decide.

Editable Regions

If you're a regular template user (and you should be), you'll find a lot of flexibility as you create editable areas for a template page. There are four types of editable areas on a template page: editable region, repeating region, optional region, and editable tag attributes. **Editable regions** are unlocked areas that you can add content in a template page. **Repeating regions** are unlocked areas that allow you to add or delete copies of the repeating regions in a template page. There are two types of repeating regions: region and table. With a table region, for example, you can to increase or decrease the rows in a table while keeping the table structure intact. **Optional regions** are unlocked areas that allow you to show or hide content in a template page. In addition to using editable regions, you can also use **editable tag attributes** to modify specific attributes related to an element. You can make some attributes editable while leaving other attributes locked.

The Internet is full of sites containing pre-designed templates. Some are quite elaborate. You can find templates for entire sites, such as shopping carts, and sites complete with Paypal pages. Listed here are a few of the sites that carry templates:

http://allwebcodesign.com/

http://www.dreamweaver-templates.org/

http://www.adobe.com/products/dreamweaver/download/templates/

Creating a Template

DW 3.3, 3.9

Templates allow you to create pages that share the same design but different content, and if you modify a template document, you immediately update the design of all pages that were created from that template. One of the best ways to create a template is to actually design a Web page, place everything where you want it to be (navigation, text areas, image areas, footers, possibly a library item, etc.), and then convert (save) the page as a template. Templates contain editable and locked areas, so they are typically enclosed within a table structure or AP elements. When you create a template, Dreamweaver saves the file by default to the Templates folder for your site and manages any links, so updates are properly maintained.

Create a Template

1. Create a document (including editable regions) that you want to use as a template.

2. Click the **File** menu, and then click **Save As Template**.

3. Save the template using the following options:

   - **Site.** Choose the site to save the template (default: working site).

   - **Existing Templates.** Choose to save as an existing template.

   - **Description.** Enter a meaningful description of the template.

   - **Save As.** Enter a file name for the template.

4. Click **Save**.

5. Click **Yes** as necessary to update the site with any needed files.

   Dreamweaver saves the template file with the .dwt extension in the default Templates folder within the local root site folder.

   NOTE *If you attempt to close a template file without an editable region, Dreamweaver warns you.*

For Your Information

Checking Template Syntax

When you insert an region in a template, Dreamweaver uses HTML comment tags, known as template tags, to specify the region in the code to make sure it remains valid HTML. For example, <!-- TemplateBeginEditable name ="..." -->. There are few important rule to be aware of: (1) white space can be any length; (2) attributes can be in any order; (3) comment and attribute name are case sensitive; and (4) all attributes need to be in quotation marks, either single or double quotes. When you save a template, Dreamweaver check the template syntax. However, you can also check it whenever you want. Open the template you want to check, click the Modify menu, point to Templates, and then click Check Template Syntax. If there are problems, an error message appears, describing the problems.

Opening a Template

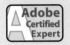 DW 3.3

After you create and save a template, you can open it using several different methods in Dreamweaver. You can use the Assets panel or the Open dialog box. When you save a template file, the default location is typically in the Templates folder of the local root site folder. When you use the Assets panel to open a template, the default location automatically appears displaying the current templates. When you use the Open dialog box, you need to navigate to the Templates folder. If you have recently saved or opened a template, you can also open it again quickly using the Open Recent submenu on the File menu. When you open a template file, the title bar in the Document window contains the word <<Template>> followed by the name of the template along with the .dwt file extension for templates.

Open a Template File Using the Assets Panel

1 Click the **Window** menu, and then click **Assets** to display the Assets panel.

2 Click the **Templates** category.

3 Open the template using one of the following options:

◆ Select the template in the Names window, and then click the **Edit** button in the Assets panel.

◆ Double click on the name of the template in the Assets panel.

Edit button

Did You Know?

You can create a blank template from the Assets panel. Open the Assets panel, click the Templates category, click the New Template button, type a name, and then press Enter (Win) or Return (Mac).

See Also

See "Creating a Web Page from a Blank Template" on page 24 for information on using a blank template.

Open a Template File Using the Open Dialog Box

1 Click the **File** menu, and then click **Open**.

TIMESAVER *Press Ctrl+O (Win) or ⌘+O (Mac).*

2 Click the **Files Of Type** list arrow (Win) or **Popup** (Mac), and then click **Template Files (*.dwt)**.

3 Locate and select the template file you want to open.

The default location is typically in the Templates folder of the local root site folder.

4 Click **Open**.

Did You Know?

You can open the template file attached to the current page file. Open the Web page based on the template you want to open, click the Modify menu, point to Templates, and then click Open Attached Template.

You can rename a template. Open the Assets panel, click the Templates category, click the name of the template, click the name again, enter a new name, and then press Enter (Win) or Return (Mac).

You can delete a template. Open the Assets panel, click the Templates category, click the template you want to delete, and then click the Delete button in the Assets panel.

Defining Editable Regions

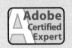
DW 3.3

When you first create a template, the entire page is locked and uneditable to the designer. Without editable areas, you would not be able to make any changes to the page. To correct this problem, you need to create editable areas in the template. Editable areas are for the designers who want to use templates to create Web pages. Web pages based on a template enable Dreamweaver users to edit parts of a Web page within the editable regions without the risk of accidentally changing the locked regions. Editable regions in Design view appear with a rectangular outline and a small tab in the upper-left corner with the name of the region. You can click the tab to select the editable region.

Define Editable Regions

1. Open the template you want to add editable regions.

2. Select the content (including tables, table cells, or AP elements) in the template you want to make editable, or click to place the insertion point.

   NOTE *If the area is going to contain text, make sure you apply any formatting options, using HTML or CSS to the area before making it an editable area.*

3. Click the **Insert** menu, point to **Template Objects**, and then click **Editable Region**.

   The New Editable Region dialog box opens.

4. Enter a unique name for the new region.

5. Click **OK**.

   The editable region appears with the name in the tab.

Did You Know?

You can remove or relock an editable region. Select the area you want to change, click the Modify menu, point to Templates, and then click Remove Template Markup.

Defining Editable Attributes

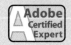
Adobe Certified Expert • DW 3.3

In addition to making regions of a page editable, you can also make specific HTML tag attributes editable (for example, the background color of the page). This combination not only gives you control over a general area such as a table, individual cell, or an AP element; you now have control over specific elements. Now that's what I call control. Use this option to allow contributors to the Web page the ability to duplicate the region. For example, creating a table that holds customer comments, and the contributor needs the ability to generate new pages, and add more rows to the table, as needed.

Define Editable Attributes

1. Open the template you want to define editable attributes.

2. Select the tag or object that you want to make editable.

3. Click the **Modify** menu, point to **Templates**, and then click **Make Attribute Editable**.

4. Select from the following options in the Editable Tag Attributes dialog box:

   ◆ **Attribute.** Select the attribute, or click the Add button and enter the attribute manually.

   ◆ **Make Attribute Editable.** Select to make this attribute editable.

   ◆ **Label.** Enter a unique name for the editable attribute.

   ◆ **Type.** Select a type from the available options: Text, URL, Color, True/False, or Number.

   ◆ **Default.** Enter the initial default value for the attribute.

5. Click **OK**.

> ### Did You Know?
>
> **You can modify the properties of an editable attribute.** Click the Modify menu, click Template Properties, select the attribute you want, make any changes, and then click OK.

Creating Repeating Regions

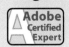

DW 3.3

Repeating regions are unlocked areas that allow you to add or delete copies of the repeating regions in a template page. There are two types of repeating regions: region and table. With a repeating region, you can specify the layout you want by duplicating repeating page elements, such as a gallery of photographs. With a repeating table region, you can increase or decrease the rows in a table while keeping the table structure intact. You can define table attributes and set which table cells are editable.

Create a Repeating Region

① Open the template you want to add a repeating region.

② Select the content in the template you want to change, or click to place the insertion point where you want it.

③ Click the **Insert** menu, point to **Template Objects**, and then click **Repeating Region**.

The New Editable Region dialog box opens.

④ Enter a unique name for the new region.

⑤ Click **OK**.

The repeating region appears with the name in the tab.

NOTE *If the area is to contain text, make sure you apply any formatting options, using HTML or CSS to the area before making it an editable area.*

Create a Repeating Table

① Open the template you want to add editable regions.

② Click to place the insertion point where you want to insert the table.

③ Click the **Insert** menu, point to **Template Objects**, and then click **Repeating Table**.

④ Select from the following options in the Inserting Repeating Table dialog box:

- ◆ **Rows.** Enter the number of rows for the table.

- ◆ **Columns.** Enter the number of columns for the table.

- ◆ **Cell Padding.** Specify the number of pixels between a cell's contents and the cell border.

- ◆ **Cell Spacing.** Specify the number of pixels between the table cells.

- ◆ **Width.** Enter the width (in pixels) or as a percentage of the browser window's width.

- ◆ **Border.** Enter the width (in pixels) for the table border.

- ◆ **Repeat Rows Of The Table.** Specify the table rows you want in the repeating region.

- ◆ **Starting Row.** Enter the row number for the first row.

- ◆ **Ending Row.** Enter the row number for the last row.

- ◆ **Region Name.** Enter a unique name for the table region.

⑤ Click **OK**.

The repeating table region appears with the name in the tab.

Creating Optional Regions

Content within an optional region may or may not be displayed, depending on certain conditions set by the template designer. Optional regions are just that: optional. Optional regions define content or editable regions that you can turn on or off (be visible or not). Optional regions, therefore, enable designers to show and hide specially marked regions. The template tab of an optional region is preceded by the word *If*. There are two types of optional regions: non-editable and editable. A **non-editable optional region** allows you to show or hide the region without the ability to edit the content, while an **editable optional region** allows you to edit the content.

Create a Non-Editable Optional Region

1. Open the template you want to add an optional region.

2. Select the item, or an AP element within the template that you want converted into an optional region.

3. Click the **Insert** menu, point to **Template Objects**, and then click **Optional Region**.

4. Click the **Basic** tab.

5. Enter a unique name for the region.

6. Select the **Show By Default** check box to toggle between showing or hiding this optional region (default: show).

7. To set values for the optional region, click the **Advanced** tab.

   ◆ Click the **Use Parameter** option, and then select a parameter from the popup, or click the **Enter Expression** option, and then write a template expression.

8. Click **OK**.

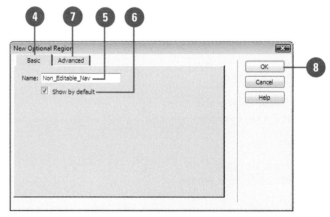

Create an Editable Optional Region

1. Open the template you want to add an optional region.

2. Click to place the insertion point where you want to insert an editable optional region.

3. Click the **Insert** menu, point to **Template Objects**, and then click **Optional Region**.

4. Click the **Basic** tab.

5. Enter a unique name for the region.

6. Select the **Show By default** check box to toggle between showing or hiding this optional region.

7. To set values for for the optional region, click the **Advanced** tab.

   ◆ Click the **Use Parameter** option, and then select a parameter from the popup, or click the **Enter Expression** option, and then write a template expression.

8. Click **OK**.

Design By Example

Creating an Optional Region

A simple use of an optional region is to allow content to either be visible or not in a page based on a template. For example, you maintain a Web site for a garden center called the Green Thumb (now that's original). The site sells three types of items: Flowers, Vegetables, and Garden Equipment. The pages are essentially the same. There will be two editable areas: one describing the product, and another for an image displaying the product. The remainder of the areas (navigation, footers, background, etc.), are all locked... except for one thing. You want a generic image on each of the pages so that the customer can identify the pages for the three products (It could even be a background image contained in an AP element). To solve this problem, you create an optional region, load all three changeable images into the area, and then let the designer of the page decide which image to use.

Creating Nested Templates

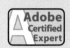

DW 3.3, 3.9

Nested templates are essentially templates within templates. Nested templates allow for different levels of control on pages created from these templates. For example, you create a Web site that has a similar overall appearance (navigation, logo, color scheme, etc.), yet also has sections that have a different appearance. For the separate sections of the site, you can make nested templates that will have common elements and layout features for that section. The differences represent a different type of page in the site. First, you create the navigation templates; each with their own differences, and save them. Next, you create the main body of the page (which will also be a template), and "nest" the navigation template into the main template. The nested template is now defined as the "child" template. Now, any time you need to make changes to the navigation, you simply edit the child template, just like any other template, and the changes will be applied specifically to the pages that contain the child. Nested templates do not increase the size of the Web page, nor do they create any additional complexity. All they do is give you control over your site.

Create a Nested Template

1 Create a normal template, the same as any other template.

This template will act as the parent template. There must be at least one editable region in the template (this is the area you will insert your nested template).

2 Click the **File** menu, and then click **Save As Template**.

3 Save the template using the following options:

- ◆ **Site.** Choose the site to save the template (default: working site).

- ◆ **Description.** Enter a meaningful description of the template.

- ◆ **Save As.** Enter a file name for the template.

4 Click **Save**.

5 Click **Yes** as necessary to update the site with any needed files.

6 Click the **File** menu, click **Close**, and then click **OK** as necessary to the alert message.

Now, you want to create a new page based on the template.

7 Click the **File** menu, and then click **New**.

8 Select from the following options in the New Document dialog box:

- ◆ Click the **Page From Template** category.

- ◆ Select the site where the template is located.

- ◆ Select the template you just saved in step 4.

- ◆ Click **Create** to open the new document.

9 Click to select the area of the document that will contain the nested template.

10 Click the **Window** menu, and then click **Assets** to display the Assets panel.

11 Click the **Templates** category.

12 Select your previously created nested template (in this example, a template that contains the navigation).

13 Click the **Apply** button in the Assets panel.

Dreamweaver adds the nested template to this new document.

14 Click the **File** menu, click **Save As Template**, and then following the instructions in step 3 thru 5 to save this template, along with its nested template.

Creating a Web Page from a Nested Template

 DW 3.3, 3.9

In addition to standard templates, you can create nested templates. A nested template is a template whose design is based on another template. By creating nested templates, you can control content in pages that share the same layout but also have slight design variations. When you open and change a nested template, it modifies that section of all the files that use the nested template without changing any other areas of the template or the pages they are attached. This takes Web page customization and reusability to the next level.

Create a Nested Template

1. Click the **File** menu, and then click **New**.

   The New Document dialog box opens.

2. Click the **Page From Template** category.

3. Select the site that contains the template you want.

4. Select the template you want to use.

5. Click **Create**.

   Dreamweaver opens a new Web page based on the selected template.

6. Add something to the new template, such as a pre-existing navigational system, an image, or possibly some changeable text.

7. Click the **Insert** menu, point to **Template Objects**, and then click **Make Nested Template**.

8. Enter a Description in the input field (optional), and then enter a name for the nested template into the Save As input field.

9. Click the **Save** button.

   Dreamweaver now saves the nested template.

Creating a Web Page from a Custom Template

 DW 3.3, 3.9

After you create your own custom template, you can use it to create Web pages. A document created from a template is known as an instance of that template. When you create a page based on a template, it contains all the attributes of the template; however, it won't be a template, it will be a Web page. When you open a page based on a template, the editable regions in Design view appear with a rectangular outline and a small tab in the upper-left corner with the name of the region. You can click the tab to select the editable region. In addition, the entire page is surrounded by a different colored outline with the template name on the tab that reminds you the page is based on a template and you can only change editable areas.

Create a Web Page from a Custom Template

1. Click the **File** menu, and then click **New**.

   The New Document dialog box opens.

2. Click the **Page From Template** category.

3. Select the site that contains the template you want.

4. Select the template you want to use.

5. Select the **Update Page When Template Changes** check box to instruct Dreamweaver to update all pages when the template changes (default).

6. Click **Create**.

   Dreamweaver generates a new document based on the selected template.

7. Edit and add content to all editable areas of the page.

8. Click the **File** menu, click **Save**, select a location, specify a name, and then click **Save** to save your new page.

Updating a Template

DW 3.3

If all you did with templates was to create new pages, based on their design; that would be very powerful. However, there's more to a template than simply streamlining the creation of a simple Web page. The power of a template is that when you change one template, you have the option of changing all the associated pages. Now, that's what I'm talking about. When you edit and save a template, Dreamweaver asks you whether you want to automatically update the page files based on that template. If you decide not to automatically update the page files, you can manually change an individual page, all the pages that use a template, or the entire site using the Update commands.

Update a Template and All the Pages Based on the Template

1. Open the template you want to update.

2. Make changes to the template, using standard editing techniques.

3. Click the **File** menu, and then click **Save**.

   The Update Templates Files dialog box opens, displaying all the page files based on the templates.

4. Click **Update** to continue the update process, or click **Don't Update** to cancel the process.

5. If you clicked Update, the Update Pages dialog box opens.

   ◆ **Look In.** Select **Entire Site** to update all the documents that use this template, or select **Files That Use** to update pages using a particular template.

   ◆ **Templates and Library Items.** Select to update templates, library items, or both.

   ◆ **Show Log.** Select to show a log upon completion.

6. Click **Start** to update the files, if necessary, and then click **Close**.

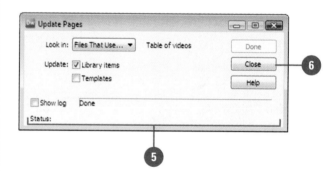

Update Pages Based on a Template Manually

① Open the template-based Web page you want to update.

② Click the **Modify** menu, point to **Templates**, and then click **Update Pages**.

The Update Pages dialog box opens.

③ Click the **Look In** popup, and then click **Files That Use** or **Entire Site**.

④ Select the **Templates** and **Library Items** check boxes to update templates and library items in the template-based files.

⑤ Select the **Show Log** check box to show a log upon completion

⑥ Click **Start** to update the files, and then click **Close**.

Did You Know?

You can manually apply template changes to a page based on the template. Open the Web page based on the template, click the Modify menu, point to Templates, and then click Update Current Page.

Design By Example

Saving Time by Using Templates

Let's say that you've just created this huge Web site for your university (I volunteered to oversee the one for my university, and it wasn't pretty). Now, the project is completed, you unveil to the students and staff, and what happens: Well in my case one of the deans decided they didn't like the look of their section of the site, and another one decided that the graphics for her section were wrong. Understand everyone signed off on the design; however, things will happen. So, now all eyes are on me... I have to get this site up and running in a week, if we're to meet our deadlines for school enrollment. I looked about the room, asked each department head to give me their changes (in writing) by 5:00PM. The next day, when the facility came in and checked the site all the changes were implemented (some people still weren't happy). How did I manage to change literally hundreds of Web pages in a single night (it actually took 3.5 hours)? How did I manage this great feat? Templates my friend, templates.

Attaching or Detaching a Template

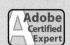 DW 3.3

If you didn't create a new page based on a template, you can still attach (apply) the template to the file later. When you apply a template to a page file, Dreamweaver tries to match the existing content to a region in the template. You can apply a template to a page using menu commands from the Document window or from the Assets panel. If you no longer want a page to be based on a template, you can detach the page from the template. The page doesn't lose any content, however, changes made to the template will not be applied to the page after it is detached.

Attach a Template to a Page

1. Open the Web page you want to apply the template to.

2. Click the **Modify** menu, point to **Templates**, and then click **Apply Template To Page**.

3. Select the template you want to apply.

4. Click **Select**.

   ◆ You can also open the Assets panel, click the **Templates** category, select a template, and then click the **Apply** button.

   If the Inconsistent Region Names dialog box opens, content on the page cannot be automatically assigned to a template region.

5. Select a destination for the content. Select a region in the new template or select **Nowhere** to remove the content.

6. To move all unresolved content to the selected region, click **Use For All**.

7. Click **OK**.

Detach a Page from a Template

1 Open the template-based Web page you want to detach.

2 Click the **Modify** menu, point to **Templates**, and then click **Detach From Template**.

The page detaches from the template, and now can be edited just like any normal Web page.

See Also

See "Setting Highlighting Color Preferences" on page 65 for information on setting highlight colors for editable regions, nested editable regions, and locked regions.

Did You Know?

You can find an editable region and select it. Click the Modify menu, point to Templates, and then select the name of the region you want to find and select. Editable regions inside a repeated region do not appear in the menu.

Importing XML into a Template

Dreamweaver provides an Import command for XML you can use to create a new document based on the template specified in an XML file. The command fills in the contents of each editable region in the new document using data from the XML file. If Dreamweaver has problems importing the data, the XML file might not have the right structure. To correct the problem, use the Export command for XML to view the file structure and then make the adjustments to the XML file you want to import.

Import XML into a Template

1 Click the **File** menu, point to **Import**, and then click **XML Into Template**.

2 Navigate to the drive and folder location where you want to import the XML file.

3 Select the XML file you want to import.

4 Click **Open**.

Dreamweaver creates a new Web page based on the template specified in the XML file. The XML data in the file is placed in the editable region in the new Web page.

Exporting Template Data as XML

DW 3.16

If you have data in a template that you want to use in another program, you can export the data as XML. The XML Export command creates an XML file with the data contained in your template's editable regions and parameters. The exported XML file includes the name of the template and editable regions for round trip purposes. You can also use the XML Export command if you are having problems importing XML data into Dreamweaver. You can export data as an XML file in order to view the file structure and then make adjustments to the XML file you want to import.

Export Template Data as XML

1. Open the template-based Web page with the data you want to export as XML.

2. Click the **File** menu, point to **Export**, and then click **Template Data As XML**.

3. Select the Notation option you want.

   ◆ **Use Standard Dreamweaver XML Tag**. Use this option if the template contains repeating regions or template parameters.

   ◆ **Use Editable Region Names As XML Tags**. Use this option if the template doesn't contain repeating regions or template parameters.

4. Click **OK**.

5. Navigate to the drive and folder location where you want to export the data as an XML file.

6. Type a name for the file, or use the suggested name.

7. Click **Save**.

Testing a Web Site

19

Introduction

Testing is an integral part of the design of a Web site. In fact, the term used to describe a good Web site is bullet proof. Without the ability to test a site, you would never know what works, and what needs help. Dreamweaver gives you a host of tools to help make sure that your visitors have a pleasant experience. Some of the things Web testing can and should look for are:

- **Validation.** Is your HTML and CSS code compatible with your visitors? Do your Web pages have any broken links? If problems arise on your site, visitors will go else where, which isn't the goal.

- **Browser Independence.** Do your Web pages load and function on the various browsers used by your visitors? Your site may be viewed in a large variety of situations: different browsers, different operating systems, or different features enabled or disabled.

- **Accessibility.** Do your Web pages conform to the standards set by the government on accessibility standards? Your site may be viewed by those with physical limitations, such as the visually impaired.

- **Speed.** Is it easy and fast to access your Web pages? Remember, visitors do not like to wait. The 8-second rule is a good guideline to remember.

All of the items are important because they make your site more compatible to your visitors. It gives them a better experience, and it helps to keep them at your site.

Finding Broken Links

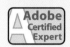

DW 4.7

One of the most absolute, worst, horrible (enough adjectives for you), is to create a Web site with links that don't work. You know what I'm talking about; you click on a link and a page pops up saying the link can't be found... I HATE it when that happens. A broken link to another site, although not acceptable, is sometimes understandable. For example, you have a link to a photography site that you like, the site goes down, and the owner never bothered to tell you. A few weeks later, you discover the problem and fix it; however, you know a lot of your visitors clicked that link. The worst types of broken links are those to pages within your own document... to pages that you created. The good news is that Dreamweaver provides you with the tools to make sure that all of your links (external and internal) function correctly using the Link Checker in the Results panel. You can check links in the current document, for the entire site, or for selected files.

Find Links

1. Open the Web page you want to find links (if you plan to check just one page).

2. Click the **Window** menu, and then click **Results** to display the Results panel.

3. Click the **Link Checker** tab in the Results panel.

   ◆ You can also click the **Site** menu, and then click **Check Links Sitewide**.

4. Select from the following Link Checker options:

   ◆ **Check Links.** Click the **Check Links** button, and then select the command you want:

     ◆ **Check Links In Current Document.**

     ◆ **Check Links For Entire Current Local Site.**

     ◆ **Check Links For Selected Files In Site.**

   ◆ **Stop.** Click the **Stop** button to stop the current link check.

Results panel

◆ **Save Report.** Click the **Save Report** button to save the report.

5 Click the **Show** popup, and then choose from the following options:

◆ **Broken Links.** Select to display a listing of all files that contain broken links (default).

◆ **External Links.** Select to display a listing of all external links.

◆ **Orphaned Links.** Select to display all the files with no incoming links (available when choosing Check Links For Entire Local Site).

Shows broken links

Shows external links

Fixing Broken Links

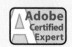

DW 4.7

After you find the broken links in your site using the Link Checker in the Results panel, you can use Dreamweaver tools to fix them. It's pretty simple. All you need to do is relink it. In the Link Checker, a broken link appears with a folder icon, which you can use to open a dialog box and select a reference to an active link. In the dialog box, you can enter a URL, select related parameters, and select whether the link is relative to the Document or Site Root. If a link changes over the entire site, you can use the Change Link Sitewide command to quickly redirect it to another place. If you want to delete a link, you can use this command.

Fix Links

1. Open the Web page you want to fix (if you plan to check just one page).

2. Click the **Window** menu, and then click **Results** to display the Results panel.

3. Click the **Link Checker** tab in the Results panel.

4. If needed, click the **Check Links** button, and then select a Check Links command.

5. Select a broken link from the Link Checker panel.

6. Click the folder icon, associated with the broken link (located to the right of the broken link).

   The Select File dialog box appears.

7. Choose to select file names from the **Site Root**, **Server**, or **Data Sources** (default: Site Root).

8. Select the correct link from the Select File dialog box, or enter the correct link directly into the URL input box.

9. Select whether the link is relative to the **Document** or **Site Root** (default: Document).

10. To add any additional parameters to the link, click **Parameters**.

11. Click **OK** to update the link.

Quick Link Change Sitewide

1. Click the **Site** menu, and then click **Change Link Sitewide**.

2. Enter a path or click the folder icon to browse and select the target file from which to unlink.

3. Enter a path or click the folder icon to browse and select the new file to link to.

4. Click **OK**.

Did You Know?

You can check links sitewide. Click the Site menu, and then click Check Link Sitewide to generate a quick report of all the links associated with the working site.

Validating Web Pages

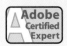

DW 4.7

The Validator in Dreamweaver allows you to quickly locate tag or syntax errors in your code. You can specify the tag-based languages against which the Validator should check, the specific problems that the Validator should check, and the types of errors that the Validator should report. Validating Web pages differs from checking for browser support in that the Validator checks for specific problems such as support for a specific version of HTML, or ColdFusion. Understanding the specific problems associated with a Web page help you to further refine the document to generate compliant code.

Set Validator Preferences

1. Click the **Dreamweaver** (Mac) or **Edit** (Win) menu, and then click **Preferences**.

2. Click the **Validator** category.

   TIMESAVER Click the Validation button on the Validation tab in the Results panel, and then click Settings.

3. Select the items that you want to validate by checking the box, located to the left of the item.

4. Click **Options**, and then select from the following validator options:

   ◆ **Display.** Select what options you want to display (**Errors**, **Warnings**, **Custom Messages**, or **Nesting Errors**).

   ◆ **Check For.** Select the options to check for **Quotes In Text** or **Entities In Text**.

5. Click **OK**.

6. Click **OK**.

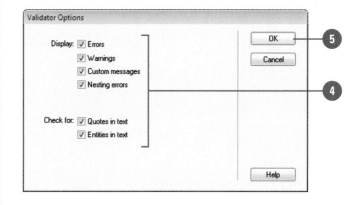

Validate a Web Page

1. Click the **Window** menu, and then click **Results** to display the Results panel.

2. Click the **Validation** tab in the Results panel.

3. Select from the following Validator options:

   ◆ **Validate.** Click the **Validate** button, and then select the validate command you want: Validate Current Document, Validate Entire Current Local Site, and Validate Selected Files In Site, Settings.

   ◆ **Stop.** Click the **Stop** button to stop the current validation check.

   ◆ **More Info.** Select an item from the validator list of errors, and then click the **More Info** button to receive more information on the selected error.

   ◆ **Save Report.** Click the **Save Report** button to save the document as an XML file.

   ◆ **Browse Report.** Click the **Browse Report** button to view an ordered listing of the current errors in your default browser.

Validate commands

Selected code related to validation

Selected validation in the Results panel

Did You Know?

You can do further validation of your Web site online. The World Wide Web Consortium gives you the ability to check your HTML and CSS according to the latest standards. Visit http://validator.w3.org/ to validate your HTML, or use http://jigsaw.w3.org/css-validator/ to check your CSS.

Checking for HTML Browser Compatibility

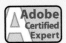

DW 2.6, 3.13

The Browser Compatibility Check (BCC) (**New!**) analyzes the HTML and CSS on the open page and determines whether it has problems in certain browsers. When you run the BCC, it scans the open page and reports any potential HTML problems in the Results panel. Each potential problem is given a confidence rating, a circle. The amount of the circle filled in—quarter, half, three-quarter, or full—determines the occurrence probability level of the problem. Browser problems fall into three categories: serious (visible problem), warning (not supported), and informational (no visible effect). In addition, you can also check browser compatibility in Code view. When you refresh a page, Dreamweaver checks the code and inserts a wavy red underline under the name of every item, creating an error in one of your predefined target browsers.

Check for HTML Browser Compatibility

① Click the **File** menu, point to **Check Page**, and then click **Browser Compatibility**.

   The Results panel appears with the Browser Compatibility Check tab, indicating any potential problems.

② Double-click an issue to select it.

   Information about the potential problem appears to the right in the Results panel.

③ To display the issue in the code, click the **Check Page** button on the Document window, and then click **Next Issue** or **Previous Issue**.

④ To exclude an issue from future checking, right-click the issue in the Results panel, and then click **Ignore Issue**.

   ◆ To edit the Ignore Issues list, click the green arrow in the Results panel, click **Edit Ignored Issues List**, delete the issue from the Exceptions.xml file, and then save and close the file.

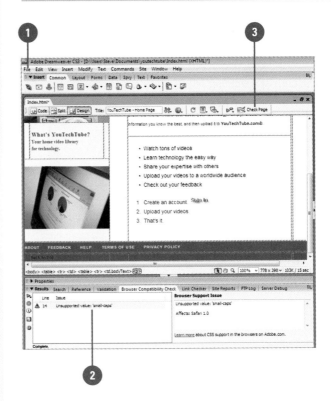

Check for HTML Browser Compatibility Using Code

① Open the document you want to check.

② Switch to Code view.

③ After making a change in Code view, click the **Refresh** button in the Properties panel, or press F5.

A wavy red underline appears under the name of every item that's an error in one of your pre-defined target browsers.

NOTE *If Dreamweaver finds no unsupported markup, then nothing is underlined, and the Target Browser Check menu icon in the Document toolbar changes to indicate that there are no errors.*

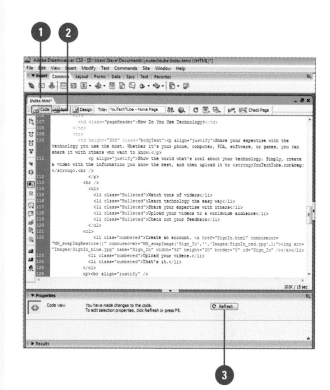

Did You Know?

You can check to see exactly what browser is not supported. Simply position the pointer to point to the red-underlined text, and a tool tip appears, indicating which browsers don't support that item.

You can select browsers to check. Click the Check Page button on the Document window, click Settings, select the browser and versions you want, and then click OK.

See Also

See "Checking for CSS Browser Compatibility" on page 238 for information on viewing and saving a BCC report.

Checking for Balanced Code

HTML is a very structured language and needs to follow specific rules to be error free. HTML code includes tags, parentheses (( )), braces ({ }), and square brackets ([ ]) that need to be balanced, meaning every opening tag, parentheses, brace, or bracket has a corresponding closing one. If HTML is not balanced, the code will not work properly and cause errors. You can use commands in Dreamweaver to make sure the tags, parentheses (( )), braces ({ }), and square brackets ([ ]) in a page are correctly balanced.

Check for Balanced Tags

1 Open the Web page in Code view you want to check.

2 Click to place the insertion point in the nested code you want to check.

3 Click the **Edit** menu, and then click **Select Parent Tag**.

The enclosing matching tags (including the contents) are selected in Code view.

4 Click the **Edit** menu, and then click **Select Parent Tag** again to continue checking tags.

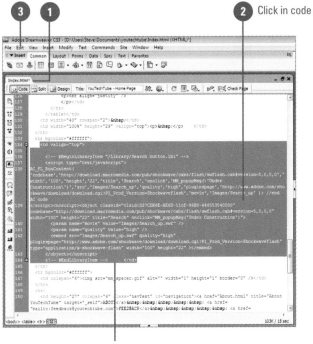

Click in code

Selected parent tag

Check for Balanced Parentheses, Braces, or Brackets

1 Open the Web page in Code view you want to check.

2 Click to place the insertion point in the code you want to check.

3 Click the **Edit** menu, and then click **Balanced Braces**.

The code between the enclosing parentheses, braces, or square brackets are selected in Code view.

4 Click the **Edit** menu, and then click **Balanced Braces** again to continue checking parentheses, braces, and square brackets.

Click in code

Selected code between parentheses, braces, or square brackets

Cleaning Up HTML

Not all HTML documents are created equal. Some HTML documents contain problems with the overall coding; empty tags, individual font tags, improperly implemented tables… the list goes on and on. The good news is that Dreamweaver can automatically remove empty tags, combine nested font tags, and otherwise improve messy or unreadable HTML or XHTML code, and more. The question to ask is where did this sloppy code come from? Did Dreamweaver generate code that subsequently must be cleaned up? The answer to that question is no. However, not all the code associated with a particular Web page is generated by Dreamweaver. For example, you might switch from Design view to Code view, and enter your own code, or (and this is more likely), you might want to insert an HTML page into your Dreamweaver site that was written by another designer, or generated by another application. If that's the case, Dreamweaver can help you straighten out the code with a click of a button. It's really that simple.

Clean Up HTML or XHTML

1. Open the Web page you want to clean up.

2. Click the **Commands** menu, and then click **Clean Up HTML** or **Clean Up XHTML**.

3. Select the Remove check boxes you want from the following options:

   ◆ **Empty Container Tags.** Removes tags that have no content.

   ◆ **Redundant Nested Tags.** Removes all redundant instances of a tag.

   ◆ **Non-Dreamweaver HTML Comments.** Removes all comments not inserted by Dreamweaver.

   ◆ **Dreamweaver Special Markup.** Removes comments related to Dreamweaver code for automatically updating templates and library-based documents.

   ◆ **Specific Tags.** Removes custom tags specified in the Adjacent text box.

④ Select the Options check boxes you want from the following options:

◆ **Combine Nested <font> Tags When Possible.** Combines two or more font tags when they control the same range of text.

◆ **Show Log On Completion.** Displays an alert with details about the changes made to the document when the cleanup is complete. A pop-up window will appear listing what actions were performed in cleaning up the document.

⑤ Click **OK** to clean up the active document.

⑥ Review the clean up summary results, and then click **OK**.

Cleaning Up Word HTML

If you have a Microsoft Word document saved as an HTML file, you can open it in Dreamweaver, and then use the Clean Up Word HTML command to convert the file into HTML compliant Web pages. The Clean Up Word HTML command removes unnecessary HTML code generated by Word. Before you convert a Word HTML file to a compliant Web page in Dreamweaver, it's a good idea to create a backup of the original Word (.doc and .htm) files, because you may not be able to reopen the HTML document in Word once you've applied the Clean Up Word HTML command.

Clean Up Word HTML

1. Open the HTML file created in Microsoft Word 97 or later you want to use in Dreamweaver.

2. Click the **Commands** menu, and then click **Clean Up Word HTML**.

3. Click the **Clean Up HTML From** popup, and then select the Word version you want to use.

4. Select from the following Basic options:

   ◆ **Remove All Word Specific Markup.** Removes Word-specific HTML code. You can select the options you want on the Details tab.

   ◆ **Clean Up CSS.** Removes Word-specific CSS.

   ◆ **Clean Up <font> Tags.** Removes HTML tags, converting the default body text to size 2 HTML text.

   ◆ **Fix Invalidly Nested Tags.** Removes the font markup tags generated by Word.

   ◆ **Set Background Color.** Replaces the gray background from Word to a color you choose (in hexadecimal).

   ◆ **Apply Source Formatting.** Uses source formatting in the HTML Format Preferences dialog box.

- ◆ **Show Log On Completion.**
  Displays an alert with details
  about the changes made to the
  document when the cleanup is
  complete. A pop-up window
  will appear listing what actions
  were performed in cleaning up
  the document.

⑤ Click the **Detailed** tab.

⑥ Select from the following
Advanced options:

- ◆ **Remove Word Specific
  Markup.** Select to enable the
  options.

  - ◆ XML from <html> tag

  - ◆ Word meta and link tags
    from <head>

  - ◆ Word XML markup

  - ◆ Conditional tags and their
    contents

  - ◆ Remove empty paragraphs
    and margins from styles

- ◆ **Clean Up CSS.** Select to enable
  the options.

  - ◆ Remove inline CSS styles
    when possible

  - ◆ Remove any style property
    that starts with "mso"

  - ◆ Remove any non-CSS style
    declaration

  - ◆ Remove all CSS styles from
    table rows and cells

⑦ Click **OK** to perform the
conversion.

⑧ Review the clean up summary
results, and then click **OK**.

Adding Accessibility

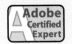 DW 2.7, 4.7

When you create accessible pages, you need to associate information, such as labels and descriptions, with your page objects to make your content accessible to all users. Web accessibility means that people with disabilities can use the Web. In addition, older people with changing abilities due to aging have better access to the Web. Web accessibility encompasses all disabilities that affect access to the Web, including visual, auditory, physical, speech, cognitive, and neurological disabilities. Dreamweaver understands the importance of Web accessibility and gives you the means to make your pages more accessible to the handicapped. As a matter of fact, Dreamweaver offers screen reader support, keyboard navigation, and operating system accessibility support. A screen reader speaks the text that appears on the computer screen. In addition, it reads non-textual information, such as button labels or image descriptions in the application. Dreamweaver supports JAWS for Windows from Freedom Scientific, and Window-Eyes screen readers from GW Micro. When designing pages to be compliant with screen readers, understand that the screen reader starts reading in the upper-left corner of the Document window. In addition, since the policy on accessibility standards changes every year, Dreamweaver gives you the ability to check your pages against the current standards. Whenever you create a new Form object, Frame, Media or Images item, a dialog box appears with accessibility options.

Set Accessibility Preferences

1. Click the **Dreamweaver** (Mac) or **Edit** (Win) menu, and then click **Preferences**.

2. Click the **Accessibility** category.

3. Select the items you want to display accessibility options for:

   ◆ **Form Objects**

   ◆ **Frames**

   ◆ **Media**

   ◆ **Images**

4. Click **OK**.

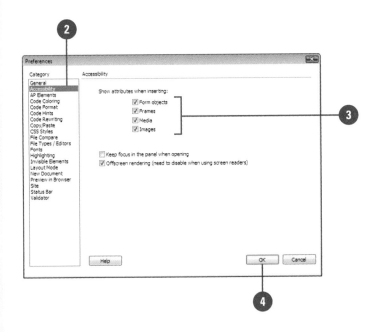

Add Accessibility

1. Open the Web page with the accessibility you want to add.

2. Add a specific item to the Web page (in this example, an image was added).

3. Select from the following options in the Image Tag Accessibility Attributes dialog box:

   ◆ **Alternate Text.** Reader programs use the text to describe the item to the visually impaired. For example, if it were a Home button, you might add the text, Home Page. In addition, the text pops up in a small window, when the visitor's mouse hovers over it.

   ◆ **Long Description.** Displays a file that contains a longer textual description of the object. For example, you might have an image of a sunset, and you want to give visually impaired readers a more in depth description. Enter the URL to the file, or click the folder icon to browse for it.

4. Click **OK**.

3 For an image

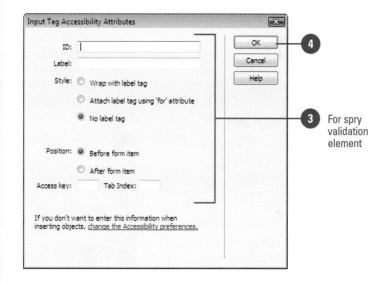
3 For spry validation element

Did You Know?

You can add accessibility to an element. If you want to add or modify accessibility options to an existing element, click the object, add the Alt tag information using the Properties panel, or right-click the object, and then click Edit Tag.

You can create an accessibility report. Click the File menu, point to Check Page, and then click Accessibility.

Running Reports to Test a Site

Dreamweaver has a lot of site reports for you to select from; for example, you can run site reports on workflow or HTML attributes, including accessibility, for the current document, selected files, or the entire site. In addition, workflow reports can improve cooperation among designers working on the same Web site. Workflow reports display checked out files and who checked them out, which files have Design Notes attached, and what, if any, files have been modified. To generate workflow reports, you need active Design notes and have access to the remote server holding the information. In addition, HTML reports enable you to compile and generate reports for HTML attributes. For example, you can check for combinable nested font tags, accessibility, missing Alt text, redundant nested tags, removable empty tags, and untitled documents. Many of the site report items have options to help you further refine what you're looking for. For example, the Recently Modified item has options to allow you to define what recently modified means. Simply select the item, and then click the Report Settings button located at the bottom of the Reports dialog box. Site reports can and should be conducted on a regular basis during the construction of any Web site, be it complex or simple.

Run Reports to Test a Site

1. Open the Web page you want to get a report (if you plan to get a report on just one page).

2. Click the **Site** menu, and then click **Reports**.

3. Click the **Report On** popup, and then select from the following options:

   ◆ **Current Document.**

   ◆ **Entire Current Local Site.**

   ◆ **Selected Files In Site.**

   ◆ **Folder.** Select the folder you want a report.

4. Select from the following site Workflow (requires remote server access) options:

   ◆ **Checked Out By.** Lists what designer checked out what files and when.

   ◆ **Design Notes.** Lists all design notes for the selected report.

◆ **Recently Modified.** Lists all files modified since the last check.

⑤ Select from the following site HTML Reports options:

◆ **Combinable Nested Font Tags.** Lists any nested font tags that can be combined to create tighter code.

◆ **Accessibility.** Lists all current accessibility standards (based on the level of HTML used).

◆ **Missing Alt Text.** Lists any missing alternate <alt> text.

◆ **Redundant Nested Tags.** Lists any redundant nested tags.

◆ **Removable Empty Tags.** Lists any empty tags.

◆ **Untitled Documents.** Lists any documents named Untitled.

⑥ To set specific options for a report, select the report, click **Report Settings**, specify the options you want (options vary depending on the report), and then click **OK**.

⑦ Click the **Run** button to generate the report.

IMPORTANT *After you run an HTML report, use the Clean Up HTML command on the Site menu to correct any HTML errors the reports listed.*

Report results

Viewing and Saving Reports

After you run a report, the results appear on the Site Reports tab in the Results panel. The Site Reports tab displays information in columns relating to the reports you selected. If you don't see enough information regarding a report item, you can display additional reference material in the Results panel. In the Site Reports tab, you can also save a report as an XML file, which you can import into a database, spreadsheet, or Web site. After you import the XML data into another file, you can print or use the report information like any other XML data.

View a Site Report

1. Create a report or display an existing one.

   ◆ **Create.** Click the **Site** menu, click **Reports,** select report options, and then click **Run.**

   ◆ **Existing.** Click the **Window** menu, click **Results,** and then click the **Site Reports** tab.

   The Results panel appears, displaying the Site Reports tab with report details.

2. The Site Reports tab in the Results panel displays the following:

   ◆ **Item Icon.** An icon appears to the left of the item indicating the type of error or problem associated with the file.

   ◆ **File.** Contains the name of the file.

   ◆ **Line.** Displays the line number of the code associated with the file.

   ◆ **Description.** Displays a description of the error.

3. To find out more information about a report item, select the report item, and then click **More Info.**

   The information appears on the Reference tab in the Results panel.

4. To open the document associated with the problem or error, double click the report item.

Site report results

474

Save a Site Report

1. Create a report or display an existing one.

   ◆ **Create.** Click the **Site** menu, click **Reports**, select report options, and then click **Run**.

   ◆ **Existing.** Click **Window**, click **Results**, and then click the **Site Reports** tab.

   The Results panel appears, displaying the Site Reports tab with report details.

2. Click the **Save Report** button in the Results panel.

3. Select a location where you want to save the site report.

4. Click **Save**.

See Also

See "Running Reports to Test a Site" on page 472 for information on creating a site report.

Gathering Download Statistics

There's an expression, and I'm sure that you've heard it before. It goes something like this: Build it and they will come. That might be true of baseball fields; however, I'm not so sure it's true of Web sites. Building it is one thing... building it in an efficient way so that visitors will stay for the experience is quite another. Dreamweaver gives you the ability to gauge how well your pages download, based on a user-defined value. For example, the rule on the Internet today is called the 8-second rule. That simply means that visitors, on average, will only wait 8 seconds for your initial (home) page to load, before they get bored and go somewhere else... that's not a whole lot of time. In response, Dreamweaver lets you view download statistics, based on the average bandwidth of your average viewer.

Change Download Statistics Preferences

1. Click the **Dreamweaver** (Mac) or **Edit** (Win) menu, and then click **Preferences**.

2. Click the **Status Bar** category.

3. Click the **Connection Speed** list arrow, and then select from the pre-defined bandwidth options, or enter in a user-defined bandwidth.

4. Click **OK**.

Did You Know?

You can quickly view Download statistics. View the file size and subsequent download time in the Download Statistics section of the Document window (located in the lower-right corner of the document window).

You can determine the speed of your file transfer rate to the Internet. Bandwidth is the amount of data that can be transferred over the network in a fixed amount of time. On the Net, it is usually expressed in bits per second (bps) or in higher units like Mbps (millions of bits per second). 28.8 modem can deliver 28,800 bps, a T1 line is about 1.5 Mbps.

Managing a Web Site

20

Introduction

In Chapter 2, you learned how to defined a site using the Basic Site Definition Wizard. With the basic settings in place, you can use the Advanced settings to fine-tune and customize the site to meet your specific needs. In this chapter, you learn how to modify advanced site definition settings to better manage and control your site.

The Advanced Site Definition dialog box allows you to define how you want your local site, remote site, and testing server to work, and set related options for updating and managing different types of files on your site.

The local site contains all the Web page files for the site as well as all images, cascading style sheet (CSS) files, templates, and other dependent files. In order to publish your site on the Web, you need to define the remote site on a Web server, and then upload the files from the local site to the remote site. If you created dynamic pages in Dreamweaver, you need to define a testing server to try it out. Dreamweaver needs a testing server to generate and display dynamic pages during development.

In addition to the main site settings for the local, remote and testing sites, you can also set related options in the following areas: cloaking, design notes, site map layout, file view columns display, Adobe Contribute compatibility, templates, and spry assets.

Setting Advanced Site Definitions

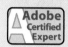
DW 2.4, 4.2. 4.3

Dreamweaver provides a choice of two methods to define a site: the Basic Site Definition Wizard and the Advanced dialog boxes. In Chapter 2, you defined a site using the Basic Site Definition Wizard. With the basic settings in place, you can use the Advanced settings to fine-tune and customize the site to meet your specific needs. The Advanced settings are organized into categories.

Set Advanced Site Definitions

1 Click the **Site** menu, point to **Manage Sites**, click **New,** and then click **Site**, or select a site, and then click **Edit**.

2 Click the **Advanced** tab.

3 Select a category, and then specify the site options you want:

- ◆ **Local Info.** Specifies the site files location and enables site management options.

- ◆ **Remote Info.** Specifies the Web site server location to upload the site files to the Web server.

- ◆ **Testing Server.** Creates a place to act like a public server to test the applications and connections to the database.

- ◆ **Cloaking.** Cloaking allows you to specify file types or specific files that you do not want uploaded to the server.

- ◆ **Design Notes.** Adds notes to files in the working site. Notes are stored in a separate file.

- ◆ **Site Map Layout.** Displays a visual layout of site pages and links, which is useful for understanding how your site files connect to one another.

- ◆ **File View Columns.** Customizes the appearance of the expanded Files panel.

Site Map Layout options

- ◆ **Contribute.** Adobe Contribute allows you to maintain and update content on existing Web sites, requiring no training or knowledge of HTML.

  - ◆ **Compatibility.** Select to enable the Contribute feature (requires the installation of the Contribute program).

- ◆ **Templates.** This option controls how templates are used within a site.

  - ◆ **Template Updating.** Select to prevent the rewriting of a document's relative path (recommended).

- ◆ **Spry.** Spry is a JavaScript library for Web designers that provides functionality that allows designers to build pages that provide a richer experience for their users.

  - ◆ **Spry Assets Folder.** Enter the path to the Spry folder, or click the folder icon to browse and select the folder on the spry folder.

④ Click **OK**.

⑤ Click **Done** to close the Manage Sites dialog box.

See Also

See "Creating a Web Site" on page 20 for information on using the Basic tab in the Site Definition dialog box.

Contribute options

Templates options

Defining Local Info for a Site

DW 2.1, 2.2, 3.18

In order for Dreamweaver to keep track of links between Web pages and dependent files, it is necessary to define a folder on the hard disk, or mapped drive, as the local root folder and to save all the files for the site in that folder. The local root folder contains the Web page files for the site as well as all images, cascading style sheet (CSS) files, templates, and other dependent files. After the site is defined, Dreamweaver creates and save pages for the site inside the local root folder. Then the contents of that local root folder are uploaded to the Web server. The local root folder and the folder on the server should have exactly the same folder structure. Dreamweaver automatically replicates the folder structure of the local root folder on the server when it uploads your files, and that make future maintenance of the site efficient and easy. When you define the site, the local folder should be easy to access.

Define the Local Info for a Site

1. Click the **Site** menu, point to **Manage Sites**, click **New,** and then click **Site**, or select a site, and then click **Edit**.

2. Click the **Advanced** tab.

3. Click the **Local Info** category.

4. Specify the following information for the Local Info category:

   ◆ **Site Name.** Enter a name for your site in the Site Name box; avoid any special characters, but it may contain capitals and spaces.

   ◆ **Local Root Folder.** Enter the path to the Local root folder, or click the folder icon to browse and select the folder that you want to contain the site files.

   IMPORTANT *Avoid using the Dreamweaver program folder as the location for the local root folder.*

- **Default Images Folder.** Enter the path to the Default Images folder, or click the folder icon to browse and select the folder you want to contain the site image files. Select a folder in the local root folder.

- **Links Relative To.** Select to set your links relative to the documents or the site's root folder.

- **HTTP Address.** Enter an HTTP address for your site.

NOTE *The HTTP Address field is useful if you are using absolute paths to refer to local files within your site, and for the link checker to determine if your links refer to your own site.*

- **Case-sensitive Links.** Select to check your links to make sure the case of the links matches the case of the filenames. This option is useful on UNIX systems where file names are case-sensitive.

NOTE *This option is only for checking in Dreamweaver, and does not impact how the links are used on the server.*

- **Cache.** Select to maintain file and asset information in a separate cache file (recommended), which speeds up most Dreamweaver operations.

5 Click **OK**.

6 Click **Done** to close the Manage Sites dialog box.

Defining Remote Info for a Site

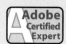 DW 1.4, 2.2, 4.2

In order to publish your site, you will first have to define the remote site, and then upload the files to a remote folder on that site. A remote folder is where you store your files for testing, and publication. Dreamweaver defines this folder as the remote site. You can define the remote server at any time during the development process. However, before you can define the remote site, you must have access to a remote Web server, such as your ISP's server, and you will need information such as: path, password, and login ID. You'll also need to find out the best access method, either FTP (File Transfer Protocol), Local/Network, WebDAV (Web-based Distributed Authoring and Versioning), RDS (Remote Data Services), or Microsoft Visual SourceSafe (a file version management system). Once you have this information, you simply add it to the setup for the working site.

Define a Remote Info for a Site

① Click the **Site** menu, point to **Manage Sites**, click **New**, and then click **Site**, or select a site, and then click **Edit**.

② Click the **Advanced** tab.

③ Click the **Remote Info** category.

④ Specify the following information for the Remote Info category:

◆ **Access None.** Select if you are not planning on moving site data to a remote server.

◆ **Access FTP.** Select if you connect to your remote server using File Transfer Protocol (FTP), which is useful for fast file transfer and working remotely.

◆ **FTP Host.** Enter the FTP address or IP address that calls the server.

◆ **Host Directory.** Enter the host directory name. The Host Directory specifies the exact folder on the server where the files will go (optional).

◆ **Login.** Enter your login name to access the server.

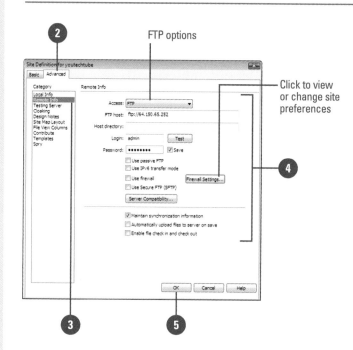

FTP options

Click to view or change site preferences

- **Password.** Enter your password to access the server.

NOTE *Click the Test button to test the connection between the local and remote server.*

- **Use Passive FTP.** Select if the server security requires the files to be transferred in passive mode.

- **Use IPv6 Transfer Mode.** Select if you are using an IPv6 (Internet Protocol version 6) enabled FTP server.

- **Use Firewall.** Select if your computer is behind a Firewall.

- **Use Secure FTP (SFTP).**

- **Maintain Synchronization Information.** Select to automatically synchronize your local and remote files.

- **Automatically Upload Files To Server On Save.** Select to transfer files to server each time the page is saved (not recommended).

- **Enable File Check In And Check Out.** Select to use the Check In/Out system to manage file development by a team.

- **Access Local/Network.** Select if the server lives on a local area network.

- **Remote Folder.** Enter the path to the Local/Network folder, or click the folder icon to browse and select the folder on the server that you want to contain the site files.

Continue Next Page

Site preferences

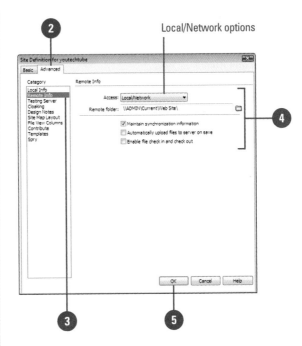

Local/Network options

Continue from Previous Page

◆ **Maintain Synchronization Information.** Select to automatically synchronize your local and remote files.

◆ **Automatically Upload Files To Server On Save.** Select to transfer files to server each time the page is saved (not recommended).

◆ **Enable File Check In And Check Out.** Select to use the Check In/Out system to manage file development by a team.

◆ **WebDAV.** WebDAV (Web-based Distributed Authoring and Versioning) allows you to manage pages to and from a WebDAV server.

◆ **URL.** Enter the address for the WebDAV server.

◆ **Login.** Enter your login name to access the server.

◆ **Password.** Enter your password to access the server.

◆ **Maintain Synchronization Information.** Select to automatically synchronize your local and remote files.

◆ **Automatically Upload Files To Server On Save.** Select to transfer files to server each time the page is saved (not recommended).

◆ **Enable File Check In And Check Out.** Select to use the Check In/Out system to manage file development by a team.

WebDAV options

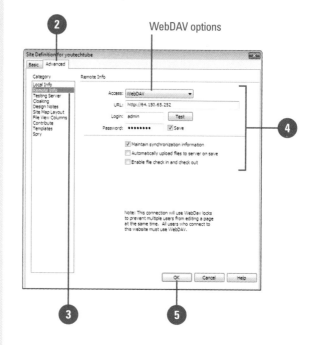

- ◆ **RDS.** RDS (Remote Data Services) allows you to work with live Web pages on the server.

  - ◆ **Settings.** Click Settings, enter in the Host Name, Port, Full Host Directory, User Name, Password for the RDS site, and then click OK.

  - ◆ **Maintain Synchronization Information.** Select to automatically synchronize your local and remote files.

  - ◆ **Automatically Upload Files To Server On Save.** Select to automatically upload files to the Web server each time the page is saved (not recommended).

  - ◆ **Enable File Check In And Check Out.** Select to use the Check In/Out system to manage file development by a team.

- ⑤ Click **OK**.

- ⑥ Click **Done** to close the Manage Sites dialog box.

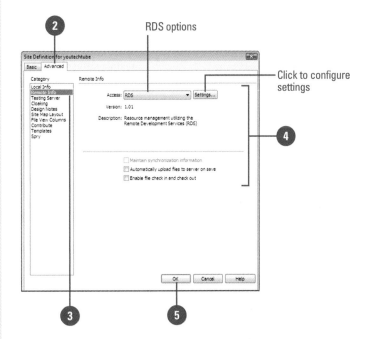

RDS options

Click to configure settings

Configure RDS server settings

Defining the Testing Server

DW 2.2

If you created dynamic pages in Dreamweaver, you need to define a testing server to try it out. Dreamweaver needs a testing server to generate and display dynamic pages during development. You can define a testing server on your local computer, a network development server, or a remote production server. For example, you can creates a place to act like a public server to test the applications and connections to the database. Before you can define a testing server, you need to define a local site folder and remote site server.

Define the Testing Server

1 Click the **Site** menu, point to **Manage Sites**, click **New,** and then click **Site,** or select a site, and then click **Edit.**

2 Click the **Advanced** tab.

3 Click the **Testing Server** category.

4 Click the **Server Model** popup, and then select a server from the available options.

◆ **Options.** ASP JavaScript, ASP VBScript, ASP.NET C#, ASP.NET VB, ColdFusion, JSP, or PHP MySQL.

5 Click the **Access** popup, and then select an access method from the available options.

◆ **Options.** FTP, Local/Network, or WebDAV.

6 Enter the URL Prefix for the location of the site's root folder on the testing server.

7 Click **OK.**

8 Click **Done** to close the Manage Sites dialog box.

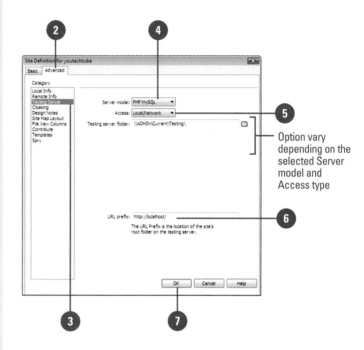

Option vary depending on the selected Server model and Access type

Defining Site Cloaking

Site cloaking allows you to exclude folders and files from certain operations, such as using Put, Get, Check In, and Check Out commands, generating reports, finding newer local and newer remote files, checking and changing sitewide links, synchronizing, using the Assets panel, and updating templates and libraries. You can cloak individual folders and specific file types; however, you cannot cloak a specific individual file. Before you can use site cloaking, you need to enable it and specify the file types you want to cloak.

Define Site Cloaking

1. Click the **Site** menu, point to **Manage Sites**, click **New,** and then click **Site**, or select a site, and then click **Edit**.

2. Click the **Advanced** tab.

3. Click the **Cloaking** category.

4. Select the **Enable Cloaking** check box to turn on cloaking.

5. Select the **Cloak Files Ending With** check box to turn on cloaking for specific file types, and then add the file extensions to the list of cloaked items. Separate multiple file types with one space (do not use a comma or semicolon). You can also enter or delete file suffixes you want to cloak or uncloak.

6. Click **OK**.

7. Click **Done** to close the Manage Sites dialog box.

Viewing a Site Map

If you like a visual approach to file management, you can view a local folder for a site using a visual map. The map is a series of icons, which are linked together. You can use the site map to add new files to a Dreamweaver site, or to add, modify, or remove links. The site map shows the site structure two levels deep, starting from the home page. It shows pages as icons and displays links in the order in which they are encountered in the source code by the use of connecting lines. The site map is an excellent choice for laying out a site's structure. You can quickly set up the entire structure of the site, and then create a graphic image of the site map. A site map is useful for understanding how your site files connect to one another.

View the Site Map

1 Click the **Site** menu, point to **Manage Sites**, and then select an active site from the available list.

2 Click **Done** to load the site.

3 Click the **Window** menu, and then click **Files** to display the Files panel.

IMPORTANT *Since the home page is the starting point of the map, you must first define a home page for your site before you can display the site map.*

4 Click the **Expand** button to display the entire Files panel.

5 Click the **Site Map** button, and then click **Map** or **Map And Files**.

The Map command only displays the site map, while the Map And Files command displays the site map and the Files panel.

6 Click the **Collapse** button to display the entire Files panel.

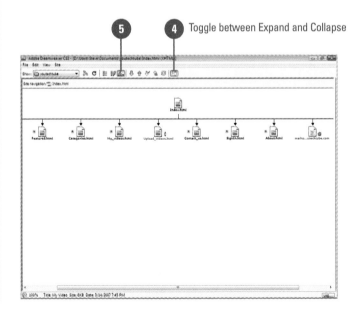

Toggle between Expand and Collapse

See Also

See "Setting the Home Page" on page 82 for information on setting a home page.

488

Work with the Site Map

① Open the site you want to view, and then display the site map.

② Click the page icon you want in the Site Map.

③ Perform any of the following options you want:

◆ **Rename.** Click the name of the file to select, click it again, and then enter a new name.

◆ **Link.** Click the link icon, and then drag it over an existing page to create a new link between the documents.

④ Right click a page icon to access the following options:

◆ **View As Root.** Select to view the selected icon as the root.

◆ **Link To New File.** Select to create a new page, with a link from the selected icon.

◆ **Link To Existing File.** Select to create a link to an existing Web document.

◆ **Change Link.** Select to change a link to the selected document.

◆ **Remove Link.** Select to remove the link from the selected document.

◆ **Show/Hide Link.** Select to show, or hide the link to the selected document.

◆ **Open To Source Of Link.** Select to open the file directly to the source of the link.

Expanded in the Files panel

Customizing Site Map View

You can use the Site Map Layout options to customize the appearance of your site map. For example, you can change the home page, the number of columns displayed in the Files panel; even the icon labels that display the filename or the page title, and whether to show hidden and dependent files.

Customize the Site Map

1. Click the **Site** menu, point to **Manage Sites**, click **New,** and then click **Site**, or select a site, and then click **Edit**.

2. Click the **Advanced** tab.

3. Click the **Site Map Layout** category.

4. Specify the following information for the Site Map Layout category:

   ◆ **Home Page.** Enter the path to the home page for the site, or click the folder icon to browse and select the home page file.

   ◆ **Number & Width Of Columns.** Enter the number of columns and their width for display of information.

   ◆ **Icon Labels.** Select between File Names, or Page Titles for the icon labels.

   ◆ **Display Files Marked As Hidden.** Select to display files marked as hidden.

   ◆ **Display Dependent Files.** Select to display dependent files.

5. Click **OK**.

6. Click **Done** to close the Manage Sites dialog box.

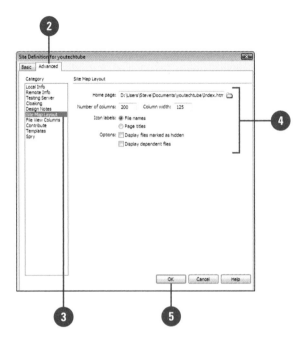

Setting File View Columns Options

When you view a Web site in the expanded Files panel, information about the files appears in columns in a similar fashion as files in Windows Explorer (Win) or the Finder (Mac). You can use the File View Columns options to customize the appearance of the expanded Files panel. For example, you can hide, add, delete, rename, and reorder columns. In addition, you can share columns with connected users, and associate columns with a Design Note.

Set File View Columns Options

① Click the **Site** menu, point to **Manage Sites**, click **New**, and then click **Site**, or select a site, and then click **Edit**.

② Click the **Advanced** tab.

③ Click the **File View Columns** category.

④ Specify the following information for the File View Columns category:

◆ **Enable Column Sharing.** Select to modify anything but the order of preexisting columns.

◆ **Column Field.** Click the Plus (+) or Minus (-) button to add/ remove columns, or select a specific column name, and then use the Up and Down arrows to change the items order.

◆ **Column Name.** Enter a name for the select column item.

◆ **Associate With Design Note.** Select a design note setting.

◆ **Align.** Click and choose how column data is aligned.

◆ **Show.** Select to show the specific column.

◆ **Share With All Users Of This Site.** Select to share with all users of the site.

⑤ Click **OK**.

⑥ Click **Done** to close the Manage Sites dialog box.

Using Design Notes

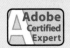 DW 3.19

Design Notes are notes that you create for the files in the working site. Although Design Notes are connected with the file they describe, they are stored separately in a file. Design Notes help you to keep track of file data related with your individual site documents. For example, if you copy a document from one site to another, you can add Design Notes for that document, with the comment that the original document is in the other site folder. In another way, Design Notes can keep track of sensitive information that you can't put inside a document for security reasons. When importing graphics into Dreamweaver, the Design Notes file is automatically copied into your site along with the graphic. Design Notes also can keep track of integration with Fireworks and Flash and allow communication on subjects ranging from the status of the page to marketing tactics. Before you can attach Design Notes to files, you need to enable it.

Enable Design Notes

1. Click the **Site** menu, point to **Manage Sites**, click **New,** and then click **Site**, or select a site, and then click **Edit**.

2. Click the **Advanced** tab.

3. Click the **Design Notes** category.

4. Select the **Maintain Design Notes** check box to active Design Notes.

5. Select the **Upload Design Notes For Sharing** check box to share your notes with others working on the site.

6. Click **OK**.

7. Click **Done** to close the Manage Sites dialog box.

Did You Know?

You can erase all Design Notes not associated with a file. In the Site Definition dialog box, click the Design Notes category, click the Clean Up button to permanently erase all Design Notes not directly associated with a file, and then click OK.

Link Design Notes with Files

1. Click the **Window** menu, and then click **Files** to display the Files panel.

2. Right-click the file you want to add notes, and then click **Design Notes**.

    The Design Notes dialog box opens.

3. Click the **Basic Info** tab, and then add notes using the following options:

    ◆ **Status.** Click the popup, and then select the current status from the available options.

    ◆ **Notes.** Enter in notes on this file.

    ◆ **Insert Date.** Click the button to add the current date to the notes.

    ◆ **Show When File Is Opened.** Select to display these notes whenever the file is first opened.

4. Click the **All Info** tab, and then view and modify notes using the following options:

    ◆ **Add/Subtract.** Click the Plus (+) or Minus (-) buttons to add or remove specific notes.

    ◆ **Info.** Displays a list of all Design Notes for the selected file.

    ◆ **Name.** Displays the name of the note, or allows you to type in a name, if this is a new note.

    ◆ **Value.** Displays the content of the note, or allows you to enter content, if this is a new note.

5. Click **OK**.

Viewing Design Notes

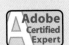 DW 3.19

After you create notes for files in your working site, you can display the files that contain notes in the expanded Files panel. A Design Notes icon appears in the Notes column. The Design Notes icons only appear in the expanded Files panel when the Notes option is set to show in the File View Columns category of the Site Definition dialog box. In the Files panel, you can double-click the Design Notes icon to open the Design Notes dialog box, where you can view the Design Notes for the selected file on the Basic Info tab.

View Design Notes

1. Click the **Window** menu, and then click **Files** to display the Files panel.

2. Use one of the following methods:
   - Right-click the file with notes you want to view, and then click **Design Notes**.
   - Double-click the yellow Design Notes icon in the Notes column of the Files panel.

   IMPORTANT *To show the yellow Design Notes, click the Site menu, click Manage Sites, select your working site, click Edit, click the File View Columns category, select Notes in the list panel, and then select the Show check box on the Advanced tab.*

   The Design Notes dialog box opens, displaying the Basic Info tab with any notes for the page. You can click the All Info tab to display HTML note information about the page.

3. Click **OK**.

Design notes for the selected page

Moving Your Site to the Internet

21

Introduction

You've worked a long time; created graphics, wrote text, built tables and layers. Now, the big moment has come... it's moving day for your Web site. However, this is not like any moving day you've ever experienced. No packing of bags, or calling the movers, because Dreamweaver has taken care of all the little details.

Dreamweaver includes a number of features for managing files and transferring files to and from a remote site (also called the remote folder). When you transfer files between local and remote sites, Dreamweaver maintains copies of the file and folder structures between the local and remote sites. If you're transferring files to the remote site, Dreamweaver will automatically create necessary folders when they do not exist. It's even possible to synchronize the files between your local and remote sites; Dreamweaver copies files in both directions as necessary and removes unwanted files when appropriate.

Dreamweaver contains features to make collaborative work on a Web site easier. You can check files in and out of a remote server so that other members of a Web team can see who is working on a file. You can add Design Notes to your files to share information with team members about a file's status, priority. You can also use the Workflow Reports feature to run reports on your site to display information on the check-in/check-out status, and to search for Design Notes attached to files.

Setting Site File Preferences

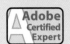 DW 4.3

Before you start transferring files from your local site to a remote site, you should specify site preferences to control the way files transfer over the Web. You can set FTP (File Transfer Protocol) connection options and firewall settings. If you're not sure how to set these options, check with your ISP (Internet Service Provider). In addition to file transfer settings, you can also set preferences for the viewing of your files in the Files panel. You can indicate which site, either local or remote, you want to always display in the Files panel, whether to prompt for confirmation when you get/check out or put/check in files, and whether to automatically save files before being put onto the remote site.

Set Site Preferences

1. Click the **Dreamweaver** (Mac) or **Edit** (Win) menu, and then click **Preferences**.

2. Click the **Site** category.

3. Select from the following options:

   ◆ **Always Show.** Indicates which site (local or remote) is always shown, and in which Files panel pane (left or right) the local and remote files appear.

   ◆ **Dependent Files.** Displays a prompt for transferring dependent files (such as images, external style sheets, etc.) that the browser loads when it loads the HTML file. The Prompt On Get/Check Out and Prompt On Put/Check In are selected by default.

   ◆ **FTP Connection.** Enter whether the connection to the remote site is terminated after the specified number of minutes has passed with no activity.

   ◆ **FTP Time Out.** Enter the number of seconds in which Dreamweaver attempts to make a connection with the remote server.

- ◆ **FTP Transfer Options.** Select whether Dreamweaver chooses the default option, after a specified number of seconds, when a dialog box appears during a file transfer and there is no user response.

- ◆ **Firewall Host.** If your site is behind a firewall, enter the address of the proxy server through which you connect to outside servers.

- ◆ **Firewall Port.** Enter the port in your firewall through which you pass to connect to the remote server. Leave Firewall host, and Firewall port blank, if you are not behind a firewall.

- ◆ **Put Options.** Select to automatically save files before being put onto the remote site.

- ◆ **Move Options.** Select to prompt you before moving files on the server.

- ◆ **Manage Sites.** Click to open the Manage Sites dialog box.

④ Click **OK**.

Click to Manage Sites

Manage Sites dialog box

Managing Site Files with the Files Panel ▶

DW 4.4, 4.5

Once a site is created, it's important to work with and organize all of the files associated with the active working site. You can organize and manage your site files and folders whether they are part of a Dreamweaver site, on a server you've connected to, or on your local drive or desktop. The Files panel gives you access to all of the files associated with the working site, and work on files and locate files within the local and remote site.

Work with the Files Panel

1 Click the **Window** menu, and then click **Files** to display the Files panel.

2 To expand the Files panel into a split window, click the **Expand** button.

3 Use any of the following options in the Files panel:

◆ Click the **Show** button to display a listing of all active Dreamweaver sites.

◆ Click the **Connect** button to create a connection between the local and remote sites.

NOTE *If you have not set up the remote site hosting information, Dreamweaver prompts you to do so before continuing.*

◆ Click the **Refresh** button to refresh the contents of the Files panel.

◆ Click the **Site Files** button to display a listing of files on the site.

◆ Click the **Testing Server** button to display a listing of all files located on the testing server.

◆ Click the **Site Map** button, and then click **Map Only** or **Map And Files** to view the files and a map, or map only.

Remote files   Local files

- ◆ Click the **Get Files** and **Put Files** buttons to receive from or send files to the remote server, respectively.

- ◆ Click the **Check Out Files** or **Check In** buttons to check files in or out.

NOTE *This option requires you to enable the file check in and out option in the Site Definition dialog box.*

- ◆ Click the **Synchronize** button to match up the files on the remote and local servers.

- ◆ Click the **Collapse** button to toggle between a split panel view (local and remote), and single view.

- ◆ Click the **Log** button to view a text log of activity performed in the Files panel.

Click to collapse Files panel

Transferring Files

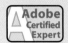
Once a remote site has been established, the next step is to begin the transfer of files from the local (working) folder, to the remote site. Since you've already defined the remote server, it's a simple question of deciding what files and folders you want to move. Dreamweaver lets you move files (Put) to the remote site, and it allows you to move files from the remote server, back to the local site (Get). The amount of time it takes to transfer your files is directly related to your bandwidth. If you're moving a large site, it might be a good idea to perform the move at night. That way the site will be moved and ready the next day.

Transfer Files to the Remote Site

1. Click the **Site** menu, click **Manage Sites**, select the site you want to use, and then click **Done**.

2. Click the **Window** menu, and then click **Files** to display the Files panel.

3. Click the **Expand** button to show local and remote sites.

4. Click the **Connect To Remote Host** button to gain access to the remote site.

5. Select files (in the right window) using one of the following options:

   ◆ Site. Click the site folder to move the entire site to the remote folder.

   ◆ Files. Ctrl-click (Win) or ⌘-click (Mac) to select the non-contiguous files for moving to the remote folder.

6. Click the **Put** button.

7. If prompted, click **Yes** to save a file or click **No** to use the existing one.

8. If prompted, click **Yes** to download dependent files along with the selected files, or click **No** to not download dependent files.

   Dreamweaver moves the entire site, or selected file/folders to the remote site.

9. To stop a file transfer, click **Cancel**.

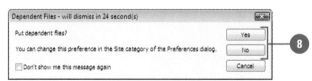

Transfer Files from the Remote Site

1 Click the **Site** menu, click **Manage Sites**, select the site you want to use, and then click **Done**.

2 Click the **Window** menu, and then click **Files** to display the Files panel.

3 Click the **Expand** button to show local and remote sites.

4 Click the **Connect To Remote Host** button to gain access to the remote site.

5 Select files from the remote site (left window) using one of the following options:

- ◆ **Site.** Click the site folder to move the entire site to the local folder.

- ◆ **Files.** Ctrl-click (Win) or ⌘-click (Mac) to select the non-contiguous files for moving to the local folder.

6 Click the **Get** button.

7 If prompted, click **Yes** to download dependent files along with the selected files, or click **No** to not download dependent files.

Dreamweaver moves the entire site, or selected file/folders to the local site.

8 To stop a file transfer, click **Cancel**.

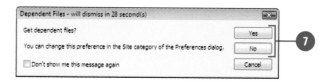

Did You Know?

You can display the FTP log. Open the Files panel, click the Options button in the upper-right corner, point to View, and then click Site FTP Log.

For Your Information

Managing File Transfers

You can cancel a file transfer or view the status of a file transfer by using the Background File Activity dialog box, which you can open by clicking the Log button at the bottom of the Files panel. In the Background File Activity dialog box, close the dialog box to cancel a transfer, click the Details expander to view more details, click Hide to minimize the dialog box, or click Save Log to save a log of the last file transfer.

Comparing Local and Remote Files

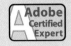 DW 4.6

If you have a third-party file comparison tool, also known as a diff tool, installed on your computer, you can use it with Dreamweaver to compare versions of the same file located on your local and remote sites. If you're not sure whether two files are the same, a file comparison tool can save you a lot of time. You can compare local and remote site versions of the same file as well as different versions of the same file on the local or remote site. Before you can use a comparison tool, you need to select it in Dreamweaver preferences. File comparison programs are designed to compare text files, not binary files, such as images. You can compare the text files you can edit in Dreamweaver, including HTML, CSS, XML, ASP.NET, ColdFusion, and PHP.

Set Compare File Preferences

1 Click the **Dreamweaver** (Mac) or **Edit** (Win) menu, and then click **Preferences**.

2 Click the **File Compare** category.

3 Select from the following File Compare options:

◆ In Windows, click **Browse** to select the comparison program you have installed on your computer.

◆ On the Macintosh, click **Browse** to select the comparison tool or script (typically located in the user/bin folder) that starts the file comparison program from the command line. Some of the tools include FileMerge, BBEdit, and TextWrangler.

4 Click **OK**.

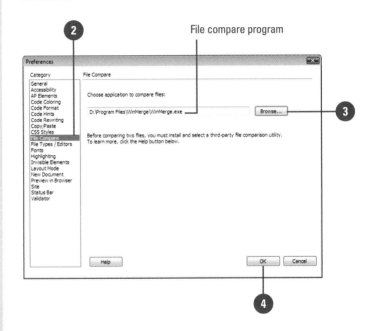

File compare program

Did You Know?

You can find a third-party file comparison tool on the Web. In your browser, perform a search for *file comparison* or *diff* tools. Dreamweaver works with most tools, including FileMerge (Mac) or WinMerge (Win). Many of them are free to download.

Compare Files

◆ **Two Local Files.** In the Files panel, select the two files on your local site, right-click the selected files, and then click **Compare Local Files**.

◆ **Two Remote Files.** In the Files panel, select the two files on your remote site, right-click the selected files, and then click **Compare Remote Files**.

◆ **Local File With Remote File.** In the Files panel, right-click a file on your local site, and then click **Compare With Remote**.

◆ **Remote File With Local File.** In the Files panel, right-click a file on your remote site, and then click **Compare With Local**.

◆ **Open File With Remote File.** Open the file in the Document window, click the **File** menu, and then click **Compare With Remote**.

Click to compare files on local site with remote site

Did You Know?

You can compare files when synchronizing. When you synchronize files from your local site to the remote site, you can also compare files. Right-click anywhere in the Files panel, click Synchronize, complete the options you want in the Synchronize dialog box, click Preview, select each file you want to compare, and then click the Compare button.

You can check for newer files without synchronizing. In the Files panel, click the Options button in the Files panel, point to Edit, and then click Newer Local or Newer Remote.

File compare complete; the files are the same

Checking Site Files In and Out

DW 4.1

It's important to understand that if you've enabled File Check In and Check Out, you can put files from the local site to the remote site, without changing the file's checked out status. Checking out a file prevents other designers from working on the same file at the same time. When a file is checked out, Dreamweaver displays the name of the person who checked out the file in the Files panel, along with a red check mark (if a team member checked out the file) or green check mark (if you checked out the file) next to the file's icon. When you or another designer has finished with the file, checking in makes the file available for other team members to check out and edit.

Use Check Out

1 Click the **Window** menu, and then click **Files** to display the Files panel.

2 Click the **Expand** button to show local and remote sites.

3 Click the **Connect To Remote Host** button to gain access to the remote site.

4 Select the file or files that you want to checkout in the remote site window on the left.

> **NOTE** *A red check mark indicates that another team member has the file checked out and a lock symbol indicates that the file is read-only (Win) or locked (Mac).*

5 Click the **Check Out** button in the Files panel toolbar.

6 If prompted, click **Yes** to download dependent files along with the selected files, or click **No** to not download dependent files.

> **NOTE** *A green check mark appears beside the local file's icon indicating that you have checked it out.*

Red check mark

Use Check In

1. Click the **Window** menu, and then click **Files** to display the Files panel.

2. Click the **Expand** button to show local and remote sites.

3. Click the **Connect To Remote Host** button to gain access to the remote site.

4. Select the file or files that you want to check in.

5. Click the **Check In** button in the Files panel toolbar.

6. If prompted, click **Yes** to download dependent files along with the selected files, or click **No** to not download dependent files.

Enable Check In and Check Out

1. Click the **Site** menu, point to **Manage Sites**, select a site, and then click **Edit**.

2. Click the **Advanced** tab.

3. Click the **Remote Info** category.

4. Click the **Access** popup, and then select a remote site type.

5. Select the **Enable File Check In And Check Out** check box.

6. Select the **Check Out Files When Opening** check box to automatically check out files when you double-click to open them.

7. Enter a check out name and an e-mail address.

8. Click **OK**.

9. Click **Done** to close the Manage Sites dialog box.

Synchronizing Site Files

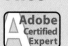

DW 4.4

In Web development, sometimes it can get confusing managing versions of files. Where is the most recent file? This question is one that you'll probably ask yourself more than once throughout the development of a site. Dreamweaver solves this problem with an option called File Synchronization. This feature compares files between the local and remote site and will determine which is the latest version. If the latest version lives on the local site, it will upload that file accordingly. File Synchronization can also delete files on either the local or remote site, if the file doesn't appear in both versions of the site. You can apply the synchronize command to selected files, or apply it site-wide.

Synchronize Files

1. Click the **Window** menu, and then click **Files** to display the Files panel.

2. Select the file or files that you want to synchronize (local or remote).

3. Click the **Synchronize** button.

   TIMESAVER *Click the Site menu, and then click Synchronize Sitewide.*

4. Select from the following synchronize options:

   ◆ **Synchronize**. Select between synchronizing the entire site, or only selected files.

   ◆ **Direction**. Select Put Newer Files To Remote (default), Get New Files From The Remote, or Get And Put Newer Files (wherever they exist).

   ◆ **Delete Remote Files Not On Local Drive**. Select to allow Dreamweaver to delete any files found on the remote server, but not on the local drive.

5 Click **Preview** to view the proposed changes.

6 Select a file or files, and make modifications using the following options:

- ◆ Mark selected files to get the remote version.

- ◆ Mark selected files to put the local version.

- ◆ Mark selected files for deletion.

- ◆ Ignore selected files during this synchronization.

- ◆ Mark selected files as already synchronized.

- ◆ Compare the local and remote versions of the selected files.

NOTE *If no synchronization is required Dreamweaver prompts you with a dialog box, asking if you want to see a list of the files, and then change them manually.*

7 Click **OK**.

Once the synchronization is complete you can save a log of the actions performed by pressing the Save Log button.

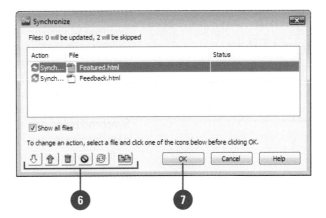

Did You Know?

You can display detailed information for a synchronized file. In the Files panel, right-click (Win) or control-click (Mac) the file you want information, and then click Display Synchronize Information. This command is available only when the Maintain Synchron- ation Information check box is selected in the Remote Info category of the Site Definition dialog box.

Cloaking and Uncloaking Files

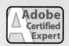 DW 4.4

Cloaking files hides the selected files from many of the file transfer commands, such as: Get, Put, Check In, and Check Out; however, it doesn't protect files when using Synchronize. For example, you have a folder on you local site that contains original uncompressed source documents, such as Photoshop and Flash. There would be no need for these files to be uploaded to the remote server, so you cloak them. Any file format you cloak remains in your local folder and will not be uploaded unless you manually override the cloak setting. In addition, cloaked files do not appear in the Assets panel. Cloaked files can be controlled by extension, such as all FLA files, or they can be controlled individually, regardless of their extension. You can cloak specific folders, even multiple ones; however, you cannot cloak all folders or an entire site.

Cloak and Uncloak Files

1. Click the **Window** menu, and then click **Files** to display the Files panel.

2. Click the **Expand** button to show local and remote sites.

3. Select the files or folder within the site files, right-click (Win) or control-click (Mac) the selection, point to **Cloaking**, and then click **Cloak** or **Uncloak**.

A red line through the folder icon appears or disappears, indicating the folder is cloaked or uncloaked.

See Also

See "Defining Site Cloaking" on page 487 for information on enabling cloaking and specifying the file types you want to cloak.

Did You Know?

You can uncloak all files at the same time. In the Files panel, select any file or folder in the local site, right-click (Win) or control-click (Mac) the selection, point to Cloaking, and then click Uncloak All.

Automating Dreamweaver

22

Introduction

You can't change time; it plods forward at sixty minutes an hour, twenty-four hours a day. Unfortunately, when you're involved in creating a complex Web site, and up against a deadline, there never seems to enough time in the day.

Adobe understands the need for efficiency in their applications, and Dreamweaver is no exception. Built into the structure of the program are ways to help you get the job done, and get it done quickly. However, it's not just about finishing a project fast, it's also about doing it right. Again, Dreamweaver creates a perfect balance between efficiency and quality.

For example, you're working along, and suddenly decide that 6 steps ago, you deleted something that should not have been deleted. No problem, just use the History panel to go back in time and correct the error. That's great, but the History panel is much more than multiple undos. It actually allows you to automate repetitive tasks by creating commands out of selected history steps.

Here's another one: You're almost finished with your site; it's 75 pages, all nicely checked out and ready to go. Then you discover a misspelling that occurs on all the pages. No problem, you simply access Find and Replace and correct the error. But Find and Replace is more that just a simple text corrector; you can search for specific source code, text within tags, even search for a specific tag. In addition, if it's something that you search for often, you can save the search as a query and use it over and over again.

What You'll Do

Examine the History Panel

Use the History Panel

Undo and Redo History Steps

Replay History Steps

Copy History Steps Between Documents

Save History Steps as Commands

Use and Manage History Commands

Record Commands for Temporary Use

Set History Panel Preferences

Use Advanced Find and Replace for Text

Use Advanced Find and Replace for Tags

Create and Use a Search Query

Examining the History Panel

The History panel helps you automate and streamline the way you work in Dreamweaver. As you work in Dreamweaver, the History panel is tracking all your steps for the entire document or only on individual or all objects behind the scenes. With the History panel, you can do any of the following:

- ◆ Undo or redo steps to correct mistakes.
- ◆ Replay selected steps for new tasks to streamline repetitive work.
- ◆ Record steps for replay from the Commands menu to automate your work.

The History panel doesn't replace the Undo, Redo, and Repeat commands on the Edit menu, it simply tracks every step you perform. When you undo or redo one or more commands, the History panel displays the results; the Undo/Redo slider moves according to the commands you select.

You can open the History panel using the Window menu like any of the other panels in Dreamweaver. Each step you take in the active document during a work session (since you created or opened the document) appears on a separate line in the History panel. The first step you perform in a work session appears at the top of the list and the last step appears at the bottom. If a red X appears in the icon for a step, it indicates Dreamweaver cannot save or replay the step. Unlike other panels in Dreamweaver, the History panel includes a slider on the left side you can use to undo/redo steps; the Undo/Redo slider initially points to the last step you performed. The bottom of the History panel includes buttons to replay selected steps, copy selected steps to the Clipboard, and create a command from selected steps. The Options button displays commands, such as Clear History, specific to the History panel.

History panel

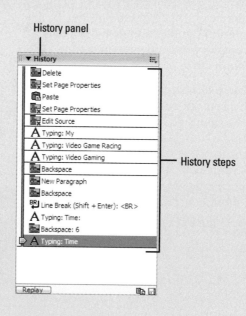

History steps

Using the History Panel

You can use the Window menu to open the History panel like any of the other panels in Dreamweaver. Each step you take in the active document during a work session appears on a separate line in the History panel. Steps you take in other Dreamweaver documents don't appear in other History panel lists. As the History panel records each step taken to the active document, it consumes memory and hard disk space. If you no longer need the steps in the History panel and want to free up some memory, you can erase the entire list. When you close a document, Dreamweaver clears the History panel.

Open or Close the History Panel

◆ To open or close the History panel, click the **Window** menu, and then click **History**.

TIMESAVER *Press Shift+F10 to open or close the History panel.*

The command toggles on and off to open and close the History panel.

◆ To show or expand the History panel, click **History** on the History panel title bar.

Click to open or close

Clear the History Panel

① Open the History panel.

② Click the **Options** button, and then click **Clear History**.

③ Click **Yes** to confirm the operation.

Options button

Undoing and Redoing History Steps

As you change the current open document you begin to see the History panel record each action you make. For example, type in a line of text and a typing layer displays in the History panel (including the text you just entered). Now select the text and change it to italic: the History panel displays the change. Each action in the document creates a new action layer in the panel. Now, continue on for a few steps, and then you realize that you didn't want to italicize the text. As long as that history step is still in the History panel, you can go back in time and undo that step. If the step you need to change is the last one, then all you need to do is press ⌘+Z (Mac), or Ctrl+Z (Win). If you change your mind you can always press ⌘+Y (Mac), or Ctrl+Y (Win) to redo the last undo... sound confusing? Not really; however, if it is, then the History palette eliminates the confusion by giving you a visual list of all your history steps.

Undo Multiple History Steps

1. Open the Web page you want to use.

2. Open the History panel.

3. Perform several actions within the document to create a running history.

4. In the History panel, perform a multiple undo using one of the following methods:

   ◆ Drag the slider on the History panel to the desired step in the History panel.

   ◆ Click the slider bar next to the step you want to undo and the slider will scroll automatically to that step.

   NOTE *Any actions performed after the undo overwrite the undone actions and create a new history for the document from that point forward.*

Redo Multiple History Steps

1. Open the Web page you want to use.

2. Open the History panel.

3. Perform several actions within the document to create a running history, and then undo one or more actions.

4. In the History panel, perform a multiple redo using one of the following methods:

    ◆ Drag the slider down on the History panel to the desired step in the History panel.

    ◆ Click the slider bar next to the step you want to revert to and the slider will scroll automatically to that step.

    NOTE *A redo can be performed only so long as you haven't performed a multiple undo, and then created new steps.*

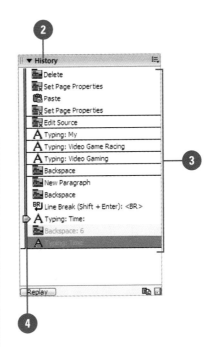

Replaying History Steps

You can replay steps from the History panel to the same object or to a different object in the document. You can replay steps only in the order in which you performed them; you can't rearrange the order of the steps in the History panel. If a red X appears in the icon for a step, it indicates Dreamweaver cannot save or replay the step.

Replay History Steps to the Same Object or Another Object

1. Open the Web page containing the steps you want to replay.

2. Open the History panel.

3. Select the steps you want:
   - **One Step.** Click a step.
   - **Adjacent Steps.** Drag from one step to another or click the first step, hold down the Shift key, and then click the last step.
   - **Nonadjacent Steps.** Hold down the ⌘ (Mac) or Ctrl (Win) key, and then click steps.

4. Select the same object used in the History steps or another object.

5. Click **Replay** in the History panel.

   The steps are replayed in order, and a new step called Replay Steps appears in the History panel.

Copying History Steps Between Documents ▶

Each document only tracks its own set of steps in the History panel. When you close a document, Dreamweaver clears the History panel. If you want to use a set of steps in another document, you need to copy them from one History panel and paste them to another document. You can use the Copy Steps button on the History panel or the same command on the Options menu to complete the task. When you paste steps into another document, Dreamweaver replays the steps and the History panel shows the steps as only one step called Paste Steps (Mac) or Paste (Win).

Copy Steps Between Documents

1 Open the Web page containing the steps you want to copy.

2 Open the History panel.

3 Perform several actions within the document to create a running history.

4 Select the steps (called a History action) that you want to copy.

5 Click the **Copy Steps** button in the History panel.

6 Click in the document to place the insertion point where you want to paste the steps or select an object to apply the steps.

7 Click the **Edit** menu, and then click **Paste**.

Dreamweaver executes the saved History steps at the insertion point of the cursor.

Saving History Steps as Commands

The History panel records the steps you take in the order in which you performed them in Dreamweaver. If you perform the same set of steps several times while you work on a document, you can save the steps in the History panel as a command on the Commands menu, which you can reuse again and again. This is where the real power is located. Dreamweaver stores the commands you save for future use in any document. While History records most actions performed while working on a page, there are some things that it can't record, such as dragging an object from one place on the page to another. If a black line separating the steps or a red X appears in the icon for a step, it indicates Dreamweaver cannot save or replay the step.

Save History Steps as a Command

1 Open the Web page you want to use.

2 Open the History panel.

3 Perform several steps within the page (in this example, a copyright notice is created using a specific font and formatting).

IMPORTANT *When selecting the text to change its formatting do not click and drag; instead use the left arrow key while holding down the shift key.*

Dreamweaver records all of the steps within a box in the History panel.

NOTE *If you see a black line separating the steps, or a red X, that indicates the steps cannot be saved or replayed as a single command.*

4 When finished creating the copyright symbol, select all of the steps that you want saved as a command, by clicking and dragging on the steps in the History panel.

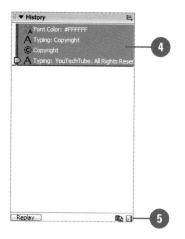

5. Click the **Save Steps** button in the History panel.

6. Enter a descriptive name for the command.

7. Click **OK**.

8. To reuse the command, click the **Commands** menu, and then click the command name.

The bottom of the Commands menu displays a list of your saved history commands.

Using and Managing History Commands

The History panel is one of those tools in Dreamweaver that many users don't take full advantage of. Most designers use it as a tool for multiple undos. While that's a fine way to use it (I love multiple undos), there's more to the History panel than that. The History panel's job is to record all the actions you make in an open document, based on a user-defined number of steps, and lets you take multiple steps backwards with the use of the panel's slider. Its real power, however, is the ability to record, play, save, and reuse user-defined commands. User-defined commands are great timesaving tools when you build complex Web sites and know that you'll do certain things over and over again. For example, you might want to insert a copyright statement at the bottom of each page. We're not talking about a library item, just some simple italicized text. That's just perfect for a command. After you save steps as a command, you can run, rename, or delete commands.

Run a History Command

1. Open the Web page you want to run (apply) a Command.

2. Click in the document where you want to run the Command.

3. Click the **Commands** menu, and then select the command from the list at the bottom of the menu (in this example, copyright).

   Dreamweaver applies the command at the insertion point of the cursor.

Manage History Commands

1 Click the **Commands** menu, and then click **Edit Command List**.

2 Select from the following options in the Edit Command List dialog box:

◆ **Rename.** Select a command from the list, and enter a new name, if desired.

◆ **Remove.** Select a command from the list, and then click the **Delete** button.

3 Click **Close** to save your changes.

Did You Know?

You can get more commands. Click the Commands menu, and then click Get More Commands. Your browser opens the Adobe Exchange, where you can pick up hundreds of specific commands (many for free).

Recording Commands for Temporary Use

If you need to quickly create a command for temporary use, such as your current working session, you can use the Start Recording and Stop Recording commands on the Commands menu. The actions you take during the recording process are stored internally by Dreamweaver and cannot be edited. Dreamweaver stores only one recorded command at a time. This means when you record a new command, the old command is erased. However, if you like a recorded command, you can save it for future use.

Record and Play a Command for Temporary Use

1. Open the Web page you want to use for recording purposes.

2. Click the **Commands** menu, and then click **Start Recording**.

   TIMESAVER *Ctrl+Shift+X (Win) or ⌘+Shift+X (Mac) to start recording.*

3. Perform the steps you want to record (the cursor changes to indicate you're recording).

4. When you're done, click the **Commands** menu, and then click **Stop Recording**.

5. To play back the recorded command, click the **Commands** menu, and then click **Play Recorded Command**.

   TIMESAVER *Ctrl+Shift+R (Win) or ⌘+Shift+R (Mac) to start recording.*

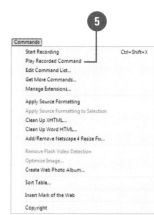

> ### Did You Know?
>
> **You can save a temporary recorded command.** Click the Commands menu, click Play Recorded Command, select the Run Command step in the History panel, click the Save Steps button, enter a name for the command, and then click OK.

Setting History Panel Preferences

By default, the History panel is set for a maximum of 50 undos. Your first job is to determine whether 50 undo steps is enough (or too many), and modify the History panel by using the General category in the Preferences dialog box. You can set the number of history steps to any number between 2 and 9999. As the History panel records each step taken in the active document, it consumes memory and hard disk space. The larger the number of history steps you specify, the more memory and hard disk space Dreamweaver consumes on your computer.

Define History Steps

1. Click the **Dreamweaver** (Mac) or **Edit** (Win) menu, and then click **Preferences**.

2. Click the **General** category.

3. Enter a numeric (2-9999) value into the Maximum Number Of History Steps box.

4. Click **OK**.

Using Advanced Find and Replace for Text

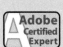 DW 3.2

Dreamweaver's Find and Replace is a powerful tool for searching for and changing HTML text, tags and their attributes within the document you are working on. Conducting a simple find/replace on text, allows you to search for a specific phrase, words or characters, and replace them. The advanced text option allows you to search for and replace text strings inside or outside of a target tag with the specific criteria you want; this acts as a filter for the search.

Conduct a Advanced Text Find and Replace

1. Open Dreamweaver (it is not necessary to open a document).

2. Click the **Edit** menu, and then click **Find And Replace**.

3. Select the following options from the Find and Replace dialog box:

   ◆ **Find In**. Click the popup to look for the find text by the desired area for the search.

   ◆ **Search**. Click the popup, and then click **Text (Advanced)**.

   ◆ **Find**. Enter the text to search.

   ◆ **Replace**. Enter the text to replace.

   ◆ **Tag**. Click the popup, click **Inside Tag** or **Not Inside**, and then select a target tag to look for text in (to the right).

   ◆ **Criteria**. Click the **Plus** (+) button or the **Minus** (-) button to add or remove search criteria.

     When you add a criteria, click to select what to look for in the tag (**With Attribute**, **Without Attribute**, or **Containing**, or **Not Containing**), and then specify the criteria you want.

     For example, with Attribute chosen, the attribute is color, and the equal sign was used to indicate we're looking for a specific color (990000).

4 Select from the following Find and Replace options:

◆ **Match Case.** Select to make the Find text case sensitive.

◆ **Match Whole Word.** Select to match whole words.

◆ **Ignore Whitespace.** Select to treat all whitespace as a single space for the purpose of matching.

◆ **Use Regular Expression.** Select to use string expressions to help locate information.

5 Click **Find Next**, **Find All**, **Replace**, **Replace All** to perform the find and replace.

6 Click **Close** to end the Find and Replace routine.

See Also

See "Finding and Replacing Text or Code" on page 122 for information on using the Find and Replace command.

Did You Know?

You can repeat the last search. Dreamweaver remembers your last search. So, if you close the Find and Replace dialog box to do additional editing, you can resume the prior search. Click the Edit menu, and then click Find Again.

Find all results

Using Advanced Find and Replace for Tags

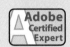

Adobe
Certified
Expert

DW 3.2

When you need to find a specific tag within the document you are working on, you can use the advanced features in the Find and Replace dialog box. The advanced options allow you to search for and replace specific tags inside or outside of a target tag with the specific criteria you want, including tag attributes. In other words, you can set conditions that act as a filter for the search. Searching the source code takes you into the code and stops at each occurrence of the search.

Conduct a Specific Tag Find and Replace

① Open Dreamweaver (it is not necessary to open a document).

② Click the **Edit** menu, and then click **Find And Replace**.

③ Select the following options from the Find and Replace dialog box:

◆ **Find In.** Click to look for the find text by the desired area for the search.

◆ **Search.** Click the popup, and then click **Specific Tag**.

◆ **Tag.** Click the list arrow, and then select the tag to look for from the list (to the right).

◆ **Tag Criteria.** Click to select what to look for in the tag (**With Attribute**, **Without Attribute**, or **Containing**, or **Not Containing**), and then specify the criteria you want.

For example, with Attribute chosen, the attribute is color, and the equal sign was used to indicate we're looking for a specific color (990000).

◆ **Criteria.** Click the **Plus** (+) button or the **Minus** (-) button to add or remove search criteria.

③

524

◆ **Actions.** Click to select from the available actions to perform, when a match is made.

④ Select from the following Find and Replace options:

◆ **Match Case.** Select to make the Find text case sensitive.

◆ **Match Whole Word.** Select to match whole words.

◆ **Ignore Whitespace.** Select to treat all whitespace as a single space for the purpose of matching.

◆ **Use Regular Expressions.** Select to use string expressions to help locate information.

⑤ Click **Find Next**, **Find All**, **Replace**, **Replace All** to perform the find and replace.

Dreamweaver looks for the specific tag and make the change you specify.

⑥ Click **Close** to end the Find and Replace routine.

See Also

See "Finding and Replacing Text or Code" on page 122 for information on using the Find and Replace command.

Find all results

Creating and Using a Search Query

If you create a complex search and want to use it again, you can save it as a query, and use it over and over again. When you save a query in the File and Replace dialog box, Dreamweaver CS3 saves the file with the extension .DWR. After you save a query, you need to load (open) it before you can use it. In addition to the .DWR extension, some queries from older versions of Dreamweaver may use the extension .DWG.

Create a Query

1. Click the **Edit** menu, and then click **Find And Replace**.

2. Create a Find and Replace search using any of the methods described in the previous sections.

3. Click the **Save Query** button.

4. Select a location for the query (default: working site folder).

5. Enter a descriptive name for the query.

6. Click **Save** to record and save the query.

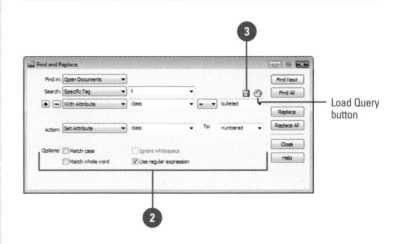

Load Query button

Use a Query

1. Click the **Edit** menu, and then click **Find And Replace**.

2. Click the **Load Query** button.

3. Select the folder that contains the query, and then select the query file you want to use.

4. Click the **Open** button to load the query into the Find and Replace dialog box.

5. Perform the Find and Replace.

Working Together with Adobe Programs

23

Introduction

Adobe programs are designed to work together so you can focus on what you need to do, rather than how to do it. In fact, the Adobe programs share tools and features for your most common tasks so you can work uninterrupted and move seamlessly from one program to another. Adobe Creative Suite 3 is an integrated collection of programs that work together to help you create designs in print, on the Web, or on mobile devices. When you install Adobe Creative Suite 3 or a stand-alone Adobe program, you also get additional shared Adobe programs—Bridge, Stock Photos, Version Cue, Device Central, and Extension Manager—to help you perform specific jobs, such as locate, download, and modify images for projects, manage files and program extensions and test files for different mobile devices.

Adobe Bridge CS3 is a program, which lets you view, open, modify, and manage images located on your computer from any Adobe Creative Suite 3 program. Adobe Bridge is literally the glue that binds Adobe Creative Suite 3 programs together with shared tools into one cohesive unit. Bridge allows you to search, sort, filter (New!), manage, and process image files one at a time or in batches. You can also use Bridge to create new folders; rename, move, delete and group (New!) files; edit metadata; rotate images; and run batch commands. You can also import files from your digital camera and view file information and metadata.

In Adobe Bridge, you can also access other Adobe programs and services. You can start Adobe Acrobat Connect, where you can start an online meeting and collaborate on any design project across platforms and programs, or Adobe Photographers Directory, where you can search for the contact information and portfolio of professional photographers around the world.

What You'll Do

Explore Adobe Programs

Explorer Adobe Bridge

Get Started with Adobe Bridge

Get Photos from a Digital Camera

Work with Raw Images from a Digital Camera

Work with Images Using Adobe Bridge

Automate Tasks in Adobe Bridge

Get Photos from Adobe Stock Photos

Manage Files Using Adobe Version Cue

Start a Meeting Using Adobe Acrobat Connect

Set Preferences in Adobe Bridge

Explore Adobe Device Central

Check Content Using Adobe Device Central

Use Adobe Extension Manager

Exploring Adobe Programs

Adobe Creative Suite 3

Adobe Creative Suite 3 (New!) is an integrated collection of programs that work together to help you create designs in print, on the Web, or on mobile devices. Adobe's Creative Suite 3 comes in different editions with different combinations of Adobe programs. The main programs for print design include InDesign and Acrobat Professional; for graphic design include Photoshop, Illustrator, and Fireworks; for video and sound design include Premiere, After Effects Professional, Encore, and Soundbooth; and for Web design include Flash Professional, Dreamweaver, and Contribute.

Working Together with Adobe Programs

When you install Adobe Creative Suite 3 or a stand-alone Adobe program, you also get additional Adobe programs—Bridge, Stock Photos, Version Cue, Device Central, and Extension Manager—to help you perform specific jobs, such as locate photo content for projects, manage files and program extensions and test files for different mobile devices.

Adobe Bridge

Adobe Bridge CS3 is a file management/batch program that frees up your Adobe program to manage and process images while you work. To use Bridge, click Browse on the File menu within an Adobe product, such as Flash, or from the desktop use the Start menu (Win) or Applications folder (Mac).

Adobe Stock Photos

Adobe Stock Photos is an integrated service available within Adobe Bridge that lets you search, view, try, and buy over one million royalty-free stock photographic images. With Stock Photos, you can download low-resolu-tion, complementary (comp) versions of images you like at no charge and edit them in Photoshop. Each stock photo includes embedded metadata about the image, such as its author, copyright, creation date, size, color space, and resolution, to make it easier to find and track. You can work with the comps until you decision to use them, at which time you can purchase and download a high-resolution image. Downloaded images are automatically saved in folders in Adobe Bridge. To display stock photos, open Bridge, click the Folder list arrow, and then click Adobe Stock Photos, or use the Favorites pane, where you can also access downloaded comps.

Adobe Version Cue

Adobe Version Cue is a file tracking management program you can use to keep track of changes to a file as you work on it. You use Adobe Bridge as a central location from which to use Version Cue. You can track Adobe and non-Adobe program files.

Adobe Device Central

Adobe Device Central CS3 allows you to test your content on a variety of mobile devices. Device Central allows you to see how your content appears on specific mobile devices. You can interact with the emulated device in a way that allows you to test your content is real-world situations. Device Central provides a library of devices and each device includes a profile with information about the device, including media and content support types.

Adobe Extension Manager

Adobe Extension Manager CS3 allows you to install and delete added program functionality, known as extensions, to many Adobe programs.

Exploring Adobe Bridge

Inspector panel
Displays or hides
Version Cue panels.

Folders panel
Displays the folders
on your computer in
a tree structure.

Preview panel
Displays a preview of
the selected image.

Favorites panel
Displays links
to common
features and
favorite places.

Filters panel
Displays files
based on filter
criteria.

Content panel
Displays the current content.

Keywords panel
Allows you to assign and
remove keywords
associated with images.

Metadata panel
Provides metadata
information about the
selected image.

Getting Started with Adobe Bridge

The Adobe Bridge CS3 is a stand-alone program, which lets you view, open, and manage images located on your computer from any Adobe Creative Suite 3 program. Adobe Bridge is literally the glue that binds Adobe Creative Suite 3 programs and shared tools together into one cohesive unit. Adobe Bridge integrates with shared tools including Adobe Version Cue, a file tracking project management program, and Adobe Stock Photos, a service that lets you search, view, try, and buy royalty-free stock photography. The Bridge program provides a set of panels that make it easy to find, view, and manage the files on your computer or network. As you work with Bridge, you'll open, close, and move (dock and undock) around the panels to meet your individual needs. After you customize the workspace, you can save the location of the panels as a custom workspace (**New!**), which you can display using the Workspace command on the Window menu. Bridge also provides some pre-defined workspaces.

Get Started with Adobe Bridge

1. Launch your Adobe product, click the **File** menu, and then click **Browse**.

   - You can also start Adobe Bridge CS3 from the Start menu (Win) or the Applications folder (Mac).

2. To open and close a panel, click the **Window** menu, and then click the panel name you want.

3. To move a panel, drag the panel tab you want to another location in the Bridge window.

4. To save a workspace, click the **Window** menu, point to **Workspace**, click **Save Workspace**, type a name, and then click **OK**.

5. To display a workspace, click the **Window** menu, point to **Workspace**, and then click the workspace you want.

6. When you're done, click the **Close** button in the Bridge window.

The Go to Bridge button on the Options bar in Photoshop

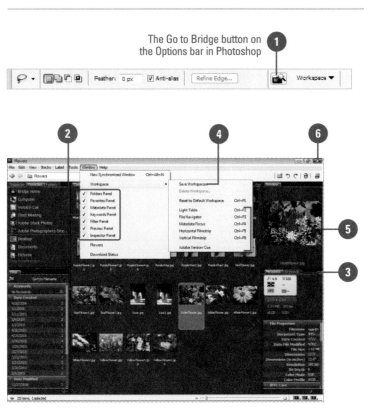

Getting Photos from a Digital Camera

If you have camera raw or other images in a digital camera, you can use the Get Photos from Camera command (**New!**) in Adobe Bridge to retrieve and copy them to your computer. The Get Photos from Camera command allows you to specify where you want to store the files, rename them, preserve metadata, or convert them to the DNG format. When you convert Camera Raw files to the DNG format, you specify preview size, compression, and whether to preserve the camera raw image or embed the original raw file.

Import Camera Raw and Other Files from a Camera

 In Adobe Bridge, click the **File** menu, and then click **Get Photos From Camera**.

 Click the **Get Photos From** popup, and then select the source camera.

 Specify the folder location and file name you want.

 To rename the files, select the method you want, and then enter the file name text you want.

 Select the options you want:

◆ **Preserve Current Filename in XMP.** Select to save the current filename as metadata in the image.

◆ **Open Adobe Bridge.** Select to open and display the files in Adobe Bridge.

◆ **Convert To DNG.** Select to convert Camera Raw files to DNG. Click Settings to set DNG conversion options.

◆ **Save Copies To.** Select to save copies to another folder for backup purposes. Click Browse to select a folder location.

 To apply metadata to the files, click **Advanced Dialog**.

 Click **Get Photos**.

The files appear in Bridge.

Working with Raw Images from a Digital Camera

Camera raw image file formats are created by most mid to high-end digital cameras and contain all the information about how the image was taken. The raw format turns off all camera adjustments, and simply saves the image information to the digital film. Using the raw format is as close to using traditional film as a digital camera can get. Raw images are larger; however, the increase in file size is actually more information that can be used by Bridge to adjust the image. In Bridge, you can open Raw, JPEG (**New!**), and TIF (**New!**) files to make image enhancements. If you're not sure what to do, you can click Auto to have Camera Raw do it or drag color sliders (**New!**) to adjust options manually. In addition, raw images can be converted into 16-bit. When a 16-bit image is opened, you have more control over adjustments, such as tonal and color correction. Once processed, raw images can be saved in the DNG, TIF, PSD, PSB, or JPEG formats. You can use the Batch, Image Processor or Create Droplet commands on the Tools menu under Photoshop in Bridge to automate the processing of camera raw files. After you make Camera Raw adjustments, you can save the settings so you can apply them to other files.

Set Camera Raw Preferences

1. In Adobe Bridge, click the **Edit** menu, and then click **Camera Raw Preferences**.

2. Select the preferences you want:

    ◆ **General.** Specify where Camera Raw file settings are stored. Use Sidecar XMP files to store settings in a separate file, or use Camera Raw Database to store settings in a central database you can search.

    ◆ **Default Image Settings.** Select options to automatically apply settings or set defaults.

    ◆ **Camera Raw Cache.** Set a cache size to shorten the loading time for Camera Raw thumbnails and previews. The cache holds about 200 images for each gigabyte of storage.

    ◆ **DNG File Handling.** Select options to ignore XMP files or update embedded content.

3. Click **OK**.

Modify a File in Camera Raw

1. Right-click the image (Camera Raw, JPEG, or TIF) you want, and then click **Open in Camera Raw**.

2. Use the **Zoom**, **Hand**, **Rotate**, **Crop**, and **Straighten** tools to change the size, orientation, and position of the image, or use the **White Balance** tools to set the image white balance or the **Color Sample** tool to sample a color, or use the **Retouch** (Heal or Clone) and **Red Eye** tools (**New!**) to fix the image.

3. Select from the available image view options:

   ◆ **Image Preview.** Displays the active image.

   ◆ **Zoom Level.** Changes the view of the active image.

   ◆ **Histogram.** Displays information on the colors and brightness levels in the active image.

4. Click the **Basic**, **Tonal Curve**, **Detail**, **Lens**, **HSL/ Grayscale**, **Split Toning**, **Len Corrections**, or **Camera Calibrate** tabs, and then click **Auto** (Basic tab) or drag sliders to modify the color and tonal values of the image.

5. Click **Save Image** to specify a folder destination, file name, and format for the processed images.

6. Select the images you want to synchronize (apply settings) in the Filmstrip (if desired, click Select All), and then click **Synchronize**.

7. Click the **Camera Raw Menu** button to **Load**, **Save**, or **Delete** a specific set of Raw settings, or to modify dialog box settings.

8. Click **Done** to process the file, but not open it, or click **Open Image** to process and open it in Photoshop. Hold Alt (Win) or Option (Mac) to use **Open Copy** or **Reset**.

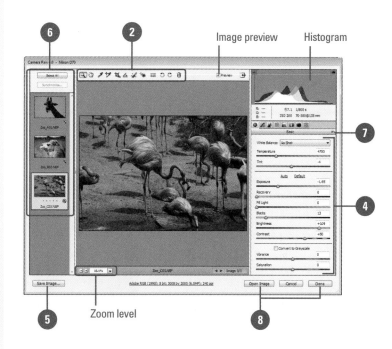

Image preview   Histogram

Zoom level

Working with Images Using Adobe Bridge ▶

With Adobe Bridge, you can drag assets into your layouts as needed, preview them, and add metadata to them. Bridge allows you to search, sort, filter (**New!**), manage, and process image files one at a time or in batches. You can also use Bridge to create new folders; rename, move, delete and group (known as stacking (**New!**)) files; edit metadata; rotate images; and run batch commands. You can also view information about files and data imported from your digital camera.

Work with Images Using Bridge

1. Launch your Adobe product, click the **File** menu, and then click **Browse**, or click the **Go to Bridge** button (if available).

2. Click the **Folder** list arrow, and then select a folder.

    ◆ You can also select Adobe Stock Photos or Version Cue.

3. Click the **Folders** tab and choose a folder from the scrolling list.

4. Click the **Favorites** tab to choose from a listing of user-defined folders, such as Pictures.

5. Click an image within the preview window to select an image.

6. Click the **Metadata** tab to view image information; including date and time the image was shot, and aperture, shutter speed, and f-stop.

7. Click the **IPTC Core** arrow to add user-defined metadata, such as creator and copyright information, or captions to an image.

8. Click the **Preview** tab to view a larger thumbnail of the selected image. Multiple images appear when you select them (**New!**).

    ◆ Click the image in the Preview tab to display a mini zoom window (**New!**). Drag it to change positions. Click it to close the window.

9. Drag the **Zoom** slider to increase or decrease the thumbnail views.

Label   Rating

10 Click the preview buttons to select a different view.

◆ **Default.** Default view, displays the images as small thumbnails with the file name underneath.

◆ **Filmstrip.** Creates thumbnails across the bottom of the preview area. Clicking on a thumbnail creates a larger view, directly above the filmstrip view.

◆ **Metadata Focus.** Displays a thumbnail of each image with metadata information details such as date created and file size.

11 Use the file management buttons to rotate or delete images, or create a new folder.

12 To narrow down the list of images using a filter (**New!**), click the criteria options you want in the Filters panel.

13 To add a label or rating to images, select the ones you want, click the **Label** menu, and then select the label or rating you want.

14 To group related images as a stacked group (**New!**), select the images, click the **Stacks** menu, and then click **Group as Stack**.

◆ Use the Stacks menu to ungroup, open, expand, or collapse stacks.

15 Double-click on an thumbnail to open it in the default program, or drag the thumbnail from the Bridge into an open Adobe document.

Stacked images

For Your Information

What is Metadata?

Metadata is information about an image file, such as its author, copyright, creation date, size, version, color space, resolution, and searchable keywords, which is stored in the file or in a separate file, known as a **sidecar file**, using a standard method called **Extensible Metadata Platform (XMP)**. Bridge and Version Cue use XMP to help you organize and search for files. Metadata is stored in other formats, such as EXIF (digital camera data), IPTC (Core data), GPS (global positioning system data), and TIFF, which are all synchronized with XMP.

Automating Tasks in Adobe Bridge

The Tools menu provides commands you can use to automate tasks in Bridge. For example, you can automate the process of renaming a group of files using the Batch Rename command. If you use Photoshop, InDesign, or Version Cue, you can use commands on submenus to run automated tasks, such as adding and synchronizing files with Version Cue or processing camera raw images with Photoshop, or can create a contact sheet of images in InDesign. You can also use the Tools menu to start other Adobe programs, such as Device Central and Acrobat Connect (Start Meeting) as well as create and edit Metadata templates, which you can use to append or replace metadata in Adobe InDesign or other XMP-enabled programs.

Rename Files Automatically in Adobe Bridge

1. In Adobe Bridge, select the files or folders you want to use.

2. Click the **Tools** menu, and then click **Batch Rename**.

3. Select the destination folder option you want, **Rename in same folder**, **Move to other folder**, or **Copy to other folder**, and then click **Browse** to specify a new folder location.

4. Click the **Element** popup, and then select an option to specify how you want to name the files.

   ◆ Text, New Extension, Current Filename, Preserved Filename, Sequence Number, Sequence Letter, Date, Time, Metadata, or Folder Name.

5. Enter the text you want to use in conjunction with the Element popup selection to name the files.

6. Select the **Preserve Current File Name In XMP Metadata** check box to retain the original filename in the metadata.

7. Select the check boxes with the operating systems you want the renamed files to be compatible.

8. Click **Rename**.

Getting Photos from Adobe Stock Photos

Adobe Stock Photos is a service that lets you search, view, try, and buy royalty-free stock photography. You can search over one million images from 23 top collections using specific keywords or browse by category and theme-based galleries for creative inspiration. All your searches are automatically saved so you can quickly retrieve files from a previous search in the Favorites panel. You can access Adobe Stock Photos directly from Adobe Bridge. When you download an image—either a free unwatermarked composite one with a lower resolution for review or a purchased one with a high resolution for full use—it's copied to your computer and available in Adobe Bridge, where you can organize and use it in your Adobe program files.

Get a Photo from Adobe Stock Photos

1. Start Adobe Bridge from the Start menu (Win) or the Applications folder (Mac).

2. In the Favorites panel, click **Adobe Stock Photos**.

   ◆ You can also start Adobe Stock Photos CS3 from the Start menu (Win) or the Applications folder (Mac).

3. Enter a keyword search or browse by category or gallery.

4. Select the image you want.

5. To download a comp, click the **Download Comp** button on the toolbar.

6. To purchase the image, click the **Add to Cart** button, and then follow the check out instructions.

7. To open the image directly in a program, right-click the image, point to **Open With**, and then select the program you want, such as Adobe Flash or Photoshop (the default).

For Your Information

Searching Adobe Photographers Directory

In Adobe Bridge, you can access the Adobe Photographers Directory, where you can search for the contact information and portfolio of professional photographers around the world. In the Favorites panel, click Adobe Photographers Directory, enter the search criteria you to use to find a professional photographer, and then click Search. If you don't find what you're looking for, click the Search tab at the top of the page to perform an advanced search.

Managing Files Using Adobe Version Cue

In Adobe Bridge, you can access the Adobe Version Cue CS3, which is a file tracking file management program you can use to keep track of changes to a file as you work on it. Adobe Bridge and Version Cue work together to allow you to access and manage Version Cue files and projects. You can use the Inspector panel (**New!**) and buttons in the Content panel to view, navigate, and access information, projects, and files on the Version Cue servers. You can check files in and out to make sure you're the only one making changes and then synchronize the changes.

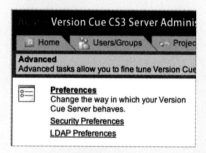

Version Cue file management provides access to projects and files. To use file management, you need to enable it. Version Cue is enabled by default in all Adobe Creative Suite programs (except Flash and Acrobat). To turn it on in an Adobe program, open the Preferences dialog box using the Edit (Win) or *program name* (Mac) menu, select the Enable Version Cue check box in one of the categories. If you disable Version Cue file management in one Adobe Creative Suite program, you disable it in all other Version Cue enabled programs, except Acrobat, Flash, and Bridge.

Before you can start using Version Cue, you need to install and configure the Version Cue Server, create a project to store master copies of files and related information, and assign users to it. The Version Cue Server gets automatically installed on your computer with Adobe Creative Suite 3 Design, Web, or Master Collection. Even though it's installed, you still need to turn it on. Click My Server in the Adobe dialog box or in Adobe Bridge, and then follow the on-screen instructions to complete the initial server administration settings (**New!**). If you're sharing files and other assets in a workgroup, you should re-install Version Cue on a dedicated network computer.

In Flash CS3 Professional

Starting a Meeting Using Adobe Acrobat Connect

In Adobe Bridge, you can access Adobe Acrobat Connect, where you can start an online meeting and collaborate on any design project across platforms and programs. In the Favorites panel, click Start Meeting (**New!**), create an account if you don't have one (sign up for a free trial), and then enter your meeting Web address along with your login and password. If you need more advanced Web conferencing, you should try Adobe Acrobat Connect Professional.

Click to start a meeting

Enter account information

Use to create a meeting

Setting Preferences in Adobe Bridge

Adobe Bridge allows you to set preferences to customize the way you work in Bridge, Adobe Stock Photos, Version Cue, and Meetings. The Preferences dialog box is organized into categories—including General, Thumbnails, Metadata, Labels, File Type Associations, Inspector, Startup Scripts, Advanced, Adobe Stock Photos, and Meetings—you can use to set specific options to suit your needs. For example, you can select options to display quick thumbnails at a lower resolution or slower thumbnails at a high resolution (**New!**).

Set Bridge Preferences

① In Adobe Bridge, click the **Bridge** (Mac) or **Edit** (Win) menu, and then click **Preferences**.

② Click the **General** category.

③ Select the appearance options and the Favorite Items you want.

④ Click the **Thumbnails** category.

⑤ Specify the performance and details options you want:

◆ **Performance.** Select the quality and size settings you want; the higher the quality, the slower the performance.

◆ **Details.** Select the metadata details you want to show with the thumbnail.

⑥ Click the **Metadata** category.

⑦ Select the check boxes with the metadata you want and clear the ones you don't want.

⑧ Click the **Labels** category.

⑨ Enter the labels you want to associate with a specific color.

10 Click the **File Type Associations** category.

The left column displays the file type and the right column displays the current default program you want to use to open the file.

11 To change the default program, click the list arrow next to the file type, and then select a program.

12 Click the **Inspector** category.

13 Select the check boxes with the Version Cue panel you want and clear the ones you don't want.

14 Click the **Startup Scripts** category.

15 Select the check boxes with the programs you want to enable and clear the ones you want to disable.

16 Click the **Advanced** category, and then specify the color management, language and keyboard, and memory cache settings you want.

17 Click the **Adobe Stock Photos** category, and then specify the downloading and purchasing settings you want.

18 Click the **Meetings** category, and then specify the login information so you don't have to enter it when you start Adobe Acrobat Connect.

19 Click **OK**.

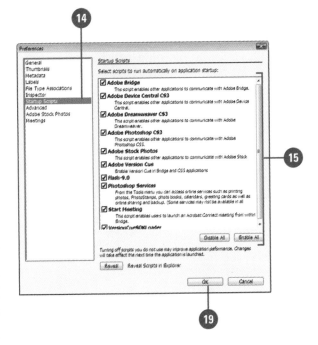

Exploring Adobe Device Central

Device Profiles tab
Displays detailed information about devices, including support details for Flash, bitmap, video, and Web.

New Document tab
Provides a way to create mobile documents in Adobe programs, such as Flash, Photoshop, or Illustrator.

Device Sets panel
Displays sets of devices for testing; availability depends on the content type.

Available Devices panel
Displays all the mobile devices that are installed with Device Central.

Emulator tab
Display a simulation of how content appears on a specific mobile devices.

Testing panels
Displays a number of panels for testing content based on the selected options.

Checking Content Using Adobe Device Central

Testing your content on as many different devices as possible allows you to reach a wider audience. Adobe Device Central (**New!**) makes it easy to test your content on a wide-variety of different mobile devices in one central place. Device Central provides a library of devices from which to choose, and each device includes a profile with information about the device, including media and content support types. Device Central uses an emulator to simulate the way your content will look on a selected device. An emulator is not the same as the real device. However, it allows you to quickly test devices to get initial results.

Check Content Using Adobe Device Central

1. Start Adobe Device Central from the Start menu (Win) or the Applications folder (Mac).

   ◆ In Bridge, right-click a file,and then click Test in Device Central.

2. From the Welcome screen or the File menu, select the option you want:

   ◆ **Open for Testing.** Opens a file for testing with the Emulator tab. Use the buttons on the mobile device to test your content.

   ◆ **Devices Profiles.** Displays mobile device profiles. In the Available Devices panel, expand a folder with devices. On the Device Profiles tab, click links to display profile information.

   ◆ **Create New Mobile.** Creates a new mobile document for Flash, Photoshop, or Illustrator; select a mobile device, and then click **Create**.

3. To change devices, select the one you want in the Available Devices panel.

4. If you're testing, select the options you want in the Testing panels.

5. When you're done, click the **Close** button in the Device Central window.

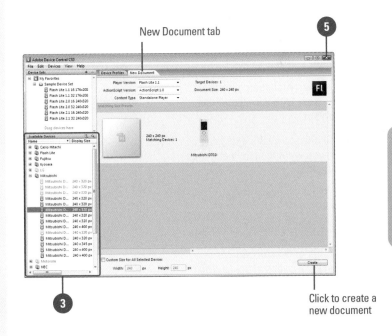

New Document tab

Click to create a new document

Using Adobe Extension Manager

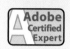

DW 2.10

The Adobe Extension Manager CS3 is a program you can use to install and delete added program functionality, known as extensions, to many Adobe programs. The Extension Manager is automatically installed when you install Flash, Dreamweaver, or Fireworks. You can use the Extension Manager to access the Adobe Exchange site, where you can locate, research, and download many different types of extensions. Some are free and some are not. After you download an extension, you can use Extension Manager to install it. Extension Manager only displays extensions installed using the Extension Manager; others installed using a third-party installer might not appear. After you install an extension, you can find and display information about it.

Download and Install an Extension

1. Start Adobe Extension Manager CS3 from the Start menu (Win) or the Applications folder (Mac).

   TIMESAVER *In Flash, Dreamweaver,or Fireworks, click the Help menu, and then click Manage Extensions.*

2. Click the **Go to Adobe Exchange** button on the toolbar.

3. Select the extension you want to download, and then save it to your computer.

4. In Extension Manager, click the **Install New Extension** button on the toolbar.

5. Locate and select the extension (.mxp) you want to install, and then click **Install**.

6. You can perform any of the following:

   ◆ **Sort**. Click a column heading.

   ◆ **Enable or Disable**. Select or clear the check in the On/Off column next to the extension.

   ◆ **Remove**. Select the extension, click the **File** menu, and then click **Remove Extension**.

7. Click the **Close** button.

Downloaded extension

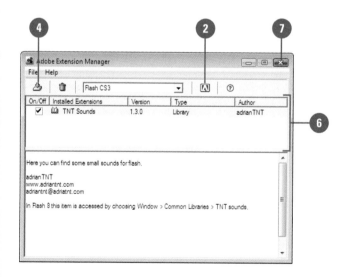

New! Features

Adobe Dreamweaver CS3

Adobe Dreamweaver CS3 means superior results faster, with new features and enhancements that help you build Web sites and Internet applications. It provides a combination of visual layout tools, application development features, and code editing support, enabling developers and designers at every skill level to create visually appealing, standards-based sites and applications quickly and easily.

Only New Features

If you're already familiar with Dreamweaver CS2 you can access and download all the tasks in this book with Adobe Dreamweaver CS3 New Features to help make your transition to the new version simple and smooth. The Dreamweaver CS3 New Features as well as other Dreamweaver 8 to Dreamweaver 8 transition helpers are available on the Web at *www.perspection.com*.

What's New

If you're searching for what's new in Dreamweaver CS3, just look for the icon: New!. The new icon appears in the table of contents and throughout this book so you can quickly and easily identify a new or improved feature in Dreamweaver CS3. The following is a brief description of each new feature and it's location in this book.

Dreamweaver CS3

- **Adobe Photoshop and Fireworks integration** (p. 138-139) Copy and paste directly from Adobe Photoshop CS3 or Fireworks CS3 into Dreamweaver CS3 to leverage assets from your prototype in your finished project.

- **Browser Compatibility Check** (p. 238-239, 462-463) Save time and ensure a more consistent experience across browsers and operating systems with the new Browser Compatibility Check. Generate reports that identify HTML and CSS-related issues in a variety of browsers, without needing to launch the browsers.

- **CSS Advisor website** (p. 238-239) Find fast solutions to browser-specific CSS issues with the new CSS Advisor website, an online community featuring a wealth of user-contributed solutions and insight.

- **CSS layouts (p. 218-219)** Easily incorporate CSS into your project with the new CSS layouts. Extensive comments in each template explain the layout, so beginning and intermediate designers can learn quickly. Each template can be customized for your project.

- **CSS management (p. 222-223)** Easily move CSS code from inline to head, from head to external sheet, from document to document, or between external sheets. Cleaning up existing CSS in older pages has never been easier.

- **AP element (p. 246)** A movable container that allows you to precisely position Web text and objects (formally known as layers).

- **Spry framework for Ajax (p. 386-404)** Visually design, develop, and deploy dynamic user interfaces using the Spry framework for Ajax. Add interactivity, speed, and usability while reducing page refreshes.

- **Spry widgets (p. 386-395)** Easily add common interface components such as lists, tables, tabs, form validation, and repeatable regions to web pages with widgets from the Spry framework for Ajax.

- **Spry data (p. 396-401)** Integrate data into web pages using XML from an RSS feed or a database. Integrated data can be easily sorted and filtered.

- **Spry effects (p. 402-403)** Easily add visual transitions to page elements to make them grow, shrink, fade, highlight, and more with the Spry effects for Ajax.

- **Adobe Bridge and Version Cue (p. 530-535, 538, 540)** Organize and browse Photoshop and other creative assets using Adobe Bridge, an independent file-management system that you can launch from within Dreamweaver. Through Adobe Bridge, you can automate workflows across Adobe Creative Suite components, apply consistent color settings across Adobe software, and access version control features, online stock photo purchase services, and other tools. You can also organize and manage your images with the Loupe tool, filters, and stacks.

- **Adobe Device Central (p. 542-543)** A new way to test content created with Adobe products on emulated mobile devices. Device Central lets you create and view artwork for display on cell phones and other mobile devices, and preview how your photos will look on different devices.

Keyboard Shortcuts

Adobe Dreamweaver CS3

If a command on a menu includes a keyboard reference, known as a keyboard shortcut, to the right of the command name, you can perform the action by pressing and holding the first key, and then pressing the second key to perform the command quickly. In some cases, a keyboard shortcut uses three keys. Simply press and hold the first two keys, and then press the third key. Keyboard shortcuts provide an alternative to using the mouse and make it easy to perform repetitive commands.

If you're searching for new keyboard shortcuts in Dreamweaver CS3, just look for the letter: **N**. The **N** appears in the Keyboard Shortcuts table so you can quickly and easily identify new or changed shortcuts.

Dreamweaver CS3 Keyboard Shortcuts		
Command	**Windows**	**Macintosh**
Menu Commands		
File		
New	Ctrl+N	⌘+N
Open	Ctrl+O	⌘+O
Browse in Bridge	Ctrl+Alt+O	⌘+Option+O
Open Recent		
Open in Frame	Ctrl+Shift+O	⌘+Shift+O
Close	Ctrl+W	⌘+W
Close All	Ctrl+Shift+W	⌘+Shift+W
Save	Ctrl+S	⌘+S
Save As	Ctrl+Shift+S	⌘+Shift+S
Print Code	Ctrl+P	⌘+P
Check Page		
Links	Shift+F8	Shift+F8

Keyboard Shortcuts (continued)

Command	Windows	Macintosh
Validate		
Markup	Shift+F6	Shift+F6
Edit		
Undo	Ctrl+Z, Alt+BkSp	⌘+Z, Option+BkSp
Redo	Ctrl+Y, Ctrl+Shift+Z	⌘+Y, ⌘+Shift+Z
Cut	Ctrl+X, Shift+Del	⌘+X, Shift+Del
Copy	Ctrl+C, Ctrl+Ins	⌘+C, ⌘+Ins
Paste Special	Ctrl+Shift+V	⌘+Shift+V
Select All	Ctrl+A	⌘+A
Select Parent Tag	Ctrl+[	⌘+[
Select Child	Ctrl+]	⌘+]
Find and Replace	Ctrl+F	⌘+F
Find Selection	Shift+F3	Shift+F3
Find Next	F3	F3
Go to Line	Ctrl+G	⌘+G
Show Code Hints	Ctrl+Space	⌘+Space
Refresh Code Hints	Ctrl+.	⌘+.
Code Hint Tools		
Indent Code	Ctrl+Shift+>	⌘+Shift+>
Outdent Code	Ctrl+Shift+<	⌘+Shift+<
Balance Braces	Ctrl+'	⌘+'
Code Collapse		
Collapse Selection	Ctrl+Shift+C	⌘+Shift+C
Collapse Outside Selection	Ctrl+Alt+C	⌘+Option+C
Expand Selection	Ctrl+Shift+E	⌘+Shift+E
Collapse Full Tag	Ctrl+Shift+J	⌘+Shift+J
Collapse Outside Full Tag	Ctrl+Alt+J	⌘+Option+J
Expand All	Ctrl+Alt+E	⌘+Option+E
Preferences	Ctrl+U	⌘+U
View		
Zoom In	Ctrl+=	⌘+=
Zoom Out	Ctrl+-	⌘+-

Command	Windows	Macintosh
Magnification		
50%	Ctrl+Alt+5	⌘+Option+5
100%	Ctrl+Alt+1	⌘+Option+1
200%	Ctrl+Alt+2	⌘+Option+2
300%	Ctrl+Alt+3	⌘+Option+3
400%	Ctrl+Alt+4	⌘+Option+4
800%	Ctrl+Alt+8	⌘+Option+8
1600%	Ctrl+Alt+6	⌘+Option+6
Fit Selection	Ctrl+Alt+0	⌘+Option+0
Fit All	Ctrl+Shift+0	⌘+Shift+0
Fit Width	Ctrl+Alt+Shift+0	⌘+Option+Shift+0
Switch Views	Ctrl+`	⌘+`
Refresh Design View	F5	F5
Server Debug	Ctrl+Shift+G	⌘+Shift+G
Live Data	Ctrl+Shift+R	⌘+Shift+R
Head Content	Ctrl+Shift+H	⌘+Shift+H
Table Mode		
Expanded Tables Mode	F6	F6
Layout Mode	Alt+F6	Option+F6
Visual Aids		
Hide All	Ctrl+Shift+I	⌘+Shift+I
Rulers		
Show	Ctrl+Alt+R	⌘+Option+R
Grid		
Show Grid	Ctrl+Alt+G	⌘+Option+G
Snap To Grid	Ctrl+Alt+Shift+G	⌘+Option+Shift+G
Guides		
Show Guides	Ctrl+;	⌘+;
Lock Guides	Ctrl+Alt+;	⌘+Option+;
Snap To Guides	Ctrl+Shift+;	⌘+Shift+;
Guides Snap To Elements	Ctrl+Shift+/	⌘+Shift+/

Keyboard Shortcuts (continued)

Command	Windows	Macintosh
Plugins		
Play	Ctrl+Alt+P	⌘+Option+P
Stop	Ctrl+Alt+X	⌘+Option+X
Play All	Ctrl+Alt+Shift+P	⌘+Option+Shift+P
Stop All	Ctrl+Alt+Shift+X	⌘+Option+Shift+X
Show Panels	F4	F4
Insert		
Tag	Ctrl+E	⌘+E
Image	Ctrl+Alt+I	⌘+Option+I
Media		
Flash	Ctrl+Alt+F	⌘+Option+F
Table	Ctrl+Alt+T	⌘+Option+T
Formed		
Named Anchor	Ctrl+Alt+A	⌘+Option+A
Special Characters		
Line Break	Shift+Return	Shift+Return
Non-Breaking	Space Ctrl+Shift+Space	Space ⌘+Shift+Space
Template Objects		
Editable Region	Ctrl+Alt+V	⌘+Option+V
Modify		
Page Properties	Ctrl+J	⌘+J
CSS Styles	Shift+F11	Shift+F11
Quick Tag Editor	Ctrl+T	⌘+T
Make Link	Ctrl+L	⌘+L
Remove Link	Ctrl+Shift+L	⌘+Shift+L
Table		
Select Table	Ctrl+A	⌘+A
Merge Cells	Ctrl+Alt+M	⌘+Option+M
Split Cell	Ctrl+Alt+S	⌘+Option+S
Insert Row	Ctrl+M	⌘+M
Insert Column	Ctrl+Shift+A	⌘+Shift+A
Delete Row	Ctrl+Shift+M	⌘+Shift+M

Command	Windows	Macintosh
Delete Column	Ctrl+Shift+-	⌘+Shift+-
Increase Column Span	Ctrl+Shift+]	⌘+Shift+]
Decrease Column Span	Ctrl+Shift+[	⌘+Shift+[
Arrange		
Align Left	Ctrl+Shift+1	⌘+Shift+1
Align Right	Ctrl+Shift+3	⌘+Shift+3
Align Top	Ctrl+Shift+4	⌘+Shift+4
Align Bottom	Ctrl+Shift+6	⌘+Shift+6
Make Same Width	Ctrl+Shift+7	⌘+Shift+7
Make Same Height	Ctrl+Shift+9	⌘+Shift+9
Timeline		
Add Object to Timeline	Ctrl+Alt+Shift+T	⌘+Option+Shift+T
Text		
Indent	Ctrl+Alt+]	⌘+Option+]
Outdent	Ctrl+Alt+[	⌘+Option+[
Paragraph Format		
None	Ctrl+0	⌘+0
Paragraph	Ctrl+Shift+P	⌘+Shift+P
Heading 1	Ctrl+1	⌘+1
Heading 2	Ctrl+2	⌘+2
Heading 3	Ctrl+3	⌘+3
Heading 4	Ctrl+4	⌘+4
Heading 5	Ctrl+5	⌘+5
Heading 6	Ctrl+6	⌘+6
Align		
Left	Ctrl+Alt+Shift+L	⌘+Option+Shift+L
Center	Ctrl+Alt+Shift+C	⌘+Option+Shift+C
Right	Ctrl+Alt+Shift+R	⌘+Option+Shift+R
Justify	Ctrl+Alt+Shift+J	⌘+Option+Shift+J
Style		
Bold	Ctrl+B	⌘+B
Italic	Ctrl+I	⌘+I

Keyboard Shortcuts *(continued)*

Command	Windows	Macintosh
Size Change		
Check spelling	Shift+F7	Shift+F7
Commands		
Start Recording	Ctrl+Shift+X	⌘+Shift+X
Site		
Get	Ctrl+Shift+D	⌘+Shift+D
Check Out	Ctrl+Alt+Shift+D	⌘+Option+Shift+D
Put	Ctrl+Shift+U	⌘+Shift+U
Check In	Ctrl+Alt+Shift+U	⌘+Option+Shift+U
Check Links Sitewide	Ctrl+F8	⌘+F8
Window		
Insert	Ctrl+F2	⌘+F2
Properties	Ctrl+F3	⌘+F3
CSS Styles	Shift+F11	Shift+F11
AP Elements	F2	F2
Databases	Ctrl+Shift+F10	⌘+Shift+F10
Bindings	Ctrl+F10	⌘+F10
Server Behaviors	Ctrl+F9	⌘+F9
Components	Ctrl+F7	⌘+F7
Files	F8	F8
Assets	F11	F11
Snippets	Shift+F9	Shift+F9
Tag Inspector	F9	F9
Behaviors	Shift+F4	Shift+F4
Results	F7	F7
Reference	Shift+F1	Shift+F1
History	Shift+F10	Shift+F10
Frames	Shift+F2	Shift+F2
Code Inspector	F10	F10
Timelines	Alt+F9	Option+F9
Show Panels	F4	F4

Command	Windows	Macintosh
Help		
Dreamweaver Help	F1	F1
ColdFusion Help	Ctrl+F1	⌘+F1
Reference	Shift+F1	Shift+F1
Files Panel Options Menu		
File		
New File	Ctrl+Shift+N	⌘+Shift+N
New Folder	Ctrl+Alt+Shift+N	⌘+Option+Shift+N
Rename	F2	F2
Delete	Delete	Delete
Preview in Browser		
Check Links	Shift+F8	Shift+F8
Edit		
Cut	Ctrl+X	⌘+X
Copy	Ctrl+C	⌘+C
Paste	Ctrl+V	⌘+V
Duplicate	Ctrl+D	⌘+D
Select All	Ctrl+A	⌘+A
View		
Refresh	F5	F5
Site Map Options		
Show/Hide Link	Ctrl+Shift+Y	⌘+Shift+Y
View as Root	Ctrl+Shift+R	⌘+Shift+R
Show Page Titles	Ctrl+Shift+T	⌘+Shift+T
Site Map	Alt+F8	Option+F8
Site		
Get	Ctrl+Shift+D	⌘+Shift+D
Check Out	Ctrl+Alt+Shift+D	⌘+Option+Shift+D
Put	Ctrl+Shift+U	⌘+Shift+U
Check In	Ctrl+Alt+Shift+U	⌘+Option+Shift+U
Cloaking		
Check Links Sitewide	Ctrl+F8	⌘+F8

Command	Windows	Macintosh
Link to New File	Ctrl+Shift+N	⌘+Shift+N
Link to Existing File	Ctrl+Shift+K	⌘+Shift+K
Change Link	Ctrl+L	⌘+L
Remove Link	Ctrl+Shift+L	⌘+Shift+L
Site Panel		
File		
New File	Ctrl+Shift+N	⌘+Shift+N
New Folder	Ctrl+Alt+Shift+N	⌘+Option+Shift+N
Rename	F2	F2
Delete	Delete	Delete
Preview in Browser		
Check Links	Shift+F8	Shift+F8
Edit		
Cut	Ctrl+X	⌘+X
Copy	Ctrl+C	⌘+C
Paste	Ctrl+V	⌘+V
Duplicate	Ctrl+D	⌘+D
Select All	Ctrl+A	⌘+A
View		
Refresh	F5	F5
Site Map Options		
Show/Hide Link	Ctrl+Shift+Y	⌘+Shift+Y
View as Root	Ctrl+Shift+R	⌘+Shift+R
Show Page Titles	Ctrl+Shift+T	⌘+Shift+T
Site Map	Alt+F8	Option+F8
Site		
Get	Ctrl+Shift+D	⌘+Shift+D
Check Out	Ctrl+Alt+Shift+D	⌘+Option+Shift+D
Put	Ctrl+Shift+U	⌘+Shift+U
Check In	Ctrl+Alt+Shift+U	⌘+Option+Shift+U
Cloaking		
Check Links Sitewide	Ctrl+F8	⌘+F8

k

Command	Windows	Macintosh
Link to New File	Ctrl+Shift+N	⌘+Shift+N
Link to Existing File	Ctrl+Shift+K	⌘+Shift+K
Change Link	Ctrl+L	⌘+L
Remove Link	Ctrl+Shift+L	⌘+Shift+L
Code Editing		
Copy	Ctrl+C,Ctrl+Ins	⌘+C,⌘+Ins
Paste	Ctrl+V,Shift+Ins	⌘+V,Shift+Ins
Paste Special	Ctrl+Shift+V	⌘+Shift+V
Cut	Ctrl+X,Shift+Del	⌘+X,Shift+Del
Surround with #	Ctrl+Shift+3	⌘+Shift+3
Delete word left	Ctrl+BkSp	⌘+BkSp
Delete word right	Ctrl+Del	⌘+Del
Select line up	Shift+Up	Shift+Up
Select line down	Shift+Down	Shift+Down
Character select left	Shift+Left	Shift+Left
Character select right	Shift+Right	Shift+Right
Select to page up	Shift+PgUp	Shift+PgUp
Select to page down	Shift+PgDn	Shift+PgDn
Move word left	Ctrl+Left	⌘+Left
Move word right	Ctrl+Right	⌘+Right
Select word left	Ctrl+Shift+Left	⌘+Shift+Left
Select word right	Ctrl+Shift+Right	⌘+Shift+Right
Move to start of line	Home	Home
Move to end of line	End	End
Select to start of line	Shift+Home	Shift+Home
Select to end of line	Shift+End	Shift+End
Move to top of file	Ctrl+Home	⌘+Home
Move to end of file	Ctrl+End	⌘+End
Select to start of file	Ctrl+Shift+Home	⌘+Shift+Home
Select to end of file	Ctrl+Shift+End	⌘+Shift+End
Copy2	Ctrl+Ins	⌘+Ins
Paste2	Shift+Ins	Shift+Ins

Keyboard Shortcuts *(continued)*

Command	Windows	Macintosh
Cut2	Shift+Del	Shift+Del
Snippets	Shift+F9	Shift+F9
Document Editing		
Quit Application	Alt+F4	Option+F4
Go to Next Word	Ctrl+Right	⌘+Right
Go to Previous Word	Ctrl+Left	⌘+Left
Go to Previous Paragraph	Ctrl+Up	⌘+Up
Go to Next Paragraph	Ctrl+Down	⌘+Down
Select Until Next Word	Ctrl+Shift+Right	⌘+Shift+Right
Select From Previous Word	Ctrl+Shift+Left	⌘+Shift+Left
Select From Previous Paragraph	Ctrl+Shift+Up	⌘+Shift+Up
Select Until Next Paragraph	Ctrl+Shift+Down	⌘+Shift+Down
Close Window	Ctrl+F4	⌘+F4
Edit Tag	Shift+F5	Shift+F5
New In Same Window	Ctrl+Shift+N	⌘+Shift+N
Preview in Primary Browser	F12	F12
Preview in Secondary Browser	Ctrl+F12,Shift+F12	⌘+F12,Shift+F12
Preview in Secondary Browser	Shift+F12	Shift+F12
Preview in Device Central	Ctrl+Alt+F12	⌘+Option+F12
Exit Paragraph	Ctrl+Return	⌘+Return
Live Data Mode	Ctrl+R	⌘+R
Print Code	Ctrl+P	⌘+P
Next Document	Ctrl+Tab	⌘+Tab
Previous Document	Ctrl+Shift+Tab	⌘+Shift+Tab
Site Window		
Close Window	Ctrl+F4	⌘+F4
Quit Application	Alt+F4	Option+F4
Preview in Primary Browser	F12	F12
Preview in Secondary Browser	Shift+F12	Shift+F12
Preview in Device Central	Ctrl+Alt+F12	⌘+Option+F12
Cancel FTP	Esc	Esc

Adobe Certified Expert

C

About the Adobe Certified Expert (ACE) Program

The Adobe Certified Expert (ACE) program is for graphic designers, Web designers, systems integrators, value-added resellers, developers, and business professionals seeking official recognition of their expertise on Adobe products.

What Is an ACE?

An Adobe Certified Expert is an individual who has passed an Adobe Product Proficiency Exam for a specific Adobe software product. Adobe Certified Experts are eligible to promote themselves to clients or employers as highly skilled, expert-level users of Adobe software. ACE certification is a recognized worldwide standard for excellence in Adobe software knowledge. There are three levels of ACE certification: Single product certification, Specialist certification, and Master certification. To become an ACE, you must pass one or more product-specific proficiency exam and sign the ACE program agreement. When you become an ACE, you enjoy these special benefits:

- ◆ Professional recognition
- ◆ An ACE program certificate
- ◆ Use of the Adobe Certified Expert program logo

What Does This Logo Mean?

It means this book will prepare you fully for the Adobe Certified Expert exam for Adobe Dreamweaver CS3. The certification exam has a set of objectives, which are organized into broader skill sets. Throughout this book, content that pertains to an ACE objective is identified with the following Adobe Certified Expert logo and objective number below the title of the topic:

 DW 3.1

Dreamweaver CS3 ACE Exam Objectives

Objective	Skill	Page
1.0	**Understanding Web technologies**	
1.1	Given an HTML tag, explain the purpose of that tag. (Tags include: <div> <span> <table> <a>)	336-337
1.2	Describe the difference between CSS classes and IDs	216-217, 235-237
1.3	Explain how JavaScript is used on the client in Web pages	358-359, 428-431
1.4	List and describe the features and functionality of ftp and how it is used in Dreamweaver	482-485
2.0	**Planning sites**	
2.1	Define a local site by using the Manage Sites dialog box	480-481
2.2	Manage site definitions for local, remote, and testing server information	480-486
2.3	Describe considerations related to case-sensitive links	170-171
2.4	Given a scenario, define the structure of a site	11, 20-21, 478-479
2.5	Given a scenario, select and set the appropriate resolution for a site	52-53
2.6	List and describe considerations related to designing a site for multiple platforms and browsers.	238-239, 462
2.7	List and describe the features Dreamweaver provides for Accessibility Standards/Section 508 compliance.	470-471
2.8	Explain how templates are used to architect for reuse and consistency	434
2.9	Create pages by using CSS starter pages	218-219
2.10	Explain how to extend Dreamweaver by using Extensions	304-309, 544
2.11	Given a scenario, set development Preferences	60-65, 214, 352-356
2.12	Given a scenario, choose the proper method to layout a page. (Methods include: tables, layers, CSS Box model)	186-189, 200-203, 216-225, 246-248, 250-253, 260-261
2.13	Incorporate graphics and rich media into a Web site	136-139, 287, 294
3.0	**Designing pages**	
3.1	List and describe how to navigate the Dreamweaver UI	42-43
3.2	Use Find and Replace including support for regular expressions	121-124, 522-525
3.3	Create and use page templates	435-450
3.4	Create and maintain Cascading Style Sheets (CSS)	218-233
3.5	Create and use reusable page objects by using library items	422-427
3.6	Explain the purpose of and how to use Server-side includes	432
3.7	Create and use code Snippets	406-413

Dreamweaver CS3 ACE Exam Objectives *(continued)*

Objective	Skill	Page
3.8	Given a method, layout a page. (Methods include: Table Layout, Layers, Expanded Tables mode)	186-189, 200-203, 216-225, 246-248, 250-253, 260-261
3.9	List and describe the options for creating and saving new pages	23-29, 80-81, 218-219, 435, 444-447
3.10	Set document properties by using the Document Properties dialog box	83-88
3.11	Layout a page by using guides	56-57
3.12	List and describe the options available for formatting the structure of a document (Options include: paragraph breaks, line breaks, non-breaking spaces, tables.)	98-99, 109-114
3.13	List and describe, and resolve issues related to browser compatibility	238-239, 462
3.14	Use JavaScript behaviors to implement page functionality (Behaviors include: Pop-Up Menus, Open Browser Window, Swap Image, Go To URL)	358-363, 370-382
3.15	Add Flash elements to a Web page (Options include: text, buttons, video, paper)	286-287, 290-297
3.16	List and describe the functionality provided by Dreamweaver for XML	396-397, 452-453
3.17	Given a coding tool or feature, describe the purpose of or how to use it (Tools or features include: Code and Design View, Code Collapse, Code Navigation, Code Hinting, and Coding Context Menu)	338-340, 342, 344-349
3.18	Discuss considerations related to naming conventions and case sensitivity (e.g., variations between UNIX and Windows)	38, 170, 481
3.19	Annotate files by using Design Notes and Comments	343, 492-494
4.0	**Managing and maintaining**	
4.1	Manage collaboration with multiple developers by using Check In-Check Out	504-505
4.2	List and describe the different methods for accessing a remote site. (Methods include: FTP, LAN, VSS, WebDAV)	478-479, 482-485
4.3	Given an access method, configure site definitions	478-479, 496-497
4.4	Transfer and synchronize files to and from a remote server. (Options include: Cloaking, background file transfer, Get, Put)	498-501. 506-508
4.5	Manage assets, links, and files for a site	74-75, 414-420 498-499
4.6	Configure preferences, and explain the process required to compare files	502-503
4.7	Validate a site prior to deployment (Options include: link checking, accessibility checking, validating markup)	470-471, 456-461

Choosing a Certification Level

There are three levels of certification to become an Adobe Certified Expert.

◆ **Single product certification.** Recognizes your proficiency in a single Adobe product. To qualify as an ACE, you must pass one product-specific exam.

◆ **Specialist certification.** Recognizes your proficiency in multiple Adobe products with a specific medium: print, Web, or video. To become certified as a Specialist, you must pass the exams on the required products. To review the requirements, go online to *http://www.adobe.com/support/certification/ace_certify.html*.

◆ **Master certification.** Recognizes your skills in terms of how they align with the Adobe product suites. To become certified as a Master, you must pass the exam for each of the products in the suite.

Preparing for an Adobe Certified Expert Exam

Every Adobe Certified Expert Exam is developed from a list of objectives, which are based on studies of how an Adobe program is actually used in the workplace. The list of objectives determine the scope of each exam, so they provide you with the information you need to prepare for ACE certification. Follow these steps to complete the ACE Exam requirement:

1 Review and perform each task identified with a Adobe Certified Expert objective to confirm that you can meet the requirements for the exam.

2 Identify the topic areas and objectives you need to study, and then prepare for the exam.

3 Review the Adobe Certified Expert Program Agreement. To review it, go online to *http://www.adobe.com/support/certification/ace_certify.html*.

You will be required to accept the ACE agreement when you take the Adobe Certified Exam at an authorized testing center.

4 Register for the Adobe Certified Expert Exam.

ACE testing is offered at more than a thousand authorized Pearson VUE and Thomson Prometric testing centers in many countries. To find the testing center nearest you, go online to *www.pearsonvue.com/adobe* (for Parson VUE) or *www.2test.com* (for Prometric). The ACE exam fee is US$150 worldwide. When contacting an authorized training center, provide them with the Adobe Product Proficiency exam name and number you want to take, which is available online in the Exam Bulletin at *http://www.adobe.com/support/certification/ace_certify.html*.

5 Take the ACE exam.

Getting Recertified

For those with an ACE certification for a specific Adobe product, recertification is required of each ACE within 90 days of a designated ACE Exam release date. There are no restrictions on the number of times you may take the exam within a given period.

To get recertified, call Pearson VUE and Thomson Prometric. You will need to verify your previous certification for that product. If you are getting recertified, check with the authorized testing center for discounts.

Taking an Adobe Certified Expert Exam

The Adobe Certified Expert exams are computer-delivered, closed-book tests consisting of 60 to 90 multiple-choice questions. Each exam is approximately one to two hours long. A 15-minute tutorial will precede the test to familiarize you with the function of the Windows-based driver. The exams are currently available worldwide in English only. They are administered by Pearson VUE and Thomson Prometric, independent third-party testing companies.

Exam Results

At the end of the exam, a score report appears indicating whether you passed or failed the exam. Diagnostic information is included in your exam report. When you pass the exam, your score is electronically reported to Adobe. You will then be sent an ACE Welcome Kit and access to the ACE program logo in four to six weeks. You are also placed on the Adobe certification mailing list to receive special Adobe announcements and information about promotions and events that take place throughout the year.

When you pass the exam, you can get program information, check and update your profile, or download ACE program logos for your promotional materials online at:

http://www.adobe.com/support/certification/community.html

Getting More Information

To learn more about the Adobe Certified Expert program, read a list of frequently asked questions, and locate the nearest testing center, go online to:

http://www.adobe.com/support/certification/ace.html

To learn more about other Adobe certification programs, go online to:

http://www.adobe.com/support/certification

Index